THE
PRACTICAL
WRITER

with Readings

THE
PRACTICAL
WRITER

with Readings

5th edition

by
Edward P. Bailey
Philip A. Powell

HARCOURT BRACE COLLEGE PUBLISHERS

Fort Worth   Philadelphia   San Diego
New York   Orlando   Austin   San Antonio
Toronto   Montreal   London   Sydney   Tokyo

Publisher	Earl McPeek
Acquisitions Editor	Julie McBurney
Product Manager	Laura Brennan
Project Editor	Claudia Gravier
Art Director	Garry Harman
Production Manager	James McDonald

Cover Image: Masterfile/Graham French

ISBN: 0-15-505502-X
Library of Congress Catalog Card Number: 98–070866

Address for Orders
Harcourt Brace College Publishers, 6277 Sea Harbor Drive, Orlando, FL 32887-6777
1-800-782-4479

Address for Editorial Correspondence
Harcourt Brace College Publishers, 301 Commerce Street, Suite 3700, Fort Worth, TX 76102

Web site Address
http://www.hbcollege.com

Harcourt Brace College Publishers will provide complimentary supplements or supplement packages to those adopters qualified under our adoption policy. Please contact your sales representative to learn how you qualify. If as an adopter or potential user you receive supplements you do not need, please return them to your sales representative or send them to: Attn.: Returns Department, Troy Warehouse, 465 South Lincoln Drive, Troy, MO 63379.

Printed in the United States of America

8 9 0 1 2 3 4 5 6 7   0 3 9   9 8 7 6 5 4 3 2 1

Harcourt Brace College Publishers

Dedicated to our families.

Preface

Now in its fifth edition, *The Practical Writer with Readings* continues to be a clear and practical guide for first-year English students. We believe students need—and appreciate—a textbook that gives them practical advice on writing and helps them gain the skills they'll need for future college courses and beyond. Using *The Practical Writer with Readings,* students will learn:

- *How to write using a clear structure.* We emphasize the importance of a clear structure throughout the book.
- *Plain English style.* Good writing doesn't need to sound like yesterday's law books. We urge our readers to write with a clear, direct style—the style most professional writers use.
- *How to use memorable supporting material.* We urge students to use detailed support—examples that readers can visualize, statistics, statements by authorities. Readers are more likely to understand—and remember—a writer's points if the writing is concrete.
- *Correctness.* Too many writers aren't comfortable with grammar and punctuation. Students should feel comfortable with these skills by the time they finish their first year of college and *The Practical Writer with Readings* helps them achieve this.

How Does *The Practical Writer with Readings* Work?

We begin by presenting the fundamentals (organization, support, unity, coherence) one at a time—in a tightly structured one-paragraph essay. The paragraph is a unit large enough for students to demonstrate their understanding of the fundamentals and small enough for them to work toward mastery. At this point, we don't overwhelm them while they're learning the fundamentals by making them struggle to find support; instead we ask them to write about personal experiences and the people and things they know well. We encourage them to be colorful, interesting, and—above all—specific.

We then move through several longer stages of writing to a 3,000- to 4,000-word research paper. By the time students complete the research block, they can write a serious paper—the kind they will have to write in other college courses and beyond—with a less mechanical structure than we required earlier. We still offer a model, of course, but it becomes a guide rather than a goal.

Parts Six and Seven—punctuation and expression—are not part of the step-by-step approach. Students can study these chapters any time, whenever they're ready for them. They aren't typical handbook material, though, because we've been careful to select only what first-year students need to learn, leaving out the skills they probably know and those they're not yet ready to apply.

The last section of the book includes paragraphs and essays written in response to our exercises throughout the years. Lots of important learning happens when students see and imitate good examples. We hope readers of this book will look at these examples and say, "I can do that!"

Throughout *The Practical Writer with Readings,* we try to avoid the "scholarly" style of writing and speak personally to students, as though we're talking to them in class. We have also included sidebars, exercises, and examples written with today's college student in mind.

What Have We Changed for This Edition?

As always, we've worked to keep the fundamentals in place and update where necessary.

- *We've brought the research section up to date.* Keeping up with the "computerized library" is nearly a full-time task these days—exciting things keep happening. For this edition, it's the Internet: much of today's research takes place on it. Our research section takes into full account the Internet and other electronic sources. We've also created a new sample research paper.

- *We've revised many of the exercises.* About 80 percent of the objective exercises are new. We've also added a number of new topics for essays—including some exercises taking advantage of E-mail and the World Wide Web. We think these new exercises should be fun and productive.

- *We've added a number of new examples.* Most of our examples were in first person writing; we now have a number in third person to illustrate different styles of writing (while retaining the clear style we've always encouraged). Also, many of the new examples are on themes that students can identify with.

- *We've added a brief section on brainstorming techniques.* These techniques will help students come up with ideas on how to develop their topics.

- *We've added new readings to Section Four.* We are always trying to gather new examples for readers to model, and several new paragraphs and essays have been added in this edition.

- *We've included a set of transparency masters.* Instructors asked for these so we've included a set to enhance the use of *The Practical Writer with Readings* in the classroom. The transparency masters include information from the text as well as new writing examples.

- *We've expanded the appendix on commonly confused words.* This appendix covers such problems as *affect/effect* and *imply/infer.*

Ancillaries

To obtain a copy of the detailed instructor's manual and the transparency masters, contact your local Harcourt Brace sales representative.

Contents

Section Three Improving Your Punctuation and Expression   309

Part Six Punctuation   311

Part Seven Expression   361

Section Four Sample Essays 429

Appendixes 485

Index 493

Acknowledgments

As a final word, we continue to express appreciation to our students, colleagues, and reviewers: Bob Baron, Mesa Community College; Jo Anne Bryant, Troy State University in Montgomery; Annie Lou Burns, Meridian Community College; Michael Connell, Kirkwood Community College; Joanne Detore-Nakamura, Brevard Community College; Catherine D. Farmer, Wallace State College; Johnanna L. Grimes, Tennessee State University; Robert Scott, DeAnza College; and Patricia D. West, North Arkansas Community/Technical College.

Special thanks to our Developmental Editor, Laurie Runion. She has been very professional and a pleasure to work with. Her ideas were extremely useful in helping us develop our approach for this edition. We'd also like to acknowledge many other helpful people at Harcourt Brace: James McDonald, Production Manager; Claudia Gravier, Project Editor; Garry Harman, Art Director; Jim Dodson, Designer; and Karen Keady, Copyeditor.

Edward P. Bailey
Marymount University

Philip A. Powell
Burke, VA

SECTION I

A Model for Writing

The One-Paragraph Essay (Stage I)

The first part of this book shows you how to write a good one-paragraph essay. Although you seldom see one-paragraph essays in publications, you'll find them remarkably handy for improving your writing for several reasons:

- They are short—you can spend your study time writing a really good one.
- At the same time, they're long enough for you to practice some fundamentals of writing.
- What you learn about one-paragraph essays transfers nicely to larger themes and even research papers.

In Part 1, you'll learn about the simplest one-paragraph essay, which we call Stage I. Later, in Part 2, you'll study the organization for a slightly more sophisticated one-paragraph essay, which we call Stage II.

Part 1 presents a tightly structured model for a paragraph. You may wonder if all good writers follow such a structure for persuasive writing. No, of course not. This structure is not *the* good way to write a paragraph, but it is *one* good way. And this way has a very real advantage: it automatically gives your paper organization so that you can concentrate on learning the other fundamentals that experienced writers already know. In addition, by working constantly with this model paragraph, you will learn organization, too, the easy way.

Support for the paragraph's main idea is also easy. Right now we don't care if you know how to find facts in the library. We're much more concerned that you can recognize and use good support once you find it. So we make finding it simple. You can use either your experiences or your imagination for support. As a result, you can have fun with your one-paragraph essays. They can be intriguing and perhaps humorous.

Writing doesn't have to be dull!

CHAPTER 1
Overview of the One-Paragraph Essay (Stage I)

For many years, teachers have given this advice to their students:

- Tell your readers what you're going to tell them.
- Tell it to them.
- Then tell them what you just told them.

Simple, isn't it? Yet even though the advice is simple, it's also extremely useful. In fact, it serves as the structure—the underlying organization—of much non-fiction writing. After all, most readers appreciate knowing at the beginning what the writing will be about. And at the end they appreciate a reminder of the writing's overall purpose. That way, all the details in the middle have a context. As a result, readers know where they are in a piece of writing and don't get lost.

You'll find that this organization is valuable to you as a *writer*, too: it gives you an easy way to get started. You'll have already solved the problem of how to organize the overall flow of your writing, and you can move on to the next step in your prewriting process.

This chapter shows you how to apply this simple organization to the one-paragraph essay. Later chapters will show you how to apply it to longer (and even lengthy) essays, including research papers. Let's turn now to the basic building block of much good writing: the one-paragraph essay. It has three main parts:

- The first sentence states the idea you want your readers to accept (your main point). We call this a *topic sentence*.
- All middle sentences present specific support for that idea.
- The last sentence rewords the topic sentence—to remind your readers of the point you've just made.

Let's look at these three points another way—as a model.

THE MODEL FOR THE ONE-PARAGRAPH ESSAY (STAGE I)

The Stage I paragraph model looks like this:

> Topic sentence
>   Specific support
>   Specific support
>   Specific support
> Reworded topic sentence

Now let's look at a "real" paragraph—one that follows the model we've just shown you:

> The Boundary Waters Canoe Area, a wilderness park in northern Minnesota, is a refreshing change from the city. Away from the din of civilization, I have canoed silently across its waters for an entire afternoon and not heard a single noise except for an occasional birdcall and the sound of waves beating against the shore. Also, my partner and I were able to navigate our way through a string of five lakes by following a campfire's scent drifting through the pure air. Most refreshing, the park is so magnificently beautiful that even the voyageurs of old were willing to endure its hardships in order to settle there. The Boundary Waters Canoe Area is thus an ideal place to clear your head of the congestion of urban life.

Look carefully at the first sentence. Notice that it states the main point of the paragraph—the idea that the rest of the paragraph supports. There were three points in the middle—a sentence for each. Now look at the last sentence. Notice that it merely rewords the first sentence. Easy, isn't it? Here's an outline of that Stage I paragraph:

> *Topic sentence*   The Boundary Waters Canoe Area is a refreshing change.
>   *Specific support*   quietness
>   *Specific support*   purity of the air
>   *Specific support*   beauty
> *Reworded topic sentence*   It's an ideal place to clear your head of the congestion of urban life.

The structure of the paragraph is absolutely clear, unmistakable, obvious. Some forms of writing (fiction, personal essays) do not necessarily benefit from an obvious organization. But in writing that takes care of the day-to-day business of the world, an obvious organization usually proves helpful to readers. As writers, then, we should take into account what works best for our readers. Getting right to the point with a topic sentence and then providing the support is a good way to keep our readers on track.

ANOTHER EXAMPLE

Here's another sample one-paragraph essay. It, too, follows the model closely:

> Even though I have never really lived there, going to my grandmother's farm always seems like coming home. The feeling begins as soon as I cross the threshold of that quaint little house and tumble into the arms of waiting aunts and cousins. The sense of welcome overwhelms me. Then there are the cozy rooms—the ceilings don't seem higher than six feet—with their crackling fireplaces that make me want to snuggle down into the feather-stuffed chairs. But the memory that always lasts the longest is the smell of Grandma's biscuits and pastries cooking in her coke-fed stove. Yes, only in Grandma's house do I feel the warmth and welcome that always seem like coming home.

Notice that the middle sentences all concern the pleasant connotation of "home" in its best sense: feeling welcome, cozy, cared for. Each of those ideas supports the topic sentence. Let's look at an outline of that paragraph:

> *Topic sentence*   Going to my grandmother's farm seems like coming home.
> *Specific support*   greeting by relatives
> *Specific support*   coziness of house
> *Specific support*   smell of home-cooked food
> *Reworded topic sentence*   Visiting Grandma's seems like coming home.

Both sample paragraphs above have exactly three items of specific support. You may wonder if that's what you should always do. No. Although three seems to work well in both of these paragraphs, sometimes five or six items are necessary to be persuasive; other times, one long example will do.

A FINAL EXAMPLE

One-paragraph essays can address topics other than personal experiences. For example, consider this one:

> Climbing Mount Everest, the highest mountain in the world, is extremely dangerous. One indication of its danger is that nobody succeeded in climbing it until Sir Edmund Hillary and Tenzing Norgay reached the summit in 1953—not all that long ago. In his best-selling book on Everest, *Into Thin Air,* Jon Krakauer points out the danger with a chilling statistic: between 1921 and 1996, 144 people died in the attempt (p. 274). Krakauer, who made it to the top, adds, "Truth be told, climbing Everest has always been an extraordinarily dangerous undertaking and doubtless always will be, whether the people involved are Himalayan neophytes being guided up the peak or world-class mountaineers climbing with their peers" (p. 274). In the case of Everest, height and danger certainly go together.

Notice that this one-paragraph essay—in the third-person style—has interesting factual content from an outside source as its support. Chapter 9 shows you a simple system for documenting outside sources. Later in the book you'll learn full-fledged techniques of documentation.

Although the sample paragraphs in the first two or three chapters of this book are good, they are intentionally fairly simple so you can easily see their basic organization. But if you don't fully understand the one-paragraph essay yet, don't worry. The next few chapters explain further.

Also, you can find a checklist for the one-paragraph essay immediately following Chapter 8. You may wish to turn to it now. It gives you a good sense of what the first eight chapters cover.

PRACTICAL WRITING

So far we have used the one-paragraph essay only as a teaching tool. But as simple as it is, it has significant value in school—and beyond.

Practical Writing in School

In school, you can easily use the pattern of the one-paragraph essay for some of your writing. Simple answers to essay questions on tests can follow this pattern. So can any one-paragraph writing—whether you're taking a course in English, history, mathematics, physics, computer sciences, or anything else. Most readers—and we can assure you this includes teachers, too—like to see the main idea up front followed by good, detailed support.

In English, for example, you might have a brief essay question like this: "What is the main feature of e. e. cummings' poetry that appeals to you?" Your answer could be this one-paragraph essay:

> I like the individual freedom that comes through in e. e. cummings' poetry. You can see that freedom right away in the lack of capitalization and normal spacing in his writing. You can also see it in the content: his poems often deal with

the carefreeness of spring and the value of the individual. Those are just two of the ways I see the emphasis on freedom I like so much in e. e. cummings' poems.

That could serve as a brief answer, if that's what your teacher expected on a test. It could be more convincing, of course, as a longer essay with detailed examples for each point.

The next chapter shows you how to use examples. And later in the book, we'll show you how to expand the one-paragraph essay into a full-length essay. You should find that especially useful in your courses beyond this one.

Practical Writing at Work

This structured approach will also be useful after you graduate. Since we wrote the first edition of this book, we've done a great deal of work with business and government writers—lawyers, accountants, auditors, doctors, bankers, military officers, government analysts, computer experts, political scientists, scientific researchers, and others of similar skill. Our main task has been to help these people—usually bright, educated, and successful professionals—express their ideas clearly.

One consistent message we tell them is this: Readers in the busy world of work strongly prefer to have the main point up front for almost everything they read. In fact, if they don't find it there—right away—they often skip to the back and start hunting for it.

Think of yourself as a reader. If you're reading a report from your doctor, wouldn't you prefer the diagnosis up front instead of three pages later, after all the lab results and all the possible illnesses you might have, but don't?

Suppose you work in an office and have a five-page report to read and comment on for your boss. Where do you, the reader, want the main point, at the end or at the beginning? Almost all of us prefer the beginning.

Let's look at an example of poor business writing—a memo that delays the main point (a recommendation) until the end. Notice how confusing it is to struggle through all the details without a main point to guide you (we've italicized the main point).

Memo with the Recommendation Last
Date: July 7
From: Fielding Brown
To: Charlotte Robinson

The copying machine was broken for three days this month—June 2, 5, and 9. During that time, nobody was able to do any of the photocopying crucial to our work. Also, it had routine maintenance two other days this month—June 15 and 30. Then, too, nobody could use the machine. Finally, Neal and Sharon had a large photocopying project that kept others from using the machine for three other days—June 1, 3, and 4. *I recommend, therefore, that we buy a second copying machine because the one we have can't meet our needs.*

It's easy to get lost in the facts of that paragraph, isn't it? If you are the boss—the one deciding whether to spend the money—you'd certainly have to read that memo *twice:* The first time you'd be hunting for the recommendation, which doesn't come until the last sentence. The second time, with the recommendation in mind, you'd read to see if the facts served as effective justification.

Writers can't expect their readers to reread. And few bosses like rereading, either. Wouldn't the memo be better with the recommendation up front, like this?

Memo with the Recommendation First
Date: July 7
From: Fielding Brown
To: Charlotte Robinson

I recommend we buy a second copying machine because the one we have can't meet our needs. Ours was broken for three days this month—June 2, 5, and 9. During that time, nobody was able to do any of the photocopying crucial to our work. Also, it had routine maintenance two other days this month—June 15 and 30. Then, too, nobody could use the machine. Finally, Neal and Sharon had a large photocopying project that kept others from using the machine for three other days—June 1, 3, and 4. For these reasons, I strongly urge that we buy a second copier.

As you can see, the memo now takes the shape of the model we gave you at the beginning of this chapter.

Practical Writing

Throughout the book, we'll point to the connections between our models and good writing outside your writing course. The connections are strong and important—for your other college courses and for the world of work.

Don't underestimate the simple structure you're learning in this chapter. It's a structure you can apply time and again for a good part of your writing as you go through life. Using a single paragraph as an essay is an artifical construction, and you won't write many one-paragraph as an essays after this course. Nevertheless, the one-paragraph essay is a great starting point for learning the writing model. The one-paragraph essay is easy for you to work with and often fun, too. We think of it as a valuable little tool, a starting point, a building block. The rest of this book builds upon that model.

EXERCISES

A. Outline the following paragraph the same way we outlined the two paragraphs in the chapter.

Three common electric distractions on my desk waste my precious study time at night. The worst distraction is my clock, constantly humming to remind me how little time I actually have. Another interruption is the "high-quality" fluorescent desk lamp that sometimes buzzes, flickers—and then goes out. And, finally, consider that fascinating little invention, the computer, that not only does all kinds of complicated math problems, but also challenges me to games and helps me write letters home. After stopping to worry about the time, fix my lamp, and play with the computer, I am too tired to study, so I just go to bed.

Topic sentence _____

Specific support _____

Specific support _____

Specific support _____

Reworded topic sentence _____

B. Outline this paragraph:

Old, stiff, and weathered, my grandfather's hands show the strenuous way of life he has known as a working man. Many hot summer days tilling the stubborn soil of West Texas have left their lasting mark in the form of a deep and permanent tan. Grandpa's hands are also covered with calluses—begun, perhaps, when he split cordwood for two dollars a day in an effort to pull his family through the Great Depression. Most striking, though, are the carpenter's scars he has collected from the days of building his house, barn, and fence and from the unending repair jobs that still occupy his every day. Although small and battered, Grandpa's hands bring back images of a time when men and women worked from dawn to dusk just to survive, a difficult but respected way of life.

Topic sentence _____

Specific support _____

Specific support _____

Specific support _____

Reworded topic sentence _____

C. Outline this paragraph:

The East Wing of the National Art Gallery in Washington, D.C., is a showplace of modern art. Inside, it houses collections of such artists as Picasso and Matisse, well known for their nonrepresentational works. Hanging from the ceiling is a mobile, normally thought of as a dangling toy parents hang above their infant's crib. This one, however, is several stories high and much more impressive to the parents (and children, too). Even the building is in keeping with its contents: it has lots of glass, open spaces, and strange angles and corners. For modern art, this wing of the gallery is an excellent place to visit.

Topic sentence _____

Specific support _____

Specific support _____

Specific support _____

Reworded topic sentence _____

D. Outline this paragraph you saw earlier in the chapter:

I like the individual freedom that comes through in e. e. cummings' poetry. You can see that freedom right away in the lack of capitalization and normal spacing in his writing. You can also see it in the content: his poems often deal with the carefreeness of spring and the value of the individual. Those are just two of the ways I see the emphasis on freedom I like so much in e. e. cummings' poems.

Topic sentence _____

Specific support _____

Specific support _____

Specific support _____

Reworded topic sentence _____

E. Outline this business memo you saw earlier in the chapter:

I recommend we buy a second copying machine because the one we have can't meet our needs. Ours was broken for three days this month—June 2, 5, and 9. During that time, nobody was able to do any of the photocopying crucial to our work. Also, it had routine maintenance two other days this month—June 15 and 30. Then, too, nobody could use the machine. Finally, Neal and Sharon had a large photocopying project that kept others from using the machine for three other days—June 1, 3, and 4. For these reasons, I strongly urge that we buy a second copier.

Topic sentence _____

Specific support _____

Specific support _____

Specific support _____

Reworded topic sentence _____

CHAPTER 2

Support: Examples, Statistics, Statements by Authorities

One-paragraph models begin with a topic sentence that is followed by support. We'll save our discussion of topic sentences for the next chapter and begin, instead, with support. Once you understand support—and how specific it must be—you'll understand much more easily how to write a good topic sentence.

This chapter discusses three kinds of support:

- examples
- statistics
- statements by authorities

EXAMPLES

Professional writers tell us, "The secret to good writing—the real secret—is using examples." Yet many teachers say, "One of the biggest problems with undergraduate writing—one that almost all students have—is that they don't use nearly enough examples." So here's a chance to solve a problem by learning a secret. Let's begin by discussing two kinds of examples: *quick* examples and *narrative* examples.

Quick Examples

You already know from your everyday experience what a quick example is: it's one instance, one occurrence of whatever you're talking about. If you're talking about the meals available at fast-food restaurants, a hamburger is one quick example. You could have named fried chicken, tacos, roast beef sandwiches, or (at the waterfront in San Francisco) even sourdough bread with crabs.

To be effective, a quick example must be specific. If you want to show that Constance Dilettante can't stick with anything, don't say, "She changes her mind a lot." Don't even say, "She changed her major frequently in college." Be still more specific: "She changed her major from philosophy to computer science to animal husbandry—all in one semester."

Do quick examples really make a difference? We think so. Consider the following:

■ Sentences *without* Quick Examples

There were many expensive cars in the school's parking lot during the football game.

You could tell spring was here because of all the flowers in bloom.

Why do lawyers use words that mean one thing to them and something entirely different in ordinary English?

■ Sentences *with* Quick Examples

There were many expensive cars in the school's parking lot during the football game: *Mercedes convertibles, low-slung Porsches, and red Ferraris.*

You could tell spring was here because of all the flowers in bloom: *tulips of all colors, yellow daffodils, and (if you want to call them flowers) even a few early dandelions.*

Why do lawyers use words that mean one thing to them and something entirely different in ordinary English *(words such as* party *and* action *and* motion)?

See the difference that quick examples make? They take general, rather abstract terms—*cars, flowers, legal words*—and make them much more concrete. It's almost as though the abstract words don't really communicate, don't really find a place to lodge in the brain cells. But the more concrete words—*Mercedes, tulip, party*—do.

Using Quick Examples

When should you use quick examples? How often do you prefer to read quick examples? Pretty often, right? And that's how often you should use them when you write.

Quick examples, of course, don't have to come at the ends of sentences. You could have a paragraph, probably a short one, that depended entirely on quick examples:

◼ A Paragraph That Depends on Quick Examples

Chairs come in many different designs. Easy chairs—designed for people who like to lounge back—usually have lots of padding, perhaps a curved back, and comfortable armrests. Straight chairs usually have minimal padding, a vertical back, and sometimes no armrests. Contemporary computer chairs known as kneelers have padding for the knees and seat, but no back at all and no armrests. So, depending on their purposes, chairs differ quite a bit.

The topic of that paragraph may not be exciting, but the quick examples—easy chair, straight chair, kneeler—certainly communicate much more than the abstract beginning: "Chairs come in many different designs."

Narrative Examples

A quick example is just one instance, one occurrence. But a *narrative* example is a brief story. A narrative example can really make an impact, so we emphasize it in this book.

Sometimes you want to emphasize an idea to help your readers understand what you mean. So you decide to run a little "motion picture"; that is, you decide to tell a story that will help your readers visualize what you are saying—as though they are watching a short movie rather than simply reading words. For example, if you want to show how to prepare for a job interview, you could give a quick example by saying, "I once did research on the Web to get ready for an interview." Or you could really make your point by telling the story:

◼ Paragraph with a Narrative Example

Last week, I got serious about hunting for a job as a computer programmer, so I began clipping ads from the newspaper and talking to some of my friends. One friend, Joanne, called me on Wednesday evening and said that her company needed someone right away, but she didn't know much about computers (or programming). If I knew the right programming language, she felt sure she could help me get an interview. The problem was that the company wanted to make its decision the next day! I went right from the phone to my computer, looked up the company's home page, and found out they have several big projects using Java. Perfect! And their home page described some of their projects in detail. The next day I showed up for the interview confident and ready.

Notice how this narrative example helps show the advantage of using a Web site to prepare for an interview. The brief example wouldn't have worked nearly as well.

A narrative example, then, is a specific incident (usually with names, dates, other details). It is not a kind of event or activity that *could* happen, such as "do research on Web pages." It is an anecdote, the story of what *has* happened (Wednesday night, Joanne, Java programming).

Let's examine another narrative example. You might find a paragraph like this in a magazine like *Time* or *Newsweek*:

■ Another Narrative Example

Alison Marks, a twenty-three-year-old graduate student in architecture at the University of Colorado, had a blood pressure of 180/120 in February. Her doctor prescribed Elavil, which Alison took for three months until she became so busy with exams that she found taking medicine too much trouble. After exams, she still neglected her medicine. As a result, her blood pressure rose so sharply that in September she was rushed to the hospital with a stroke.

Do we care that this patient was an architecture student, or that she was twenty-three, or that she was named Alison Marks? Yes, somehow we do. Through this information, Alison becomes more real to us, someone we can sympathize with. And, because Alison's case becomes believable and typical, we begin to believe that people with high blood pressure should take their medicine. The narrative example has helped convince us.

Now let's apply what we've learned about narrative examples to the one-paragraph essay. Suppose you're sitting in your room trying to write your first college English paper—the one for this course. You remember your professor's words: "I want to see examples—*specific* examples—whatever else you do on this paper." She's told you to write about something that distracts you. You look aimlessly around the room, your eyes suddenly brighten, and you slap down this sentence:

My roommate distracts me when I try to study.

Now you need some examples. Let's see. She has that tape player going again, she's smacking her gum, and you remember all those dumb questions she asks every few minutes. Here goes:

■ First Try

Although my roommate is a helpful companion at times, she is a distracting nuisance whenever I try to study. Throughout the evening, her tape player blares in my ears. Even worse, she insists on smacking her gum. She also interrupts me with questions that have nothing to do with homework. At any other time, my roommate is a friend, but while I'm studying, she's my greatest enemy.

"Pretty good," you say. "I think I'll show it to my roommate to see what she— on second thought, . . ."

Now, suppose you're sitting in your room a couple of days later, ego deflated by a low grade, trying to rewrite that paper. Your examples seemed specific enough to you—record player, gum, questions—but they obviously weren't. You used quick examples when a narrative example might have been more effective.

Instead of presenting a list of things your roommate does to distract you, you could have used a narrative example—a story of something that *actually did happen* at a particular time and a particular place. In other words, you could have written about one specific study period; you could have told us not just that her tape player was going—you could have told us what tape she was playing. You could have told us what kind of gum she was chewing. You even could have told us what specific "dumb" questions she asked you. In other words, you could have written this paragraph:

■ Better Version with a Narrative Example

Although my roommate is a helpful companion at times, she is a distracting nuisance whenever I try to study. Just last Wednesday night, Anna decided to spend the evening playing her "classic" Bob Dylan tapes. While I was trying desperately to integrate a math function, all I could hear was that the answer was somewhere "blowin' in the wind." Even worse, the entire time Dylan was rasping away, Anna accompanied him by smacking and popping her Bazooka bubble gum. I'd finally given up on math and started my struggle with chemistry when she abruptly asked (loudly, of course, so I could hear her over the music), "Do you think any Cokes are left in the Coke machine?" My stomach started rumbling and my throat suddenly felt dry—even drier than the chemistry text I was trying to read. As I dropped the change into the Coke machine, I realized that although Anna is usually a friend, while I'm studying she is my greatest enemy.

Now we can picture you, and Anna, and all those distractions. You've told us the *story* (a narrative example) of your evening trying to study, helping us to *see* you and *feel* your frustration. That's communication. So remember the secret that all professional writers know: *examples*.

STATISTICS

Examples are an important form of support to help convince your readers and make your paper more interesting. Examples alone, though, may not be enough. Sometimes we need something else: *numbers*. Who doesn't love numbers, trust them, believe in them? Give us a statistic we don't suspect is phony, and we are probably convinced right there. Alison Marks and her trouble with high blood pressure may move us emotionally, but we will more likely be persuaded by a medical report like this:

■ Paragraph with Statistics

Recent statistics show convincingly that jogging is saving the lives of many Americans. Of the 12.5 million who jog at least ten miles per week, 78 percent have a pulse rate and blood pressure lower than nonjoggers of the same age. Estimates indicate that these joggers can expect to live to an average age of 77—more than three years longer than the average age of their contemporaries. The lesson seems clear, doesn't it?

To be convincing, statistics must be unambiguous. We aren't necessarily alarmed, for example, to hear that seven of fifty-four football players were injured in a practice session because we have no way of knowing how serious the injuries were. Perhaps six of the players were treated with Band-Aids. We would certainly be alarmed, however, to hear that seven of fifty-four football players were hospitalized for at least one night following a practice session. The second statistic defines *injury* more clearly, so it is more convincing than the first.

STATEMENTS BY AUTHORITIES

The last kind of support we'll consider is the statement by an authority, a person who is in a position to know about a subject. If people we trust tell us something, we just might believe them because we trust *them:* their character, their judgment, and their knowledge of the subject.

We have no reason to believe Alison Marks, the architecture student who forgot to take her pills, if she tells us that shark hunting is one of the safest sports, but we might listen to her if she tells us that patients with high blood pressure should take their medicine. We also might believe the president of the American Medical Association, a research specialist in high blood pressure, or a cardiologist—people who know what they're talking about.

People whose unsupported opinions about high blood pressure would fail to convince us are those whose character, judgment, or knowledge of the subject is questionable:

- We wouldn't trust the unsupported opinion of the druggist convicted of selling overpriced drugs to people who didn't need them anyway.
- We wouldn't trust the doctor being investigated for gross incompetence by the American Medical Association.
- And we wouldn't trust our roommate, who thinks blood pressure is measured by a thermometer.

The first has doubtful character; the second, doubtful judgment; and the third, doubtful knowledge.

Citing an authority is particularly important when you present statistics. Remember all those impressive figures about people who jog? For all you know, they came from a sixth-grade creative writing class. Unless the writer reveals the source of the statistics, readers don't know whether or not to trust them.

Here's a revision of the paragraph about joggers. Notice the use of authorities (in italics), including one that cites statistics:

■ Authority and Statistics

Recent statistics show convincingly that jogging is saving the lives of many Americans. *According to the Congressional Subcommittee on Physical Fitness,* 78 percent of the 12.5 million people who jog at least ten miles per week have a pulse rate and blood pressure lower than nonjoggers of the same age. *This committee* estimates that these joggers can expect to live to an average age of 77—more than three years longer than the average age of their contemporaries. *Dr. Hans Corpuscle, chief adviser to the committee,* says that joggers are "the single healthiest group of people in America today." The lesson seems clear, doesn't it?

COMBINED TYPES OF SUPPORT

A paragraph that uses one type of support—examples, maybe—is often convincing, but many good paragraphs contain several types: a couple of examples and some statistics, or a statement by an authority and an example, and so on.

The following paragraph says that people attend yard sales for entertainment. Can you identify the types of support?

■ Combined Support

Although you might think that most people attend yard sales for the bargains, the main reason they attend is for the entertainment they find there. For example, consider what happened to my family last summer when we held a yard sale to get rid of some old things before moving to a new place. Many people came, but few bought. Each new carload of people disgorged a new group that would while away an hour or so on a Saturday by caressing the sun-faded curtains, thumbing through ancient *National Geographic* magazines, and carefully considering sweaters eight sizes too small for them or anyone else in their group. Then the group would gather around a folded section of the classified ads and pick the next sale they'd visit. My suspicions about why those people came to our sale were confirmed a few months later by a survey I read in *Psychology Monthly.* The survey showed that seven of ten people who attended yard sales admitted they did so "just for the fun of it." The psychologist who conducted the survey reached a conclusion I could have told him last summer: "The real bargain that people seek at yard sales, if only subconsciously, is not another frying pan or partially burned plastic spatula, but just a little weekend entertainment."

Notice that the statement by the authority is an effective rewording of the topic sentence, so that no separate concluding sentence is necessary for this paragraph.

The above paragraph uses all three kinds of support—all of it invented by the writer. Sufficient statistics and statements by authorities are not difficult to find when you invent support for class exercises or when you research it in books or magazines. When you write paragraphs based on personal experiences, however (like many samples in this section of the book), you will rely heavily on examples rather than statistics and authority statements. Fortunately, the example is one of the most colorful and convincing kinds of support.

Of course, writing can succeed without personal examples. Consider this paragraph from the first chapter:

> Climbing Mount Everest, the highest mountain in the world, is extremely dangerous. One indication of its danger is that nobody succeeded in climbing it until Sir Edmund Hillary and Tenzing Norgay reached the summit in 1953 — not all that long ago. In his best-selling book on Everest, *Into Thin Air*, Jon Krakauer points out the danger with a chilling statistic: between 1921 and 1996, 144 people died in the attempt (p. 274). Krakauer, who made it to the top, adds, "Truth be told, climbing Everest has always been an extraordinarily dangerous undertaking and doubtless always will be, whether the people involved are Himalayan neophytes being guided up the peak or world-class mountaineers climbing with their peers" (p. 274). In the case of Everest, height and danger certainly go together.

This paragraph combines a statistic and a statement by an authority. Interesting factual content can be every bit as compelling as examples.

INVENTED SUPPORT

Before you begin the exercises, let's discuss invented support, which can greatly simplify the learning process for you in two ways:

- You don't have to struggle to find real support at the same time you're trying to figure out just what good support is. In fact, you don't have to search any further than your own mind.
- You can be as specific as you like.

But remember, inventing evidence for a class is just an exercise, a convenience for you and your instructor.

Rules for Inventing Support

Please follow these rules when you invent your support:

- Never write invented support unless your readers know that what they are reading is invented.
- Never write invented support unless your instructor approves.

If you're careful, you can have fun with your writing. Most of the examples we used in this chapter were invented; you could easily tell that. So try to be imaginative. At the same time, though, be somewhat realistic. Don't, for instance, try to convince us that the Grand Junction School of Cosmetology is noted for its scholarly excellence because it had thirteen Rhodes scholars last year. The school may be good, but such an exaggerated figure is bound to raise eyebrows.

PRACTICAL WRITING

Good support has practical value for any kind of writing. In the previous chapter, we showed you a one-paragraph essay on e. e. cummings' poetry. It might have served as a good short answer for a test, but it didn't have enough support to be effective in many other circumstances. So let's add some specific support—in this case, quick examples—to improve it:

> I like the individual freedom that comes through in e. e. cummings' poetry. You can see that freedom right away in the lack of both capitalization and normal spacing in his writing. Just look at the way he writes his name—no capital letters! Already he seems like a rebel (as he certainly was). You can also see his emphasis on individual freedom in his content: his poems often deal with the carefreeness of spring and the value of the individual. Consider, for example, the first lines of one of his most famous poems: " 'sweet spring is your / time is my time is our / time for springtime is lovetime / and viva sweet love.' " The value of spring and the individual certainly comes through in those lines, doesn't it? Format and content are two elements that reveal the emphasis on freedom that I like so much in e. e. cummings' poetry.

The examples make a lot of difference in the paragraph's impact, don't they? You can use the same technique—good support—in virtually all of your writing in school, whether you're writing about poetry, computers, or laser optics. All readers need the concreteness that good examples give.

The need for good support also carries over into your writing after you graduate. In fact, a common problem with business writing is that it leaves out the convincing support and relies instead on generalizations.

Suppose you are president of a business and you've had some people inspecting your company. A section of the inspection report contains this generalization with only poor support:

■ Poor Support: A Generalization

We made many random observations of the workforce. Much of the time, workers were not productive.

"That's interesting," you may say, "but I'm hardly convinced. Where's the proof?" Let's consider a rewrite, this time adding some statistics:

■ A Little Better: With Statistics

During June, we made *118 random observations* of the workforce. *At least 78 times,* the workers were not productive.

"Hmmm," you might say. "So, what do you mean by 'not productive 78 times'? Can you tell me more?"

The inspector can tell more—and should have in the first place. Let's look now at what should have been the first version. This time, it has not only statistics but some quick examples, too:

■ Much Better: With Statistics and Quick Examples

During June, we made 118 random observations of the workforce. At least 78 times, the workers were not productive. These are some of our observations:

- After clocking in, about 20 employees routinely left their workshops in company vehicles and went to the cafeteria. Some stayed more than an hour.
- During one five-day period, 9 of 19 employees didn't work a full shift. They arrived as much as 30 minutes late, left as much as 30 minutes early, or both.
- On June 19, about 40 employees returned to the shop area 30 to 60 minutes before the end of the work day.
- On June 20, some employees parked for over 40 minutes behind the library. Others drove company vehicles for long periods without stopping to do any work.

From our inspection, we believe these observations in June are typical of what goes on year round.

The inspectors seem much more convincing now, don't they? So, remember: detailed support is a key to communication at school and on the job.

EXERCISES

A. For each of the topic sentences below, invent (in other words, simply make up) a quick example (1 sentence), a narrative example (3–5 sentences), a statistic (1–2 sentences), and a statement by an authority (1–2 sentences), as required. Use the sample paragraph on yard sales, which has invented support, as a model.

1. *Grizzly bears are a big threat to campers in Montana.*

   a. **narrative example** _____

   _____

   b. **statistic** _____

   _____

   c. **statement by an authority** _____

   _____

2. *Browsing the Internet can be a real time-saver.*

   a. **statistic** _____

   _____

   b. **narrative example** _____

   _____

   c. **statement by an authority** _____

   _____

3. *Some of today's music carries a valuable message for young children.*

   a. **quick example** _____

   _____

   b. **quick example** _____

   _____

    c.   **statement by an authority** _____

    _____

B. Follow the same instructions for these topic sentences:

    1. _Grizzly bears aren't much of a threat to campers in Montana._

        a   **statement by an authority** _____

        _____

        b. **quick example** _____

        _____

        c. **narrative example** _____

        _____

    2. _Browsing the Internet can be a real waste of time._

        a. **narrative example** _____

        _____

        b. **statistic** _____

        _____

        c. **statement by an authority** _____

        _____

    3. _Some of today's music carries a poor message for young children._

        a. **quick example** _____

        _____

        b. **quick example** _____

        _____

        c. **statement by an authority** _____

        _____

C. Invent support for the same topic sentence four different ways:

1. *Pizza is surprisingly good for you.*

    a   statistic _____

    _____

    b. statistic _____

    _____

    c. statistic _____

    _____

2. *Pizza is surprisingly good for you.*

    a. **statement by an authority** _____

    _____

    b. **statement by an authority** _____

    _____

3. *Pizza is surprisingly good for you.*

    a. **quick example** _____

    _____

    b. **quick example** _____

    _____

    c. **quick example** _____

    _____

4. *Pizza is surprisingly good for you.*

    a. **narrative example** _____

    _____

b. narrative example _____

_____

D. Answer these questions about Exercise C:

1. Which form of support was most effective? Why?
2. Which form of support was least effective? Why?
3. What combination of support (statistics, statements by authorities, quick examples, narrative examples) would you recommend for the topic sentence in Exercise C? Why?

E. Look at the paragraph on yard sales in the chapter. Now intentionally destroy the effectiveness of the paragraph: rewrite the good example (the second through the fifth sentences) by making it too general.

F. Now reverse Exercise E. Here are some topic sentences followed by examples that are too general. Improve each italicized example by converting the dull generality into a narrative example. You'll need several sentences for each one.

1. Vacations to other states can be educational. *Last summer, for example, I learned some interesting things.*
2. Diets are hard to stick to. *One time I couldn't resist some snacks when I went out.*
3. Books can help young people develop character. *Some books help a lot.*

G. In Exercises A, B, and C you outlined several paragraphs. Choose the one that interests you the most and use the support you invented to write the paragraph. Appendix A to this book gives you a suggested format.

CHAPTER 3
Topic Sentence

Now we move to the first sentence of the Stage I one-paragraph essay: the topic sentence. Think of the topic sentence as the main idea of the paragraph—the point you're making, the generalization that the rest of your paragraph will support.

Writing texts use a variety of terms to define *topic sentence*: it is the writer's "viewpoint" of the topic, the writer's "judgment" about the topic, the writer's "conviction," the writer's "assertion." The topic sentence is all these things. However, we prefer the term *opinion*: the topic sentence is a precise statement of the opinion you wish to persuade your readers to accept.

Why do we associate a topic sentence with the word *opinion*? An opinion is a judgment that seems true only for the person who believes it. Imagine for a moment that you're telling a friend something you believe—a viewpoint, a judgment, a conviction, an assertion you hold to be true. Your friend replies, "That's just your opinion." She's not denying that you believe what you say, but she is letting you know that you'll have to persuade her to agree with you. She's placing the burden on you to support your belief so that she can accept the idea as you do.

A similar relationship exists between you (the writer) and your readers. Your topic sentence stands as a statement of your opinion *until* you persuade your audience to accept it fully. Recognizing that the topic sentence is a statement of opinion will help you remember your obligation to support your idea.

Why should the topic sentence be an opinion instead of a fact? If you state your idea and your readers respond with, "Oh, yes, that's true" or "That's a fact," what more can you say? Suppose you write this topic sentence:

William Shakespeare wrote *Hamlet.*

In your paragraph you could discuss Shakespeare or his play, but you wouldn't be trying to convince a reader to accept the topic sentence itself; that Shakespeare wrote *Hamlet* is accepted as fact. And statements of fact (or at least what everyone accepts as fact) make poor topic sentences because they leave the writer nothing important to say. On the other hand, suppose you try this topic sentence:

Francis Bacon wrote *Hamlet.*

Now you've stated an opinion. Unfortunately, hardly anyone believes it. You've crossed into such extreme controversy that you'll really have to work to convince readers to accept your topic-sentence opinion.

Your topic-sentence opinion doesn't need to arouse instant doubt. You don't need to take outrageous stands like these:

Dogs are really man's greatest enemy.

A toupee is better than real hair.

In fact, most good topic sentences bring neither instant acceptance nor instant doubt. Usually readers have not formed their own judgments, and they're willing to accept yours if you persuade them. For example, consider this topic sentence:

Today's toupees are so well made that they look like a person's own hair.

The writer is stating what he believes to be fact. Although readers have no reason to doubt him, they are not obliged to believe him either. They probably will agree with what he says once he provides specific support for his opinion. And it *is* his opinion—until he persuades readers to accept it as fully as he does.

When you write a one-paragraph essay, you'll begin with a topic sentence and follow it with specific support (examples, statistics, or authoritative statements). If you structure the topic sentence well and support it well with specifics, you'll persuade your readers to accept your idea fully. The rest of this chapter shows you how to write a good topic sentence.

A Good Topic Sentence

A good topic sentence has two parts:

- a *limited* subject
- a *precise opinion* about that subject

LIMITING THE SUBJECT

The first step in writing a good topic sentence is to choose a subject limited enough to support in a single paragraph. If you try to support a large subject in a one-paragraph essay, your argument is not likely to be convincing: your subject will probably demand more support than you can develop in one paragraph. Thus, limiting the subject is the first step toward writing a good topic sentence.

Let's look at a sample. Suppose you begin with a general subject: advertising. Because the topic is obviously too large for a one-paragraph essay, you must limit it. Of the many types of advertisements (television, radio, newspaper, billboard, and the like), you choose one—for instance, magazine advertising.

As you glance at the advertisements in your favorite magazine, three attract your attention. In one advertisement, you see a scantily clad woman holding a tape recorder she wants you to buy. In another, a muscular man is looking manfully at a bottle of cologne. And in a third ad, a couple embrace in delight as they hold cigarettes in their free hands. You see a common element in each sales pitch: the advertisers use sex appeal to make you want the things you see before you. In this way you limit the subject from *advertising* to *magazine advertising* to *sex appeal in magazine advertising*.

Consider the process you just went through. You might have noticed the lack of color in the tape-recorder advertisement, the large amount of space wasted in the cologne ad, or the small print that obscures the Surgeon General's warning in the cigarette advertisement. Instead, you focused your attention on sex appeal in the ads, thereby limiting the subject.

STATING THE PRECISE OPINION

The second part of the topic sentence expresses your opinion about the limited subject. Although limiting the subject is a step toward precision, an opinion about even a limited subject will remain vague unless you tell your readers what your idea is exactly.

The precise-opinion part of the topic sentence is a word or phrase that makes a judgment, such as *dangerous* or *exciting*. But a warning is necessary here, for not all judgment words will express precise opinions. Words like *interesting, nice, good,* or *bad* start to take a stand but remain vague. What do you really mean when you say something is "interesting"? What have you said about a person you call "nice"? Such vague judgments make imprecise opinions. On the other hand, precise judgments combine with a subject to define your opinion about the subject.

Again, let's apply this theory to our sample case, sex appeal in magazine advertising. So what if advertisers support sales with sex appeal? You look again at the ads that will support your argument only to find another common element: sex appeal isn't really related to the items for sale. The ads hold your attention because sex appeal was connected to nonsexual items. You are irritated because the advertisers are trying to manipulate your senses so that you will buy whatever they put in the advertisements. Thus, you are ready to state precisely your opinion about sex appeal in these three advertisements: it is *irrelevant*.

Again, consider the process you used. You had to make a judgment about sex appeal in the advertising; you had to establish your precise opinion about the subject. Because you didn't like the sex appeal in the ads, you might have said that the sex appeal was bad. But what would *bad* mean? Did the sex appeal disgust you? Did it appeal to your prurient interests in a manner not consistent with community standards (whatever those might be)? Did the sex appeal in the ads merely irritate you? Just what was the *badness?* When you made the precise judgment that sex appeal in some magazine advertisements is *irrelevant to the product,* you established your exact stand on the subject.

WRITING THE TOPIC SENTENCE

When you have limited the subject and have decided precisely your opinion about it, you have formed the two basic parts of the topic sentence: a *limited subject* and a *precise opinion* about that subject. You can easily structure a topic sentence by stating the precise opinion in some form after the sentence's subject, as in the following:

> For me, dieting is futile.

Dieting, the subject of the sentence, is the limited subject, and *futile,* which follows, is the precise opinion about it.

Now we can write the topic sentence for the paragraph on sex appeal in magazine advertisements.

> The sex appeal in many magazine advertisements is irrelevant.

We can see, then, that the basic pattern for the topic sentence is "*limited subject* is *precise opinion.*" Consider these examples:

> Arcade video games are challenging.

> Restoring old houses is rewarding.

In the first sentence, *arcade video games* is the limited subject and *challenging* is the precise opinion. In the second, you intend to persuade readers that *restoring old houses* (the limited subject) is *rewarding* (the precise opinion).

REFINING THE TOPIC SENTENCE

Even though this pattern is basic for a topic sentence, you aren't restricted to it. Perhaps the model seems too mechanical. You can easily convert the model to a slightly more sophisticated form. Look at the following topic sentence in the basic pattern:

Overpackaging of supermarket items is seriously wasteful of natural resources.

Here is the same idea in another form:

Overpackaging of supermarket items seriously wastes natural resources.

Notice that the precise opinion *wasteful* (the basic pattern) became the verb *wastes* in the second sentence form. Now look at a topic sentence from an earlier chapter:

Even though I have never really lived there, going to my grandmother's farm always seems like coming home.

That sentence almost exactly follows our basic model:

Going to my grandmother's farm is like coming home.

In another topic sentence we may say this:

Hitchhiking is dangerous.

But we may also state the sentence more imaginatively:

Hitchhiking has proved to be the last ride for many people.

The important point is that refined topic sentences, such as those above, always can be converted to the basic model: "*limited subject* is *precise opinion.*" When you write a topic-sentence form beyond the model, take a moment to make sure that you still can convert it to the two basic parts.

Whatever the pattern of the topic sentences, the result is the same. When you have limited your subject and precisely defined your opinion about it, you have created an assertion that will guide both you and your readers through the supporting material of the paragraph.

PRACTICAL WRITING

As we discussed in Chapter 1, topic sentences are useful beyond this course. Did the topic sentence about e. e. cummings follow the basic model?

I like the individual freedom that comes through in e. e. cummings' poetry.

No—but we can convert it to the basic model:

The poetry of e. e. cummings is about individual freedom.

Starting with a good topic sentence can be useful in a paper in college about literature. In fact, a good topic sentence is a great start for just about any paper you write on any subject. Think of any other college subject, and you'll quickly see that there's usually a need to clearly express your idea—your opinion—about something in that subject. For example:

- *History.* What were the main causes of the Civil War?
- *Astronomy.* What is the probable composition of the Great Red Spot on Jupiter?
- *Chemistry.* What is the most efficient way to identify an unknown substance?
- *Computer sciences.* What is the best way to network computers over a wide area?

A topic sentence gives focus to your paper, for your reader and for you. Understanding the value of topic sentences should be of immense value to you as a communicator.

EXERCISES

A. Place a check mark by the sentences that would not make good topic sentences because they don't state opinions or because the opinions aren't precise.

_____   1. Pets are neat.

_____   2. Pets are popular in impoverished countries.

_____   3. The Rocky Mountains challenged the navigational abilities of early pioneers.

_____   4. Competitive parachuting takes place this weekend.

_____   5. Competitive parachuting can be surprisingly safe.

_____   6. Accurate weather forecasting requires tremendously sophisticated computers.

_____   7. Years ago, state fairs were great!

_____   8. Years ago, state fairs helped farmers develop a sense of community.

_____ 9. Desert states have less than 10 inches of rainfall per year.

_____ 10. Desert states have explosive population growth because of the effects of modern technology.

B. For these topic sentences, underline the subject once and the opinion twice. Also, circle any subjects that aren't limited enough and any opinions that aren't precise enough.

1. Death Valley is the lowest point in the United States.

2. Death Valley is attractive to winter tourists.

3. Many airports have high-tech features.

4. Delaware's state bird is the blue hen chicken.

5. Fatty foods are unhealthful.

6. Jack Dempsey, the famous heavyweight boxer, was tough.

7. Summer evenings with friends are neat.

8. The outer planets are inhospitable to any species on Earth.

9. Firefighters' tactics are based on scientific research.

10. Trips to foreign countries are usually fun.

C. Limit the general subjects below and then state a precise opinion about each limited subject:

Example: **General subject**   traveling

_____*Hitchhiking*_____ is/are _____*a danger to us*_____
        (Limited subject)   (Precise opinion)

1. **General subject**   medical breakthroughs

_____ is/are _____
        (Limited subject)   (Precise opinion)

2. **General subject**   travel

_____ is/are _____
        (Limited subject)   (Precise opinion)

3. **General subject**   insects

   _____ is/are _____
          (Limited subject)   (Precise opinion)

4. **General subject**   communication devices

   _____ is/are _____
          (Limited subject)   (Precise opinion)

5. **General subject**   entertainment

   _____ is/are _____
          (Limited subject)   (Precise opinion)

6. **General subject**   pets

   _____ is/are _____
          (Limited subject)   (Precise opinion)

CHAPTER 4

Unity

You know a topic sentence presents a precise opinion about a limited subject. Now we can go to the next step in good writing: unity.

Think about the word *unity* for a moment. It means *oneness*, doesn't it? For a paragraph to have unity, it must have *oneness*. More specifically, each idea in the paragraph should clearly support the "one main point," the topic sentence. Normally your writing should exclude any ideas that are irrelevant, that don't support the point of the paragraph.

If, for example, you're writing about the dullest class you ever took, you'd destroy the unity by talking about the fascinating lectures and exciting field trips. Or, if you want to show that your mynah bird is an ideal pet, the friendliness of the boa constrictor is off the subject and, therefore, irrelevant. In other words, everything you say in a paragraph must support your main point. Can you find the two places in this next paragraph where the writer loses her sense of unity?

■ Poor Unity

My most frustrating job was cooking for the dorm cafeteria during my freshman year. No matter how hard I tried, I never could cook what the menu said because the food company always delivered the wrong food or brought it late. I also was frustrated because I had trouble estimating how much food to cook. Many times we ran short of hamburgers or had to throw away pounds and pounds of french fries. Sometimes we ate the extra french fries, though, and we'd sit around, joking and having a good time. The worst thing, however, was the condition of my clothes after the meal was over. Even if I hadn't spilled anything (and I usually had spilled spaghetti or something worse), my clothes smelled awful. I'd want to go home to change before going anyplace else. Some of the other students who didn't work in the cafeteria also spilled food and had to change, too. No wonder, then, I thought cooking for the dorm cafeteria was frustrating.

Two sentences violate the unity of the paragraph. The first is about eating french fries and having a good time; the second is about other students spilling food on themselves and having to change clothes. Neither of those sentences has anything to do with the main topic of the paragraph: working in the cafeteria is *a frustrating job*. Here's a diagram showing what we mean:

> **Topic sentence**
> My job as cook was frustrating.
> **Support**
> Wrong food was delivered.
> **Support**
> I had trouble estimating amounts.
> **Support**
> Had fun eating extra food.
> **Support**
> My clothes were messy.
> **Support**
> Other students changed clothes, too.
> **Conclusion**
> Therefore, my job as cook was frustrating.

Now let's fix the unity of that paragraph:

■ Good Unity

My most frustrating job was cooking for the dorm cafeteria during my freshman year. No matter how hard I tried, I never could cook what the menu said because the food company always delivered the wrong food or brought it late. I also was frustrated because I had trouble estimating how much food to cook—many times we ran short of hamburgers or had to throw away pounds and pounds of french fries. The worst thing, however, was the condition of my clothes after the meal was over. Even if I hadn't spilled anything (and I usually had spilled spaghetti or something worse), my clothes smelled awful. I'd want to go home to change before going anyplace else. No wonder, then, I thought cooking for the dorm cafeteria was frustrating.

Note the difference: the writer sticks to the subject. All the examples help show that being a cook for the dorm cafeteria was frustrating. A diagram of this paragraph looks unified, showing that all the blocks fit:

> **Topic sentence**
> My job as cook was frustrating.
> **Support**
> Wrong food was delivered.
> **Support**
> I had trouble estimating amounts.
> **Support**
> My clothes were messy
> **Conclusion**
> Therefore, my job as cook was frustrating.

As you can see, the idea of unity is simple: stick to the point. Don't be led astray by a word or idea in one of your sentences the way the writer was in the first paragraph. Make sure everything in your paragraph belongs there. That way, your reader won't be distracted—or worse, confused.

EXERCISES

A. Read these paragraphs and underline the precise opinion in each topic sentence. Then identify those sentences that don't help support the precise opinion.

1. (1) Preparing a house for sale is exhausting work. (2) First, you have to repaint everything—inside and out. (3) Then you have to clean the carpets and floors. (4) Sometimes you find neat things in the house you haven't seen for years! (5) And, last, you have to get the yard completely in shape. (6) Getting a house ready for sale really is tiring.

    The irrelevant sentence is _____.

2. (1) Albert Bierstadt was a pioneer as a landscape painter. (2) He desired to paint unusual places so much that he left his home in Europe—in the middle of the nineteenth century—and moved to the United States. (3) He painted mainly traditional landscapes before he left Europe. (4) He was also a pioneer in that he traveled to the far west of the United States to do his most famous paintings: large pictures of Yosemite. (5) Albert Bierstadt's drive to paint the unusual made him a pioneer.

    The irrelevant sentence is _____.

3. (1) Walt Disney was a creative genius. (2) He created the first animated film with talking characters, the first color animated film, and

the first full-length animated film. (3) Surprisingly, he wasn't much of a cartoonist himself. (4) Disney also created the idea of theme parks—including Disneyland and Disney World. (5) He earned a lot of money from his ideas. (6) He really was a very creative person.

The irrelevant sentence is _____.

B. In the following examples, provide unified support for the topic sentence. If you need to, invent specific details for your support.

1.

> **Topic sentence**
> Maps use colors well.
> > **Support**
> > **Support**
> > **Support**
> **Reworded topic sentence**
> Therefore, maps use colors well.

2.

> **Topic sentence**
> Classrooms need comfortable furniture.
> > **Support**
> > **Support**
> > **Support**
> **Reworded topic sentence**
> Therefore, classrooms need comfortable furniture.

3.

> **Topic sentence**
> Breakfast is usually my poorest meal.
> > **Support**
> > **Support**
> > **Support**
> **Reworded topic sentence**
> Therefore, breakfast is usually my poorest meal.

C. Write a paragraph on one of the topic sentences in Exercise B; use your invented support. Add two irrelevant sentences to destroy the paragraph's unity, and underline them.

CHAPTER 5
Coherence

A one-paragraph essay needs more than unity. It also must have coherence. The best way to define *coherence* is to look at its opposite: *incoherence*. If a woman runs into a room screaming, "Fire! Dog! House!" we call her incoherent. Does she mean that a dog is on fire in the house? Or that the house is on fire with the dog inside? Or that a doghouse is on fire? We don't know. Although the woman apparently has some important ideas she wishes desperately to communicate, she has left out the essential links of thought. Coherence requires including those links.

This chapter discusses three important ways to achieve coherence in a one-paragraph essay:

- explanation of the support
- reminders of the opinion in the topic sentence
- transitions

These important techniques will help your readers move smoothly from idea to idea within your paragraph. Then, when your doghouse catches on fire, you'll know exactly how to call for help.

EXPLANATION OF THE SUPPORT

Don't assume that your readers are specially gifted people able to read minds. You must not only present the support to the readers but also explain how it is related to the topic sentence. In other words, you must link your support—clearly and unambiguously—to the topic sentence. The author of the following paragraph does not try to explain his support at all, apparently hoping that his readers are clairvoyant:

■ First Try

In the early morning, I am easily annoyed by my roommate. I have to shut the ice-covered windows. A white tornado of dandruff swirls around the room. A mass of smoke from cigarettes hovers near the door. No wonder I find my roommate annoying.

No wonder, indeed! The paragraph is incoherent because the author has failed to explain how his support relates to the topic sentence. Does he mean that his roommate is annoying because he does not close the window in the morning? Or is he annoying because he opens the window every night, even in winter, thus causing the writer to be cold in the morning? And who has dandruff, and who smokes? Is it the roommate, or is it the author, who is upset because the roommate does not understand? After all, the author may be doing the best he can to get rid of the dandruff, and he is smoking heavily only because he is trying to distract himself after waking up every morning in a cold room. By being incomplete, by not explaining the support fully, the paragraph demands too much of readers. Let's guess what the writer really meant and revise the paragraph to add coherence.

■ Second Try

In the early morning, I am easily annoyed by my roommate. I have to shut the ice-covered windows *that John, my roommate, insists on opening every night, even during the winter.* A white tornado swirling around the room *shows me that his dandruff problem is still in full force.* A mass of smoke *from John's pack-a-day habit* hovers near the door. No wonder I find my roommate annoying.

We have now explained that John, the roommate, is guilty of the indiscretions. The coherence is improved greatly, but the paragraph still needs work.

REMINDERS OF THE OPINION IN THE TOPIC SENTENCE

In the preceding section, we learned not to assume that readers can read minds. In this section, however, we will make an assumption about readers: readers, like all of us, prefer being mentally lazy. They don't like remembering too much at once. While they read the support, they like occasional reminders of the opinion in the topic sentence so that they will remember why they are reading that support. We can remind them of the topic sentence's opinion with either of two techniques at the beginning of each item of support:

- We can repeat the exact words of the opinion.
- We can use other words that suggest the opinion.

In the sample paragraph about the roommate, we can use the word *annoy* in presenting each example, or we can use words such as *disgusted* or *choking on stale smoke,* which *suggest* annoyance. Notice the reminders in the revised paragraph:

■ Third Try

In the early morning, I am easily annoyed by my roommate. I *am annoyed* each time I have to shut the ice-covered windows that John, my roommate, insists on opening every night, even during the winter. A *disgusting* white tornado swirling around the room shows me that his dandruff problem is still in full force. A *choking mass of stale smoke* from John's pack-a-day habit hovers near the door. No wonder I find my roommate annoying.

By reminding the readers that each example presents something annoying, the paragraph becomes more coherent.

TRANSITIONS

Each example in the sample paragraph now has a clear explanation of the support and a reminder of the opinion in the topic sentence, but the paragraph is still rough. It moves like a train with square wheels, chunking along abruptly from idea to idea. To help the paragraph move more smoothly, we must add transitions.

Transitions are like road signs that tell readers where they are going. If you live in Louisville and wish to drive north to Indianapolis, you don't want to stop to ask people to find out if you are on the right road. You would rather have road signs.

Similarly, readers don't want to run into an example that slows them because they don't understand how it relates to the previous example or, worse yet, how it relates to the topic sentence. In a paragraph, the road sign could be *however* to tell readers that the next idea is going to contrast with the one just presented; or it could be *also* to tell readers that another idea like the preceding one is about to be presented; or it could be *therefore* to tell readers to prepare for a conclusion.

These and other transitions will keep your reader from losing valuable time because she has to stop, or, if she takes a chance and presses on, from arriving nowhere, which is where she may end her trip through a paragraph without transitions.

Common Transitions

To *add an idea:* also, and, another, equally important, finally, furthermore, in addition, last, likewise, moreover, most important, next, second, third

To *give an example:* for example, for instance, as an illustration, as a case in point, consider . . .

To *make a contrast:* and yet, but, however, instead, nevertheless, nonetheless, on the contrary, on the other hand, still

To *begin a conclusion:* as a result, clearly, hence, in conclusion, no wonder, obviously, then, therefore, thus

A paragraph must have transitions, but where should you place them?

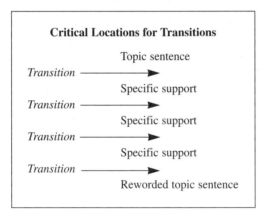

Critical Locations for Transitions

Transition ⟶ Topic sentence

Transition ⟶ Specific support

Transition ⟶ Specific support

Transition ⟶ Specific support

Reworded topic sentence

Sometimes you will find that no transition is necessary between the topic sentence and the first item of specific support because the second sentence of the paragraph is so obviously an example that a transitional expression seems too mechanical. For instance, you might be able to leave out the first transition in this final revision of the sample paragraph about the roommate. The remaining transitions, however, are all desirable.

■ Final Version

In the early morning, I am easily annoyed by my roommate. *For example,* I am annoyed each time I have to shut the ice-covered windows that John, my roommate, insists on opening every night, even during the winter. I am *also* disgusted by a white tornado swirling around the room, which shows me that his dandruff problem is still in full force. *Most bothersome, though,* is the choking mass of stale smoke from John's pack-a-day habit that hovers near the door. *No wonder* I find my roommate annoying.

Our sample paragraph is finally coherent. We have:

- explained the support
- reminded the reader frequently of the opinion in the topic sentence
- added transitions at the critical locations

You're so familiar with the above paragraph by now, and it's so simple, you may believe the transitions aren't really necessary. Perhaps you're right. But what if you read a paragraph that begins like this?

■ Poor Coherence

If you've ever bought a pomegranate, you probably know that it's one of the most difficult foods to eat. The juice is delicious and a beautiful ruby color. It drips everywhere, staining whatever it hits. The bitter, inedible pulp seems impossible to avoid. . . .

By now, you're probably lost. If the writer has trouble eating a pomegranate, then why start by telling us how delicious and beautiful it is? The writer knows why, but the readers don't because there aren't any transitions. Let's put them in:

■ Revised for Effective Coherence

If you've ever bought a pomegranate, you probably know that it's one of the most difficult foods to eat. *Although* the juice is delicious and a beautiful ruby color, it *unfortunately* drips everywhere, staining whatever it hits. *Also frustrating,* the bitter, inedible pulp seems impossible to avoid. . . .

The transitions (and the reminder *frustrating*) make the writer's point easy to understand the first time through.

Good writing shouldn't be an IQ test or a guessing game for the readers, so let them know what you're thinking as your ideas shift directions. For now, use the three techniques demonstrated in this chapter, even if they seem mechanical. As you gain experience as a writer, you will learn more subtle ways to link your ideas to each other and to the topic sentence. Your immediate goal now, though, is to communicate coherently with your readers.

Three Techniques for Coherence

- explanation of the support
- reminder of the opinion in the topic sentence
- transitions

EXERCISES

A. Outline this paragraph and indicate the transitions by filling in the blanks below. Summarize the topic sentence, the support, and the reworded topic sentence rather than writing them in full.

A significant change I have noticed in myself since entering college is a fear of mathematics. The mere sight of a 350-page math text, for instance, causes a cold shiver to run the length of my spine. As I cautiously open the front cover of the text, myriad complex formulas spring at me, quickly eliminating any trace of confidence I may have had. My dread of math is also strengthened each time I enter the small, dismal classroom. I can find no consolation in watching my classmates cringe behind open briefcases as they prepare to do battle with a common enemy capable of engulfing us all in a blanket of confusion. Finally, my greatest fears are realized as my instructor self-consciously adjusts his glasses and admits that he majored in English and never truly mastered, or even understood, calculus. Then I suddenly realize that the Cartesian plane has snared me in its nightmarish world for another semester.

Topic sentence _____

   Transition _____

   Specific support_____

   Transition _____

   Specific support_____

   Transition _____

   Specific support_____

   Transition _____

Reworded topic sentence _____

The opinion the above paragraph demonstrates is *fear*. Circle all *reminders* of that opinion in the paragraph; that is, circle all words that either repeat the word or suggest the meaning of *fear*.

B. Outline the following paragraph and show the transitions by filling in the blanks. Again, summarize the topic sentence, the support, and the reworded topic sentence rather than writing them in full.

Travis McGee, the main character in many adventure novels by John D. MacDonald, is more than just a tough guy. For one thing, he often depends on his mind, not his physical gifts, to outsmart the villains— who are often financial connivers—by beating them at their own game. Another way he's not just a tough guy is that he always gets emotionally involved with the people in the case, often fancying himself, deprecatingly, as Don Quixote doing battle with windmills. A final reason is that, unlike many tough guys, he's intensely loyal to his friends, willingly helping them when they've reached bottom, celebrating with them when they gain success, risking his life for them when they're in danger. So, as you can see, McGee is far more than a guy with more than his share of physical toughness.

Topic sentence _____

    Transition _____

    Specific support_____

    Transition _____

    Specific support_____

    Transition _____

    Specific support_____

    Transition _____

Reworded topic sentence _____

The opinion in the above paragraph is *more than just a tough guy*. Circle all reminder words that either repeat that phrase or suggest its meaning.

C. Using another paragraph in this book assigned by your instructor, underline all transitions and circle all reminders.

D. Rewrite the following paragraph, adding transitions and reminders of the opinion in the topic sentence. You also may need to add some support to fully explain the relationship of the support to the topic sentence.

The city of Stockholm is among the loveliest in the world. Slum districts, prevalent in almost all large cities, are nearly nonexistent in Stockholm, having been replaced by government housing. The citizens are careful to dispose of their litter properly and to pick up litter other people may have dropped. Stockholm has a unique layout: it is built on twenty-three islands. Water winds throughout the city. The beauty of Stockholm makes it one of the most alluring cities in the world.

E. Follow the same instructions as for Exercise D:

Overnight camping can be disenchanting if you are a novice. Whether you hike in (carrying pounds and pounds of food and equipment on your back) or whether you drive (with all the monotony car trips are infamous for), you will probably be tired once you are ready to set up your camp. When you settle back to admire the stars at the end of the day, you will probably be besieged by bugs—mosquitoes and sand flies seem to prefer making their homes in scenic places. When you go to bed, you may find that your sleeping bag, especially if you have a cheap one, is noticeably uncomfortable. Camping for newcomers can be quite different from a purely romantic adventure.

F. Write a paragraph that convinces readers that *something* (not some*one*) has a particular characteristic. On the final copy, underline all transitions and circle all reminders. Make sure you have met the other requirement for coherence by explaining your support fully. (The paragraph in Chapter 1 on the Boundary Waters Canoe Area could have been a response to this exercise.)

G. Write a paragraph that convinces readers of one significant way in which a friend of yours has changed. Use examples from your experience with that person as support. On the final copy, underline all transitions and circle all reminders. Make sure you have met the other requirement for coherence by explaining your support fully.

H. Write a paragraph that convinces readers of one important characteristic you like your friends to have. Use examples from your experience as support. On your final copy, underline all transitions and circle all reminders. Make sure you have met the other requirement for coherence by explaining your support fully.

I. Think about the other courses you're taking now. Write a paragraph that describes one intriguing idea from one of those courses. On your final copy, underline all transitions and circle all reminders. Make sure you have met the other requirement for coherence by explaining your support fully.

J. If you've held a job, try this exercise: Describe one important characteristic workers need at the place you work (or worked)—Patience? Stubbornness? Endurance? Intelligence? Something else? On your final copy, underline all transitions and circle all reminders. Make sure you have met the other requirement for coherence by explaining your support fully.

K. Exercise B is about Travis McGee, a popular character in American literature. Write a one-paragraph essay about one of your favorite characters from a book or story you've read.

L. Choose a topic much in the news. Devise a thesis statement giving your opinion about it. Use information from newspapers, magazines, or editorials to write a Stage I one-paragraph essay. This is a good chance to bring in statistics and statements by authorities (not just examples). Be sure to put quotation marks around any words that come directly from your sources. If you choose this topic, read the section called "Preliminary Documentation" in Chapter 9.

M. If you're doing Exercise F, G, H, I, J, K, or L, here's a way to practice a good writing process. If you have access to E-mail, get a partner and send a draft of your paragraph via E-mail. At the same time, your partner will send you a draft. Critique each other's draft and send comments via E-mail. Accept or ignore your partner's comments (it's your paper). Be sure to send a courtesy copy of all your E-mail to your instructor, who may observe silently or occasionally offer extra advice.

CHAPTER 6
Tips on the Writing Process

So far, we've concentrated on what the final *product* of your writing should look like—a paragraph with a topic sentence, good support, unity, and coherence. This chapter will give you a few tips on the *process* for producing a piece of writing. To do that, we'll answer two questions:

- What is the writing process?
- What are some ways to think of ideas?

THE WRITING PROCESS

The traditional way to think about the writing process is to divide it into three parts: *prewriting, writing,* and *rewriting.* Most teachers today think the process is more complicated than that, and we certainly agree with them. Nevertheless, these three parts give us a convenient way to talk about the process in general.

Prewriting

Prewriting is the process of gathering your thoughts and preparing to write. You choose your topic, refine it, and consider ways of supporting it. You don't have to think your way all the way through the paper. In fact, most writers have trouble envisioning the entire paper—even only a one-paragraph essay—before the pencil hits the page. That's why writers do a little prewriting as part of the writing process.

Try some of these strategies to help with your prewriting:

- If you have no idea of a topic, and your instructor hasn't given you one, browse through some popular magazines. Just let your mind wander. You may write about something that isn't even in the magazines, but they can trigger ideas for you. Even better, browse through an encyclopedia.

- If you still don't have a good topic, talk to your friends. Tell them about your paper and start a general discussion. You might be surprised how some random conversation can get your mind going in the right direction.

- When you have a general topic, try refining it into a good topic sentence (remember: a limited subject and a precise opinion). We suggest you actually write it down and then play around with it until it's just right.

Now you need the support. One technique for getting good support—especially if the topic is about your personal experiences or uses invented material—is to brainstorm on paper. That is, spend a few minutes jotting down whatever comes to mind. Don't be judgmental at this point ("That idea doesn't make sense at all!"). Just let your thoughts flow. When you're through, look at what you have. Often you'll find something useful.

Another way to get good support is to try a little free writing. That is, just start writing. Don't stop to think and don't stop writing. Make yourself write for perhaps five minutes, saying whatever comes to mind. If you're like us, a lot of absolute nonsense will appear on your page. But buried in that nonsense may well be a few nuggets that will become the actual support in your paper.

These techniques are all standard fare in the writing game—well known and often used. They take a little time, but only a little. And that small investment gets your brain in gear, ready to write.

Writing

So you have your ideas. Now is the time to get them on paper. If you already have some ideas on paper from free writing or brainstorming, it's time to bring law and order to the page. Here are some strategies for the writing stage:

- Have an outline. You don't need a formal one for your one-paragraph essay, but you should have at least an informal one you've jotted down.

- Next, remind yourself of the requirements for the one-paragraph essay so you'll meet the requirements of your assignment.

- Then . . . just start writing. Don't worry about errors and spelling—you can take care of them later. Just try to get the whole thing on paper, warts and all. Your goal here is to have a good flow of ideas. Try to write fairly quickly.

- Stop if your ideas aren't working at all, as any further writing will just waste your time. Instead, try some of the techniques of prewriting again. (Or take a break. Not too long, though!)

When you have a complete draft, breathe a sigh of relief. You have more work to do, but the hard part is finished.

Rewriting

In the writing stage, you put a premium on speed—getting everything down on paper. In the rewriting stage, the premium is on care. Few people slap down an "A" paper in one burst of creative effort. Most need to add some polish. Here are some suggestions:

- First, check for the larger matters: Does your writing make sense? Does it follow the requirements for the one-paragraph essay? Is it unified? Coherent? Interesting?
- Next, check for the smaller matters: Have you spelled the words correctly? Is your punctuation correct? Do your word choices seem good? These matters are small, but they can get big fast.
- Read your paper aloud. Don't read silently. Actually say the words. It's amazing how awkward phrases, missing ideas, and poor sentence structure stand out when you actually hear the words. Do you know that we read this entire book out loud several times when we prepared the first edition? And we're glad we did!
- Finally, set your writing aside. Do something else. Then come back to it. Your mind will be cleared of all the ideas you had when writing, and now you can see your writing through the eyes of someone else—or at least have a more objective view of what you wrote. Add the final polish that turns the funny-looking rock into a real gem.

We began by saying the writing process is more complicated than prewriting, writing, and rewriting. That's true. The process often loops back and forth. For example, you might get stuck while you're in the writing stage. That's a good time to head back for a few minutes in the prewriting stage. Or you might do part of your paper and then set it aside. Before going on with more writing, you might begin (as we often do) by doing a little rewriting. That helps you ease into the actual writing by refamiliarizing yourself with what you've already completed.

WHAT ARE SOME WAYS TO THINK OF IDEAS?

Sometimes you have a topic you must write on but can't think of what to say. The problem may not be lack of information, but, rather, no inspiration on how to tackle it. This section will give you some ideas:

- Brainstorm with a classmate.
- Browse through material on your topic.
- Try free writing.

Brainstorm with a Classmate

This will probably be your best way to get ideas. Suppose you want to write a paragraph about a place you've visited. You've visited lots of places: the local zoo, your grandparents' farm, the neighboring states—even some countries in Europe. Your problem isn't a lack of information; your problem is that you don't yet have a good place to start. Try bouncing ideas off a friend:

"So I have to write this paper about a place I've visited, but I can't think of anything to say."

"Well, have you been anyplace you've really, really liked?"

"Yeah—a friend and I spent a month last summer touring Europe. Hey, that might be something to write about!"

"Was there anyplace you'd really like to go back to?"

"Lots of places—Switzerland was neat. So was Sweden. I guess I like the colder places."

"I've been to Sweden. You must have visited Stockholm. Did you like it there?"

"Oh, yes. It was lovely."

Aha! A *topic sentence* emerges! And the result was the paragraph you read in the previous chapter:

> The city of Stockholm is among the loveliest in the world. Slum districts, prevalent in almost all large cities, are nearly nonexistent in Stockholm, having been replaced by government housing. The citizens are careful to dispose of their litter properly and to pick up litter other people may have dropped. Stockholm has a unique layout: it is built on twenty-three islands. Water winds throughout the city. The beauty of Stockholm makes it one of the most alluring cities in the world.

The brainstorming conversation may seem a little contrived, but brainstorming works. And it often works about that quickly. There's a great synergistic effect when two or three people purposefully bounce ideas off each other. In fact, your instructor may want to allow time in class for a brainstorming exercise. And several exercises in this book ask you to look at each other's drafts (via E-mail, if possible), in part to help brainstorm better ways to develop ideas you've already started to write about.

Browse through Material on Your Topic

Say you've decided to write about Stockholm. You've been there. You liked it. You remember it well. But you're still having trouble getting going. Look through an encyclopedia. Visit the Web. What you see there will probably trigger thoughts, often reminders of what you already know. You may even find some facts you want to include in your writing, things you didn't know but that bear a good relationship to what you want to say. Perhaps you already knew Stockholm had twenty-three islands. Or maybe you just remember that there seemed to be a lot of water.

If you include something that isn't readily available as common knowledge (Stockholm's twenty-three islands is obviously readily available), be sure to document it. Chapter 9 gives you a quick and easy way to do that.

Try Free Writing

People who study writing often characterize it as a way of *learning* about something, not just recording what you already know. The concept is "writing as a way of discovery." You've perhaps had that happen to you already: you thought you knew what you wanted to write, but somehow your ideas didn't convert easily into words. That is, you couldn't get your ideas from your head to the page. Sometimes the problem is that the ideas really aren't clear yet.

One person who has studied writing, Peter Elbow, says this about the writing process on page 15 of *Writing without Teachers:*

> Meaning is not what you start out with but what you end up with. Control, coherence, and knowing your mind are not what you start out with but what you end up with. Think of writing then not as a way to transmit a message but as a way to grow and cook a message.

Elbow also says on page 82 that "Producing writing . . . is not so much like filling a basin or a pool once, but rather getting water to flow *through* till it finally runs clear."

Elbow recommends a technique called free writing to help you discover ideas and approaches to a topic. Essentially, you start with a blank piece of paper (or a computer screen) and write for a set amount of time—say two minutes. Even if you don't have anything to say, you write something, anything related to your topic, even if you keep repeating yourself like a broken record. After the set amount of time, chances are you've opened a door you didn't know was there, discovering an idea or an approach you can use. Free writing doesn't work for everybody, but it takes only a little bit of time, and the results can be surprisingly good!

EXERCISE

Use one of the brainstorming techniques for the next paper you write.

PART 2

The One-Paragraph Essay (Stage II)

In this section you'll learn a slightly more sophisticated way to organize a one-paragraph essay. You'll find out later in the book that this new type of paragraph is actually a stepping-stone to larger themes and research papers. When you've learned how to write a Stage II paragraph, you'll find the full-length essay simple to learn.

CHAPTER 7
Overview of the One-Paragraph Essay (Stage II)

So how are Stage I and Stage II paragraphs different from each other? A Stage I paragraph has only one opinion, whereas the Stage II paragraph has more than one:

- the opinion in the topic sentence (which is the main opinion)
- the opinions in the subtopic sentences (these opinions help support the main opinion in the topic sentence)

Subtopic sentences are generalizations *within* the paragraph that help support the overall generalization: the topic sentence. Let's look at an example. Here's a Stage II paragraph (we've italicized the subtopic sentences):

▨ A Stage II Paragraph

Old-style computer manuals can be really frustrating to use. *For one thing, the indexes are usually frustrating because they are hard to decipher.* I remember when I was trying to find out how to print my paper: I tried to find the word *print* in the index. Believe it or not, the word wasn't even there. I finally asked the person next to me, who said the term for printing in that manual isn't *print*; instead, it's "concatenate." No wonder I had trouble! *Aside from the indexes, the general quality of writing in the manuals themselves is frustrating.* The manual for my old spreadsheet program doesn't have any diagrams at all, asking me to visualize what a spreadsheet looks like. And my old word processing manual assumes I know as much as the software developers do. As you can tell, I think older computer manuals were user-UNfriendly.

See how the subtopic sentences support the topic sentence? Here is an outline of that paragraph:

Topic sentence	Older computer manuals are frustrating.
Subtopic sentence	Indexes are hard to use.
Specific support	One index didn't use the word *print*.
Subtopic sentence	General quality of writing is poor.
Specific support	Spreadsheet program has no diagrams.
Specific support	Word processing program assumes too much.
Reworded topic sentence	Older computer manuals needed work.

Notice that each subtopic sentence has the kind of specific support we discussed in Chapter 2. We use examples here (a narrative example for the first subtopic sentence and two quick examples for the second one). But statistics and statements by authorities would do as well.

Notice also that if you remove the subtopic sentences above, you would have a Stage I paragraph. Sometimes the relationship between Stage I and Stage II paragraphs is not so simple. You could add subtopic sentences to the Boundary Waters Canoe Area paragraph in Chapter 1, but you would end up with a worse paragraph because the support is so meager—the paragraph would have more topic and subtopic sentences than support sentences. Also, some Stage I paragraphs cannot become Stage II paragraphs because they were never divided into subtopic ideas. The paragraph about fearing mathematics in Exercise A in Chapter 5, for example, does not have subtopic ideas, so you could not easily convert it into a Stage II paragraph.

Let's look now at a general model of the Stage II paragraph:

> **Model of the Stage II Paragraph**
>
> Topic sentence
>   Subtopic sentence
>   Specific support
>   Specific support
>   Subtopic sentence
>   Specific support
>   Specific support
> Reworded topic sentence

This outline is not rigid, of course. Your Stage II paragraph may have several subtopic sentences, and each subtopic sentence may have several items of support, depending on the subject and your approach to it. Consider this Stage II paragraph, for example:

■ Another Stage II Paragraph

Although apparently just an assortment of oddities from the National Museum of American History, a special exhibit called "The Nation's Attic" struck me as a tribute to American ingenuity. *One part of the exhibit demonstrated the ingenious ways Americans have found to shape everyday items.* For instance, a large collection of sewing accessories—hundreds of thimbles, needle cases, sewing cases, and pincushions—showed how simple things could be made more useful, more beautiful, or more entertaining. *More imaginative, though, were the things made apparently just because Americans wanted to accept the challenge of making them.* There was an intricate model of the U.S. Capitol constructed entirely of glass rods. Someone else had engraved the Lord's Prayer on a single grain of rice. And a group of chemical engineers even had managed to do the proverbial "undoable": they actually had created a silk purse from a sow's ear—just to prove it could be done. *The most interesting part of the exhibit to me, however, was some of the bizarre but ingenious failures among the models submitted for approval to the U.S. Patent Office.* I haven't been able to forget an early attempt at creating an electric razor. The inventor had mounted some razor blades on a rotating wheel so it looked something like the paddle wheel of a riverboat, and this wheel was attached to a small hand-held electric motor. There were no guards to control the depth at which the blades cut, so anyone foolish enough to use the razor no doubt would have lost much more than a few whiskers from his face. Still, although I would never have sampled this inventor's work, I had to respect his resourcefulness. This invention, like the other unusual items in "The Nation's Attic," showed the mark of American ingenuity.

Here is an outline of the paragraph:

Topic sentence   "The Nation's Attic" was a tribute to American ingenuity.
  Subtopic sentence   Some everyday items were ingenious.
    Specific support   Sewing items.
  Subtopic sentence   Some items made just for the challenge were imaginative.

Specific support	Capitol from glass rods.
Specific support	Lord's Prayer on grain of rice.
Specific support	Silk purse from sow's ear.
Subtopic sentence	Some bizarre failures were ingenious.
Specific support	Attempt to create electric razor.
Reworded topic sentence	The unusual items showed American ingenuity.

You might notice that the last sentence of the sample paragraph ties together the last item of support with all those that preceded it. That's not a necessary attribute of a reworded topic sentence, but it works nicely here. Notice also that even though a paragraph follows a model, as does the paragraph above, it can still be good writing.

Can a Stage II paragraph be in the third-person style? Of course. Here's the topic of climbing Mount Everest again—with entirely different supporting ideas:

■ A Final Example of a Stage II Paragraph

Climbing Mount Everest, the highest mountain in the world, is extremely dangerous. One reason it's dangerous is the scarcity of oxygen at the top (which is 29,028 feet above sea level). When climbers lack oxygen, they can barely summon the strength to put one foot in front of the other and have little energy to deal with emergencies. Also, the lack of oxygen produces a condition called "hypoxia," which greatly reduces a climber's ability to think clearly. A second reason it's dangerous to climb Everest is that the weather at the top (often actually in the jet stream) is horrendous. Jon Krakauer, author of *Into Thin Air,* tells what it was like camping near the top: "The gale threatened to blow the tent apart. Every time the door was opened, the shelter would fill with blowing spindrift, so everything inside was covered with an inch-thick layer of snow" (p. 208). As you can see, height—with the lack of oxygen and bad weather— easily equals danger when it comes to mountain climbing.

EXERCISES

A. Outline this paragraph.

To play water polo well, you have to learn to cheat. The only way you can keep the ball is by making a few slightly illegal moves. Pushing off your opponent's stomach can give you the elbow room necessary to make a good pass or score a goal. Likewise, kneeing your attacker in the ribs can keep him from stealing the ball while you are setting up a play. When the opposing team does get possession, the unapproved solution for retrieving the ball is again through cheating. Pulling back on your adversary's leg is an effective means of slowing him down to give you a fairer chance at guarding him. But the most effective method of getting the ball is simply to pull his suit down, which immediately stops all his competitive activity. Fortunately, water polo is played in the water, which hides the cheating all players must do in order to be successful.

Topic sentence _____

    Subtopic sentence _____

        Specific support _____

        Specific support _____

    Subtopic sentence _____

        Specific support _____

        Specific support _____

Reworded topic sentence _____

B. Outline this paragraph:

Giving a good speech takes a lot of work. For instance, it takes hard work just to prepare the content—to write it. Last year I had to give a speech to our entire graduating class in high school. I wanted to impress my friends and their families, of course, but the words I wrote always sounded phony—too "elevated" in tone. I wrote and wrote and rewrote until I finally decided not to be impressive, but just to say the good things I felt about the school. I spent more than hours; I spent days getting the words right. Once I had the words, the hard part started: practicing my delivery. I gave my speech to my empty room. I gave my speech to my mirror. I gave my speech to my twin sister. I even gave my speech to my parents! So don't let anybody tell you that giving a speech is easy.

Topic sentence _____

    Subtopic sentence _____

        Specific support _____

    Subtopic sentence _____

        Specific support _____

Specific support _____

Specific support _____

Specific support _____

Reworded topic sentence _____

C. Outline this paragraph you saw in Chapter 2:

I like the individual freedom that comes through in e. e. cummings'
poetry. You can see that freedom right away in the lack of both capitalization and normal spacing in his writing. Just look at the way he writes
his name—no capital letters! Already he seems like a rebel (as he certainly was). You can also see his emphasis on individual freedom in his
content: his poems often deal with the carefreeness of spring and the
value of the individual. Consider, for example, the first lines of one of his
most famous poems: " 'sweet spring is your / time is my time is our / time
for springtime is lovetime / and viva sweet love.' " The value of spring
and the individual certainly comes through in those lines, doesn't it? Format and content are two elements that reveal the emphasis on freedom
that I like so much in e. e. cummings' poetry.

Topic sentence _____

Subtopic sentence _____

Specific support _____

Subtopic sentence _____

Specific support _____

Reworded topic sentence _____

D. Outline this paragraph you saw earlier in this chapter:

Climbing Mount Everest, the highest mountain in the world, is extremely
dangerous. One reason it's dangerous is the scarcity of oxygen at the top
(which is 29,028 feet above sea level). When climbers lack oxygen, they
can barely summon the strength to put one foot in front of the other and
have little energy to deal with emergencies. Also, the lack of oxygen produces a condition called "hypoxia," which greatly reduces a climber's
ability to think clearly. A second reason it's dangerous to climb Everest is
that the weather at the top (often actually in the jet stream) is horrendous. Jon Krakauer, author of *Into Thin Air*, tells what it was like camp-

ing near the top: "The gale threatened to blow the tent apart. Every time the door was opened, the shelter would fill with blowing spindrift, so everything inside was covered with an inch-thick layer of snow" (p. 208). As you can see, height—with the lack of oxygen and bad weather—easily equals danger when it comes to mountain climbing.

Topic sentence _____

    Subtopic sentence _____

        Specific support _____

        Specific support _____

    Subtopic sentence _____

        Specific support _____

Reworded topic sentence _____

CHAPTER 8

Support: Subtopic Sentences

Subtopic sentences are like topic sentences:

- Both state opinions that need support.
- Both have two parts: the subject (which must be limited) and the opinion (which must be precise).

Topic Sentences and Subtopic Sentences

A *topic* sentence is the main idea of your paragraph. A *subtopic* sentence is the main idea of one part of your paragraph. Theoretically, if you can persuade your readers to accept each subtopic sentence, they should accept your topic sentence as well.

The precise opinion in each subtopic sentence is usually identical to the precise opinion in the topic sentence. For example, we showed you a sample Stage II paragraph in the previous chapter. These were the two subtopic sentences; notice that the opinions in them are identical:

For one thing, the indexes are usually *frustrating* because they are hard to decipher.

Aside from the indexes, the general quality of the writing is *frustrating* in the manuals themselves.

In this chapter you'll learn about three different kinds of subtopic sentences: subtopic sentences that answer the questions "Why?" "How?" or "When?" There are other kinds of subtopic sentences, of course, but these three can get you started quickly.

SUBTOPIC SENTENCE: "WHY?"

One of the easiest ways to find a subtopic sentence is to state the topic sentence and then ask, "Why?" Suppose this is your topic sentence: "Vegetable gardens take a lot of planning." If you ask yourself, "Why do vegetable gardens take a lot of planning?" you might come up with these two subtopic sentences:

Vegetable gardens take a lot of planning because the soil needs to be prepared.

Vegetable gardens take a lot of planning because the vegetables need to be planted at specific times.

Here is a possible outline, including the specific support you might want to use:

Topic sentence	Vegetable gardens take a lot of planning.
Subtopic sentence	They take planning because the soil needs to be prepared.
Specific support	Soil should be tilled in the fall, after the last harvest.
Specific support	Soil should be tested in the spring, especially for acidity and nitrogen.
Subtopic sentence	Vegetables need to be planted at specific times.
Specific support	Last year, I planted the lettuce too late, so that by the time it should have been ready for harvest, it had died from the heat.
Reworded topic sentence	Therefore, you should plan your garden in advance.

In this outline, the subtopic sentences give reasons why the topic sentence is true; the specific support follows with concrete support for the subtopic sentences.

By the way, subtopic sentences that answer the question "Why?" always can be joined to the topic sentence with the word *because*:

Vegetable gardens take a lot of planning *because* the soil needs to be prepared.

Vegetable gardens take a lot of planning *because* the vegetables need to be planted at specific times.

You needn't actually use *because* to join the "Why?" subtopic sentence to the topic sentence, but you could. Whenever you write "Why?" subtopic sentences, you might want to test them by joining them to the topic sentence with *because*.

Notice that you can support your subtopic sentences with the same kind of specific support you learned in Chapter 2: examples (quick or narrative), statistics, and statements by authorities.

SUBTOPIC SENTENCE: "HOW?"

Another common type of subtopic sentence answers the question "How?" Notice that the italicized subtopic sentences answer the question "How does rush hour traffic bring out the worst in drivers?":

> Heavy rush-hour traffic brings out the worst in many drivers. *Traffic conditions make some drivers overly nervous.* Uncle Billy, usually a calm and careful driver, becomes so flustered in rush-hour traffic that he can't carry on a conversation, and he forgets to check the rearview mirror when he changes lanes. A 1987 study of traffic flow in the Los Angeles area showed that the average waiting time at freeway entrance ramps increased to 1.5 minutes during rush hour because of the number of drivers who were afraid to merge into the heavy stream of cars. *Also, heavy rush-hour traffic reinforces the aggressiveness of some drivers.* Often drivers follow too closely during rush hour because they're afraid other drivers might slip in ahead of them. Drivers continue into intersections on yellow lights even though they will get caught there and block cross traffic. A psychologist who has studied driver reactions concluded that "stress conditions of rush-hour traffic cause physical and emotional reactions like those of a soldier in combat." Rush-hour traffic conditions show many drivers at their worst.

As you can see, these subtopic sentences answer the question "How?" and not the question "Why?" "Why?" subtopic sentences probably would state something about the cause-effect relationship between rush-hour traffic and the way drivers present themselves in it; "How?" subtopic sentences, on the other hand, show the results of the traffic on driver behavior.

We need to add a word of caution here. Sometimes subtopic sentences clearly answer "Why?" and sometimes they clearly answer "How?" At other times the questions appear to overlap. In other words, sometimes we can't be sure which of these two questions the subtopic sentences answer. Don't worry. Such fine distinctions are more fitting for a class in philosophy or semantics than for one in composition. Treat these questions for what they are—a quick and effective way to find subtopic sentences.

SUBTOPIC SENTENCE: "WHEN?"

Another type of subtopic sentence answers the question "When?" For example, to show that your roommate is constantly sleepy, you could ask yourself

"When?" You might answer in a paragraph such as this (we've italicized the subtopic sentences):

> My roommate is constantly sleepy. *He is sleepy in the morning when he gets up.* He fumbles with the alarm clock. He once put his trousers on backward. *He is sleepy when he is in class.* He once fell asleep in Math III and crunched his jaw on the desk. He does not even remember the subject of the lecture he attended yesterday morning in biology. *He is sleepy in the evening.* His typical study position is a comatose sprawl with his head on his desk. He is always in bed by 8:30 P.M. My roommate is sleepy all the time.

Each of the italicized sentences answers the question, *"When* is my roommate sleepy?"

PARALLEL SUBTOPIC SENTENCES

In the examples in this chapter, all subtopic sentences within a one-paragraph essay answer the same question: "Why?" "How?" or "When?" Your Stage II paragraphs should do the same.

If you are supporting the idea "Hitchhiking is dangerous" in a Stage II paragraph, don't answer the question "Why?" for one subtopic sentence ("Hitchhiking is dangerous because too many drivers are deranged") and the question "When?" for another subtopic sentence ("Hitchhiking is dangerous at night, when the streets are poorly lighted"). These ideas may both work to support your topic sentence, but they don't work well together. They are not parallel and seem like a mixture of apples and oranges when you are selling only apples. When you have outlined your Stage II paragraph, be sure your subtopic sentences answer the same question: "Why?" or "How?" or "When?"

Remember the exercise about Travis McGee at then end of Chapter 5? Here's a revised version—now a Stage II paragraph. Notice that each subtopic sentence answers the question "How?"

> Travis McGee, the main character in many adventure novels by John D. Mac-Donald, is more than just a tough guy. For one thing, he often depends on his mind, not his physical gifts, to outsmart the villains—who are often financial connivers—by beating them at their own game. For example, in *Pale Gray for Guilt,* McGee uses skillful lawyers, a sharp businesswoman, and the economist who is his best friend to financially destroy the people who had effectively killed another good friend of his. Another way he's not just a tough guy is that he always gets emotionally involved with the people in the case, often fancying himself, deprecatingly, as Don Quixote doing battle with windmills. Again, in *Pale Gray for Guilt,* his dead friend was a bumbling nice guy who had been McGee's friend in college. McGee avenged his death for no reason

except to nail the people who had needlessly destroyed his friend. A final reason is that, unlike many tough guys, McGee is intensely loyal to his friends, willingly helping them when they've reached bottom, celebrating with them when they gain success, risking his life for them when they're in danger. In *Dress Her in Indigo,* McGee takes a complex and ultimately dangerous case only because his economist friend, Meyer, clearly wants him to. As you can see, McGee is far more than a guy with more than his share of physical toughness.

EXERCISES

A. For each of these topic sentences, invent subtopic sentences and specific support. Be sure all your subtopic sentences answer the same question: "Why?" "How?" or "When?"

1. *Television has warped my mind.*

    Subtopic sentence (Why? or How? or When?)

    _____

    _____

    Specific support (quick example)

    _____

    _____

    Subtopic sentence (Why? or How? or When?)

    _____

    _____

    Specific support (statistics)

    _____

    _____

Specific support (statement by authority)

_____

_____

2. *Goldfish make good pets for children.*

   Subtopic sentence (Why? or How? or When?)

   _____

   _____

   Specific support (narrative example)

   _____

   _____

   Subtopic sentence (Why? or How? or When?)

   _____

   _____

   Specific support (statistics)

   _____

   _____

   Specific support (statement by authority)

   _____

   _____

3. *My computer has more capability than libraries of two decades ago.*

   Subtopic sentence (Why? or How? or When?)

   _____

   _____

Specific support (statistics)

_____

_____

Specific support (statistics)

_____

_____

Subtopic sentence (Why? or How? or When?)

_____

_____

Specific support (quick example)

_____

_____

Specific support (quick example)

_____

_____

B. Outline the opposite of all the above topic sentences:

1. Television has warped my mind.

2. Goldfish make good pets for children.

3. My computer has more capability than libraries of two decades ago.

Use whichever type of subtopic sentence ("Why?" "How?" or "When?") and whichever type of specific support (examples, statistics, statements by authorities) you wish.

C. In Exercises A and B you outlined several Stage II paragraphs. Choose the one that interests you the most and use the support you invented to write the paragraph.

D. Write a Stage II paragraph to convince us that someone you know has a positive (pleasant, good) or a negative (unpleasant, bad) characteristic. Because you're writing about someone you know, don't use invented support for this exercise.

E. Write a Stage II paragraph that explains how something you have observed impressed you. The sample paragraph in Chapter 7 about "The Nation's Attic" could have been a response to this exercise. Because you're writing about something you've observed, don't use invented support for this exercise.

F. Write a Stage II paragraph about one of these topics. Use invented support if you like.

sailing	dancing
time travel	mythological beasts
a television star	travel by ship two hundred years ago
a wild animal	

G. Write a Stage II paragraph about one of these topics. Don't use invented support.

a current event	a local celebrity
a historical event	a recent sports event
a classic movie	a foreign country
a person from your past	a person you recently encountered

H. Think about the other courses you're taking. Choose a focused topic from one of those courses and write a Stage II paragraph based on it. For example, in history, you could give two reasons why the Battle of Gettysburg was a disaster for the South. Or in physics, you could tell about two occasions when scientists applied one of Newton's laws for practical benefits. Or in computer sciences, you could briefly explain two ways modern programming techniques help programmers.

I. If you've held a job, try this exercise. Write a Stage II paragraph characterizing your first day there. Were you nervous? Confident? Frustrated? Confused? Impressed? Some other feeling?

J. At the end of Chapter 5 (Exercise B), you read a short paragraph about Travis McGee, a popular character in American literature. Write a Stage II paragraph about one of your own favorite literary characters. If you wrote a paragraph about one for Chapter 5, revise it into a Stage II paragraph.

K. Choose a topic much in the news—but different from the topic you used at the end of Chapter 5. Devise a thesis statement giving your opinion about it. Use information from newspapers, magazines, or editorials to write a Stage II paragraph. This is a good chance to bring in statistics and statements by authorities (not just examples). Be sure to put quotation marks around any words that come directly from your sources. If you choose this topic, read the section called "Preliminary Documentation" in Chapter 9.

   If your instructor agrees, make this a team project (just as the exercise suggested at the end of Chapter 5). You and your partner will each write a Stage II paragraph (on different topics). You'll critique each other's draft (in writing). Accept or reject whatever advice you receive, as you deem appropriate, but hand in four items:

   • your paper
   • your partner's critique of your writing
   • a brief statement explaining why you accepted or rejected each piece of advice from your partner
   • the critique you wrote evaluating your partner's Stage II paragraph (the quality of your writing and critiquing is important)

   Use E-mail, if you wish, to critique each other's writing, but hand in printed copies. Your grade will be based on this entire project, not just on your own Stage II paragraph.

CHECKLIST FOR THE ONE-PARAGRAPH ESSAY

Topic sentence

_____ Does your paragraph begin with a topic sentence?

_____ Does your topic sentence have a limited subject?

_____ Does your topic sentence have a precise opinion?

Support

_____ Does your support begin with the second sentence of the paragraph?

_____ Is your support detailed enough?

_____ Do all your items of support clearly belong with the topic sentence (unity)?

_____ Do you explain your support fully so the relation to the topic is clear (coherence)?

_____ Does each item of support include a reminder of the opinion in the topic sentence (coherence)?

_____ Do you have transitions at the critical locations (coherence)?

Conclusion

_____ Does the last sentence of the paragraph reword the topic sentence?

Other

_____ Is your paragraph convincing?

_____ Is your paragraph interesting?

_____ Have you checked the spelling of words you're unsure of?

_____ Is your paper neatly done so that it's easy to read?

PART 3

The Five-Paragraph Essay

A five-paragraph essay is a handy device for learning to write longer papers. The first and last paragraphs are the introduction and conclusion, two types of paragraph most longer papers need. The three central paragraphs provide enough material to justify a full-length introduction and conclusion but still keep the paper short enough to be manageable—for both you and your instructor.

You'll begin writing about more serious topics in this part. So far you've depended on your own experiences for much of your support; you'll still present your experiences here, but you'll supplement them with occasional support from books and magazines. Of course, we don't expect you to learn the fundamentals of the multiparagraph essay and the fundamentals of documentation at the same time, so we present in this section a simplified system of documentation you can use until you study the research paper in Part 5.

CHAPTER 9

Overview of the Five-Paragraph Essay

Are your paragraphs turning into monsters? Are they getting longer and longer, seeming more like small themes than one-paragraph essays? If so, you're ready to take the next step: learning to write the five-paragraph essay. Actually, the five-paragraph essay is much like a Stage II paragraph. This diagram shows you how they resemble each other:

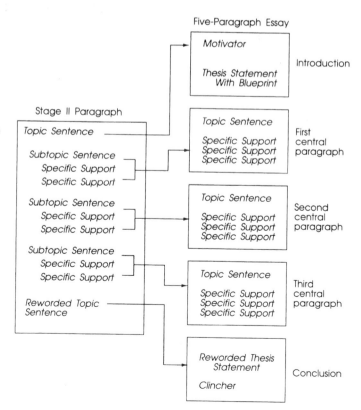

Parts of a Five-Paragraph Essay

A five-paragraph essay has these parts:

- an introduction (1 paragraph)
- central paragraphs (3 paragraphs)
- a conclusion (1 paragraph)

Let's look at each of these briefly. (We'll discuss them in greater detail in the next few chapters.)

Introduction

An introduction is, of course, the first paragraph of the essay. In a way, the topic sentence of your one-paragraph essay served as an introduction, but now that you're about to write longer papers, you'll want something more substantial at the beginning. Introductions have three parts: a *motivator,* a *thesis statement,* and a *blueprint.*

Motivator

A motivator is the beginning of the introductory paragraph. Its purpose is simply to get the reader interested in reading more—in other words, in *motivating* the reader.

Thesis Statement

Just as a topic sentence carries the main idea of a one-paragraph essay, a thesis statement carries the main idea of the five-paragraph essay.

Blueprint

A blueprint is simply a short list of the main points you're about to present in the essay. Because a five-paragraph essay has three central paragraphs, your blueprint will have three points, one for the topic of each central paragraph.

Central Paragraphs

A five-paragraph essay has three central paragraphs, and each central paragraph supports the essay's main point (or thesis statement). A central paragraph is like a one-paragraph essay, with a topic sentence at the beginning and specific support following. However, central paragraphs generally lack reworded topic sentences.

Conclusion

Remember the reworded topic sentence at the end of a one-paragraph essay? That sentence gave your one-paragraph essay a sense of finality. The conclusion—the last paragraph of a five-paragraph essay—also gives a sense of finality. A conclusion has two parts: a *reworded thesis statement* and a *clincher.*

Reworded Thesis Statement

A reworded thesis statement simply does what it says: rewords the thesis statement. It's intended to remind your readers, saying, in effect, "You've just been reading my three central paragraphs. Once again, I will tell you what those three paragraphs were supporting." Then you tell them.

Clincher

A clincher is a finisher, a final sentence or two that leaves no doubt in the reader's mind that the essay has reached its end.

A SAMPLE FIVE-PARAGRAPH ESSAY

Now let's look at a "real" five-paragraph essay. As you read it, notice the points we've been discussing: the motivator, the blueprint, and so forth (an outline following this essay shows all these points).

> Do you realize that newly born children are not even aware that parts of their bodies belong to them? I learned this fascinating fact in my psychology course from a book that says a baby "lies on his back, kicking his heels and watching the little fists flying past his face. But only very slowly does he come to know that they are attached to him and he can control them" (Mary Ann Spencer Pulaski, *Understanding Piaget,* p. 21). Children have a lot of learning to do before they can see the world—and themselves—through grown-up eyes. As children pass through this remarkable process of growing up, they often do humorous things, especially in learning to speak, in discovering that all objects do not have human characteristics, and in trying to imitate others around them.

Not surprisingly, one area in which children often are unintentionally humorous is in learning to speak. I remember one time I was talking to a friend on the phone while my little sister, Betsy, seemed to be playing inattentively on the floor nearby. After I hung up, Betsy asked me, "Why is the teacher going to give Janet an old tomato?" At first I couldn't figure out what Betsy was talking about. When I asked her what she meant, she said, "You said if Janet doesn't hand in her homework, the teacher is going to give her an old tomato." Finally I caught on. The word I had used was *ultimatum!*

Children also can be funny in the way they humanize the objects around them. According to my psychology book, "Up to four or five years old, the child believes anything may be endowed with purpose and conscious activity. A ball may refuse to be thrown straight, or a 'naughty' chair may be responsible for bumping him" (Pulaski, *Understanding Piaget,* p. 45). I, myself, still can remember one vivid and scary afternoon when I was sure the sun was following me around, just waiting for the right moment to get me. I also can remember a time, not scary, when Betsy stood at the top of the stairs and yelled to her shoes at the bottom, "Shoes! Get up here!"

Another way in which children are sometimes funny is in their attempts to imitate what they see around them. All children look pretty silly when they dress up like their mothers and fathers and play "house." My psychology book tells of a more interesting example, though. The famous psychologist Jean Piaget wrote of the time his sixteen-month-old daughter quietly watched a visiting little boy throw a tantrum in trying to get out of his playpen. Piaget's daughter thought it would be fun to try the same thing: "The next day, she herself screamed in her playpen and tried to move it, stamping her foot lightly several times in succession. The imitation of the whole scene was most striking" (quoted in Pulaski, *Understanding Piaget,* p. 81).

Little children are funny creatures to watch, aren't they? But as we laugh, we have to admire, too, because the humorous mistakes are but temporary side trips that children take on the amazingly complicated journey to maturity—a long way from the beginning, when they lay in wonder, silently watching the strange, fingered spacecraft passing back and forth before their infant eyes.

Now let's look at an outline of that essay:

Introduction

Motivator	Children have many things to learn and adjust to as they grow up—including awareness of the parts of their bodies.
Thesis	Children often do humorous things . . .
Blueprint	. . . in learning to speak, in discovering that all objects do not have human characteristics, and in attempting to imitate others.

First Central Paragraph

Topic sentence	Children often are unintentionally humorous in learning to speak.
Specific support	Betsy mistook *ultimatum* for *old tomato.*

Second Central Paragraph

Topic sentence	Children humanize the objects around them.
Specific support	Book says children blame balls and chairs as though the things were conscious.
Specific support	I thought the sun was out to get me.
Specific support	Betsy ordered her shoes to climb the stairs.

Third Central Paragraph

Topic sentence	Children attempt to imitate what they see.
Specific support	They dress like their parents.
Specific support	Piaget's daughter imitated a tantrum that a visiting child threw.

Conclusion

Reworded thesis	Children are funny creatures to watch.
Clincher	Reminder of the motivator that children have a lot of learning and adjusting to do.

PRELIMINARY DOCUMENTATION

Until now, you've been writing most of your papers based on your personal experience. Those papers can be interesting and important. At some time in your life, though, you need to learn to write about other topics—about the ideas and the words of other people. When you use the ideas and words of others, you need to let the reader know which parts of your writing are your own and which contain the ideas and words of others. In short, you need to include documentation.

You must document any time you use the ideas or words of other people. To simplify the process of learning both the fundamentals of the five-paragraph essay and the fundamentals of documentation, we've devised what we call a "preliminary system of documentation"—a temporary and easy way for you to acknowledge your sources. Later in the book we devote two chapters to a more formal way of documenting your writing. Here's our preliminary system:

1. Put quotation marks around all words you take directly from a source.
2. At the end of every sentence or multiple-sentence quotation in which you use someone else's words or ideas, identify the source in parentheses. To identify the source, simply use the author's name (if there is one), the title of the book or article, and the page number.

Here are some examples of the documentation you could put after sentences when you use someone else's words or ideas:

(Dick Francis, *Forfeit*, p. 143)
(*The Columbia-Viking Desk Encyclopedia*, pp. 45–58)
(George Miller, "The Magical Number 7, Plus or Minus 2," p. 81)

Proper documentation serves two purposes:

• It tells your readers that you are using ideas or words of others.
• It tells your readers where they can find your source.

Our preliminary system serves only the first purpose well, because your parenthetical information simply isn't complete. As a result, your instructor may ask you to keep your sources handy. The sample essay in this chapter has examples of preliminary documentation. If you have any questions at all, please ask your instructor.

Practical Writing

You don't find many five-paragraph essays in the everyday writing you read, but you sometimes see variations that come close. Let's look more at practical uses of the five-paragraph essay in school and at work.

Practical Writing in School

You can use the idea of the five-paragraph essay to help you organize much of your school writing. You may not end up with five paragraphs, of course, but you can often end up with an introduction that includes a thesis and blueprint, central paragraphs with topic sentences, and a conclusion. Let's continue with our example on the poetry of e. e. cummings. Here is a five-paragraph essay you might write for a freshman literature class:

SOCIETY AND THE INDIVIDUAL:
FREEDOM IN THE POETRY OF E. E. CUMMINGS

A constant tension exists between the values of society and the values of the individuals who compose it. We saw that in our country in the 1920s after World War I turned traditional values upside down and brought new values that emphasized the individual. We certainly saw it again in the 1960s with the hippies, flower children, and other, more violent, expressions. During both of those decades, the poetry of e. e. cummings was quite popular. And—no surprise—his poetry emphasized a break from traditional values and a move toward individual freedom. We can find that emphasis on freedom in the typographical layout of his poems, their frequent antigovernment content, and the celebration of the individual in his poetry on spring.

Perhaps the most obvious example of individual freedom is the freedom cummings himself took in the typographical layout of his poems. For example, consider this first line from one of his poems:

here's a little mouse)and

The poem begins without a capital letter! It has a closed parenthesis without an opening one, and it has no space after the closed parenthesis mark! This freedom from traditional typographical conventions is *typical* of cummings' poems—not just an occasional technique he used.

Another example of cummings' emphasis on the freedom of the individual is his scorn for governments that try to control that freedom. In one poem, a speaker delivers a clichéd political speech. This is the last line of the poem:

He spoke. And drank rapidly a glass of water.

The context of the poem makes it clear that the hypocritical speaker—praising the government—needs to wash the unclean words out of his mouth. Such antigovernment content is common in e. e. cummings' poetry.

Finally, we can see the emphasis on individual freedom in the delight cummings takes in the carefreeness of spring—a month when we like to "free" ourselves of "cares" and allow our emotions and passions to express themselves. One of my favorites has these first lines:

sweet spring is your
time is my time is our
time for springtime is lovetime
and viva sweet love

Beautiful lines, aren't they? You can *feel* the freedom and value of the individual coming through those lines.

You can see that cummings' poetry broke from traditional values by moving toward individual freedom. We find it in the layout of his poems, their antigovernment content, and his celebration of the freedom that spring brings. Although his poems were especially popular during certain decades, the tension between society and the individual always exists. And that is why cummings has been able to speak not just for a generation or two but—at times in our lives—for all of us.

The five-paragraph essay is a tightly structured way to write, but it doesn't need to take the life or meaning out of what you have to say. That's why a highly structured five-paragraph essay can talk effectively about one of our least structured writers—e. e. cummings—and still be effective. You can easily find applications for the principles of the five-paragraph essay in virtually all of your college courses that require writing.

Practical Writing at Work

You will also find applications for the principles of the five-paragraph essay once you graduate. Not that all your memos, letters, and reports will be exactly five paragraphs long, but the underlying structure—which is why we teach you the five-paragraph essay—is extremely useful. For example, busy readers usually like the main point up front—for the document as a whole and for the sections of a document. In other words, something like a thesis statement at the beginning of a document is helpful. And something like topic sentences at the beginnings of sections can be helpful, too.

When a document has sections, it's useful to name those sections up front, right after the main point. Naming the sections is (you guessed it) a blueprint. Business writers sometimes call it a "road map." Let's look at an example of business writing that resembles our five-paragraph essay. Here's the situation: A manager writes a memo to his boss, asking permission to buy an expensive kind of printer and software that does fancy word processing. This is the memo:

■ Using the Principles of the Five-Paragraph Essay

From: Ed Malone
To: Janet Chambers
Subject: A proposal for a color printer and desktop publishing
         capabilities

We need to improve the quality of the documents and proposals we're producing in our division. To add the polish and professional look we need, I recommend we buy a color printer plus additional purchases that will let our secretaries do desktop publishing. This memo will cover why we need the printer, why we need the additional purchases, and what our implementation plan will be.

First, I recommend we buy a color printer. The cost would be $3,400. The printer will give us two main benefits: First, it will add graphics capabilities to both our graphics work and our desktop publishing. In fact, desktop publishing almost requires a color printer for professional impact. Second, the color printer is also fairly fast, so it will give us crucial speed for rapid turnaround of final documents and proposals. It will make possible those last-minute additions and changes that often improve final presentation.

Next, we'll need additional purchases to do desktop publishing on the printer. Here's specifically what we'll need:

2 copies of graphics software
1 training slot

The desktop publishing software will give our documents a professional appearance, and it can easily combine text and graphics. That way the appearance of our documents will truly express the professional quality of our work. The training will allow staff members to make the most effective use of both hardware and software.

When we get a color printer and the additional purchases, here's what our implementation plan will be: We'll add the color printer to our network to make it widely available to the staff. We'll install the other hardware and software on the workstations belonging to the two secretaries. One secretary is ready to start desktop

> publishing as soon as we get her a mouse and a graphics board. She already has software, training, and experience publishing a proposal. The other secretary needs to take the training first. That training is offered three weeks from now. When he's trained, we should have an excellent start for desktop publishing.
>
> I'll be glad to talk this over with you whenever you like.

The principles of the five-paragraph are all there. Did you notice the main point and blueprint in the first paragraph? The topic sentences at the beginning of each major paragraph? The detailed support?

Now try to imagine that memo another way—*without* those good techniques of organization. And imagine you're the vice president getting it (and you're having a busy day). You'd have to read it slowly, wouldn't you? And you'd probably have to struggle with it, too. So even though the five-paragraph essay is a learning tool, the principles it teaches can help you all your life.

EXERCISE

Outline this five-paragraph essay:

> When we think of an old-time, small-town doctor, we usually envision a mannerly, dignified gentleman. However, this image did not fit my Uncle Rodney, a doctor in the small town of Bandon, Wyoming. Instead, Dr. Rodney was an obnoxious person because he had an annoying habit of speaking in crude, incoherent sentences; he had sloppy eating habits; and he was a messy smoker.
>
> Probably Dr. Rodney's most irritating trait was his crude way of speaking. For example, I recall a particularly embarrassing moment during a family reunion at my mother-in-law's house when Dr. Rodney was asked to say a blessing before dinner. He managed a "Hump, bump, grump," or so it sounded, and almost immediately added, "Goddammit," as he knocked over a bowl of grated corn he was grabbing. As a result, my mother-in-law—a deeply religious

person—was mortified. On another occasion, Dr. Rodney's nurse said, "It's a good thing I can interpret what Dr. Rodney says and smooth over the rough feelings, or we would be out of patients."

Additionally, Dr. Rodney bothered many people with his messy eating habits. He shoveled food into his mouth at such an alarming rate that often he could not catch his breath. My brother-in-law once remarked, "When I see Uncle Rodney eat, I think of jackals devouring their kill." Furthermore, Dr. Rodney always finished his meal long before anyone else; then he would make a nauseating slurping sound by sucking air and saliva through the gaps between his top front teeth while he waited for everybody else to finish. Because of his atrocious eating habits, none of Dr. Rodney's neighbors invited him to dinner.

Dr. Rodney also was disliked because he was an inconsiderate smoker. Everywhere he went, he left a trail of ashes, a terrible stench, and wet, chewed-up cigar butts. After his death, the office cleaning lady confided that the townspeople used to bet on how many days would pass before anyone saw Dr. Rodney without a spot of tobacco juice on his shirt. All the local children learned not to be downwind from him because no one could easily tolerate his odor of stale tobacco.

Clearly, Dr. Rodney was an obnoxious person whose talking, eating, and smoking habits alienated him from even his own family. He was indeed lucky that the town had only one doctor, or he might not have been employed.

Introduction

Motivator
Thesis Statement
Blueprint

First Central Paragraph

Topic sentence
  Specific support
  Specific support

Second Central Paragraph

Topic sentence
    Specific support
    Specific support
    Specific support
    Specific support

Third Central Paragraph

Topic sentence
    Specific support
    Specific support
    Specific support

Conclusion

Reworded thesis
Clincher

CHAPTER 10
Alternative Techniques of Layout

This chapter offers some alternatives to the traditional layout of the five-paragraph essay. They are optional. You'll find that some instructors prefer these techniques; others don't.

The computer has allowed most of us more capability on our desks than most professional print shops had a couple decades ago. Today, we are more and more concerned with the layout of our document, trying to help readers *see* its parts easily. Here are three suggestions on layout for you to consider:

- headings
- short paragraphs
- indented lists (like this one)

Let's look more closely at these three layout techniques.

HEADINGS

The word just above this sentence *(Headings)* is a heading—the name for the "title" of a section of writing. In fact, we like to think of a heading as a *label* for a section's content. One advantage of a heading is that it adds some white space to your text, signaling your reader that you're moving to a new topic. In that way, your layout visually reinforces your words.

Another advantage is that a heading gives the main idea of the section. In the five-paragraph-essay model we just showed you, paragraphing identified new ideas. But sometimes paragraphs have minor changes in thought within them. If you've used headings to announce the topic of a section, you then can have paragraphs *within* that section. That way, the reader can see all minor shifts in organization, such as moving to a new item of specific support. And the reader shouldn't get confused: the headings clearly show the various major sections of the paper.

You may wonder how to make headings. One simple way is to begin with a capital letter at the left margin. Here's a sample paper using headings of this type:

A SAMPLE PAPER WITH HEADINGS

xxxxx xxxxxxxxxx xxxxxx xxx xxxxxxxxxx xxxx xxxxxx xxxxxxx
xxxxxxx xxxxxxxxxxxxxx xxxxxx xxxxxxxxxx xx xxxxxxxxxxx
xxxxx xxxxxxxxxx xxxxxx xxxxxx xxx xxxxxxxxxx xxxx xxxxxx
xxxxxxx xxxxxxx xxxxxxxxxxxxxx xxxxxx

This is a Heading

xxx xxxxxxxxxx xxxx xxxxxx xxxxxxx xxxxxxx xxxxxxxxxxxxxx
xxxxxx xxxxxxxxxxx xx xxxxxxxxxxx xxx xxxxxxxxxx xxxx xxxxxx
xxxxxxx xxxxxxx xxxxxxxxxxxxxx xxxxxx xxxxxxxxxxx xx
xxxxxxxxxxx xxx

xxxxxxxxxx xxxx xxxxxx xxxxxxx xxxxxxx xxxx xxxxxx xxxxxxx
xxxxxxx xxx xxxxxxxxxx xxxx xxxxxx xxxxxxx xxxxxxx
xxxxxxxxxxxxxx xxxxxx xxxxxxxxxx xx xxxxxxxxxxx xxx
xxxxxxxxxx xxxx xxxxxx xxxxxxx xxxxxxx xxxxxxxxxxxxxx xxxxxx
xxxxxxxxxxx xx xxxxxxxxxxx

This is Another Heading

xxx xxxxxxxxxx xxxx xxxxxx xxxxxxx xxxxxxx xxxxxxxxxxxxxx
xxxxxx xxxxxx xxx xxxxxxxxxx xxxx xxxxxx xxxxxxx xxxxxxx
xxxxxxxxxxxxxx xxxxxx xxxxxxxxxx xx xxxxxxxxxxx xxxxx
xxxxxxxxxx xxxxx xxxxxxxxxx xx xxxxxxxxxx xxx xxxxxxxxxx
xxxx xxxxxxxxxx

xxx xxxxxxxxxx xxxx xxxxxx xxxxxxx xxxxxxx xxxxxxxxxxxxxx
xxxxxx xxxxxxxxxxx xx xxxxxxxxxxx xx xxxxxxxxxxx xxxxx
xxxxxxxxxx xxxxxxxxxxxxxxxxxx xx xxx xxxxxxxxxx xxxx xxxxxx
xxxxxxx xxxxxxx xxxxxxxxxxxxxx xxxxxx xxxxxxxxxxx xx
xxxxxxxxxx

You can have a single paragraph or several paragraphs under a heading.

Tips on Making Headings

These are some common standards for making headings:

- If you use a computer or newer typewriter, make all your headings bold. Don't use bold elsewhere in the paper (simply underline or use italics) or else you'll distract your reader's eyes from your headings.
- Put one more space above a heading than below it. That way your heading is visually part of the text it labels.
- Use at least two of each type heading—never only one. Headings show subordinate ideas so—just as with outlines—you need two or more.
- Don't put a heading all by itself as the last line on a page. Include at least two lines of the text after the heading. You may need to move a heading to the top of the following page.

SHORTER PARAGRAPHS

When you use headings, you can use shorter paragraphs that show breaks in thought. For example, consider this paragraph from our sample five-paragraph essay in the last chapter:

■ Sample Paragraph without Organizational Breaks

Children also can be funny in the way they "humanize" the objects around them. According to my psychology book, "Up to four or five years old, the child believes anything may be endowed with purpose and conscious activity. A ball may refuse to be thrown straight, or a 'naughty' chair may be responsible for bumping him" (Pulaski, *Understanding Piaget,* p. 45). I, myself, still can remember one vivid and scary afternoon when I was sure the sun was following me around, just waiting for the right moment to get me. I also can remember a time, not scary, when Betsy stood at the top of the stairs and yelled to her shoes at the bottom, "Shoes! Get up here!"

If that paragraph had a heading (and the paragraph after had another heading), we could show the small organizational breaks this way:

■ Sample Paragraph with Organizational Breaks

Discovering Objects Aren't Human

Children also can be funny in the way they "humanize" the objects around them. According to my psychology book, "Up to four or five years old, the child believes anything may be endowed with purpose and conscious activity. A ball may refuse to be thrown straight, or a 'naughty' chair may be responsible for bumping him" (Pulaski, *Understanding Piaget,* p. 45).

I, myself, still can remember one vivid and scary afternoon when I was sure the sun was following me around, just waiting for the right moment to get me. I also can remember a time, not scary, when Betsy stood at the top of the stairs and yelled to her shoes at the bottom, "Shoes! Get up here!"

The second paragraph signals a shift from one item of specific support (a statement by an authority) to another item of specific support (a quick example). We'll know when the next topic sentence occurs because a heading will announce it.

INDENTED LISTS

Lists help *show* a series of items. That is, if you have two or three or more items in series in a sentence, consider breaking them out into an indented list. The term for the broken-out list is a "bulleted" or an "indented" list.

Tips on Making Indented Lists

To make an indented list (like this one):

- Use a bullet symbol (a hyphen will do fine, as will a lowercase letter *o*).
- Align the text in second and following lines with the text above—don't go all the way back to the left margin.
- Put the bullet symbol about .5 inch from the left margin.

- Tab over .2 inch from the bullet symbol to the text.
- Double-space between bulleted items.

There is no standard way to capitalize or punctuate bulleted items. The system you see in this book (no capital letters or punctuation unless the items are full sentences) is very common. Just be consistent.

A SAMPLE FIVE-PARAGRAPH ESSAY WITH ALTERNATIVE LAYOUT

Now let's see what these alternative layout techniques can do for a paper we saw in the previous chapter.

HUMOROUS THINGS CHILDREN DO

Do you realize that newly born children are not even aware that parts of their bodies belong to them?

I learned this fascinating fact in my psychology course from a book that says a baby "lies on his back, kicking his heels and watching the little fists flying past his face. But only very slowly does he come to know that they are attached to him and he can control them" (Mary Ann Spencer Pulaski, *Understanding Piaget,* p. 21).

Children have a lot of learning to do before they can see the world—and themselves—through grown-up eyes. As children pass through this remarkable process of growing up, they often do humorous things, especially:

- in learning to speak
- in discovering that all objects do not have human characteristics
- in trying to imitate others around them

Learning to Speak

Not surprisingly, one area in which children often are unintentionally humorous is in learning to speak. I remember one time I was talking to a friend on the phone while my little sister, Betsy, seemed to be playing inattentively on the floor nearby. After I hung up, Betsy asked me, "Why is the teacher going to give Janet an old tomato?"

At first I couldn't figure out what Betsy was talking about. When I asked her what she meant, she said, "You said if Janet doesn't hand in her homework, the teacher is going to give her an old tomato." Finally I caught on. The word I had used was *ultimatum!*

Discovering Objects Aren't Human

Children also can be funny in the way they humanize the objects around them. According to my psychology book, "Up to four or five years old, the child believes anything may be endowed with purpose and conscious activity. A ball may refuse to be thrown straight, or a 'naughty' chair may be responsible for bumping him" (Pulaski, *Understanding Piaget,* p. 45).

I, myself, still can remember one vivid and scary afternoon when I was sure the sun was following me around, just waiting for the right moment to get me. I also can remember a time, not scary, when Betsy stood at the top of the stairs and yelled to her shoes at the bottom, "Shoes! Get up here!"

Imitating Others Around Them

Another way in which children are sometimes funny is in their attempts to imitate what they see around them. All children look pretty silly when they dress up like their mothers and fathers and play "house."

My psychology book tells of a more interesting example, though. The famous psychologist Jean Piaget wrote of the time his sixteen-month-old daughter quietly watched a visiting little boy throw a tantrum in trying to get out of his playpen. Piaget's daughter thought it would be fun to try the same thing: "The next day, she herself screamed in her playpen and tried to move it, stamping her foot lightly several times in succession. The imitation of the whole scene was most striking" (quoted in Pulaski, *Understanding Piaget,* p. 81).

Conclusion

Little children are funny creatures to watch, aren't they? But as we laugh, we have to admire, too, because the humorous mistakes are but temporary side trips that children take on the amazingly complicated journey to maturity—a long way from the beginning, when they lay in wonder, silently watching the strange, fingered spacecraft passing back and forth before their infant eyes.

It looks good, doesn't it? And those of you who use computers can play around with the layout of your paper until you get it just right.

SINGLE SPACING AND DOUBLE SPACING

In the past, all school papers had to have double-spaced lines. A double-spaced paper gives your instructor room to make detailed comments. However, some instructors prefer single spacing, particularly if the paper has headings in it. Single spacing allows the instructor to understand the organization better—more words and ideas are on each page. Ask your instructor which spacing to use.

EXERCISE

Apply the three techniques of layout to a modified version of a paper we showed you in the previous chapter:

From: Ed Malone
To: Janet Chambers
Subject: A proposal for a color printer and desktop publishing capabilities

    We need to improve the quality of the documents and proposals we're producing in our division. To add the polish and professional look we need, I recommend we buy a color printer plus additional purchases that will let our secretaries do desktop publishing. This memo will cover why we need the printer, why we need the additional purchases, and what our implementation plan will be.

    First, I recommend we buy a color printer. The cost would be $3,400. The printer will give us two main benefits: First, it will add graphics capabilities to both our graphics work and our desktop publishing. In fact, desktop publishing almost requires a color printer for professional impact. Second, the color printer is also fairly fast, so it will give us crucial speed for rapid turnaround of final documents and proposals. It will make possible those last-minute additions and changes that often improve final presentation.

Next, we'll need additional purchases to do desktop publishing on the printer. Here's specifically what we'll need:

2 copies of graphics software
1 training slot

The desktop publishing software will give our documents a professional appearance, and it can easily combine text and graphics. That way the appearance of our documents will truly express the professional quality of our work. The training will allow staff members to make the most effective use of both hardware and software.

When we get a color printer and the additional purchases, here's what our implementation plan will be: We'll add the color printer to our network to make it widely available to the staff. We'll install the other hardware and software on the workstations belonging to the two secretaries. One secretary is ready to start desktop publishing as soon as we get her a mouse and a graphics board. She already has software, training, and experience publishing a proposal. The other secretary needs to take the training first. That training is offered three weeks from now. When he's trained, we should have an excellent start for desktop publishing.

I'll be glad to talk this over with you whenever you like.

CHAPTER 11
Thesis Statement with Blueprint

The thesis statement with blueprint is an essential part of your five-paragraph essay. As the name suggests, it has two components:

- the main idea (thesis statement)
- the outline of your support (blueprint)

Let's look at each of these two components in more detail.

THESIS STATEMENT

The thesis statement is the main idea of your five-paragraph essay, the single idea your entire essay will support. Sound familiar? The *topic sentence* was the main idea of a one-paragraph essay. The *thesis statement* is the main idea of anything larger than a one-paragraph essay—in this case, the main idea of the five-paragraph essay. Like the topic sentence, the thesis statement can take the form of *"limited subject* is *precise opinion."* In the following introduction to our sample five-paragraph essay we've italicized the thesis:

■ Introduction with Thesis Statement

Do you realize that newly born children are not even aware that parts of their bodies belong to them? I learned this fascinating fact in my psychology course from a book that says a baby "lies on his back, kicking his heels and watching the little fists flying past his face. But only very slowly does he come to know that they are attached to him and he can control them" (Mary Ann Spencer Pulaski, *Understanding Piaget,* p. 21). Children have a lot of learning to do before they can see the world—and themselves—through grown-up eyes. *As children pass through this remarkable process of growing up, they often do humorous things,* especially in learning to speak, in discovering that all objects do not have human characteristics, and in trying to imitate others around them.

The limited subject is *children as they grow up;* the precise opinion is *humorous.*

BLUEPRINT

What is a blueprint for an essay? As we mentioned in the previous chapter, a blueprint is a summary of the main points you are about to present in the body of your paper. In other words, *the blueprint is a list of the ideas in your topic sentences.*

Blueprint

As the name *blueprint* suggests, the blueprint is like an architect's pattern for the structure she intends to build . . . only in this case, you are the architect, and the structure you intend to build is your essay.

Suppose you have this organization in mind for your five-paragraph essay:

Thesis statement	Streetlights installed at least ten feet high is a good idea.
Topic sentence	They can light up a wider area.
Topic sentence	They are harder to vandalize.
Topic sentence	They don't block people's view.

Now, to form a blueprint, simply list the basic ideas from the three topic sentences:

> Because they light up a wider area, they are harder to vandalize, and they don't block people's view, . . .

Now let's combine the blueprint with the thesis statement to get the result this chapter is about—the thesis statement with blueprint:

> Because they light up a wider area, they are harder to vandalize, and they don't block people's view, streetlights installed at least ten feet high is a good idea.

Finally, let's look at the introduction to the sample theme from Chapter 9, with the blueprint italicized:

■ Introduction with Thesis and Blueprint

Do you realize that newly born children are not even aware that parts of their bodies belong to them? I learned this fascinating fact in my psychology course from a book that says a baby "lies on his back, kicking his heels and watching the little fists flying past his face. But only very slowly does he come to know that they are attached to him and he can control them" (Mary Ann Spencer Pulaski, *Understanding Piaget,* p. 21). Children have a lot of learning to do before they can see the world—and themselves—through grown-up eyes. As children pass through this remarkable process of growing up, they often do humorous things, *especially in learning to speak, in discovering that all objects do not have human characteristics, and in trying to imitate others around them.*

BLUEPRINTS ANSWERING "WHY?" "HOW?" "WHEN?"

Because the five-paragraph essay is an expanded Stage II paragraph, you can use the same kinds of support for both of them. Let's examine sample blueprints that answer each of the questions "Why?" "How?" and "When?"

"Why?" Blueprint

If we ask "Why?" about a thesis statement, the answer will usually begin with *because*. Let's look an example: "Why do vegetable gardens take a lot of planning?"

■ Blueprint Answering "Why?"

Because the soil needs to be prepared, *because* the vegetables need to be planted at the right times, and *because* the fertilizing must take place on schedule, [the thesis follows].

"How?" Blueprint

A "How?" blueprint usually can begin with *by, with,* or *through*. Also, since "How?" blueprints are sometimes similar to "Why?" blueprints, they both can begin with *because*. For example: "How does Wanda distract you?"

■ Blueprints Answering "How?"

By singing, eating, and talking as I try to study,

   or

With her singing, her eating, and her talking,

   or

Through her singing, her eating, and her talking,

   or

Because of her singing, her eating, and her talking,

"When?" Blueprint

"When?" blueprints usually begin with the word *when.* "When is your room-mate constantly sleepy?"

■ Blueprint Answering "When?"

When he gets up in the morning, sits in class, or studies in the evening,

DIFFERENT FORMS OF THE THESIS WITH BLUEPRINT

So far, we've shown you blueprints as part of the same sentence as the thesis, with the blueprint coming at the beginning of that thesis:

■ Thesis with Blueprint in the Same Sentence

Because they light up a wider area, they are harder to vandalize, and they don't block people's view, streetlights installed at least ten feet high is a good idea.

Actually, though, you can present the thesis with blueprint many different ways:

■ Different Forms of the Thesis with Blueprint

Installing streetlights at least ten feet high is a good idea because they light up a wider area, they are harder to vandalize, and they don't block people's view.

   or

Installing streetlights at least ten feet high is a good idea: they light up a wider area, they are harder to vandalize, and they don't block people's view.

or

Installing streetlights at least ten feet high is a good idea. They light up a wider area. They are harder to vandalize. And they don't block people's view.

Please notice, though, that for each example, each item in the blueprint has the same structure. In the last example, each was an entire sentence.

The following is a poor blueprint because the blueprint items do not have the same structure:

■ Poor Blueprint

Installing street lights at least ten feet high is a good idea because they light up a wider area and they are harder to vandalize. Also, they don't block people's view.

A reader probably would be confused. Is the writer going to discuss two ideas or three? There seem to be three ideas (wider area, vandalizing, better view), but only two blueprint sentences follow the thesis statement. You can avoid confusing your reader by using the same structure—all sentences, all clauses, or all phrases—for each of your blueprint items. If you want more information, see the chapter on parallelism in Part 7.

PRACTICAL WRITING

A blueprint is useful for much of your writing at school or work. Remember the five-paragraph essay on e. e. cummings' poetry? It included this thesis with blueprint:

■ A Thesis with Blueprint from a College Paper

We can find that emphasis on freedom in the typographical layout of his poems, their frequent antigovernment content, and the celebration of the individual in his poetry on spring.

Blueprints are also common in specialized journals. Here's a sample from a journal article on computers, *UNIX Review:*

■ A Blueprint on Problems with Computer Security

I've organized the problems into five categories:

- What can I do to mess up one of those system configuration files?
- You mean there's something special about setup programs?

- What's so important about physical security anyway?
- Are these manuals really useful for installing a system?
- That can't be a security breach! I've got a provably secure UNIX system!

The article includes sections on each of the blueprint items.

EXERCISES

A. Combine the thesis statement and ideas for topic sentences to produce a thesis with blueprint.

1. **Thesis** Whales need friends, too.

   Idea for topic sentence travel in groups

   Idea for topic sentence talk to each other

   Idea for topic sentence mourn loss of another whale

   Thesis with blueprint _____

   _____

2. **Thesis** Deserts are distinctive from other geographical areas.

   Idea for topic sentence climate

   Idea for topic sentence plants

   Idea for topic sentence animals

   Thesis with blueprint _____

   _____

3. **Thesis** Detergents attack dirt in several ways.

   Idea for topic sentence wet the material you want to clean

   Idea for topic sentence remove the dirt through a chemical reaction

   Idea for topic sentence suspend dirt in water so you can rinse it away

Thesis with blueprint _____

_____

4. **Thesis**   American "hard-boiled" mysteries have many things in common.

   Idea for topic sentence   tough private eyes

   Idea for topic sentence   uncooperative police

   Idea for topic sentence   lying clients

   Thesis with blueprint _____

   _____

5. **Thesis**   Scientists disagree on why dinosaurs became extinct.

   Idea for topic sentence   climate became too cold

   Idea for topic sentence   giant asteroid destroyed important sources of food worldwide

   Idea for topic sentence   new plants developed that dinosaurs couldn't eat

   Thesis with blueprint _____

   _____

B. Choose any one of the items from Exercise A and write a thesis statement with blueprint three different ways. See the last section of the chapter, "Different Forms of the Thesis with Blueprint," for some ideas.

C. Each item below gives a thesis statement. Invent your own support or look in an encyclopedia or on the Web to get a few ideas for how to develop the thesis. Combine those ideas with the thesis statement to produce a thesis statement with blueprint. If you use an outside source, document it briefly (see Chapter 9).

   1. **Thesis**   There are useful ways for people to overcome disabilities.

      Topic sentence _____

      Topic sentence _____

Topic sentence_____

Thesis with blueprint_____

_____

2. **Thesis**   Each part of a tooth serves important purposes.

Topic sentence _____

Topic sentence _____

Topic sentence _____

Thesis with blueprint _____

_____

3. **Thesis**   Telescopes have several important capabilities.

Topic sentence _____

Topic sentence _____

Topic sentence _____

Thesis with blueprint _____

_____

CHAPTER 12
Central Paragraphs

A five-paragraph essay has three central paragraphs, and each one helps prove your thesis statement. Essentially, then, central paragraphs are simply one-paragraph essays that each support one item in your blueprint. In fact, each central paragraph is like a Stage I or Stage II paragraph.

Specific support in a central paragraph supports the paragraph's topic sentence, and the three topic sentences, taken together, support the thesis. Therefore, if each central paragraph supports its own topic sentence, and if the topic sentences are properly related to one another and to your thesis, then the central paragraphs should persuade the readers to accept your thesis statement. We'll discuss introductions and conclusions later; for the moment assume that a five-paragraph essay looks like this:

> Thesis statement with blueprint
> First central paragraph
> Second central paragraph
> Third central paragraph
> Thesis statement with blueprint

This chapter deals with two differences between central paragraphs and the one-paragraph essay:

- omission of the reworded topic sentence
- additions to the topic sentence

OMISSION OF THE REWORDED TOPIC SENTENCE

Every Stage I and Stage II one-paragraph essay, a unit complete in itself, has three basic parts:

- a topic sentence
- specific support
- a reworded topic sentence

The reworded topic sentence provides a mark of finality to the argument.

A central paragraph, however, doesn't require this same mark of finality. Because a central paragraph doesn't present the entire argument of the essay, a reworded topic sentence at the end of each central paragraph is unnecessary. After you've presented your last item of specific support, you go on to the next paragraph.

ADDITIONS TO THE TOPIC SENTENCE

Like a topic sentence for a one-paragraph essay, the topic sentence for a central paragraph presents the *main idea of the paragraph* in the basic form of *"limited subject* is *precise opinion."* However, the topic sentence for a central paragraph has two important additions:

- a *transition* from the preceding paragraph
- a *reminder* of the thesis

The first addition, the *transition,* provides coherence. Just as sentences within any paragraph must move smoothly from one to another, paragraphs within a theme must also flow together.

The second addition to the topic sentence, the *reminder of the thesis,* helps fit the central paragraph's main idea to the theme's main idea. The total argument will come together more easily if each central paragraph's idea (its topic sentence) connects to the theme's idea (the thesis statement). This addition, then, helps provide both coherence and unity. Therefore, the topic sentence for a central paragraph should have these three parts:

- a transition
- a reminder of the thesis statement
- the main idea of the paragraph

EXAMPLES OF CENTRAL PARAGRAPHS

Let's look at some examples of central paragraphs. Here's the first central paragraph from the sample theme in Chapter 9. Can you find the three parts of the topic sentence?

■ First Central Paragraph

Not surprisingly, one area in which children often are unintentionally humorous is in learning to speak. I remember one time I was talking to a friend on the phone while my little sister, Betsy, seemed to be playing inattentively on the floor nearby. After I hung up, Betsy asked me, "Why is the teacher going to give Janet an old tomato?" At first I couldn't figure out what Betsy was talking about. When I asked her what she meant, she said, "You said if Janet doesn't hand in her homework, the teacher is going to give her an old tomato." Finally, I caught on. The word I had used was *ultimatum!*

Here are the three parts:

Transition	one area
Reminder	children often are unintentionally humorous
Main idea	learning to speak

Notice also the specific support for the topic sentence: a narrative example telling the brief story of Betsy's funny question. A central paragraph should have the same detailed support as a one-paragraph essay. Now let's look at the *second* central paragraph from the sample theme:

■ Second Central Paragraph

Children also can be funny in the way they humanize the objects around them. According to my psychology book, "Up to four or five years old, the child believes anything may be endowed with purpose and conscious activity. A ball may refuse to be thrown straight, or a 'naughty' chair may be responsible for bumping him" (Pulaski, *Understanding Piaget,* p. 45). I, myself, still can remember one vivid and scary afternoon when I was sure the sun was following me around, just waiting for the right moment to get me. I also can remember a time, not scary, when Betsy stood up at the top of the stars and yelled to her shoes at the bottom, "Shoes! Get up here!"

Here are the three parts of the topic sentence:

> *Transition*   also
> *Reminder*   children can be funny
> *Main idea*   the way they humanize objects

This paragraph has a variety of support: a statement by an authority and two quick examples. Finally, let's look at the *third* central paragraph:

■ Third Central Paragraph

Another way in which children are sometimes funny is in their attempts to imitate what they see around them. All children look pretty silly when they dress up like their mothers and fathers and play "house." My psychology book tells of a more interesting example, though. The famous psychologist Jean Piaget wrote of the time his sixteen-month-old daughter quietly watched a visiting little boy throw a tantrum in trying to get out of his playpen. Piaget's daughter thought it would be fun to try the same thing: "The next day, she herself screamed in her playpen and tried to move it, stamping her foot lightly several times in succession. The imitation of the whole scene was most striking" (quoted in Pulaski, *Understanding Piaget,* p. 81).

Here are the three parts of the topic sentence:

> *Transition*   Another way
> *Reminder*   children are sometimes funny
> *Main idea*   their attempts to imitate what they see around them

This paragraph has an interesting form of support: a narrative example that's stated by an authority—Piaget.

Because you must have space to develop your argument, you break it into parts—the arguments of the central paragraphs. Yet, like a jigsaw puzzle, a theme will never seem complete unless you connect the pieces. The additions to the topic sentence of each central paragraph help you fit the central paragraphs to one another and to your thesis statement.

EXERCISES

A. Let's say you're writing a five-paragraph essay with this thesis statement:

Thesis   Termites have special roles to play.

For each topic sentence below, identify the transition, the reminder of the thesis, and the main idea.

First topic sentence   For one thing, the soldier termites have the special role of defending the colony.

Transition _____

Reminder _____

Main idea _____

Second topic sentence   A second special role for termites is doing the routine work of destroying your house.

Transition _____

Reminder _____

Main idea _____

Third topic sentence   A final special role for termites is reproducing to keep enough termites in the colony.

Transition _____

Reminder _____

Main idea _____

B.   Follow the instructions for Exercise A with this thesis statement:

Thesis   Driving a car requires constant attention.

First topic sentence   For one thing, drivers must constantly look at the gauges on the dashboard.

Transition _____

Reminder _____

Main idea _____

Second topic sentence   As if that's not enough, drivers also must pay attention to the route they are traveling.

Transition _____

Reminder _____

Main idea _____

Third topic sentence   And drivers have to keep a sharp lookout for other traffic, including pedestrians.

Transition _____

Reminder _____

Main idea _____

C. Follow the instructions for Exercise A with this thesis statement:

Thesis   Television meteorologists—more commonly known as TV weather forecasters—need special expertise.

First topic sentence   Television forecasters, most importantly, have to understand weather data.

Transition _____

Reminder _____

Main idea _____

Second topic sentence   They also must know how to operate computer equipment to design their weather shows.

Transition _____

Reminder _____

Main idea _____

Third topic sentence   Further, they need to understand the proper behavior required on camera for giving forecasts in front of thousands of viewers.

Transition _____

Reminder _____

Main idea _____

D. Here's a thesis statement and three main ideas for central paragraphs.
Use these main ideas to write complete topic sentences—including transitions and reminders of the thesis.

Thesis   Sailing requires adjusting the sails.

Main idea   into the wind

Main idea   across the wind

Main idea   with the wind

First topic sentence _____

   Transition _____

   Reminder _____

Second topic sentence _____

   Transition _____

   Reminder _____

Third topic sentence _____

   Transition _____

   Reminder _____

E.   Follow the instructions for Exercise D with this thesis and three main ideas:

Thesis   Some musical instruments are hard to play.

Main idea   guitar

Main idea   violin

Main idea   trombone

First topic sentence _____

   Transition _____

Reminder _____

Second topic sentence _____

  Transition _____

  Reminder _____

Third topic sentence _____

  Transition _____

  Reminder _____

F. For Exercises A–E, you've written topic sentences for a number of central paragraphs. Choose the one that interests you the most, and—inventing the support—write one central paragraph.

G. Recall the sample theme in Chapter 9 on the humorous things children do. In a way, the writer of that theme was an "expert" on children's funny behavior: she had been a child herself, and she had observed her sister (and other children) growing up. She didn't depend in that theme on any expertise in psychology, only on the behavior of children she had observed. The expertise she did use—from the book on Piaget—was highly interesting, of course, but it wasn't an essential part of the thesis statement, nor was it the only support.

    You, too, are probably an "expert" in something. Perhaps you play golf well or understand how to tune an automobile engine or know every song the Beatles recorded. Choose a topic you know well and a significant idea related to it. Think of something important to say about your topic and turn that statement into a thesis statement with blueprint. Letting the thesis statement with blueprint serve as both the introduction and the conclusion, write the three central paragraphs of a five-paragraph essay (you'll write the full-length introduction and conclusion later as exercises for Chapters 13 and 14).

    Be sure to use detailed support for each central paragraph, just as you would for a one-paragraph essay, and be sure that each of your topic sentences contains a transition from the previous paragraph, a reminder of the thesis statement, and the main idea of the paragraph.

    If you use outside sources, use them only to find support, not to find a thesis. Otherwise, you'll merely be paraphrasing someone else. Also, be sure to place quotation marks around all words you borrow directly. At the end of every sentence that contains borrowed words or ideas, acknowledge your source in parentheses (see Chapter 9 if you've forgotten the rules for the preliminary documentation system). If you have any questions about documentation, be sure to ask your instructor.

H. Think about the other courses you're taking and some of the interesting ideas you are learning in those courses. From those ideas, devise a thesis statement with blueprint.

   Letting the thesis statement with blueprint serve as both the introduction and the conclusion, write the three central paragraphs of a five-paragraph essay (you'll write the full-length introduction and conclusion later as exercises for Chapters 13 and 14).

   Be sure to use detailed support for each central paragraph, just as you would for a one-paragraph essay, and be sure that each of your topic sentences contains a transition from the previous paragraph, a reminder of the thesis statement, and the main idea of the paragraph.

   This exercise, in particular, will probably require some documentation. So be sure to place quotation marks around all words you borrow directly. At the end of every sentence that contains borrowed words or ideas, acknowledge your source in parentheses (see Chapter 9 if you've forgotten the rules for the preliminary documentation system). If you have any questions about documentation, be sure to ask your instructor.

I. Using your first job (or any job you've held) as a topic, devise a thesis statement. Perhaps your thesis could be about an important lesson you learned at work, what you learned not to do, or how the job changed your attitude toward school, your friends, or your parents.

   Let the thesis with blueprint serve as both the introduction and the conclusion. Write the three central paragraphs of a five-paragraph essay (you'll write the full-length introduction and conclusion later as exercises for Chapters 13 and 14). Be sure to follow the advice for support and documentation in Exercise G.

J. Find a Web site that particularly interests you. Next, devise a thesis statement that captures your opinion of that Web site. Develop a blueprint. Letting the thesis statement with blueprint serve as both your introduction and the conclusion, write the three central paragraphs of a five-paragraph essay (you'll write the full-length introduction and conclusion later as exercises for Chapters 13 and 14). Be sure to follow the advice for support and documentation in Exercise G.

CHAPTER 13

Introduction

Your introduction serves two important purposes:

- It gets your reader's attention.
- It tells your reader what your main idea is (and how you will develop it).

The part of your introduction that gets your reader's attention is called a *motivator*. The part that tells your reader what your main point is (and how you will develop it) is called the *thesis statement with blueprint*. We discussed thesis statements with blueprints in Chapter 12. In this chapter we'll concentrate on motivators.

Here's the introduction from our sample theme in Chapter 9. Can you find the motivator—the part that gets the reader's attention?

■ Introduction to a Five-Paragraph Essay

Do you realize that newly born children are not even aware that parts of their bodies belong to them? I learned this fascinating fact in my psychology course from a book that says a baby "lies on his back, kicking his heels and watching the little fists flying past his face. But only very slowly does he come to know that they are attached to him and he can control them" (Mary Ann Spencer Pulaski, *Understanding Piaget*, p. 21). Children have a lot of learning to do before they can see the world—and themselves—through grown-up eyes. As children pass through this remarkable process of growing up, they often do humorous things, especially in learning to speak, in discovering that all objects do not have human characteristics, and in trying to imitate others around them.

The motivator is all but the last sentence. The writer hopes to interest you by telling you something intriguing—that infants don't know that parts of their bodies belong to them. As you practice writing and look carefully at the writing of others, you'll find many good ways to motivate your reader. Here are three good ways that we'll discuss in this chapter:

- the opposite opinion
- a brief story
- an interesting statement

THE OPPOSITE OPINION

An easy way to begin your paper is to state the opinion your paper opposes followed by a transition to your thesis statement with blueprint. In other words, your introduction has this flow to it:

- what the opposition says
- transition
- what you say

Transitions with the Opposite Opinion

The transition is particularly important in this kind of introduction because you must move clearly from the position you oppose to the position you support.

Here's a sample introduction to an essay showing that smoking is a disgusting habit:

> Some people think that smoking makes them appear sophisticated and mysterious, perhaps even seductive. They become Humphrey Bogart in *Casablanca* or Lauren Bacall in *To Have and Have Not*. Those people, however, are wrong. As far as I am concerned, smoking is really a disgusting habit—messy, irritating to others, and even harmful to nonsmokers.

Notice the strong transition ("Those people, however, are wrong.") And notice that the thesis statement and blueprint are obvious. Readers know clearly they have read the main idea of the paper and how it will be developed.

Here is another introduction using the opposite opinion as the motivator:

> As I was walking down the hall yesterday, I overheard a professor complaining about computers: "Those things are going to ruin the writing of our students. A computer is just a fancied-up TV and arcade game disguised as an

'educational tool.' " But my experience with computers is entirely different. As word processors, for example, they can be immensely helpful with each stage of the writing process: prewriting, writing, and rewriting.

A BRIEF STORY

We all enjoy stories, so one of the most interesting ways to begin a paper is to tell your readers a brief story somehow related to your thesis statement. In that way, you engage their attention right from the start. By the time they've finished the story, sheer momentum carries them into the rest of your paper. Here's a sample introduction that begins with a brief story:

> I walked into the living room, picked up a magazine, and settled back into my chair. When I opened the cover, I was confronted by the image of a slender, elegant woman staring confidently into the distance and holding a cigarette in one hand. "Smoke cigarettes," she seemed to be saying, "and you, too, can be slender and elegant." I wanted so much to be like her. But I never took up smoking because—elegance and slenderness notwithstanding—I've always thought of it as a disgusting habit: messy, irritating to others, and even harmful to nonsmokers.

Notice that the introduction has a transition ("But I never took up . . .") between the motivator and thesis with blueprint.

Some introductions need a transition—like the one above, and all those that begin with opposite opinions—whereas others move smoothly from the motivator to the thesis with blueprint without any explicit transition words:

> I remember the first time I used a computer—or "word processor"—to do some writing. I was at a neighbor's house, so I just began a "letter" (one I wasn't planning to mail) to a friend. Instead of pausing frequently to think of things to say, I just wrote. The words seemed to come easily because I knew I could make changes later with no problem. Since then, I've used computers for most of my writing, and I've come to believe that they can be immensely helpful to us at each stage in the writing process: prewriting, writing, and rewriting.

AN INTERESTING STATEMENT

Another easy way to get your reader's attention is to begin with a statement that's interesting, either because the idea is intriguing or because, perhaps, the tone is angry. The introduction to the five-paragraph essay in Chapter 9 begins with an interesting statement, one that's intriguing: "Do you realize that newly born children are not even aware that parts of their bodies belong to them?"

The next example is a motivator that's interesting because the tone is angry (after all, if we're walking along and hear somebody yelling, we would probably stop because we're curious):

> I'm sick of smokers flicking ashes on my desk and throwing ashes on the rug. Long after these people have left, their messes remain, together with the foul smoke they have exhaled from their tar-coated lungs. Let's face facts: smoking is a disgusting habit—messy, irritating, and even harmful to nonsmokers.

The following example is only two sentences long and shows that an introduction can be effective even if it's short:

> Computers can *really* make a difference in how quickly and how easily you can get words on paper. In fact, computers—used as word processors—can be immensely helpful with each stage of the writing process: prewriting, writing, and rewriting.

The motivator for this introduction is interesting because the writer seems enthusiastic. If you convey your enthusiasm for your topic, your beginning most likely will be interesting, too.

When you are writing the introduction to your paper—whether you choose the opposite opinion, a brief story, or an interesting statement—be sure you fulfill the two important purposes of all introductions: interest your readers and tell them the main idea of your paper (and how you will develop it).

EXERCISES

A. In Exercise A for Chapter 11 ("Thesis Statement with Blueprint"), you wrote five thesis statements with blueprints. Choose one and write three introductions for it: one with the opposite opinion, one with a brief story, and one with an interesting statement.

B. For Exercises G, H, I, and J in Chapter 12 ("Central Paragraphs"), you wrote a thesis statement with blueprint followed by three central paragraphs. Now, using any of the three types of motivators we just discussed, write a full-length introduction for one of those exercises (G, H, I, or J). You may need to change the wording of the original thesis statement with blueprint to make it fit smoothly with your motivator, but don't change the essential meaning.

CHAPTER 14
Conclusion

The conclusion, like the introduction, serves two purposes in an essay:

- It reminds the reader of the main point of your essay.
- It gives the reader a sense of finality.

The part that reminds the reader of the main point is the *reworded thesis statement*. The part that gives finality is the *clincher*. Below is the conclusion to the sample five-paragraph essay you saw in Chapter 9. Locate the reworded thesis and the clincher.

■ Conclusion of a Five-Paragraph Essay

Little children are funny creatures to watch, aren't they? But as we laugh, we have to admire, too, because the humorous mistakes are but temporary side trips that children take on the amazingly complicated journey to maturity—a long way from the beginning, where they lay in wonder, silently watching the strange, fingered spacecraft passing back and forth before their infant eyes.

The reworded thesis is the first sentence; the clincher is the last one. You already know how to write a reworded thesis statement: it resembles the reworded topic sentence that you worked with on the one-paragraph essay. Therefore, this chapter concentrates on the clincher. We'll discuss two types:

- the reference to the motivator
- the interesting statement

THE REFERENCE TO THE MOTIVATOR

The simplest—and most common—clincher reminds the readers of the motivator you used in your introduction. This clincher has the advantage of bringing the paper full circle, an unmistakable signal that the paper is over.

The previous chapter showed you three sample introductions with the thesis that smoking is disgusting. Let's look at those introductions again. Notice that each conclusion:

- begins with a reworded thesis statement
- finishes by referring to the motivator

Introduction to Essay 1 (opposite opinion)

Some people think that smoking makes them appear sophisticated and mysterious, perhaps even seductive. They become Humphrey Bogart in *Casablanca* or Lauren Bacall in *To Have and Have Not*. Those people, however, are wrong. As far as I am concerned, smoking is really a disgusting habit—messy, irritating to others, and even harmful to nonsmokers.

Conclusion to Essay 1

I am glad I never began such a disgusting habit, and I wish others had not started, either. I hope my sophisticated friends soon find out that Humphrey Bogart and Lauren Bacall were mysterious and appealing in spite of their habit, not because of it.

Introduction to Essay 2 (brief story)

I walked into the living room, picked up a magazine, and settled back into my chair. When I opened the cover, I was confronted by the image of a slender, elegant woman staring confidently into the distance and holding a cigarette in one hand. "Smoke cigarettes," she seemed to be saying, "and you, too, can be slender and elegant." I wanted so much to be like her. But I never took up smoking because—elegance and slenderness notwithstanding—I've always thought of it as a disgusting habit: messy, irritating to others, and even harmful to nonsmokers.

Conclusion to Essay 2

I am glad I never began such a disgusting habit, and I wish others hadn't started, either. I no longer have the magazine with the elegant woman. But I don't miss her, the magazine, or smoking.

Introduction to Essay 3 (interesting statement)

I'm sick of smokers flicking ashes on my desk and throwing ashes on the rug. Long after these people have left, their messes remain, together with the foul smoke they have exhaled from their tar-coated lungs. Let's face facts: smoking is a disgusting habit—messy, irritating, and even harmful to nonsmokers.

■ Conclusion to Essay 3

I'm glad I never began such a disgusting habit. If other people hadn't started smoking, then neither their houses nor mine would be littered with smokers' messes, and we would all be healthier.

An Interesting Statement

The previous chapter showed you how to *begin* papers with interesting statements; an interesting statement is a good way to *end* a paper, too. Your statement might be interesting because of the information or because of the tone. Here's a conclusion that includes a statement interesting for its information:

> I am glad I never began such a disgusting habit, and I wish others had not started, either. I hope my sophisticated friends soon find out that Humphrey Bogart, mysterious and appealing though he might have been, unfortunately died of cancer of the throat—possibly caused by smoking.

And here's a conclusion with an interesting—even angry—tone:

> I am glad I never began such a disgusting habit, and I wish others had not started, either. Then the only smoking would take place at the fire-eater's show at the carnival—a spectacle that would give smoking the kind of dignity it deserves.

To finish your five-paragraph essay, simply reword the thesis statement and end with unmistakable finality: the clincher.

A Note of Caution

When you write your conclusion, be careful not to state any new, unsupported generalizations that your reader might question.

An Example of a Five-Paragraph Essay

Now that you've read about all the parts of a five-paragraph essay, let's finish by looking at one more. In Chapter 5 you saw a version of this (about Travis McGee) as a Stage I paragraph; in Chapter 8, we expanded it to a Stage II paragraph. Now look at it as a five-paragraph essay:

> One of the most compelling characters in popular American fiction in the twentieth century was Travis McGee. McGee appeared to be just a beach

bum, owning a fifty-foot houseboat at the Bahia Mar Marina in Fort Lauderdale, lazing around, and living the good life. And he also appeared to be a tough-guy beach bum; six feet four inches tall, incredibly quick, and in good shape, he was able to take on bullies from motorcycle goons to psychopathic killers and hammer them into submission. But McGee's main appeal is that he's more than just a beach bum and a tough guy. You can see that through his clever and tricky schemes to defeat villains, his emotional involvement with his cases, and his total loyalty to his friends.

For one thing, McGee often depends on his mind, not his physical gifts, to outdo the villains. For example, in *Pale Gray for Guilt,* McGee uses skillful lawyers, a sharp businesswoman, and the economist who is his best friend to financially destroy the people who had effectively killed another good friend of his, Tush Bannon. And he does it by getting the main conniver to invest everything he owns and everything he can borrow into the same type of land scheme the conniver had used on Bannon. McGee thus avenged his friend by outsmarting the culprit—hurting him far more than a punch to the body could ever have done.

Another way McGee's not just a tough guy is that he always gets emotionally involved with the people in the case, often fancying himself, deprecatingly, as Don Quixote doing battle with windmills. Again, in *Pale Gray for Guilt,* his dead friend, Tush Bannon, was a bumblingly nice guy. Bannon started a moderately successful marina that, unfortunately, was in the middle of some land the local power structure wanted to develop. The result was Bannon's death and McGee vowed to avenge it. This is what McGee told his girlfriend the day he discovered the murder:

> Maybe he [Bannon] didn't listen very good, or catch on soon enough. I listen very good. I catch on. And when I add up this tab and name the price, I'm going to look at some nice gray skin, honey. Gray and pale, oily and guilty as hell, and some eyes shifting around looking for some way out of it. But every damned door will be nailed shut (p. 39).

Finally, McGee demonstrates that he isn't just another tough guy through his intense loyalty to his friends. In *Dress Her in Indigo,* McGee takes a complex and ultimately dangerous case only because his economist friend, Meyer, clearly wants him to. McGee doesn't want to, but lets his friendship with Meyer overcome his reservations: "But I could see that it had racked my friend Meyer, and that if I continued to drag my feet, he was going to say please, and then I would be unable to help myself, so I agreed before he had a chance to say the magic word friends should not have to use on one another" (page 13).

So, as you can see, McGee is far more than a tough beach bum. Tough? Sure. A beach bum? Of course. But a clever, emotional, and loyal human being? Absolutely!

You can see that the same topic—Travis McGee—can become a Stage I paragraph, a Stage II paragraph, or a five-paragraph essay. It all depends on how much you want—or need—to develop your idea. Notice that the type of introduction this essay uses is the *interesting statement*. And the type of conclusion is the *reference to the motivator*. (By the way, you can search the Web for Travis McGee if you want to find out more about him.)

EXERCISES

A. Chapter 13 presents three introductions to a paper about computers. Using the *reference to the motivator* as a clincher, write a conclusion to each one.

B. Again, for the sample introductions to a paper about computers in Chapter 13, choose one introduction and write a conclusion that has an *interesting statement* as your clincher.

C. At the ends of Chapters 5 and 8 are exercises that ask you to write about a favorite literary character. Now use the same character and convert your paragraph into a full-fledged five-paragraph essay.

D. For Exercise B in Chapter 13 you wrote an introduction to the three paragraphs you had written for Exercises G, H, I, or J in Chapter 12. Now finish your five-paragraph essay by writing the conclusion. Use either type of clincher.

E. Choose a nonfiction book you've read and write a five-paragraph essay about it. You've seen examples of Stage I and Stage II paragraphs that come from factual material about Mount Everest (from Jon Krakauer's *Into Thin Air*). Find similarly interesting material from your chosen nonfiction book. For this exercise, use third-person point of view throughout (that is, don't use pronouns such as *I, me, my, we, you,* and *your*.

F. Choose a topic currently in the news—but different from the topics you used at the end of Chapters 5 and 8. Devise a thesis statement giving your opinion about it. Use information from newspapers, magazines, or editorials to write a convincing five-paragraph essay urging your point of view. This is a good chance to bring in statistics and statements by authorities (not just examples). Be sure to follow the advice for support and documentation in Chapter 9.

If your instructor agrees, make this a team project (just as the exercise suggested at the end of Chapter 8). You and your partner will each write a response (on different topics). You'll critique each other's draft (in writing). Accept or reject whatever advice you receive, as you deem appropriate, but hand in four items:

1. your paper
2. your partner's critique of your writing
3. a brief statement explaining why you accepted or rejected each piece of advice from your partner
4. your written critique of your partner's five-paragraph essay—including a copy of the draft you evaluated (the quality of your writing and critiquing is important)

Use E-mail, if you wish, to critique each other's writing, but hand in printed copies. Your grade will be based on this entire project, not just on your own five-paragraph essay.

CHECKLIST FOR THE FIVE-PARAGRAPH ESSAY

Introduction

_____ Does your introduction begin with a motivator?

_____ Does your introduction have a thesis statement with blueprint?

_____ Does your thesis statement have a limited subject?

_____ Does your thesis statement have a precise opinion?

_____ Are the items in your blueprint in the same order as your central paragraphs?

_____ Do the items in your blueprint all answer the same question: "Why?" or "How?" or "When?"

Central paragraphs

_____ Does each central paragraph begin with a topic sentence?

_____ Does each topic sentence have a transition from the previous paragraph?

_____ Does each topic sentence have a reminder of the thesis?

_____ Does each topic sentence state the main idea of the paragraph?

_____ Is your support specific enough to be convincing?

_____ Do all your items of support clearly support the topic sentence (unity)?

_____ Do you explain your support fully to make the relation to the topic sentence clear (coherence)?

_____ Does each item of support include a reminder of the opinion in the topic sentence (coherence)?

_____ Do you have transitions at critical locations (coherence)?

Conclusion

_____ Does your conclusion have a reworded thesis statement?

_____ Does your conclusion end with a clincher?

Other

_____ Is your essay convincing?

_____ Is your essay interesting?

_____ Have you checked the spelling of words you're unsure of?

_____ Is your paper neatly done so it's easy to read?

SECTION II

Beyond the Model Essay

PART 4

More Patterns of Development

In Part 3 you began your transition to the research paper by learning how to write longer papers and how to use a simple method of documentation. You'll continue that transition here, learning two new skills:

- First, you'll find out about four different ways to develop a paper: comparison and contrast, cause and effect, classification, and process.
- Second, you'll learn some easy ways to vary from the five-paragraph essay. Our sample essays in this part clearly grow out of the five-paragraph essay model, but they all have differences from it.

Throughout this part, you'll apply the principles of the five-paragraph essay—but, as you'll see, those principles can easily apply to papers longer than five paragraphs. You'll continue to use the following:

- an introduction that describes the structure of your paper
- paragraphs that begin with topic sentences
- conclusions that wrap things up

CHAPTER 15

Comparison and Contrast

Comparison and contrast aren't new to you; they are extremely common ways of thinking. Whenever you examine how things are similar, you *compare* them. And when you look at their differences, you *contrast* them.

Sometimes you use comparison and contrast to describe something new: by telling your readers how a thing is similar to or different from something they know, you can help them understand the new thing. For instance, to explain a rotary automobile engine, you'd probably compare and contrast it to the conventional automobile engine. However, besides explaining something new, comparison and contrast also appear frequently in decision making: because A and B share some characteristics but differ in others, one is better and the other worse. You compare and contrast brands when you shop for groceries, stereos, automobiles, and so forth. When you chose the college you're attending, you probably compared and contrasted available schools, and most likely you'll use comparison and contrast again when you choose your major. The list of examples could be endless. The comparison-and-contrast theme, then, is really quite practical.

THESIS

Comparison and contrast lead logically to a thesis because you usually won't bother to compare and contrast unless you have some purpose in mind. You could, of course, stop once you note that A is like B or C is different from D. But your readers probably will want to know what the similarity or difference amounts to. You could write this for a thesis:

> The rotary automobile engine is different from the conventional automobile engine.

However, once you've noted the difference, readers will see that you've merely stated the obvious. Much more useful would be one of the following:

> Although the mechanical structure of the rotary automobile engine is obviously different from that of the conventional automobile engine, the rotary engine offers little worthwhile improvement.

or

> Although they both depend on internal combustion. the rotary automobile engine is a significant improvement over the conventional automobile engine.

Thus, although comparison or contrast for its own sake is generally pointless, both are useful to develop support for a thesis.

APPROACHES TO COMPARISON AND CONTRAST

As you may have noticed in the preceding sample thesis statements, two general approaches apply to the comparison-and-contrast paper. First, you can briefly note the difference between items but *concentrate on their similarity* (comparison).

> Although the mechanical structure of the rotary automobile engine is obviously different from that of the conventional automobile engine, the rotary engine offers little worthwhile improvement.

Here the writer acknowledges that the engine types are different. Does the difference mean that the newer one—the rotary engine—is better? The writer says it isn't; the engines are truly comparable. We can expect the theme to concentrate on the similarities of the engines.

For the second approach you can briefly note the similarity between items but *concentrate on their differences* (contrast).

> Although they both depend on internal combustion, the rotary automobile engine is a significant improvement over the conventional automobile engine.

Now the writer acknowledges one similarity—that the two engines have the same type of combustion—but he is concerned with showing that the rotary engine is better than the conventional engine.

Notice that with either similarity or difference you acknowledge the opposite. Why? You need to establish a reason for bringing the two items together. Noting that the items seem different gives you a reason for comparing them, and noting that the items appear to be similar establishes a reason for contrasting them. In both cases, the opposite can provide the motivator section of your theme's introduction.

At the same time, you must decide where in the essay you're going to discuss the similarities and differences. The thesis establishes your primary purpose, which you'll concentrate on; you'll obviously discuss that side in the central sections.

Yet, how will you deal with the opposite? You have two choices. If the opposite is well known, let the introduction handle it. But if the opposite is not generally understood, you may need to develop it in the body of the theme. In that case cover it first in your central sections. Structuring your presentation this way leaves the primary idea in the position of emphasis, the end of the theme.

Organizing Your Central Paragraphs

When you've decided whether to concentrate on comparison or contrast, you still must decide *how* to do it. Suppose you want to contrast two brands of automobile to decide which to buy; you'll consider such subtopics as price, miles per gallon, and maintenance record. You must decide whether to devote the central paragraphs:

- to whole items (a paragraph for each of the cars)
- or to their various elements (separate paragraphs for price, miles per gallon, and maintenance record).

The diagram shows the two most likely organizational types (we've used two items with three elements per item, but other combinations are certainly possible):

Type I	Type II
Introduction	Introduction
Item A	Element 1
Element 1	Item A
Element 2	Item B
Element 3	Element 2
Item B	Item A
Element 1	Item B
Element 2	Element 3
Element 3	Item A
Conclusion	Item B
	Conclusion

Which pattern is preferable? Well, notice that the Type I organization gives a sense of each item as a whole; however, the readers may have difficulty relating the elements. For example, suppose you compare a Ford and a Chrysler on the basis of seven elements. By the time the readers get to element five of the second car, the Chrysler, they've forgotten what they read about element five of the Ford. As a result, Type I organization is better for short papers dealing with only a few items and elements.

On the other hand, Type II organization destroys the sense of the whole item as it builds the relationships of the elements. Still, Type II development can handle more items and more elements, so it's more useful than Type I for a longer comparison or contrast paper.

Order of Your Subtopics

Whether you choose the Type I or Type II organization for the central sections of your theme, make sure that you always cover the same subtopics in the same order. As with parallelism within a sentence (see Chapter 37), this symmetry will clearly show the relationships that are important for your ideas.

So which type is better? There's no absolute answer, but you'll see more papers using Type II organization, probably because people are more concerned with element-by-element similarities and differences.

Type I

To demonstrate the difference, we've included a Type I essay that compares kinds of school classes. Note how the writer, one of our students, deals first with one kind of class and its elements (teacher, students, results), then another. The essay is short enough that we as readers don't get lost in all the differences.

LEARNING OR NOT: ACTIVE AND PASSIVE CLASSES

Everyone who has gone to school knows that some classes are better, more interesting, livelier than others. We have all sat through classes where we learned little except the facts and to be quiet. We also have been part of classes where we actively learned by being challenged by teachers and the subject to learn for ourselves.

Although classes often seem outwardly alike in having a teacher, in having some students, and in producing some results, the differences between passive and active classes are enormous.

Passive Classes

The passive kind of class usually has a teacher who lectures, puts outlines and terms on the chalkboard, and dispenses information to the students. Like my sophomore biology teacher, Mrs. Noguida, who rarely looked up from the orange notebook in which she had carefully typed all her lectures, teachers in a passive classroom simply dictate information and answers. They tell the students how to think and what to think. They pour facts into the students like water into a sieve. The students are forced, usually by the teacher's authority, to sit, listen, take notes, and regurgitate only what the teacher has said.

The only kinds of questions are about form: "What is the work in subpoint 3.a.(1)?" or "How do you spell *minuscule?*" The results in such a class are measured by multiple-choice or true-false questions, or questions that require memorized answers: "What is Newton's First Law?" "What are the three causes of the American Civil War?" The results in such classes are also measured by how quickly the students forget the facts they had poured into them.

Active Classes

The other kind of class, the active kind, usually has a teacher who stimulates the students to learn for themselves by asking students questions, by posing problems, and most of all by being a student, too. Such a teacher might plan the outline of a course, but doesn't force the class in only one direction. Instead, like Ms. Cerrillo, my junior history teacher, a teacher in an active class uses the discussion to lead to learning. Instead of lecturing on the causes of the Civil War, Ms. Cerrillo gave us a list of books and articles and said, "Find out what caused the Civil War." We had to search for ourselves, find some answers, then discuss what we found in class. From the discussions, we all learned more than just the facts; we also learned how complex the causes were.

Students in active classes like that become more involved in their learning; they ask questions about why and how. The results in the active class are usually measured by essay answers, individual projects, and a change in attitude on the students' part. Learning becomes fun; although students may forget the facts just as quickly, their attitudes toward learning and their excitement in developing answers for themselves don't end with the last class.

We all remember having to learn that "4 × 9 = 36" and having to memorize dates such as 1914–1918, 1776, and 1492. And those kinds of classes are important for laying some groundwork, but not much true learning takes place there. There is a difference between *knowing* a fact and *understanding* it. Despite their outward similarities, the passive kind of class is clearly inferior to the active one for helping students understand the world around them.

Type II

Here's a sample theme that compares two characters in literature. As you'll see, a theme that compares two fictional characters is fairly easy to organize. Notice how well the Type II organization works for comparing a large number of subtopic elements, even though there are only two items.

HOLMES AND DUPIN

Although Sir Arthur Conan Doyle created Sherlock Holmes in 1886, Holmes remains one of the most popular of detective characters. Moreover, Holmes' personality influenced the characterizations of other fictional detectives, both in Doyle's time and later. For example, Agatha Christie's Hercule Poirot is similar to Holmes.

Yet many readers of the Holmes stories don't realize that Holmes isn't entirely original. Holmes is much like Chevalier C. Auguste Dupin, a character Edgar Allan Poe introduced in 1841. Of course, Holmes and Dupin have their differences; Holmes himself calls Dupin "a very inferior fellow" (Doyle, *A Study in Scarlet and The Sign of Four*, p. 25).

Nevertheless, pushing aside Holmes' criticism of Dupin, we can find numerous similarities between the two characters. Both in the conditions of their work and in personality, Holmes is nearly a copy of Dupin.

Conditions of Their Work

The conditions under which Dupin and Holmes work are alike. Both Dupin and Holmes are "consulting detectives," to use Holmes' name for the profession (Doyle, p. 23). This may not seem important, but we should notice that most other detective characters take cases on their own. Yet Dupin works on cases for Monsieur G—, Prefect of the Parisian police, and Holmes (at least when he first appears) works on cases that have stumped Scotland Yard detectives.

In addition, both characters dislike the policemen they work for, and for the same reason. In "The Purloined Letter," Dupin says that the police are "persevering, ingenious, cunning, and thoroughly versed in the knowledge which their duties seem chiefly to demand," but that they fail because they cannot adapt their methods "to the case and to the man" (Poe, *Great Tales and Poems of Edgar Allan Poe*, pp. 208–09). Similarly, Holmes says the Scotland Yard detectives are "both quick and energetic, but conventional—shockingly so" (Doyle, p. 28).

Still, Dupin and Holmes somehow control their scorn while they solve cases for the police. The "consulting detectives" have the satisfaction of solving puzzles, but they let the police steal the glory.

Their Personalities

Holmes' personality also matches Dupin's. Both characters are loners; they accept the company of the narrators of their stories, but of no one else. Poe writes in "The Murders in the Rue Morgue" that Dupin is "enamored of the night for her own sake"; in fact, Dupin and the narrator close the shutters of their house during the day and usually go out only at night (Poe, pp. 106–07). This love of darkness emphasizes Dupin's physical withdrawal from society. In Holmes' case, the withdrawal and gloominess lead to cocaine addiction; when Holmes isn't on a case, he withdraws from ordinary life as well as from society.

Of course, the detectives become active in society to solve cases, but each withdraws again when his case is over. At the opening of the second Dupin story, the narrator says that after his first case, Dupin "relapsed into his old habits of moody revery" (Poe, p. 144). And Holmes, at the end of *The Sign of Four,* calls for his cocaine so he, too, can withdraw.

Even when Dupin and Holmes actually enter society to solve puzzles, they remain mentally separate from other characters. On a case, both Dupin and Holmes show energy unknown to most people. This energy involves them in society, but it doesn't mean that they actually join society. Instead, each stays separate by remaining unemotional; unlike ordinary men, they appear to be minds without feelings. In "The Murders in the Rue Morgue" the narrator describes the working Dupin as "frigid and abstract," with eyes "vacant in expression" (Poe, p. 107).

Doyle is more obvious about Holmes. In *The Sign of Four* Holmes says that "detection is, or ought to be, an exact science and should be treated in the same cold and unemotional manner" (Doyle, p. 137). Like Dupin, then, Holmes prefers to have a mind free of emotions.

Holmes as Copy

Thus, the number of similarities between the two characters shows that the 1886 Holmes is a copy of the 1841 Dupin. They take their cases for the same reason and handle them with the same dislike for their police associates. Neither character can stand the world of normal men, choosing instead to withdraw into a secret shell. And even when they work with ordinary men, they remain aloof, emotionless. These similarities are too numerous to be accidental. Clearly Doyle owes a large debt to Poe.

VARYING FROM THE MODEL ESSAY

This chapter includes two sample essays, the one on active and passive classes and the one you just read on Holmes and Dupin. Both follow the general form of the five-paragraph essay rather closely. These are the main differences:

- They use *sections* instead of *paragraphs* (like most of the other sample essays you've seen in this part). Both samples have two central sections.
- They use headings to help readers see the organization. This is especially useful in longer papers—beyond the five-paragraph essay.

Their similarities to the five-paragraph essay are these:

- They have a thesis statement and blueprint in the introduction.
- They begin each section with a topic sentence.
- They use detailed support throughout the sections.
- They conclude with a reminder of the thesis statement.

So although they show some variation from the five-paragraph essay, they show a lot of similarity, too.

EXERCISES

A. For each of the two topics below, first limit the topic and then write two thesis statements, one for each approach to a comparison-and-contrast paper. Here's an example to get you started:

Topic   automobiles

Limited topic   the bodies of sports cars

Acknowledge the difference and concentrate on the similarity.

Although there are many different designs for the bodies of sports cars, most of them have a great deal in common.

Acknowledge the similarity and concentrate on the difference.

Although the bodies of sports cars have a great deal in common, there are some important differences.

1. **Topic**   fiction

   Limited topic_____

   Acknowledge the difference and concentrate on the similarity.

   _____

   _____

   Acknowledge the similarity and concentrate on the difference.

   _____

   _____

2. **Topic**   college living arrangements

   Limited topic_____

   Acknowledge the difference and concentrate on the similarity.

   _____

   _____

   Acknowledge the similarity and concentrate on the difference.

   _____

   _____

B. Choose one of the thesis statements you developed for Exercise A and outline the central sections for a theme to support the thesis. Make your outline conform to either the Type I or the Type II organization: for each central section you will need to show a topic item with subtopic elements (Type I) or a topic element with subtopic items (Type II).

C. Here are some possible topics for comparison-and-contrast papers:

famous trials	shopping centers
recent inventions	sports
ethnic groups	jewelry
trains	a current event

First, limit the topic; then write a thesis that concentrates on comparison or contrast. Organize your support with the Type I or Type II pattern, and write the essay. If you wish to vary from the model, do so. If you use outside sources for support, be sure to document them (you can use the preliminary system we showed you in Chapter 9, as the second sample theme in the chapter does).

D. Think about the other courses you're taking. Choose a topic and write a comparison-and-contrast paper. And if you use outside sources for support, be sure to document them (you can use the preliminary system, as the second sample theme in the chapter does).

Chapter 16

Cause and Effect

Remember the "Why?" subtopic sentences you studied in Chapter 8? Maybe you didn't realize it at the time, but you were studying one kind of cause-and-effect paper. We'll examine cause-effect papers more closely in this chapter.

A *cause* is a reason something happens; an *effect*, then, is whatever happens. As a simple example, we might say, "Because the television set is unplugged, it doesn't work." The *cause* is that the set is unplugged; the *effect* is that the set doesn't work.

Kinds of Cause-Effect Papers

You can write three kinds of cause-effect papers:

- You can state that the effect is true and examine the *cause* in detail.
- You can state that the cause is true and examine the *effect* in detail.
- Or you can try to show that the *entire cause-effect statement* is true.

EXAMINING THE CAUSES

In some cases the cause is the controversial part of a cause-effect statement, so the paper naturally examines that part in detail. Let's say you've decided to write about this thesis: "The aggravated assault rate here at Gila Monster Maximum Security Prison has decreased dramatically because of the warden's innovations."

The effect—that the aggravated assault rate has dropped—shouldn't be controversial, so take care of that part quickly with a statistic or two in your introduction: "In the last year, the aggravated assault rate at Gila Monster Maximum Security Prison has plummeted from nineteen per month to only four per month." After dispensing with the effect, spend the rest of your paper telling us about the warden's policies and why they work. How? Write a section about each of the warden's important policies. Your outline might look something like this:

Thesis	Because of the warden's innovations, the aggravated assault rate at Gila Monster Maximum Security Prison has decreased dramatically.
Topic sentence	The warden's new leathercraft shop allows inmates a constructive way to spend their time.
Topic sentence	The warden has started an intramural sports program that permits the prisoners a physical outlet for their pent-up emotions.
Topic sentence	The new co-ed jail cells allow the inmates the chance to discuss relevant social issues with members of the opposite sex.

Did you notice that the thesis begins with *because?* That word clearly established that the essay will examine cause and effect. Another way of saying it is this: if you want to write a cause-and-effect paper, you must be able to have the word *because* somewhere in the thesis statement.

Of course, you don't need to have exactly three central sections. Two especially well-developed sections or four or five shorter ones could work also. Let's look at an example that uses two central sections:

COMPUTER PRESENTATIONS: ANOTHER REVOLUTION!

Computers have affected almost every facet of our lives: houses, cars, and certainly the workplace have changed dramatically because of them. Years ago, people could have predicted many of these changes, but few would have predicted that the computer could actually revolutionize giving speeches. It has! Using a computer, speakers can now project whatever is on their computer monitor onto a large screen in front of the audience—thus letting the audience see miracles at work! And, with today's technology, the room can be brightly lit. Because computer presentations are easy to design and easier for audiences to understand, they are definitely part of the computer revolution.

One reason computer presentations are part of the revolution is that they're easy to design. Many years ago, presenters who wanted to use visual aids had to depend on a graphics shop for the design and, often, service bureaus for the final product. Thirty-five-millimeter slides, for example, were expensive and arduous to produce. As a result, few speakers actually used them and then only for especially important presentations. A few years later, overhead transparencies became more popular. They were cheap and readily available, but they often looked homemade (unless graphics shops and service bureaus were involved). Today, though, typical workers can use simple programs such as PowerPoint to produce colorful slides, often with interesting graphics, right at their desks! They transfer their file via an intranet or disk to the conference room's computer, and they're ready to go. There's no more dependence on the graphics shop and no more dependence on service bureaus!

Another reason computer presentations are part of the revolution is that audiences often understand the presentations better. Partly that's because computer presentations are often more attractive than old-fashioned presentations—so audiences actually pay attention to what's going on. Also, computer presentations allow speakers to build a slide one element at a time. For example, instead of showing all four bullets on a slide at once, speakers can show them one at a time. That way, audiences aren't looking at the third bullet while the speaker is still talking about the first one. As a result, audiences are typically looking at the same thing on a slide that the speaker is talking about, with no built-in distractions. Audiences can therefore pay attention to the right thing at the right time—thus understanding the presentation better.

When you think of a speaker today, don't automatically picture someone behind the lectern . . . or (even worse) a disembodied voice from the darkened room delivering a 35-millimeter slide show to a dozing audience. Instead, picture a colorful screen in the front of the room, filled with images, everything unfolding just as the audience needs to see it.

EXAMINING THE EFFECTS

Sometimes the cause is fairly straightforward, but the effect needs elaboration. What if your thesis is that "Because Napoleon's wars killed many young men who otherwise could have worked a lifetime, Europe's standard of living dropped markedly"? Not many people would doubt that the wars killed many young men who could have done a lot of work, but people still might doubt that the standard of living actually did drop. You need to state the cause as a fact and then elaborate upon the effect.

You then could begin the theme by mentioning in the introduction (perhaps using the "striking statement" motivator) how many young men were slaughtered. You could develop the theme by discussing the effect ("Europe's standard of living dropped markedly") in three or four European countries. Here's a possible outline

Thesis	Because Napoleon's wars killed many young men who otherwise could have worked a lifetime, Europe's standard of living dropped markedly.
Topic sentence	After Napoleon's wars, Russia had a lower standard of living.
Topic sentence	Austria also had a lower standard of living.
Topic sentence	Even Napoleon's home, France, had a lower standard of living.

Sometimes you have to deal with ideas that require a little more complexity. The cause may be a general assertion, but the effects are real and often complicated. The following sample paper by one of our students, though it deals with technical matters and borrowed ideas, contains a thesis with blueprint and three central ideas.

THE SEARCH FOR EXTRATERRESTRIAL LIFE

When the first hominid stood upright, we speculate, that it must have looked up to the heavens in wonder, for we find ourselves doing so today. As we look at the nighttime sky with all its stars and spaces, we can't help wondering about life out there.

Perhaps the curiosity, the need to know, which motivated our ancestors to explore this planet, to go into the most forbidding jungles, or to sail the most hazardous seas, also motivates us. We think that what happened here on Earth might have happened elsewhere in the cosmos, and we follow our interest to press farther into the universe, searching for life.

Because of our enduring quest to know the unknown, our search for extraterrestrial life, a search that already has taken people to the moon, will grow in the years ahead. Whether in the form of space probes, radio and radar signals in outer space, or interstellar travel, the human race will continue to look up to the heavens looking for life beyond this Earth.

Space Probes

"The search for extraterrestrial life," according to Isaac Asimov, "took its first flying leap in 1969 when man walked on the moon" (*Extraterrestrial Civilization,* p. 183). This great step proved that we were not destined to spend the rest of our existence earthbound.

Subsequent successful moon landings demonstrated our race's ability to traverse space to the moon and return safely. More distant planets also were out there to be explored. Viking I and II, for example, were sent to Mars in 1975 to test the planet for the possibility for life. Landing in 1976, they found Martian soil not unlike Earth's "but richer in iron and less rich in aluminum" (Asimov, p. 59). The bad news was the absence of carbon, which is essential for life as we know it. Consequently, the search for life beyond Earth turned to other planets and other means—long-distance radio and interstellar travel.

Radio and Radar Signals

Attempts at interstellar communications have been going on for many years, but they take a long time. Because radio waves travel at the speed of light, it would take more than one hundred years for a question to be asked and answered from a near star only fifty light-years away. And when we send out radio signals, we have no way of knowing if anyone is even listening.

But despite the long delays, astronomers have been sending radio signals for almost twenty years using "single or arrayed radio techniques, sensitive radio detectors, advanced computers for processing received information, and the imagination and skill of dedicated scientists" (Carl Sagan, "The Quest for Extraterrestrial Life," *Smithsonian,* May 1978, p. 39). They listen for meaningful sounds from outer space because scientists theorize that any civilization akin to ours would learn to use radio signals most readily. The largest listening dish in the world—in the Russian Caucasus—is devoted to this search for intelligent life beyond our planet (Sagan, p. 43).

Interstellar Travel

An even more dramatic attempt to find life in space will come with interstellar travel. However, the barriers to interstellar exploration are both technically and humanly enormous. For example, according to NASA, an interstellar spacecraft would need a totally efficient fuel, one that hasn't been developed yet. It may even have to wait for the discovery of antimatter. Almost certainly such a fuel would require metal alloys to withstand heat beyond anything we now know (NASA, *Interstellar Communications,* 1963, pp. 144–50). Both these problems likely will be overcome; human intelligence and the quest for knowing probably will meet those challenges as we have in the past.

The real barrier to interstellar travel, however, is that same human being. We do not know if humans can endure the extreme deprivations of space travel. Not only would travelers be confined to cramped quarters with limited exercise and have little variety to see, but also the crew might well suffer mentally from the confinement.

Furthermore, if Einstein's theory of relativity is correct, the phenomenon of "time delation" will mean that the Earth from which travelers leave will be far different from the one to which they return. "Time delation" means that the rate at which time seems to progress slows with increased speed; this phenomenon would mean that a traveler hurtling through space would live what seemed to him or her a normal lifetime, while five thousand years elapsed on Earth (Asimov, pp. 231–32). Thus, travelers searching for life on other stars would return to an Earth that no longer had their families or friends, perhaps not even the nation that sent out the explorers.

Continuing the Search

Despite the barriers (and the limited success), the search for extraterrestrial life will continue. The chances seem too great that somewhere in the estimated 280 billion planetary systems in our galaxy (Asimov, p. 109) intelligent creatures also have developed.

With the technological advances we already have made united with the never-ending quest to explore the unknown, our search for extraterrestrial life in the great expanse of space will go on. It must, just as it was inevitable that the first hominids would look up to the heavens so long ago.

EXAMINING THE ENTIRE CAUSE-EFFECT STATEMENT

Sometimes cause-effect papers examine the entire statement instead of only half of it. Perhaps both cause and effect are controversial, or perhaps neither is controversial but the fact that they have a cause-effect relationship is.

Let's look first at a cause-effect statement in which both parts are controversial and need elaboration. What if we say that "Because Colorado land developers have no long-term stake in the developments they sell, customers often end up with property they cannot inhabit"? We'll have to persuade the readers of two ideas: that the developers have no long-term interests in their developments and that the new landowners can't live on their property. Both parts need support.

One simple way to organize the support is to write a section on the cause and a section on the effect. We could show in the first central section that Colorado developers lack any long-term interests in the land; in the next section, then, we could show that the new owners often can't use their property.

However, we probably could write a better paper by examining both parts of the cause-effect statement in the same section. How? We could use examples. We'll make each central section a narrative example of the entire cause-effect statement.

One section might be about Pyrite Acres, a development bulldozed out of the desert at the base of the Sangre de Cristo mountains. The developer, after selling the last site, disappeared into Arizona with all the money. He had neglected to tell the new owners that the underground water supply was so low it could last for only another year or two. If our thesis is valid, we should be able to present a section on each of two or three similar situations with other developers. Extended examples can be effective any time both the cause and effect need support.

Extended examples can help in another case—one in which both the cause and the effect are fairly straightforward, but their relationship is not. Consider this statement: "Because many mountain climbers are elated after a difficult climb, they are in danger from carelessness after the difficulty is past." We can accept easily that climbers are elated after a difficult ascent; we also can accept that climbers who are careless afterward are in danger. We probably would like to see support for the idea that the elation from a difficult climb produces that carelessness. The following sample theme uses extended examples to provide such support.

THE MATTERHORN EFFECT

Only a little more than a century ago, some people in Europe thought that the Matterhorn—that awesome, beautiful pinnacle—was the highest mountain in the world. Many climbers from many nations had raced to climb it, but none had succeeded. Then, in 1865, Englishman Edward Whymper and six others reached the summit, but only Whymper and two others lived to tell about it. The rest, careless from elation and fatigue, died when one climber slipped on a relatively easy part of the descent and carried three others over a four-thousand-foot cliff.

That carelessness, a mental letdown that climbers tend to experience after succeeding at something hard, is called the "Matterhorn effect." I've seen it myself.

The Matterhorn Effect—and Me

I remember how pleased I was when I first climbed Borderline, a hard route up a 150-foot spire in the Garden of the Gods, Colorado. Only six others had ever climbed it. My forearms were so cramped from exertion that I could barely pull the rope up as my climbing partner, Leonard Coyne, seconded the route.

After reaching the top, Leonard mentioned that he knew the descent route was fairly hard, though the previous climbers had disdained using a rope for it. Filled with overconfidence, I simply tossed the rope to the ground below. *We* had just done the tough ascent, so surely *we* did not need a rope either. Then I started down the nearly vertical face.

Suddenly Leonard yelled, "Your handhold is loose! Grab my leg!" There I was—unroped, 150 feet above the ground, and apprehensively holding a couple of loose flakes of rock—when my *foothold* broke. I still don't know what kept me on the rock, but apparently as my foothold gave way, my foot slipped into a barely visible toehold. I didn't fall, but if I hadn't been overconfident from the hard ascent, I would never have ventured into that dangerous position without a rope.

The Matterhorn Effect—and Leonard

I've seen the Matterhorn effect almost claim Leonard, too. Last summer, he, Gary Campbell, and I had just finished climbing the northwest face of Half Dome, a magnificent two-thousand-foot vertical cliff in Yosemite, California. We'd been climbing, eating, and sleeping on the face for three days, and finally we were on top—well, almost. Actually we were about thirty feet from the top, but that part was really easy. We untied, coiled the ropes, and stowed our climbing hardware. Leonard slung on one of the packs—a rather unwieldy thing with a sleeping bag tied precariously to the outside—and started up the last thirty feet. As he began to haul himself onto a five-foot shelf, the pack shifted on his back, almost jerking him off the rock.

Two thousand feet above the ground, he balanced—like a turtle about to flip on its back—for what seemed like a minute before he rolled slowly forward onto the shelf. Three days of numbing fatigue and the elation of doing such a hard climb had caused us all to have a mental letdown; we had put away the ropes too soon. That letdown almost cost Leonard his life.

The point is clear to me: the Matterhorn effect is real for anybody who has just done something hard, but especially for climbers. I've seen it in myself too many times and too many times in others. But—so far, at least—I've been fortunate not to learn about it in the way Edward Whymper and his companions did.

Each extended example in this sample theme presents the entire cause-effect relationship. The cause (the author's elation and fatigue on Borderline and Leonard's on Half Dome) seems to lead quite naturally to the effect (the near accidents).

PITFALLS OF THE CAUSE-EFFECT THEME

In earlier chapters, you learned not to choose a subject that is too general for your paper. That advice is also true for cause-effect papers. For example, a theme would not allow you the space or time to convince disbelievers of this thesis: "Because the United States wanted to ensure the freedom of South Vietnam, it went to war against North Vietnam." You'd need a book, or a substantial chapter in one, to support that statement.

You also must be careful that your cause-effect statement presents the important cause and not just a secondary one. We'd be foolish to blame a field-goal kicker for losing an important game just because he missed a thirty-two-yard attempt during the last five seconds. The team may have lost in part because of that missed attempt, but what about the quarterback who threw an interception during the first quarter, the defensive lineman who missed a key tackle, or the coach who canceled practice last Wednesday? Be sure, in other words, that your cause is the main cause.

VARYING FROM THE MODEL ESSAY

As you saw in the preceding chapters, one of our purposes in Part 4 is to help you learn how to vary from the model essay. How does our sample about the Matterhorn effect differ from the model five-paragraph essay you learned in Part 3? Before we discuss the differences, look back at that sample and underline the thesis, blueprint, and topic sentences. Then read on.

You probably underlined this sentence as the thesis: "That carelessness, a mental letdown that climbers tend to experience after succeeding at something hard, is called the 'Matterhorn effect.' " It doesn't exactly state the main idea of the paper (that the Matterhorn effect is real), but certainly it implies it. Readers expect the rest of the paper to convince them that the Matterhorn effect exists.

Did you find a blueprint? The last sentence of the introduction—"I've seen it myself"—is not really a blueprint of the topic ideas for each section, but it certainly *implies* the development. We know we are about to read some examples.

The topic sentence for the first central section also is implied, not by any one sentence but by the heading for the entire section. A stated topic sentence isn't nearly as important as unified support and coherence. You can eliminate a topic sentence as long as the section is sufficiently unified that you *could* write a topic sentence—and as long as the readers have no doubt what they are reading and why.

EXERCISES

A. Use these topics to answer the items below:

    an actor or actress   the state you're living in
    charity   a country or state you've visited
    nursing homes   a job you've held
    traffic jams   your favorite music

1. Write a cause-effect thesis with a cause that is controversial but an
    effect that isn't. Write three proposed topic sentences to show how
    you could develop your thesis.

    Thesis _____

    _____

    Topic sentence_____

    _____

    Topic sentence_____

    _____

    Topic sentence_____

    _____

2. Write a cause-effect thesis with an effect that is controversial but a
    cause that isn't. Again, write the topic sentences you'd use.

    Thesis _____

    _____

    Topic sentence_____

    _____

    Topic sentence_____

    _____

    Topic sentence_____

    _____

3. Write a cause-effect thesis that has both a controversial cause and a controversial effect. Write the proposed topic sentences.

Thesis _____

_____

Topic sentence _____

_____

Topic sentence _____

_____

Topic sentence _____

_____

B. Find your own support and write a cause-effect theme using your favorite sport or hobby as a topic.

C. Choose something that had a significant effect on you and write a cause-effect paper. If you use outside sources for support, be sure to document them. You can use the preliminary system you learned in Chapter 9.

D. Choose one of the topics in Exercise A (not necessarily one you outlined) and write the paper. If you use outside sources for support, be sure to document them. You can use the preliminary system you learned in Chapter 9.

E. Think about one of your other courses and write a cause-effect paper based on something you've learned in that course. If you use outside sources for support, be sure to document them. You can use the preliminary system you learned in Chapter 9.

CHAPTER 17
Classification

Often we find ourselves with a long list of items to discuss but with no simple way to discuss them. We know we could handle the items if we put them into three or four groups. This process of grouping a long list into categories is *classification*.

Consider this example. At the end of classes on Friday you look for a way to tackle all the studying you need to do over the weekend. Some of the work is so simple that you can do it right away before you go to a movie. You want to save some of the assignments for Sunday so the lessons will be fresh in your mind on Monday morning. And you have a couple of small research projects that would be good for a library session on Saturday. To cope with the amount of studying you have to do, you classify the assignments under these headings:

> things to study Friday
>
> things to study Saturday
>
> things to study Sunday

Now you've reduced a long list to three groups, but the important idea is that the groups all answer the same question: When is a good time to do this work? In other words, you've classified according to *one* characteristic related to all the items in the list.

If you classify on the basis of a different characteristic related to the items, you'll get a different listing. For example, as usual you don't study as hard over the weekend as you planned to on Friday afternoon; late Sunday night you find yourself with most of the work to do. Perhaps you make a new list, like this:

> put off until next weekend
>
> put off until final exams
>
> put off until forever

Now the groupings are based on how long you can avoid doing the work, and this listing will differ from the one you made on Friday afternoon.

Classifying

Dozens of times each week we organize items by classification. We classify when we sort laundry into piles for machine wash, hand wash, or dry clean; or when we put the machine wash into piles for hot water, cold water, or medium temperature. We think of automobiles in groupings by size (subcompact, compact, intermediate, and so on), by cost (under $15,000, $15,000–$20,000, and so on), or by expected use (individual, family, or commercial).

Because classification is such a common way of thinking, it is also a popular type of essay development. The groupings automatically provide us with the essay's *organization* and help us see what we want to say about the groups, our *thesis*.

ORGANIZATION

Because it breaks a topic into packages, classification results in a simple pattern that matches the model for the multiparagraph essay. Each category forms a central section:

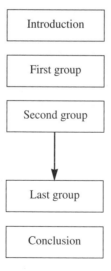

You'll see an essay using a pattern similar to this one later in the chapter.

Yet, easy as the pattern of development is, you need to avoid its three potential pitfalls. You can tumble into any one of them if you're not careful when you classify.

The first problem is to limit the subject you intend to classify. A subject that is too broad could contain hundreds of items. You could put these hundreds into two or three groups, but the groups probably wouldn't be useful because each would still include a long list of items. On the other hand, you could classify hundreds of items into a large number of groups (say, fifteen), but then you'd have to write an essay with fifteen central paragraphs. In either case, you might as well not classify. Instead, limit the subject until it includes a workable number of items. For example, suppose you choose "Ethnic Groups" as your subject. The world has too many ethnic groups for you to work with. You limit to "Major Ethnic Groups in the United States," but the number of items still seems endless. Limiting the subject to "Major Ethnic Groups in Iowa City" should solve the problem.

The second and most common problem is related to unity. Remember that classification means grouping on the basis of *one* characteristic related to each item. If more than one kind of grouping shows up in your essay, you've failed to maintain unity; and readers who are troubled by the groupings themselves probably will not be convinced by your argument. Consider this list of categories for types of car:

American

Italian

Japanese

Luxury

German

"Luxury" is not a country of origin. The grouping is unacceptable.

Finally, you need to realize that many classifications that work well for grouping items actually have minor flaws. For instance, we often put motorized passenger vehicles that run on land into three convenient groups: cars, trucks, and buses. Yet this classification does not cover the special vehicle that looks like a large station wagon (a car) but is built on a truck chassis (a truck) and can carry nine adults (a small bus). There's no simple rule for dealing with the problem of exceptions; however, there is a reasonable procedure to follow when you find an exception to your classes:

- First, judge the importance of the exception. If the exception destroys the point you are trying to make (the thesis of your argument), then rethink your groupings.
- If a single exception brings to mind dozens more, then, again, you must regroup.
- If the exception remains a minor flaw, you may want to simply acknowledge the complication somewhere in your paper.

You also may be able to exclude the exception by the way you word your subject. For example, if you write about "Religions on My Campus," you'll have to deal with all of them, including that of the single student who has made an idol of the oak tree on the campus mall; but if you write about "Major Religions on My Campus," you eliminate the minor exceptions to your categories.

THESIS

Classification leads logically to one of two types of thesis. The classification may itself be the thesis. Or the classification may be only the means of organizing the argument that persuades readers to accept the thesis. The first is easier to write, but the second generally makes a better essay.

If your classification reveals striking groupings, the classification itself may be the thesis. Such a thesis takes the general form of "There are *(number of groups)* for *(topic)*." For example, "There are three types of teacher," or "There are two types of politician." Not very interesting, really. Still, sometimes the groupings themselves reveal your stand on the topic. In such cases the "there are" thesis may work. Consider this example:

Today there are two types of politician: the dishonest and the half-honest.

Implicit in these classes is the thesis that no politician today is completely honest.

Often, however, the "there are" thesis fails to satisfy by itself. Readers yawn and mutter, "So what?" What they are really asking is why the writer bothered to classify items. Consider this thesis:

There are four types of door locks available for home use.

If your readers happen to be interested in locks, the thesis may work. Probably more interesting would be an essay that uses the types of door locks to make a more important point, such as this:

Although there are four types of door locks available for home use, an expert burglar can fool any of them.

Now the thesis is that the locks are not foolproof; the writer will develop the essay with a central section for each type of lock, but she'll be showing in each case that the locks will not stop a determined burglar.

When you develop a subject by classification, you'll have to judge the value of your classification. Will the readers care that you've identified groups? Or do the groups merely help reveal something more important? Here's a sample essay in which the classification serves as an organizational stepping-stone to the thesis idea:

THE WAISTLAND OF TV ADVERTISEMENTS

Like thousands of Americans, my compulsive drive to eat keeps me continually on a diet. When I told a friend that I eat if I'm happy, sad, or just sort of blah, he said I need to occupy my mind.

He suggested that when I'm hungry I should watch television. This solution seemed particularly appropriate, for I enjoy television when I'm happy, when I'm sad, and when my mind is too dull to feel much of anything. My friend was right about the television shows; even the worst of them draws my attention away from food.

But my friend forgot about the advertisements. Whether commercials for food in restaurants or for food to take home, these television advertisements represent cruel and all-too-usual punishment for the dieter.

Ads for Restaurants

Numerous restaurant ads provide seemingly continuous reminders of a world of eating enjoyment, all of it forbidden on my 1,200-calorie diet. There are so many restaurant ads that I can turn from channel to channel during commercial time and usually be assaulted with only one laundry detergent ad, one pet food ad, but four ads for restaurants.

After a week on my diet, I'm jealous of the kitten in the cat chow commercial; imagine what the barrage of restaurant ads does to me. I see commercials for steak (with salad, potato, and toast), pizza (thick or thin crust, with dozens of toppings to choose from), fish or clams, chicken (with fixin's), hamburgers (with or without cheese, decorated with catsup and mustard, sprinkled with chopped onions and lettuce, topped with a pickle, stuffed in a lightly toasted bun), roast beef or ham sandwiches (for a change from the hamburger habit), and tacos or burritos (as well as related Mexican foods that I've never heard of but begin to crave anyway when I see them on TV).

Need I go on? Probably by now even your stomach has started to rumble, and you've had more for supper than my spoonful of cottage cheese on half a small peach (made more appetizing by a scrap of wilting lettuce for decoration).

Ads for Take-Home Food

Less numerous than restaurant ads but more enticing are the commercials for the foods I can buy to take home. When I've been starved for carbohydrates for a few days, the convenience of take-home foods appeals to the remnants of my ability to reason. You see, if my willpower wavers and I go to a restaurant—even a quick-order place—someone who knows I'm dieting may catch me, but it's easy to dart into a grocery store, ice-cream parlor, or doughnut shop and dash home without being seen.

Besides, the TV ads for foods to take home are so inviting. For example, you may remember seeing the advertisement for one of the doughnut shops in town. As the TV camera pans slowly across a counter laden with bakery goodies, I begin to drool. The commercial's soundtrack broadcasts a man calling to his wife to run to the TV to see the panorama of food laid out before his—and my—impressionable eyes.

He says that the sight of the doughnuts will "drive him crazy," and his voice sounds as though he's already slightly deranged because of what he sees. He proclaims the scene "heavenly," but I know it's a dieter's hell.

I've always assumed he demands that his wife give him her car keys so he can rush to the doughnut shop; I say "assumed" because I've never stayed at my TV set long enough to hear the end of the commercial. I'm on my way out the door to beat that crazy fool to the best of the doughnuts.

Just Deserts

You're reading the ravings of a dieter too often distracted by hunger and too long provoked by TV commercials for food. Yes, I confess—stop the torture—the ads are obviously effective. I salivate right on cue for all the food advertisers. But in my few remaining rational moments, I can still judge those advertisements for restaurants and take-home foods: To the dieter they're cruel. They play on the dieter's weakness, the compulsion to eat.

But I'll have my revenge, in my own limited way. My friend has invited me to his apartment tomorrow to watch TV, as he puts it, "to relieve the depression" of my latest diet. I'll sit calmly in his favorite chair; I'll stare innocently at his television. But when the first commercial for food comes on, I'm going to cut the plug off his set. While he's paralyzed by shock, I'll go into his kitchen to make myself a sandwich.

Behind the writer's humorous mask is a pattern of development dependent upon classification. Because he recognizes that there are too many different food ads to deal with individually, the writer has classified them into two groups—foods to eat in restaurants and foods to eat at home.

Are you bothered by the fact that some of the foods he classifies as restaurant foods could be taken home? Probably not, because the inconsistency will not damage his thesis. And besides, for him the classification may well be valid; some types of foods he consistently eats at restaurants (though he could take them home) and some types he buys for his pantry.

What we should recognize is this: classifications are arbitrary, but they do allow us a reasonable means to organize material. All in all, the classification in this essay is reasonable. It allows the writer to package his support material so that he can get to his thesis.

VARYING FROM THE MODEL ESSAY

Did you notice the minor differences in the sample essay for this chapter? For one, the thesis is not a simple statement of *"limited subject* is *precise opinion,"* but we could still tell that the writer would need to show that the food ads are numerous and that they are "cruel." You may have noticed that the first central section is the Stage I type, whereas the second central section, which uses subtopic ideas, is a Stage II type. Finally, no single sentence in the conclusion fully restates the thesis; nevertheless, the first five sentences of the conclusion as a whole do remind us of the thesis. As you can see, the general pattern of the multiparagraph essay remains, even though there are deviations from the model.

EXERCISES

A. Circle the class in each list below that breaks the unity of the classification.

   1. **Topic** insects
       Classes ants
                   scorpions
                   spiderwebs
                   roaches

   2. **Topic** science
       Classes astronomy
                   Newton's laws
                   geology
                   biology

   3. **Topic** ocean dwellers
       Classes shrimp
                   stingrays
                   sharks
                   seaweed

   4. **Topic** medical profession
       Classes ambulance attendant
                   emergency room
                   physician
                   medical technologist

B. Each subject below is too broad to classify easily. Limit the subject and name at least three classes.

Example

Topic	music	
Limited topic	classical music	
Classes	early Renaissance	solo
	late Renaissance OR	small group
	Eighteenth Century	symphonic
	Romantic	
	Early Modern	

1. **Topic**   magazines

   Limited topic _____

   Classes _____

   _____

   _____

   _____

2. **Topic**   clothes

   Limited topic _____

   Classes _____

   _____

   _____

   _____

3. **Topic**   advertising

   Limited topic _____

   Classes _____

   _____

   _____

   _____

4. **Topic**   travel

   Limited topic _____

   Classes _____

   _____

   _____

   _____

C. Choose one of the limited topics from Exercise B and write an essay that you organize by classification. Remember that you can make your writing more interesting if you use classification to develop a thesis other than the classification itself.

D. Use classification to develop an essay about one of the following topics. You'll need to limit the topic before you attempt to classify it, just as you did in Exercise B.

   electronic devices
   future travel
   lessons we learn
   friends (or enemies)
   a famous work of art

   If you use outside sources for support, be sure to document them with the preliminary system you learned in Chapter 9.

CHAPTER 18

Process

There are two kinds of processes. The first is simply how to do something—instructions. A description of such a process could be:

- a recipe that tells us how to cook something
- a computer manual that tells us how to execute a task on a computer
- the Internal Revenue Service instructions that tell us how to prepare our taxes (well, sort of . . .)

And so forth.

Scientists and engineers will tell you of another kind of process description: how some*thing* works. For example:

- How does an automobile engine work?
- Or a telescope?
- Or even photosynthesis?

Describing either kind of process (how to do something or how something works) can be a real challenge. You'll find, though, that the structure we've presented throughout this book works nicely to help you meet this challenge.

DESCRIBING HOW TO DO SOMETHING (INSTRUCTIONS)

Let's look first at instructions—telling people how to do something. Here are some terrible instructions (an ugly but genuine example):

Attributes may be assigned to the elements of a document either directly or indirectly; these two ways of assigning attributes are referred to as "direct-formatting" and "styles." Direct formatting has a direct effect on document layout. Assigning a style tells the word processor to look on a style sheet to acquire direct formatting.

Would you like to try following those instructions?

Here are some suggestions for preparing instructions that could have made those instructions better:

1. *Organize the instructions into a step-by-step procedure.* If you truly understand the instructions you are about to give, this should be easy to do. Steps are much easier for the reader to follow than continuous narrative. We are using steps right now.

2. *Start each step with a verb (as in this sentence).* Instructions tell people what to do, what action to take. Verbs are action words. Starting each step with the specific action gets right to what the reader needs to know. Virtually all good computer manuals (and there are many good ones) begin each step with a verb.

3. *Use a layout that clearly shows the steps.* Headings, bulleted paragraphs, and numbered paragraphs are all easy techniques to let the reader see the steps in the process you're describing.

4. *Test your instructions on somebody else.* Try to choose somebody who is typical of the people you really plan to instruct. It's amazing how easy it is to leave out steps when you're writing. Early computer manuals gained their deservedly terrible reputation because they didn't test the instructions adequately. Now the top-notch computer companies test their manuals extensively before publishing them.

The following sample essay applies the first three of those steps:

GETTING READY TO PAINT A ROOM

Painters will tell you that the hardest parts of painting are getting ready and cleaning up—the painting itself is pretty easy. Painters will also tell you that getting ready properly can make cleaning up lots easier and prevent disasters, too. So if you have to paint something (and nearly everyone has to paint a room at some time or other—at home, in a dorm, in a first apartment), you can make the painting simpler if you follow these steps to get ready.

Protect Furnishings in the Room

Clearly, the best time to paint a room is when it's empty. If you're in that fortunate situation, skip to the next step. But if your room isn't empty, your first step is to protect what's there:

1. *Move the furniture.* Get it away from the walls and into the center of the room, stacking wherever possible to use as little floor space as you can.
2. *Use drop cloths.* Cover all furniture and the floor. The best drop cloths have fabric on the top and plastic on the bottom. Drop cloths that are all plastic don't absorb spilled paint, so they stay messy. On the other hand, drop cloths that are all fabric can leak through to what's underneath.

Remove Electrical Covers

The next step is to remove cover plates for wall switches and outlets. The covers are usually held in place with one or two screws, so remove the screws and place them in a plastic bag.

Use Drafting Tape

Tape over anything you want to stay free of paint—windows, woodwork, door hinges, door knobs, and such. Use a sharp knife to cut the tape precisely rather than just tearing it. Also, check the stickiness of the tape—some is so sticky that it can remove the paint underneath it, the paint you want to save! "Drafting tape," which is only slightly sticky, is best.

Profit from Your Preparations

These few steps can be time consuming, but anyone who has tried skipping them can tell you a cautionary tale with the moral of "haste makes waste." The time you spend preparing is saved many times over during the next two stages of the painting process: putting the paint on the wall and (especially) cleaning up!

Simple and efficient, isn't it? Notice the obvious organization that echoes the clear structure you learned for the five-paragraph essay: the brief introduction tells what's coming; each step begins with the main point (in a heading).

DESCRIBING HOW SOME*THING* WORKS

The second kind of process paper tells how some*thing* works. Describing this kind of process uses basically the same guidelines as for writing instructions:

- Organize the process into steps.
- Use an appealing layout on the page.

Essentially, you divide whatever you're describing into parts—and then describe each one. For example, if you decide to tell, in broad terms, how a computer works, you'd no doubt divide it into at least these parts:

- the central processor
- the memory
- the hard drive
- the keyboard (or other input device, such as a mouse)
- the viewing device (such as the monitor)

Although this kind of description couldn't go into any real detail, it could certainly be valuable, a good overview of the main parts and how they work together. Your paper would probably begin by setting out your subject (describing the computer). Next you'd probably give a blueprint, naming the parts (such as central processor). Then you'd have a section on each of those parts.

VARYING FROM THE MODEL ESSAY

The five-paragraph essay you learned earlier in this book is highly organized—and so are descriptions of processes. The sample in this chapter (painting a room) differed from the model because it didn't start with a blueprint and didn't always use topic sentences—it depended on the headings to convey the topic ideas. Those are all common techniques in process papers.

However, by now in the course, although you've no doubt seen that a clear structure is important, you know that you needn't follow it to the letter. Just be sure you and your reader know where you are in the paper at all times. The models here help you do that. They help you get started and often serve as the actual structure for what you write.

You're now ready to begin the next section of the book: writing research papers!

EXERCISES

A. Let's say you're going to give instructions on how to get ready for class or work in the morning. Without writing the paper, simply list the various steps, in order, that you think someone should follow (or that you actually do follow).

B. Now let's say you're going to describe how something simple, such as a mercury thermometer, operates. Choose something other than a thermometer, go to an encyclopedia (or other source) if necessary, and do a little research. Then outline how that "something" works.

C. Now, write the paper for Exercise A. Be sure to follow the conventions on documentation we discuss in Chapter 9.

D. Write the paper for Exercise B. Be sure to follow the conventions on documentation we discuss in Chapter 9.

E. Everyone knows something other people don't know but might be interested in. Perhaps you're good at golf, computers, or gardening. Choose something you know how to do and write a clear, concise set of instructions that tells your readers how to do it. You might try out these instructions on a friend before you hand in your paper. It's amazing how easily people (including all of us, of course) can go wrong unless the instructions are absolutely unambiguous.

    One caution: Most instructors prefer that you avoid simply writing instructions for a "recipe." That can get pretty boring. Be sure to choose something that doesn't simply paraphrase from a book—something you already know about!

F. You can probably get some good ideas for a description of a process from other courses. For example, in astronomy you've probably learned how the universe may have developed (a *large* process). In geology perhaps you've learned how mountains or canyons developed. In sociology, you might have learned how one culture meshes with another. In journalism you might've learned how to write a good lead.

    Think of a good process and write about it. Choose either how some*one* does something or how some*thing* does something. Be sure to follow the conventions on documentation we discuss in Chapter 9.

PART 5

The Research Paper

Y ou've probably been having nightmares about the research paper ever since we first mentioned it. Actually, you already know most of the skills involved. You know the fundamentals of organization and support, and you may have looked at the punctuation and expression chapters. You've even used some outside sources and a simple method of documentation. The only new skills you need to learn are efficient ways to find your support, organize it, use it in the paper, and document it. You'll find these new skills demand more time and patience than you needed for your earlier papers, but they are not difficult to learn.

CHAPTER 19

Overview of the Research Paper

Sooner or later we all write the longer paper, usually because it's assigned, or perhaps because we find ourselves interested in a subject. But regardless of the reason, we all face the same problem: How do we discuss anything intelligently for five or ten pages or more?

Either we write about a subject we know intimately, or we go to some other source—an interview with an eyewitness, perhaps, or a book in the library. When we must use sources outside our own minds or experience, we rely on research.

Unlike some of the earlier exercises and paragraphs in this book, the research paper has no invented evidence. You must find the specific support for your research paper by consulting real sources, not imaginary ones.

By now you may be worried because of stories you've heard about research papers. A research paper can be long, and it can be a lot of work. It can be particularly troublesome if you put it off until the last minute. The process of research and writing requires a number of careful steps. You'll find it hard to compress all of them into a long night's work—or even a day or two.

What a Research Paper Is and Isn't

It's not:

- a rehash of encyclopedia articles
- a string of quotations, one after another, like sausages
- a mass of invented support
- a mystical kind of writing that's more difficult than the kinds you've been doing

It is:

- an organized statement (with limited subject and precise opinion) about a topic, using support from sources outside your own experience
- a paper that credits sources with thorough documentation
- a normal requirement in many college courses and professional jobs
- the next step in your development as a writer

THE SHAPE OF THE RESEARCH PAPER

Like the writing you did for Part 4, the research paper is an expanded form of the five-paragraph essay. Although it's longer, the basic structure is still the same. The chart on the next page shows the relationship between a five-paragraph essay and a longer research paper.

Not every paragraph must have exactly three items of specific support, nor must every main idea have exactly three paragraphs of support. Some may have more and some less. Whatever the number, the support paragraphs help persuade your readers to accept one of the major topic sentences in the same way specific support helps persuade them to accept the topic sentences in a five-paragraph essay. And the major topic sentences in the research paper help convince your readers of the thesis. By now you've learned that a model is simply a guide, a handy way to begin thinking about your paper. Treat this model the same way.

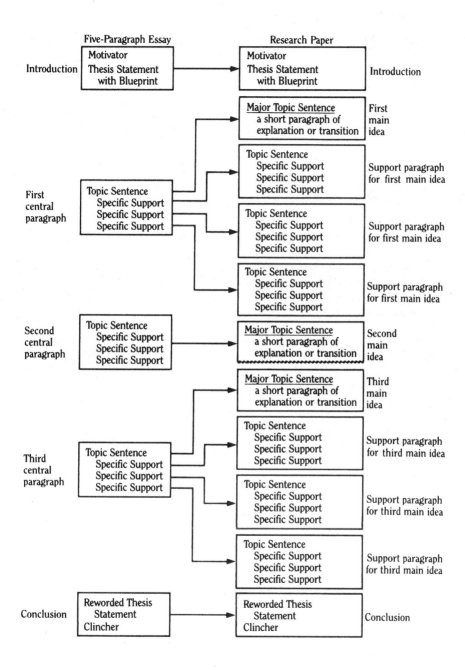

THE RESEARCH PAPER'S PURPOSE

Why write a long paper? In a research paper you could:

- explore a particular problem (leading to a thesis identifying the major cause of the British defeat at Singapore in World War II, for example)
- inform readers about a development (with a thesis, for example, about the effects of an increase in the minimum wage)
- trace the history of a situation (perhaps developing a thesis identifying why America became involved in the history of the Panama Canal)
- present the solution to a problem (with a thesis on how Americans can deal with lethal crimes among the nation's youth, for example)

Research papers are a means of presenting a large amount of information about a particular topic, information gathered from outside the writer's own knowledge and experience. And the purposes of these papers can be as varied as the reasons for presenting large amounts of information.

Practical Applications for Research Papers

A research paper is more than just a classroom exercise. It has many practical uses. Businesses use research reports as marketing studies and reports to stockholders. The military services call them staff studies and intelligence reports. Inspectors and auditors call them reports of findings. Doctors call them case studies. Professors sometimes call them monographs. Whatever the names, reports that present large amounts of information from research or investigations of some sort are likely to remain part of your life beyond the classroom.

A SAMPLE RESEARCH PAPER

To see what is possible in a research paper of about four thousand words, look at the sample paper that follows. Comments on pages facing the paper highlight points you'll learn more about in subsequent chapters.

For the most part, the page layout in the sample paper follows the guidance in the fourth edition of the *MLA Handbook for Writers of Research Papers*. In a few places, however, we've departed from the MLA page-format guidance because it restricts layout techniques. Nevertheless, we've noted those places in the comments facing the pages so you'll know the MLA rules if your instructor wants your paper to adhere strictly to MLA format. Of course, we've also explained why we departed from the MLA format to help you judge the effect of the alterations.

Some instructors want their students to submit outlines with their final papers. Chapter 22, which discusses outlining, shows a formal sentence outline for this sample research paper.

The MLA research paper format, which your instructor may want you to use, does not include a title page, but many instructors have requested that we include a sample. If you want to follow the MLA format completely, your paper will begin with the first page of the body (that is, without a title page and without an abstract). You'll provide identifying information at the top of the first page of the body, flush left with the paper's left margin, one inch from the top edge of the paper, and with all identification elements double spaced. Provide the following: your full name, your instructor's name, the course title, and the date. After this information you'll double space to find the line on which to type your paper's title.

A

GRANT'S REGRETTABLE ASSAULT AT COLD HARBOR

by

Lawrence Henderson

for
English 111
Professor Collier
12 December 1997

B   The MLA research paper format does not call for an abstract. Again, numerous instructors have requested that we include a sample. For this reason the sample paper includes an informative abstract, providing it after the title page and before the paper's body, much like an executive summary. Chapter 22 discusses informative and descriptive abstracts.

B

Henderson ii

ABSTRACT

The Union army assault on the morning of 3 June 1864 against Confederate entrenchments at Cold Harbor, Virginia, resulted in terrible Union losses in less than two hours. General Grant afterwards indicated twice that he regretted ordering the assault. Nevertheless, examination of the strategy Grant was pursuing, his attitude toward the requirements of war, and the progress of the Wilderness Campaign preceding the 3 June assault show that Grant had reason to imagine that an attack might prove successful, though errors in timing, lack of planning, and poor execution brought disaster instead. Grant changed the Union's military strategy from the territorial emphasis of his predecessors to an emphasis on coordinated pursuit and destruction of the South's armies in the field. He understood that winning the war would require "complete conquest" of the South and that destroying the Confederate armies would necessitate heavy Union losses. Throughout the Wilderness Campaign in 1864, ending in the Battle of Cold Harbor, Grant tried to force Lee's Army of Northern Virginia into an open battle. Yet, as Grant drove Lee toward Richmond, Lee's forces always managed to stay ahead and to entrench successfully as they moved. Union losses in the Wilderness and at Spotsylvania were quite heavy, though assaults at Spotsylvania seemed to suggest that Lee's field works could be breached. At North Anna, Lee's position was so strong that Grant never ordered a major assault. The move to Cold Harbor was the last one possible before Lee would be forced into Richmond's fortifications, and both Lee and Grant wanted to destroy the other's army before accepting the stalemate of a siege. This situation plus early fighting at Cold Harbor that appeared to justify further assault led Grant to order the disastrous attack; errors in timing, planning, and execution caused a poor assault twenty-four hours late, ensuring the high Union losses. Once the disaster had occurred, Grant accepted the blame and expressed his regret that nothing had been accomplished to justify the cost; then he turned his attention to moving the Union army to the south of the James River to begin the siege of Petersburg and Richmond.

C The MLA page format, which your instructor may want you to use, calls for your last name and the page number one-half inch from the top of each page and flush with the right margin. You'll see this style illustrated on page 2 and subsequent pages of the sample paper. MLA guidance calls for this information on page 1 as well, but we've deleted it. Traditionally the first page of a document bears no page marking.

MLA guidance directs you to type the title of the paper and double space to begin the first line of text in the body of your paper. The result is a solid-looking mass of type that provides no visual separation for the paper's title. We've added extra space after the title, setting it off for readers to see. Using white space in this way is a simple design technique that enhances the appearance of a paper.

D The thesis statement for this paper answers the question that precedes it: "Why . . . did Grant order the assault for the morning of 3 June 1864?" The thesis indicates "that Grant had reason to imagine that an assault might prove successful, though errors in timing, lack of planning, and poor execution brought disaster instead."

Combined with the thesis statement and preceding it is the blueprint: "Examination of the strategy Grant was pursuing, his attitude toward the requirements of war, and the progress of the Wilderness Campaign preceding the 3 June assault . . ." The paper also discusses the 3 June assault itself and why Grant ordered it; these two discussion areas are implicit in the thesis, so they did not need to be mentioned separately in the blueprint. Because of the combined thesis statement and blueprint, readers can tell where the paper is going and how it will get there.

E Marked here is a first-level (or major) heading. In Chapter 10 you saw what a single level of headings could do to help readers grasp the information in a short paper. A longer paper may need more levels—this one has two.

The heading at the beginning of the first block of "body" text provides a benefit for the introduction as well. That heading also is at the end of the introduction, showing readers the move from introduction to body paragraphs.

MLA page format does not address headings. However, MLA guidance does call for consistent double spacing throughout the research paper. Presumably, then, it would allow no extra space before or after headings within the body of the paper. As you can see, we advise using white space with headings to set them off.

Spacing is an important design technique. White space signals a move to a new topic and sets off the heading, focusing on the title it provides for the following material. In this way, layout reinforces your words.

F The research paper uses the MLA's parenthetical documentation scheme, which places source references in parentheses in the body of your paper rather than employing footnotes or endnotes. However, you may need an occasional footnote for an explanatory digression from the main line of your text. This

GRANT'S REGRETTABLE ASSAULT
AT COLD HARBOR

In May and June 1864, Lieutenant General Ulysses S. Grant directed a series of Civil War battles that collectively are called the Wilderness Campaign.[1] The last battle of the campaign, according to historian Bruce Catton, has "one of the hard and terrible names of the Civil War, perhaps the most terrible one of all: *Cold Harbor*" (257–58). Cold Harbor was terrible, and so memorable, because of the tragic results of the Union assault on Confederate entrenchments on the morning of 3 June 1864, when Union casualties approached 7,000 in less than two hours, while Confederate casualties were fewer than 1,500 (Catton 267; Foote 292; Krick, Andrus, and Ruth 56). That night, according to Horace Porter, of Grant's staff, Grant apologized to his staff: "'I regret this assault more than any one I ever ordered'" (qtd. in Maney 192). And years later Grant wrote in his memoirs: "I have always regretted that the last assault at Cold Harbor was ever made. . . . At Cold Harbor no advantage whatever was gained to compensate for the heavy loss we sustained" (2:276). Why, then, did Grant order the assault for the morning of 3 June 1864? Examination of the strategy Grant was pursuing, his attitude toward the requirements of war, and the progress of the Wilderness Campaign preceding the 3 June assault show that Grant had reason to imagine that an assault might prove successful, though errors in timing, lack of planning, and poor execution brought disaster instead.

GRANT'S STRATEGY

The Union's military strategy for the first part of the Civil War was the Anaconda Plan put forth by General Winfield Scott before he left the position of general-in-chief. That plan required a naval blockade of Southern ports to isolate the Confederacy, opening the Mississippi River under Union control, and capturing Richmond (Murray 181). The emphasis was on territory. By 1864 the Union navy was maintaining an adequate blockade and the Mississippi

---

[1] This series of battles also is known as the Overland Campaign of 1864 and the Virginia Campaign of 1864.

page illustrates how such a footnote is accomplished. Chapter 24 covers foot-notes such as this one as well as parenthetical documentation as a whole.

G   Documenting borrowed material is one of the new skills you'll learn in studying the research paper. Notice that the information from Geoffrey Perret's book has an introduction ("As biographer Geoffrey Perret indicates . . .") so that readers can tell where the borrowed material begins. The parenthetical reference at the end of the borrowing—"(301)"—marks where the borrowing ends and tells specifically which part of Perret's book the writer drew upon. Notice also that the parenthetical reference—the page number in parenthe-ses—comes before the period that ends the sentence. You'll learn more about presenting and documenting borrowed material in Chapters 23 through 25.

H   See the parenthetical reference at the end of the second sentence, "(Murray 183)"? Where did the summary begin? You want readers to be able to tell what is borrowed material and what represents your own thinking. No problem here: Clearly the borrowed material begins at the start of the paragraph. How-ever, if you think readers may question where your borrowed material begins, introduce the borrowing by mentioning the source's author or title.

The third sentence of the paragraph ("Banks against Mobile . . .") is the writer's own. Readers can tell that because the second sentence ends with a parenthetical reference and the fifth sentence introduces another borrowing, the Sherman quotation.

Henderson 2

was open, but Richmond had not been taken and the Confederates still maintained large armies in the field.

When Grant became general-in-chief in 1864, he added his own strategy to the Anaconda Plan. Earlier operations had lacked coordination from theater to theater, allowing the Confederates to move troops to strengthen this army or that one when any was threatened. As biographer Geoffrey Perret indicates, Grant wanted to have all the Union armies operating together as "powerful, converging columns, designed to apply pressure on the Confederacy from various directions, in season and out, the movements of each column coordinated with the advance of the rest" (301). Grant's strategic emphasis would be on destroying the South's armies.

The military strategy Grant set in motion involved five Union armies. In the west, General Banks was already pursuing an operation in Louisiana; Grant thought it pointless and wanted it ended as quickly as possible so Banks could threaten Mobile, Alabama (Murray 183). Banks against Mobile would tie up Confederate forces that otherwise could support General Joseph Johnston, General Sherman's objective. Grant met with Sherman in March 1864 in Cincinnati and the two friends reviewed Grant's strategic plan. Years later Sherman summarized the strategy simply: " 'He was to go for Lee and I was to go for Joe Johnston. That was the plan' " (qtd. in Jaynes et al. 26).

In the east, General Meade, in command of the Army of the Potomac since just before Gettysburg, retained his command, though General Grant decided to keep his own headquarters in the field and close to Meade's—recognition of the importance of Meade's target, General Robert E. Lee and the Army of Northern Virginia. In a letter of instruction to Meade dated 9 April 1864, Grant wrote: "Lee's army will be your objective point. Wherever Lee goes, there you will go also" (Grant 2:135). General Butler was to move up the James River to threaten Richmond and Petersburg from the east, so forces protecting Richmond could not be used to reinforce Lee (Murray 183). In addition, if Meade and the Army of the Potomac could not destroy Lee's army before it reached Richmond, then Grant intended to join Meade's and Butler's forces and move them south of the James River, to hit Petersburg and the rail

This paragraph illustrates a number of parenthetical reference formats. The first one—"(Murray 181)"—is a "standard" parenthetical reference. It includes the name of the author of the source (*Murray*) and a page reference for the Murray source (*181*). The next reference, however, says simply "(McPherson)." Checking the Works Cited list for the sample paper shows that the McPherson source is an Internet electronic reference work that lacks pagination. For this reason, referring to the entire source is the only reference possible. Following that is another standard reference—"(Murray 181)"—and then just "(181)." The latter reference comes at the end of a borrowing that begins, "As Murray notes. . . . " Because Murray is indicated at the beginning of the borrowing, the parenthetical reference needs only a page number (*181*). The final two parenthetical references for the paragraph are "(1:368)" and "(2:131)." Both of these show no author because the author, Grant, is included in the opening for each borrowing. These two parenthetical references show a volume number as well as a page number because the Grant source consists of two volumes. You'll learn more about all types of parenthetical references in Chapter 24.

Henderson 3

lines supporting Richmond from the south. This would force either Lee's surrender or movement of his forces out of the Richmond area defenses, so Grant's forces could destroy them (O.R. Ser. 1, Vol. 34, Pt. 1:18). Finally, General Siegel was to operate in the Shenandoah Valley of Virginia, again to keep Lee from being reinforced (Murray 183).

As operations played out, only the Sherman and Meade parts of Grant's plan worked. Banks became bogged down in Louisiana, allowing Johnston to be reinforced. Butler threatened Richmond but allowed a small force to bottle him up in the Bermuda Hundred east of Richmond; his force was secure, but so were Richmond and Petersburg for the Confederates—and troops from Richmond reinforced Lee. General Siegel was defeated at New Market, allowing a Confederate force from the Shenandoah Valley to reinforce Lee. These failures made Sherman's and Meade's tasks more difficult but did not wreck Grant's strategy, and Confederate forces still could not be moved between Johnston and Lee.

GRANT'S FRAME OF MIND

In addition to understanding Grant's intention to pursue and destroy the South's armies in the field, it is important to realize how far Grant was willing to push warfare. The American Civil War introduced rifled muskets and rifled artillery to the battlefield. The rifled musket extended the normal killing range of an infantry soldier by 300 to 400 yards (Murray 181), making the Napoleonic tactics then part of American military training and used at the beginning of the Civil War obsolete. Moving regiments of soldiers in close order toward regiments of their foes on an open field now just spent manpower, so soldiers learned to entrench to help protect themselves from the rifled muskets and artillery (McPherson). By 1864 trench warfare was the norm, though effective *offensive* tactics against soldiers in trenches were not developed until late in World War I (Murray 181). This meant for Grant's armies that not only did an attacker need superior forces and firepower, such as Grant controlled, but the leader taking the offensive had to be prepared to accept heavy losses. As Murray notes, after the losses Grant's forces sustained at Shiloh in April 1862, Grant was criticized for the heavy

J   Quotations that require four or fewer lines of typing in your paper will be incorporated into the flow of your paper but set off with quotation marks to designate the exact words from your source. Longer quotations, like this one, are indented as a block. Notice that the indented quotation does not begin and end with quotation marks; the block indentation functions in the place of quotation marks to set off the exact words of the source from your own words.

Notice also that the parenthetical reference—"(1:368)"—comes *after* the ending punctuation for the quotation. For long, indented quotations, space after the ending punctuation of the quotation, provide the parenthetical reference, and put *no* punctuation after the closing parenthesis of the reference. Note: this is the style *only* for quotations set off with block indentation.

K   This short quotation from Shelby Foote's book is incorporated into the flow of the student writer's work. Notice that the quoted material, which is set off with quotation marks, does not begin with a capital letter. That is, the first portion of the quotation is itself not a full sentence, although it is set into the student's writing so that there is a complete sentence structure. You can, and should, trim the material you quote to fit it into your own writing as support for your points. The quotations should fit into the grammar and sense of your own writing. Of course, it's *not* acceptable to edit the original material in such a way that you misrepresent what its author said or wrote—for example, by leaving out *not* or *never*. Chapter 23 explains techniques for dealing with quotations: omitting words, adding words, adding emphasis, verifying quotation accuracy, altering initial capitalization, and altering final punctuation.

Notice also that the parenthetical reference here—"(20)"—follows the quotation marks but precedes the ending punctuation for the sentence. This technique applies to quotations incorporated into the flow of your paragraphs, but not to long, indented quotations.

Henderson 4

casualties. "But Grant at least sensed the depth of Southern hostility and its implications after the slaughter at Shiloh" (181). Whereas the McClellans of the American military still believed that a decisive victory would end the war, Grant understood the reality the North had to deal with. In his memoirs Grant provided this summary of his frame of mind after Shiloh:

> Up to the battle of Shiloh I, as well as thousands of other citizens, believed that the rebellion against the Government would collapse suddenly and soon, if a decisive victory could be gained over any of its armies. Donelson and Henry were such victories. . . . But when Confederate armies were collected which not only attempted to hold a line farther south . . . , but assumed the offensive and made such a gallant effort to regain what had been lost, then, indeed, I gave up all idea of saving the Union except by complete conquest. (1:368)

Grant accepted that the North could win the Civil War only by destroying armies in the field and by going one step further: by destroying the resource base that supported the armies. Thus, at the outset of operations in 1864, he already was considering the type of destructive operations Sherman would carry out on his March to the Sea and that Grant later would send General Sheridan to perform in the Shenandoah Valley. Grant's written instructions to Sherman, dated 4 April 1864, told him "to move against Johnston's army, to break it up and to get into the interior of the enemy's country as far as you can, inflicting all of the damage you can against their war resources" (2:131).

As for the Army of the Potomac, according to historian Shelby Foote, Grant felt it was accustomed to defeat not because of the brilliance of Robert E. Lee and Stonewall Jackson, but because it lacked "self-confidence, which seemed to him an outgrowth of aggressiveness, an eagerness to come to grips with the enemy and a habit of thinking of wounds it would inflict rather than of wounds it was likely to suffer" (20). At the outset, Grant expected to pound Lee's army continuously, which the Army of the Potomac did day after day during the Wilderness Campaign from the Wilderness, through Spotsylvania, North Anna, and Cold Harbor, the major battles of the campaign. And Grant expected losses—not because he

L   This block quotation illustrates alteration of initial capitalization and use of ellipsis points, the three spaced periods (. . .). The student writer needed to fit the Eggleston quotation into the flow of his own writing. The word *by* did not start a sentence in the Eggleston source, but the writer needed a full sentence there. Therefore, he presented the first letter of *by* in square brackets: [*B*], which shows that the writer has altered the capitalization of the opening of the quotation. The writer also did not need all of Sergeant-Major Eggleston's words to make his point, so he trimmed some out of the quotation, replacing the missing words with the ellipsis points. The meaning of what Sergeant-Major Eggleston wrote has not been altered; the writer has simply trimmed the wording to get to the point he wants to make more rapidly and more directly. Both of these alterations, as Chapter 23 discusses, are legitimate ways of modifying quoted material to make it fit into your writing.

Henderson 5

wished them, but because they were a necessity of the type of warfare he understood was required. Grant wrote the following about his expectations for the period beginning with the Wilderness Campaign: "This was not to be accomplished, however, without as desperate fighting as the world has ever witnessed; not to be consummated in a day, a week, a month, or a single season. The losses inflicted, and endured, were destined to be severe" (2:177). Sergeant-Major George Eggleston, of Lamkin's Virginia Battery, wrote of the Southern military man's view of what Grant intended:

> [B]y the time that we reached Cold Harbor we had begun to understand what our new adversary meant, . . . that Grant was not going to retreat; that he was not to be removed from command because he had failed to break Lee's resistance; and that the policy of pounding had begun, and would continue until our strength should be utterly worn away.

PROGRESS OF THE WILDERNESS CAMPAIGN

Grant and Meade faced the same problem that every commander of the Army of the Potomac since McClellan had faced: how to get across the Northern Virginia rivers and pull Lee's forces out of their defensive works to fight where the Union's superior numbers and firepower could triumph. Bruce Catton notes that Grant would have preferred to go to his right (around Lee's left flank) because the terrain there was suitable for "quick movement and sharp maneuvering, carried out as if such words as 'attrition' and 'hammering' had never been invented" (154). Grant settled instead on moving to his left (around Lee's right flank) because this direction allowed protection of the supply lines of the Army of the Potomac. Moving to the left continued to be the preferred choice throughout the campaign for the same reason; indeed, Grant was able to change supply bases several times to make use of Virginia's waterways and thereby shorten the distance support forces had to haul supplies by land. Moving to his left also put the Army of the Potomac increasingly closer to Butler's forces to the east of Richmond.

M   "The Wilderness" and the three headings that follow are second-level (or minor) headings. The heading style in this sample research paper demonstrates one good way to make headings in a paper. The major headings, which are centered and all in uppercase letters, stand out more on the page than the minor headings do.

N   Tables and figures often fail to fit exactly where you'd like them in your final paper. For that reason, it's best to prepare them to "float" freely within the paper—that is, so that you need not place them in only one particular place. Refer to a table (or figure) by number—as with "(see Table 1)." Then place the table (or figure) where you'd like it to go if it will fit there. If it won't fit, you can place it intact at the top of the next page (or on a separate page for a large table or figure).

O   Prepare a table as the sample paper shows it. Give the table a number and a title; show the source, if necessary, at the end of the table, set off by a two-inch line dividing it from the table contents. You may want to put tables and figures within boxes to separate the graphics from your text; most computer word processing programs provide such a capability. Illustrated here is a technique of setting the table off with single lines above and below—a layout technique you can achieve with only a standard typewriter.

The MLA format for a table differs somewhat from what you see here. If you need to follow MLA guidance exactly, make these changes: Type the table designator and title on separate lines as shown, but place them flush left at the left margin of your paper. Double space throughout the table. Use full-ruled lines (margin to margin) in the place of the italics you see in this sample table. Do not use either italics or boldface type. Do not set the table off from your text with lines or a box, and do not provide extra space above or below the table. Finally, provide a full Works Cited entry for the source rather than the shortened form illustrated in the sample (which has the same information that you would find in a parenthetical reference in the body of the paper).

Henderson 6

The Wilderness

The Army of the Potomac began the Wilderness Campaign with 147,000 persons, over 122,000 of them infantry, artillery, or cavalry "effectives"; the Army of Northern Virginia began with about 62,000 effectives (Foote 133). The Army of the Potomac began moving across the Rapidan River and through the Wilderness on 3 May 1864. Grant hoped to be through the Wilderness—without major conflict—by 6 May. Lee hit the Union forces on 5 May (Perret 306–08). After two days of vicious fighting, the Union had lost 17,666, against some 7,800 Confederate losses (Foote 188). Union losses were carefully recorded in various reports (see Table 1), whereas Confederate losses were not and therefore can be only rough estimates. On the night of 7 May, Grant began moving the army to the left, around Lee's right flank again. Lee began moving his army the same night when Union movement was detected.

Table 1
Union Killed, Wounded, and
Missing in the Wilderness Campaign

Battle	Aggregated Losses
The Wilderness (5–7 May)	17,666
Spotsylvania Court House (8–21 May)	18,399
North Anna, Pamunkey crossing, Totopotomoy (22–30 May)	3,986
Cold Harbor and related battles (31 May–15 June)	12,738
Separate but related cavalry operations	2,137
Total	**54,926**

Source: O.R. Ser. 1, Vol. 36, Pt. 1: 188.

Spotsylvania Court House

Both Grant and Lee moved toward Spotsylvania Court House for the same reason. It was a critical crossroads on the way from the Wilderness to Hanover Junction, and Hanover Junction was Lee's supply base, where the Richmond, Fredericksburg, and Potomac

Henderson 7

Railroad and the Virginia Central Railroad intersected. If Grant could control Spotsylvania, he would be between Lee and Richmond and would threaten Lee's supplies. Lee would have either to attack or to move on to Richmond on less capable roads (Jaynes et al. 82).

Unfortunately for Grant, Lee won the race to Spotsylvania, and the Army of Northern Virginia quickly entrenched before Grant was ready to attack. The entrenchments were the most formidable that Lee's forces had constructed to that time (Jaynes et al. 90). Nevertheless, the Union commanders felt the line had weaknesses, and on 10 May a young West Point graduate, Colonel Upton, was allowed to try a creative new massed attack against a salient the Confederates called the Mule Shoe. Upton's assault succeeded, but he was forced to retreat later because the supporting force failed (Jaynes et al. 89–91; Perret 317). Nevertheless, Upton's assault showed that a strong entrenchment could be successfully assaulted under certain conditions. A larger assault two days later was also successful for a time, though it failed ultimately (Perret 318). Nevertheless, the lesson that strong entrenchments could be assaulted under certain conditions must have been on the Union commanders' minds in the following weeks.

On the night of 20 May, Grant began moving again to his left, this time toward the crossings of the North Anna River. Spotsylvania cost the Union 18,399 to something more than 10,000 for the Confederates (Foote 241–42), approximating the 2:1 ratio that was typical for the Wilderness Campaign as a whole (except for 3 June at Cold Harbor, when Union losses approached 5:1). Given that the Union forces usually were attacking entrenched Confederates, Grant would have considered 2:1 losses acceptable; he expected heavy losses from aggressive operations.

North Anna

When Grant's army reached the North Anna River crossings, they found the Confederates entrenched. Lee deployed his forces in an inverted *V*, with the tip of the *V* at an unassailable point on the south side of the North Anna River. Because of the *V* and the terrain, Grant's forces would have to cross the river twice to reinforce

Henderson 8

from one side to the other, while Lee's forces could move easily from side to side (Foote 273). After a couple of days of sparring to determine how strong Lee's defenses were, Grant decided not to assault Lee's lines and began moving away on 26 May.

Grant tried another minor movement to the left, crossing the Pamunkey River at two points on 28 May (Krick, Andrus, and Ruth 13). A cavalry battle at Haw's Shop showed Lee that Grant had crossed the Pamunkey, and Lee moved his forces to the south side of Totopotomoy Creek, a strong defensive position (Krick, Andrus, and Ruth 16).

At this point both Grant and Lee were aware that they were running out of room to maneuver, with Richmond defenses less than 15 miles away. On 30 May Lee told one of his corps commanders, General Early: "'We must destroy this Army of Grant's before he gets to [the] James River. If he gets there it will become a siege, and then it will be a mere question of time'" (qtd. in Krick, Andrus, and Ruth 17). Early attacked one of Grant's corps on the 30 May at Bethesda Church, but the attack was poorly executed and unsuccessful.

Cold Harbor

On 31 May, Lee sent cavalry and an infantry division to Cold Harbor, while Grant sent General Sheridan's cavalry to the same point. Cold Harbor was at the junction of five roads, none leading directly to Richmond, but important for movement between Grant's forces and their new supply base at White House Landing on the Pamunkey River. Lee had learned on 30 May that Grant was about to be reinforced by another corps—some 16,000 men—from Butler's forces east of Richmond and that the troops would arrive at White House Landing. Lee saw that Grant could extend his lines on his left (at Cold Harbor) beyond Lee's ability to counter these lines, effectively flanking Lee (Foote 281). Control of Cold Harbor became critical.

Sheridan won the battle for Cold Harbor on 31 May, began to retreat because he didn't think he could hold the position, and received word from Grant to control the crossroads at any cost. He was promised support from two infantry corps (Krick, Andrus, and

Henderson 9

Ruth 21). The first of June began with a weak attack by Confederate infantry against Sheridan's dismounted cavalry and ended with a more serious battle between Confederate infantry and parts of two Union corps. The afternoon attacks by the Union against rough, unfinished Confederate entrenchments cost about 2,200 casualties but positioned the Union forces for an attack on 2 June (Krick, Andrus, and Ruth 44–46; Catton 258). Bruce Catton explains: "Grant could see only what was visible across the murky flats in the battlefield twilight; and what he saw, dimly but unmistakably, was opportunity" (258).

3 JUNE AT COLD HARBOR

Grant ordered a third corps to join the two in place at Cold Harbor and to attack early on 2 June, but nothing went right. General Hancock's corps, moving all night to join General Smith's and General Wright's corps, became lost and arrived both late and exhausted. General Smith's troops lacked sufficient ammunition for an attack. Grant delayed the 2 June assault once to four in the afternoon, and delayed it again until four-thirty on the morning of 3 June (Catton 259–60). As Bruce Catton puts it: "Now the army was twenty-four hours late for the offensive that might have won the war. This was not anybody's fault, in particular. The army was just late" (259).

The delay allowed Lee's forces to dig in well. The entrenchments not only were formidable, but they apparently did not appear to be so. Wayne Maney describes them:

> The defensive positions on the Confederate right flank were unlike anything yet constructed. . . . [E]very physical trait had been turned into an elaborate defensive puzzle. . . . [P]ossible lanes of approach would bring the unwary into natural funnels where crossfires covered every spot. The entrenchments overlapped and used each modulation to advantage. From across the empty lowlands, Union soldiers could have no idea of the interlacing ditches and abatis that awaited them. (125–26)

Then, compounding the problem of timing errors, the assault went without serious planning and without coordination. General Meade formed no overall plan, leaving each corps commander on

P   This heading sets off the summary analysis of why Grant ordered the assault that he subsequently regretted. From this analysis the research paper passes to a short conclusion, showing that, having expressed his regret for the mistake, Grant moved on—a fitting end for the paper. No additional heading is needed because the final material of the body flows smoothly into the conclusion of the paper. If a smooth transition had not existed, the author could have added another heading to set off the conclusion.

Henderson 10

his own. The corps commanders did not conduct a thorough reconnaissance of what awaited them (Perret 330). As Geoffrey Perret notes, "Only strong columns well supported by artillery had any chance of breaking through if the enemy proved to be well dug in. But there were no assault columns. The attack would be made almost entirely by men advancing in line—the simplest formation but the one with the least chance of success" (330).

The result was extreme Union losses in short order. Each corps assault moved on a separate approach, so both artillery and musket fire caught each group of advancing men both in front and in cross-fires. "Survivors remembered that to be out there was like being in the heart of an exploding thundercloud, like trying to fight a battle in the center of a volcano, like something language had no words for: the ultimate storm, more terrible than anything men had seen before" (Catton 263–64).

"I HAVE ALWAYS REGRETTED . . ."

Despite the mistakes in timing, planning, and execution—which explain the extent of the disaster on the morning of 3 June—there remains the issue of why Grant ordered an assault on Lee's well-fortified position at all. The most obvious reason has to do with geography and terrain. Grant had, from the beginning of the Wilderness Campaign, been attempting to draw Lee out of fortifications for a fight in the open. At the start were fortifications in the Fredericksburg region of Virginia that Lee's troops had developed for years; at the end lay well-developed fixed fortifications around Richmond. Between were ad hoc entrenchments, built while Lee's army was on the move, which would seem to offer the next best option after open terrain, and clearly Lee would no longer opt for open battle. After Cold Harbor, the next Union move would push Lee into the Richmond defenses. As Shelby Foote puts it, "Grant's decision to . . . attack was arrived at by a process of elimination. This was coffin corner" (285). Thus, Grant could assault Lee's position one last time, or he could accept the challenge of Lee in Richmond. The latter meant he "would, in short, be mounting a siege, which at this stage he wanted as little as Lee did, since it represented the

Henderson 11

stalemate he had avoided from the start" (Foote 285). A stalemate, combined with the cost of Grant's campaign, would strengthen the hand of the Peace Democrats who were trying to put President Lincoln out of office—the greatest hope the South had at the time of "winning" the war.

Another way of looking at the assault is that put forward by Robert Krick and his associates: "to attack was Grant's 'way' while in Virginia. His tireless system of pushing and driving had brought him to within a dozen miles of the Confederate capital, and there was no reason to suspect that June 3 would be much different" (50). Operations on 1 June had offered hope of success, and assaults at Spotsylvania, although costly, had suggested that Lee's defenses could be breached. Had the assault on 2 June gone as planned, success might have offset the costs. Or had the corps commanders adequately reconnoitered their fronts, they might have convinced Meade and Grant that the task was too hard. Or had there been a well-developed plan of attack, coordinated movement of the corps. . . . But this last possibility would imply that anyone at the time knew how to attack well-prepared entrenchments. As James McPherson notes, "tactics lagged behind technology," with commanders to the end of the Civil War ordering assaults that "became increasingly suicidal, especially for Union attackers running up against Confederate trenches, which by 1864 were almost as elaborate as those on the western front in World War I."

Grant's expression of regret about Cold Harbor merits a review. In his memoirs Grant wrote: "I have always regretted that the last assault at Cold Harbor was ever made." He then noted that he could say the same about an assault he ordered at Vicksburg, yet he explained that the situation at Vicksburg offered "reasons justifying the assault" (2:278). At Cold Harbor, on the other hand, "no advantage whatever was gained to compensate for the heavy loss we sustained. Indeed, the advantages other than those of relative losses, were on the Confederate side" (2:276). Clearly, what Grant regretted was not the fact of casualties—for he expected those from an assault on a fortified position—but casualties when no benefits resulted for the Union.

Henderson 12

Grant also noted that the 3 June assault benefited the Confederates because it "seemed to revive their hopes temporarily" (2:277).
Confederate troops in Richmond created a ditty about their advantage at Cold Harbor:

> The man in the North,
> He pledged his troth,
> To find a Richmond barber,
> But the man in the South,
> He mashed his mouth
> At a place they call Cold Harbor. (Fraser)

Grant's reaction to the failure at Cold Harbor was typical of his
way of dealing with a crisis: he set to work on his next move. On
5 June he wrote General Halleck, the Chief of Staff of the Army, in
Washington, of his plans. Having failed to pull Lee out of entrenchments for an open battle "after more than thirty days of trial," Grant
felt that "Without a greater sacrifice of human life than I am willing
to make, all cannot be accomplished that I had designed outside of
the city" (O.R. Ser. 1, Vol. 36, Pt. 3: 598). He would hold his
infantry in position at Cold Harbor to allow increased opportunity
of success for cavalry actions against rail lines to the north and
northwest of Richmond, then move his force to the south of the
James River, join it with Butler's remaining troops, and attack
Petersburg and the rail lines supplying Richmond from the south.
On the night of 12 June, Grant began that process, ending the
Wilderness Campaign and moving toward the siege of Petersburg
and Richmond. The 3 June assault at Cold Harbor became a regrettable part of Grant's and the Union's past.

Q The Works Cited page begins on a separate page from the text of the research paper. Chapter 25 explains in detail the styles for Works Cited entries.

If you need to follow MLA page-layout guidance exactly, begin the section title—"Works Cited"—one inch from the top of the paper, and double space to get to the line for the first entry. That is, do not provide additional space between the section title and the beginning of the entries. We've shown extra space for the same reason we set off the paper's title, the headings, and the table—to let white space signal breaks and highlight the material set off.

WORKS CITED

Q

Catton, Bruce. *Grant Takes Command.* 1969. New York: Book-of-the-Month Club, 1994.

Eggleston, George Cary. "Notes on Cold Harbor." N.d. *Civil War: America's Epic Struggle.* Ed. Marc J. Schulman. Vers. 2.0. CD-ROM. New Rochelle: MultiEducator, 1997.

Foote, Shelby. *Red River to Appomattox.* 1974. New York: Vintage-Random, 1986. Vol. 3 of *The Civil War: A Narrative.* 3 vols.

Fraser, Kathie. "Mother Lincoln's Melodies." N.d. Online. Internet. Available <http://www.erols.com/kfraser/melodies.html> (29 Aug. 1997).

Grant, Ulysses S. *Personal Memoirs of U. S. Grant.* 2 vols. New York: Charles Webster, 1885.

Jaynes, Gregory, et al. *The Killing Ground: Wilderness to Cold Harbor.* Alexandria: Time-Life Books, 1986.

Krick, Robert E. L., Michael Andrus, and David Ruth. "Grant and Lee, 1864: From the North Anna to the Crossing of the James." *Blue & Gray Magazine* April 1994: 10–22, 44–58.

Maney, R. Wayne. *Marching to Cold Harbor: Victory and Failure, 1864.* Shippensberg, PA: White Mane, 1995.

McPherson, James M. "Civil War (US)." *The Reader's Companion to American History.* 1991 ed. Encarta article A14200155. Online. Internet. Available <http://trial.encarta.cognito.com/cgi-bin/cgi_appl.cgi/4/9/83094/34?xrn-311> (17 Aug. 1997).

Murray, Williamson. "What Took the North So Long?" *Experience of War: An Anthology of Articles from "MHQ: The Quarterly Journal of Military History."* Ed. Robert Crowley. New York: Norton, 1992. 177–86.

Perret, Geoffrey. *Ulysses S. Grant: Soldier & President.* New York: Random, 1997.

The War of the Rebellion: A Compilation of the Official Records of the Union and Confederate Armies. 128 vols. Washington: GPO, 1880–1901. *The Civil War CD-ROM.* Vers. 1.5. CD-ROM. Carmel IN: Guild, 1997. NOTE: Civil War historians refer to the volumes collected on this CD-ROM as the *Official Records,* or O.R.; this convention has been maintained in the documentation for this research paper.

PREVIEWING THE RESEARCH PAPER PROCESS

You already know what a good thesis looks like—a precise opinion about a limited topic. Research papers, too, require a good thesis, but because the research paper is longer and uses other people's ideas, we might call the thesis a thoughtful assertion about the limited topic. That means the research thesis is more than just an opinion: it's opinion supported by facts, ideas, and words of other authorities. To help you devise a good thesis, we'll preview the research process here.

Although you might be an intuitive writer and settle immediately on the exact thesis statement you'll use in writing your paper, that would be very unusual. If you're an ordinary mortal like most of us, this will be more common: You pick a topic, narrow it enough to make the scale of research reasonable, and move slowly toward the final thesis statement as your research goes along. For example, the writer of the sample research paper began with *The American Civil War,* narrowed that to the *Wilderness Campaign,* and—after research and analysis of what he could focus on—settled on *why General Grant ordered the 3 June 1864 assault of the Battle of Cold Harbor,* an assault that Grant later indicated he wished he had never ordered. Answering the question of why Grant ordered the assault became the basis for the writer's thesis statement.

In the next six chapters we'll go into more detail, but here's the research paper procedure we recommend to start you on your way:

- *Select a general topic* that interests you.
- *Do some preliminary reading* in handy, reliable sources to find out whether your topic and your ideas about it seem to be based on accurate assumptions and whether reliable, relevant sources appear to be available. If you're unhappy about your topic at this point, choose something else.
- *Develop a working thesis statement* to set a reasonable scope for research. As you find sources and think about what you've learned, constantly refine your working thesis by checking to see whether the subject is precise. Keep your mind open so that you can refine the working thesis when necessary.
- *Find supporting sources* that deal with your topic. You needn't limit your search to library sources, although the time available to work on your paper may prevent you from conducting interviews or tests. Be sure to evaluate your sources for relevance and reliability rather than blindly trusting what you read and hear. And be sure to keep accurate records about your sources; you'll need information about them when you document your paper.
- *Gather supporting facts and opinions* from your sources. You won't be able to remember every detail, and you'll need some sort of system to

match information with sources so you'll be able to document what you borrow. (We'll discuss two different ways of accomplishing these objectives.)

- *Organize your thoughts and support.* You should develop working outlines as you conduct your research; they help you see where you're going with your investigation—especially where you need more material. Before you draft your paper, however, you'll need to develop some sort of final outline to guide your writing. Moreover, many instructors require their students to submit formal outlines either before they begin writing or with the final paper.

- *Write a first draft.* The writing step is much like you've done for shorter papers, but you'll also be incorporating borrowed material from your research. As you write, you can insert the appropriate parenthetical references in the text for part of the documentation process. You'll also write and organize Works Cited entries for the listing that ends your research paper.

- *Revise the draft*—as many times as necessary to get the paper right.

- *Prepare the final version of your paper to hand in.*

POSSIBLE TOPICS

Now we'll look at some topics that may stir your imagination. Any of these broad topics could lead to a good narrow topic and thesis, or they may suggest similar topics that interest you. All, however, need to be narrowed carefully. Moreover, you'll do yourself and your readers a real favor if you stay away from some kinds of topics. Avoid writing about contemporary politics or religion—such topics often are too personal to write a research paper about. Thus, they are frequently ineffective from the beginning.

Remember, the topics that follow all need deliberate limiting. And, of course, before you can develop a thesis, each needs a thoughtful assertion—a precise opinion—made about it.

Acid Rain	Changes in Europe	Drugs in Sports
Adoption	Chemical Fertilizers	Drug Testing
AIDS Research	Child Abuse	Endangered Species
Auto Safety	Child Custody	Environmental
Ballet	Commercial Satellites	Legislation
Bicyclling	Corporate	Flemish Painting
Cable Television	Downsizing	Gambling
Censorship	Digital Technology	Global Warming

Hazardous Wastes

Hospices

Insulation

International Terrorism

Islamic Movement

Junk Bonds

Learning Disorders

Midwives

Minoans

Missing Children

Operation Desert Storm

Organ Donation

Panama Canal

Pollution

Prison Overcrowding

Rain Forests

Refugees

Savings and Loan Banks

Space Station Mir

Speech Disorders

Strip-mining

Tax Reform

Teen Alcoholism

Trojan War

Urban Transportation

Vegetarianism

Volcanoes

Worker Productivity

Yoga

CHAPTER 20

Finding Support

Sometimes when you have to write a research paper you won't know much about the subject, so you won't know what you want to say until you've studied the subject enough to narrow it to a manageable size, to a thesis. For example, from the broad subject of *pollution,* you might narrow to *pollution from plastics* and even further to the narrower thesis that *fast-food restaurants are the primary source of plastics pollution in North America.*

WHERE TO BEGIN

One way both to narrow your topic and to get a lead on information you need is to do some preliminary research in general reference tools such as encyclopedias. Even here, keep an informal record of your research by listing briefly the title and headings or subjects you looked under. This step is especially important if later you want to return to pick up the bit of information you remember reading but neglected to write down.

You may be in for some surprises as you continue working on your subject; what you find may take you in unexpected directions. Despite your initial belief, you might find, for example, that two of the fast-food chains have stopped using plastics and are active in research to prevent their products from contributing to pollution. When such a change happens, you must revise your thesis. In this case, you might say something like, "Although many people think fast-food chains are destructive polluters, some are actually working hard to prevent pollution caused by their products."

Once you have a working thesis, you're ready to begin the more formal research process. The problem is to know where to begin among all the resources available.

You may want to conduct a survey or series of experiments. Your research could involve audio or video tapes or viewing a series of television programs.

Or perhaps you'll want to interview participants in a relatively recent event of some importance—or business executives involved in an ongoing project. Finding sources for a research paper can include any search for information relevant to a topic and thesis.

Most college research paper projects today, however, involve a mixture of library and online computer research. Research usually is limited to books and articles that are available in the college library and to similar materials available online through the Internet or electronic information services. The limitation is the time you have available to conduct your research and prepare your paper. For this practical reason, our discussion of finding sources focuses on the college library and the Internet. Fortunately, though, what you're learning about conducting research and writing a research paper applies just as well to other types of research you might conduct if you had more time.

College libraries today provide a mixture of online data bases, CD-ROMs, and shelved books and periodicals. Research tools, in particular, probably are automated in your school's library, though some of the most useful reference guides may be on CD-ROM or in book form, depending on your library's holdings. In addition, your library may have one or more online information services, providing automated access to reference works and periodical articles. You probably have online computer access available either where you live or through some facility at your college. In this chapter we discuss what most likely is available to you and point out what you should look for. Still, knowing what resources you actually have available will require a little exploration on your own.

Books

The Catalog

Traditionally, the primary guide to a library's book collection has been called the "card catalog," because all the library's books were listed on index cards filed in long, narrow drawers. Today your library probably doesn't have such cards, but it will have a catalog of some sort, perhaps on microfilm, but most likely in a computer file. Whatever the form and name, it will provide essentially the same information as did the traditional card catalog. Because most college libraries now have computerized catalogs, we'll deal with those first.

The Computerized Catalog

To begin using your library's computerized catalog of books, you'll need to follow the directions either near the computer or on the screen. The directions can lead you in several ways to find books you need for your research. Generally, those directions tell you to enter an author's name, a book's title, or the subject you're interested in. Here's a sample of the first screen you might find in a library:

What type of search do you wish to do?
1. TIL = Title, journal title, series title, etc.
2. AUT = Author, illustrator, editor, organization, etc.
3. A-T = Combination of author and title.
4. SUB = Subject heading assigned by library.
5. NUM = Call number, ISBN, ISSN, etc.
6. KEY = One word taken from a title, author, or subject.
Enter number or code, then press RETURN.

You can see that this list also includes the combination of author and title, the call number (the number the library files the book under in the book stacks), or a keyword search. If you're looking for books by one author, naturally you'd try an author search. If you know a book's title, you can ask the computer to get the call number you need.

But the computer can help you in other ways by searching the index for you. You could ask for a subject or a keyword search. Let's say you decide to ask for a keyword search for *pollution*. Here's what you might get:

TITLE KEYWORD SEARCH

Your Title Keyword: Pollution

Matches 385 titles

		No. of citations in entire catalog	Your Lib
1	2nd Soviet-Swedish Symposium on the Pollution of the Baltic>	1	1
2	Acid rain and emissions trading: implementing a market appr>	1	1
3	Aerophysics of air pollution/	1	1
4	Against pollution and hunger; [proceedings]	1	1
5	Air pollution.	9	9
6	AIR POLLUTION-1970	5	5
7	Air pollution and acid rain: the biological impact/	1	1
8	Air pollution, acid rain, and the future of forests/	1	1
9	Air pollution and athletic performance/	1	1
10	Air pollution, the automobile, and public health/	1	1
11	Air pollution control/	4	4

Type a number to see more information -OR-
    FOR - move forward in this list   CAT - begin a new search
    CMD - see additional commands

With 385 titles that include your keyword, you might have more information than you can use. So, let's go back to the computer to look at a subject search for *pollution*. This search lists all titles that the library has filed under that subject. With this search you get eighty-six entries:

	No. of citations in entire catalog	Your Lib
1 Pollution.	91	86
2 Pollution Abstracts Periodicals.	1	0
3 Pollution Addresses, Essays, Lectures.	2	2
4 Pollution Bibliography.	4	4
5 Pollution Bibliography Periodicals.	1	1
6 Pollution British Columbia Congresses.	1	1
7 Pollution Congresses.	13	13
8 Pollution Control Equipment.	3	3
9 Pollution Control Equipment Handbooks, Manuals, etc.	1	1
10 Pollution Control Equipment Linings.	1	1
11 Pollution Control Equipment Maintenance and Repair.	1	1

If you then ask for a listing of number 4 above, "Pollution Bibliography," you see a short title list of the four entries catalogued under that subject heading:

		matches 4 citations (All in this library)
Ref # Author	Title	Date
1 Burk, Janet L.	Environmental concerns: a bibliogr>	1995
2 Kiraldi, Louis, 1911–	Pollution: a selected bibliography>	1991
3 McDonald, Rita	Guide to literature on environmenta>	1990
4 Rehfus, Ruth	Mercury contamination in the natura>	1990

If we want to see more about a source on air pollution, different keystrokes give a short entry for one of the books identified in our earlier search. This short entry gives the author, title, and call number and indicates that the book is in the library—all important bits of information.

AUTHOR: Lynn, David A.
TITLE: Air pollution, threat and response/David A. Lynn
IMPRINT: Reading, Mass.: Addison-Wesley Pub. Co., c1976.

Location	Loan Type	Cpy #	Status
BKSTAX	BOOK	1	In Library

Call Number: TD883.L96

But just being in the library isn't quite enough (either for you or for the book); you need more information. One more keystroke gives a full entry, one that tells how big the book is, whether it has a more detailed bibliography, and another subject ("air pollution") you might search for.

AUTHOR:	Lynn, David A.
TITLE:	Air pollution, threat and response/David A. Lynn
IMPRINT:	Reading, Mass.: Addison-Wesley Pub. Co., c1976
PHYSICAL FEATURES:	x, 388 p.: ill.; 24 cm.
NOTES:	CALL NO.: TD 883.L96 *includes index. *Bibliography: p. 349–364.
SUBJECTS:	Air—Pollution.
CALL NUMBER:	TD 883.L96 *TD 883.L96

Without leaving the computer terminal, then, you can get a list of the books the library has on your subject, their call numbers, and other detailed information about them. Unlike the card catalog, this computer catalog even tells whether the book is available for checkout.

The Card Catalog

Your library may have the traditional card catalog. Cards come in three kinds: author, title, and subject. If you know a book's author or title, look for one of those. But as you look for support for your research paper, you may know only a general subject, say, *architecture*. Then you can look at cards filed under that heading.

The information on the card catalog cards, like that in the computerized catalog, will save you time. All three kinds of cards start as author cards. A title card has the title typed across the top so it can be alphabetized by title easily, and a subject card has the subject typed on top so it can be alphabetized by subject. Beyond that top line, however, the contents of the cards are the same.

If you were trying to find out something about building styles of ancient civilizations, you could look for books on architecture, specifically on the history of architecture. In the card catalog under the subject heading "Architecture—History" you might find this card:

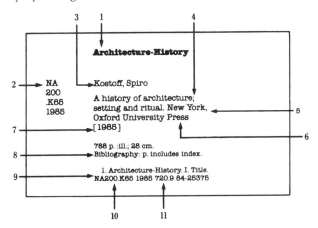

1. Subject heading. A title card would have the book's title instead. The basic author card would have nothing in this position.

2. Call number. The library where we found this card uses the Library of Congress classification system for filing its books. If it had used the Dewey decimal classification system, "720.9" would have appeared in this position.

3. Author's name.

4. Title.

5. Place of publication.

6. Publisher.

7. Publication date.

8. Notes on special contents. The book is illustrated, has a bibliography, and is indexed. Information about the number of pages may prove useful in evaluating the potential value of the book. The bibliography is especially important, for it can lead to other related books.

9. Recommended subject headings.

10. Recommended Library of Congress number.

11. Recommended Dewey decimal number.

Besides finding this card under "Architecture—History," you would find it under the author's name and the book's title. Depending on how a library files its cards, the three card types may be integrated in the same catalog or filed separately.

PERIODICALS

Your library's book catalog, whatever its form, is only one way to find the support material you need for your research. Periodicals—popular magazines, professional journals, and newspapers—are also basic sources, sometimes the most important ones. Even the most recent book is at least a year out of date by the time it appears, and the information in it may be several years old. If you're writing about the Battle of Hastings in 1066, books could be your principal sources. But if your topic requires last-minute, up-to-date information, you'll probably want to use some periodicals.

How do you find what you need? You could leaf through some recent magazines in hope of finding an article that will help. But even looking at the table of contents in each issue of a single magazine or journal would take more time than you can afford. You need access to reference tools that will help you find the right articles the way the book catalog helps you find the right books. Among the numerous ways to track down periodical resources, the most useful (if your library has one) probably will be the computerized periodical index.

Computerized Index

The samples of computer screens we'll look at next are adapted from a college library in a large city; the library belongs to a consortium of college libraries in the metropolitan area. The book and periodical catalogs for these libraries are interrelated so that a student can search the data bases for all the college libraries in the consortium at once—greatly increasing the number of research sources available. Here's the base screen for the computer system at one of the schools:

LIBRARY DATA BASE SELECTION MENU
On this terminal, you may search the data bases below. Choose a data base by entering its four-letter label. You may change data bases at any time by typing CHO (CHOOSE) and the four-letter label.

CATS   Consortium Libraries Catalog
GENL   Periodical Indexes (multisubject)
PAPR   Newspaper Index (U.S. newspapers only)
ERIC   ERIC (Educational Resources Information Center)
ABII   ABI/Inform (Business & Management Index)

Select a data base label from above

Choosing *CATS* would allow us to search the combined computerized book catalogs for the college libraries in the consortium. *PAPR* would allow us to search among abstracts for thousands of newspaper articles in major newspapers across the United States. *ERIC* would give us access to a specialized index for sources in the education field. And *ABII* would put us in a specialized index for business and management. We'll choose *GENL*, which takes us to a collection of aggregated general indexes for magazines and journals.

Periodical Indexes
Introduction

INTRODUCTION TO PERIODICAL INDEXES (GENL)

GENL is the online version of several well-known indexes to periodical literature. All indexes are searched simultaneously.

BP   Business Periodicals Index   From July 1982–
GS   General Science Index   From May 1984–
HU   Humanities Index   From February 1984–
IL   Index to Legal Periodicals   From August 1981–
RG   Readers' Guide   From January 1983–
SS   Social Sciences Index   From February 1983–

From any citation, you may type HOL and press <RETURN> to determine if the periodical is held by a consortium library.
To search by: Title   T =   Author   A =
                 Subject S =   Keyword   K =
                          Enter search command

As this screen indicates, we can search for a title, an author, a subject, or a keyword. Let's try a keyword search for *pollution*.

```
Search Request:  K=POLLUTION                              Periodical Indexes
Search Results:  15531 Entries Found                         Keyword Index

         DATE    TITLE                          AUTHOR
  1      1997    After oil damage, Carolinas look to fe   Jensen, Charles      RG
  2      1997    Agreement will shield corporation fro                         GS
  3      1997    Air pollution and federal law changes                        GS
  4      1997    Appeals Court questions federal guid     Lockabill, Richard   BP
  5      1997    Barge in oil disaster had been conde     Bottom, Eleven R     RG
  6      1997    Big oil spill fouls beaches on Atlantic                       RG
  7      1997    Boat in oil dumping incident operated    Donaldson, James     RG


STArt over           Type number to display record              <F8> FORward page
HELp                 MARk
OTHer options
```

This search yields 15,531 articles—far more that we want to consider looking at one by one. Let's narrow the search by looking for *pollution and air,* which limits "pollution" to "air pollution."

```
Search Request:  K=POLLUTION                              Periodical Indexes
Search Results:  5041 Entries Found                          Keyword Index

         DATE    TITLE                          AUTHOR
  1      1997    Agreement will shield corporation fro                         RG
  2      1997    Air pollution and federal law changes                        GS
  3      1997    Cutting pollution from semis             Robertson, Charles   GS
  4      1997    Denver officials charge several firms                         BP
  5      1997    Detroit starts to listen to protests fro  Stockland, Peter    BP
  6      1997    Detroit views air pollution as everybo                       BP
  7      1997    Federal court decision may force clea    Eggen, Steven        BP


STArt over           Type number to display record              <F8> FORward page
HELp                 MARk
OTHer options
```

Searching for *pollution and air* cuts the number of articles available to 5,041, but that's still too many to view. If we limit the search to articles for a particular year by specifying *(pollution and air) and 1997,* we see the following results:

```
Search Request:  K=(POLLUTION AND AIR) AND 1997          Periodical Indexes
Search Results:  42 Entries Found                              Keyword Index

            DATE     TITLE                             AUTHOR
    1       1997     Agreement will shield corporation fro              GS
    2       1997     Air pollution and federal law changes              GS
    3       1997     Cutting pollution from semis      Robertson, Charles    GS
    4       1997     Denver officials charge several firms               BP
    5       1997     Detroit starts to listen to protests fro  Stockland, Peter   BP
    6       1997     Detroit views air pollution as everybo             BP
    7       1997     Federal court decision may force clea  Eggen, Steven     BP

    STArt over           Type number to display record        <F8> FORward page
    HELp                 MARk
    OTHer options
```

This time our search limits the number of articles to forty-two. Because some may be difficult to locate or obtain, this is a good time to see just what the articles are and whether they are available. Let's look at information about the third article in the list above.

```
Search Request: K=(POLLUTION AND AIR) AND 1997           Periodical Indexes
3 of 42 Entries Found                                         Long View

    AUTHOR(S):              Robertson, Charles

    TITLE:                  Cutting pollution from semis.

    SOURCE:                 Life With Health v. 3 (Jan/Feb'97) p.16–8

    SPECIAL FEATURES:       p. 16–8

    SUBJECT DESCRIPTORS:    Air pollution—Control.
                           Trucks.
                           Oil fuel.

    STArt over      HOLdings         MARk        <F6> NEXt record
    HELp            BRIef view                   <F5> PREvious record
    OTHer options   INDex
```

Now we see the author, the article title, and information about the periodical that contains the article. We also see a list of subjects under which the article is indexed; a list such as this may help in our own search by suggesting subjects we might want to search for.

One other piece of information is important to us at this point: Does our library, or another nearby library, hold this article? Asking for *HOLdings* gives another screen that tells us which libraries in the consortium have the particular issue of the magazine with this article and where they hold it (on the shelf, in microform, or on CD-ROM). When we check for this article, we find that our own library holds the issue on microfilm.

Data Base Searches

When you search an electronic data base, whether online or on CD-ROM, take a few minutes to see how the system allows you to search. Most search systems employ limiting terms from Boolean logic (and often are called "Boolean queries"). The Boolean operators are *and, or,* and *not.* (Some search systems change *and* and *not* to *with* and *without.*)

If we search a group of articles with two terms linked by *and,* the system finds all articles that contain both terms. If we connect the search terms with *or,* the system finds all the articles that contain either term. And if we use *not,* the system finds all the articles for the first term but deletes those that also contain the second term.

Here's a sample: We searched a CD-ROM collection about countries of the world for articles with references to Menachem Begin, prime minister of Israel from 1977 to 1983. We didn't want to use his first and last names as search terms since many references would have only his last name. Unfortunately, his last name is also an English verb, as in "Egypt will *begin* building . . ." So we decided to use as our search terms *Begin* and *Israel* (search systems usually disregard case, so capitals or lowercase letters give the same results).

A search for *Begin* yielded 564 articles, while *Israel* gave 401. *Begin or Israel* gave 861 articles (less than the sum of *Begin* plus *Israel* since some articles would have both). *Begin and Israel* yielded 99 articles.

Our search system also allowed searches for two terms (with an *and* relationship) within a given word range. We selected a 50-word range, figuring this would give us articles about Menachem Begin that mentioned *Begin* in context with *Israel* (thereby excluding instances such as "Egypt will begin building . . ."). A search of *Begin [50] Israel* yielded 28 articles. Why 28 articles for *Begin [50] Israel* when *Begin and Israel* yielded 99? The 99 articles include a number with references such as "Israel will begin building . . . " Thus, the most useful search for our purposes proved to be *Begin [50] Israel.*

Common Indexes

If your library doesn't have an automated search capability for common periodical indexes, you'll need to look for indexes in book or CD-ROM form. Among the more common reference tools, you may find these in your library:

- *Annual Bibliography of English Language and Literature.* Indexes articles and books about authors and literature written in English.
- *Biography Index.* An index to biographical material on living and historical figures.
- *Book Review Digest.* A summary of book reviews for modern literature; useful for finding out how a book was received.
- *Business Periodicals Digest.* As the title indicates, an index of business and economics articles.
- *Education Index.* For articles dealing with education research and development.
- *MLA International Bibliography.* Published annually by the Modern Language Association; covers scholarly journals and books about language and literature in English and other languages.
- *New York Times Index.* A key, comprehensive index to all news events in the *New York Times;* a basic tool, good for almost any topic including books reviewed in the *New York Times Review of Books.*
- *PAIS (Public Affairs Information Services) International in Print.* In January 1991, the *PAIS Bulletin* merged with the *PAIS Foreign Language Index* to become *PAIS International.* It indexes some 1,300 periodicals of general interest as well as some books.
- *Readers' Guide to Periodical Literature.* Indexes some two hundred magazines and journals considered to contain articles of general (or "popular") interest: *Time, Newsweek, U.S. News and World Report, Jet, Good Housekeeping, Popular Mechanics,* and the like.
- *Social Sciences, Humanities, and General Sciences Indexes.* A family of indexes covering scholarly and professional journals on these subjects. (The *International Index,* published 1907–65, became the *Social Sciences and Humanities Index,* which split in 1974 into the *Social Sciences Index* and the *Humanities Index;* the *General Sciences Index* joined the family in 1978.)

Even if your library has an automated search capability for periodical articles, you still may want to look for some of these indexes. For example, the automated data base we searched in our sample earlier in this chapter included five of the indexes above. Yet, if our topic concerned language or literature, we'd still want to look at the *Annual Bibliography of English Language and Literature* and the *MLA International Bibliography.*

Other good sources of help are subject bibliographies. Whereas the indexes above are generally for an academic or business field, published bibliographies serve many more limited subjects, such as Vincent van Gogh, the Arab-Israeli wars, novels in early America, or the refugee problem. Consult an experienced librarian for help finding a bibliography for your particular subject.

Abstracts

Another kind of reference tool, an abstract, may help your research. An abstract summarizes the contents of a technical or scholarly article, and the summary is much longer than the brief comment you may find in a general index. In addition to summarizing the contents of the article, the abstract provides source information you'll need to find the work the abstract covers.

Hundreds of abstracts, such as *Biological Abstracts, Chemical Abstracts, Historical Abstracts,* and *Psychological Abstracts,* cover thousands of topics. Consider consulting collections of specialized abstracts for your field.

Remember that an abstract is not an article, but a summary only. Like a metal detector, it can tell you that something is there, but not how valuable it is. To use the article you must read it. As a general rule, don't cite abstracts in your parenthetical references or Works Cited listing. Go to the original.

ELECTRONIC SOURCES

Portable Electronic Sources

Portable electronic sources include CD-ROMs, diskettes, and magnetic tapes, with CD-ROMs certainly the most widely available of the three. These electronic sources may compile material also published in printed form, material with no printed counterpart, or a mixture of both. Because portable electronic sources are high-volume storage devices, each can include the equivalent of hundreds of books and articles. Finding what portable electronic sources your library has to offer will prove a valuable use of a few minutes of your time.

In addition, many CD-ROMs and diskettes are available for home use. Several multimedia encyclopedias are on CD-ROM, and most of these include links to online Internet data bases that update material on the CD-ROM or connect to online sources for expanded research. Other reference tools are available as well, including indexes to information on the Internet. Also on CD-ROM are collections of text, pictures, sound, and video on specialized topics. Some popular magazines such as *Time* and *National Geographic* are in CD-ROM collections that provide the type of historical archives otherwise available only from the publisher. Thus, a CD-ROM drive connected to your home computer can give you access to volumes of research material that a few years ago would not have been accessible even in a well-endowed library.

Online Electronic Sources

Online electronic sources also offer massive amounts of research data that any student conducting research a few years ago would have envied. Online electronic sources include information services and material accessible on the Internet. Like portable electronic sources, the online variety offer materials that have a printed counterpart as well as materials that have not appeared in print.

Your college library may have access to one or more of more than twenty online information services that offer full-text search and retrieval of articles from a wide variety of print sources. Among the leading systems are DIALOG, Data-Star, and NEXIS. DIALOG, for example, has hundreds of full-text data bases that provide access to thousands of sources, including magazine, journal, and newspaper articles; news wires; reference books (including many common and specialized indexes and abstract collections); newsletters; government documents; and conference papers and reports. Be sure to find out what information services your library makes available and what they contain.

Various information services are available online for home use: America Online, Prodigy, and CompuServe, for example. These offer online multimedia encyclopedias, news services, electronic magazines (E-zines), and, of course, connection to the Internet, the so-called "information superhighway." Connection to the Internet also is available from numerous Internet service providers.

The Internet offers a wide variety of information types. Many government agencies, military organizations, commercial businesses, private and international organizations, and colleges and universities have information files available online through various types of access: gopher and telnet searches, file transfer protocol (ftp) access, and World Wide Web access. Synchronous communication connections make possible electronic mail (E-mail), group discussions of topics through chat groups, and Usenet news group postings on thousands of subjects.

You can find some information about virtually any subject somewhere on the Internet. Does that mean that online sources make library research unnecessary? No, not by a long shot. No governing body controls Internet content to ensure that topics are covered thoroughly, nor is there even a comprehensive organizational scheme for the material available online. You might find anything you could ever want to know about one topic, but only bits and pieces of information for another. Moreover, access to some information sites is limited to persons or organizations that have been given passwords, while some other sites charge a fee for access. Most authorities today agree that for academic research the Internet is a valuable complement to library resources.

Searching the World Wide Web

The World Wide Web has hundreds of thousands of information sites, so how do you find what you want? The best way is to use one or more of several easily available indexes or search engines. Here are some of the most common ones, with their electronic addresses (Uniform Resource Locators, or URLs):

AltaVista <http://www.altavista.digital.com/>

Excite <http://www.excite.com/?x-a-b3>

Galaxy <http://galaxy.einet.net/search.html>

HotBot <http://www.hotbot.com/index.html>

InfoSeek <http://www.infoseek.com:80/home>

Lycos <http://www.lycos.com>

Magellan <http://magellan.mckinley.com>

OpenText <http://index.opentext.net>

ProFusion <http://www.designlab.ukans.edu/profusion/>

WebCrawler <http://www.webcrawler.com>

Yahoo! <http://www.yahoo.com>

What search engines and indexes find depends on what has been indexed into them, so the results will not be exactly the same with each search tool in response to the same instructions. You may want to use more than one of them.

What they find also depends on how you tell them to look. Many have both simple and advanced search capabilities. We've learned one thing about all of them: you need to take a few minutes to learn how they're set up for searches. Look for a file of useful information, a help file, search instructions, or a FAQ (frequently asked questions) file.

Learning a little about how a particular search tool works can save you a great deal of time in actually locating research material on the Web. The previous text box told you about data base searches and Boolean operators. Search engines also use these operators—but they sometimes have special rules that affect which ones you use as well as when and how you use them.

We can illustrate the importance of learning how search engines work with a simple tale about what happened to a friend of ours, a man in charge of the Internet program office for his organization. He spent an uncomfortable morning explaining to one of the senior executives in his organization why that executive couldn't find data he knew was available at his own organization's Web site. The executive had wanted some data about the SG-10 item in his organization's inventory, so he had instructed the search engine to find "SG-10." The response to the query pointed to information on other "SG" items, the SG-9, SG-12, and SG-15—but nothing for the SG-10. Our friend was puzzled until he reviewed the rules for querying the search engine. This particular search tool allowed for shortcuts in writing queries, with a minus sign representing the Boolean term "not." A hyphen and a minus sign are the same keyboard character. Thus, by typing "SG-10," the executive had actually asked for information on all SG items *except* the SG-10.

EVALUATING YOUR SOURCES

Some sources are more valuable than others. Understanding the differences between *primary sources* and *secondary sources* can help you evaluate the material you find and determine how to use it in supporting your own points.

Primary Sources

A primary source is an original source of basic facts or opinions on your subject: eyewitness accounts, official investigations, newspaper articles of the time. If you conduct original research—personal interviews, for example—the material you gather falls in the primary source category.

The following is an excerpt from page 443 of volume 1 of the *Personal Memoirs of U. S. Grant* (published by Charles L. Webster & Company of New York in 1885); here Ulysses S. Grant is explaining why he risked operations against Vicksburg without first setting up a protected logistics base:

> Marching across this country in the face of an enemy was impossible; navigating it proved equally impracticable. The strategical way according to the rule, therefore, would have been to go back to Memphis; establish that as a base of supplies; fortify it so that the storehouses could be held by a small garrison, and move from there along the line of railroad, repairing as we advanced, to the Yallabusha, or to Jackson, Mississippi. At this time the North had become very much discouraged. Many strong Union men believed that the war must prove a failure. The elections of 1862 had gone against the party which was for the prosecution of the war to save the Union if it took the last man and the last dollar. Voluntary enlistments had ceased throughout the greater part of the North, and the draft had been resorted to to fill up our ranks. It was my judgment at the time that to make a backward movement as long as that from Vicksburg to Memphis, would be interpreted, by many of those yet full of hope for the preservation of the Union, as a defeat, and that the draft would be resisted, desertions ensue and the power to capture and punish deserters lost. There was nothing left to be done but to *go forward to a decisive victory*. This was in my mind from the moment I took command in person at Young's Point.

If you're writing a paper about the Battle of Vicksburg, or perhaps about General Grant's strategic planning of Civil War campaigns, then Grant's own words showing his thoughts about the Vicksburg campaign are particularly important. Other writers might tell you what Grant probably was thinking, but Grant on Grant's thinking provides one of the best sources. Primary sources are not always easy to find, but they're worth looking for.

Secondary Sources

A secondary source is secondhand, removed at least one step from primary sources. It uses primary sources or other secondary sources as its basis. Thus a 1998 article about Grant's Vicksburg campaign would be a secondary source, drawing perhaps from Grant's *Memoirs* but also from the writing of other people who were at Vicksburg and from other books and articles analyzing the Vicksburg operations.

Compare these two lists:

Primary Source	Secondary Source
• The Panama Canal Treaty printed in the *Congressional Record*	• An article about the Panama Canal Treaty in *Time*
• Shakespeare's Sonnet 73	• A critical analysis of Shakespeare's sonnets
• The transcript of a trial	• An article in *Newsweek* about that trial
• An 1865 newspaper article about Lincoln's assassination	• A 1997 book about Lincoln's assassination

The distinction isn't always clear-cut. The last primary source might have been considered a secondary source in 1865, if the writer wasn't somehow connected to the assassination. Today we'd call it a primary source because a journalist in 1865 had greater opportunities for investigating true primary sources (such as eyewitnesses) and also could capture the feelings of the time.

Secondary sources select, filter, evaluate, and analyze material from primary sources (as well as other secondary sources). That is both their value and their weakness. Primary sources are more likely to provide "unfiltered truth," but primary sources generally lack the scope provided by secondary sources, which draw on multiple primary and secondary sources. That is, secondary sources are valuable because their writers already have done a lot of work for you, but at the same time you have to be cautious and guard against the biases of the writers who selected and filtered truth for you.

So which source type should you look for? Both. Try to find as many primary sources as you can. If you're writing about a topic for which witnesses are available near you, try to arrange an interview. And look into old newspaper files if they're available.

But look for secondary sources, too. Each type of source—primary and secondary—has its own strengths and weaknesses. And each type can help you evaluate the other. Details from primary sources can help you determine the validity of the conclusions in secondary sources; secondary sources, on the other hand, can help you understand the primary sources by telling you what to look for.

No matter what type of source you find, you need to decide whether it is *relevant* (of value for your treatment of your topic) and *reliable*.

Relevant Material

What you find about a potential source in a catalog, index, or abstract can suggest that a source will have information important for your thesis, but you'll have to get the work in hand before you can be sure.

In a book
- Review the table of contents.
- Skim the index.
- Read the preface, foreword, or author's introduction (if the book has these). Students often overlook prefaces, forewords, and introductions, but these can be valuable indicators of relevance. Frequently they discuss the range of material in a book and the author's intentions in writing it. Scope and intentions also can help you judge the source's reliability.

In an article
- Skim headings (if the article has them) and starts of paragraphs.

In an electronic source
- Examine what the source contains (a contents page or FAQ file, if one is present).
- Examine the organization of files or pages (another way to get an idea of contents).
- Review a "read me" file for a portable electronic source (if one is present).

And if the electronic source has a search tool, be sure to see how it works. Doing so may not help you judge relevancy, but understanding how to use the search tool can make the difference between whether you locate available relevant material or never actually find it. Also notice whether an electronic source contains links to other sources that cover the same topic. These links can provide connections from one site with relevant material to others with more of the same or similar material. Locating overlapping information has a lot to do with reliability, which we'll discuss next.

Reliable Material

You must always ask yourself, "Can I trust what I'm reading?" Just because something is printed or appears on screen doesn't make it so.

How do you know when to be suspicious? You always should be a little wary, but be especially so if the tone of a source—the personality an author projects—raises questions. Forewords and the like can be particularly important for evaluating an author's objectivity.

For example, consider the problem with sources about the battle of the Alamo, when a group of Texans stood up against a larger, better armed Mexican force. Most of us know stories about the battle and its heroes—and that's part of the problem with source reliability. The event is surrounded with numerous legends, a scarcity of eyewitness reports, self-serving accounts from some individuals associated with the event, and numerous secondary source evaluations that treat the people and related events from various perspectives.

In one book about the Alamo, for example, we find a foreword in which the book's author touts the noble motives of the Texans and the glory they deserve. In the foreword to another book we find an author commenting on the difficulty of gathering trustworthy material about the event. Do these forewords prove anything about the books? No, but we could be more comfortable at the outset about the objectivity of the author of the second book. Of course, we still would have to evaluate the reliability of the information as we read.

Date of publication can be helpful in evaluating the reliability of information. It's not as simple, though, as believing that newer sources are more reliable than older ones. But, for example, a book or article published shortly after the Soviet reactor failure at Chernobyl is less likely to be accurate about the long-term effects of that disaster than one written in 1998. (And one in 2050 will have a greater advantage on this same point.) So don't exclude older sources, but look for recent ones when the data you want is recent.

Reliability and the Internet

Be particularly on guard regarding information from the Internet.

Publishers of printed publications—books, journals, magazines, and newspapers—usually have editors or boards charged with attempting to verify the authenticity and accuracy of the material they publish. Most portable electronic sources are produced under the same controls. Do they ensure reliability? Not absolutely, of course. Some trade publications, for example, work on the edge of reliability, and we've all heard about the editorial practices of tabloid newspapers and magazines. Still, the existence of editorial standards among most publishing sources helps us somewhat with reliability.

But the Internet is quite different. You may recall that earlier we said the Internet has no governing body controlling content. Indeed, anyone who wants to pay the costs of supplying material for the Internet can do so. Material appearing in chat room discussions and posted on many Usenet news groups costs the originators little or nothing; they face virtually no barriers except good taste. (And the Internet offers numerous examples of poor taste in action!) Some discussion groups and Usenet news groups have moderators, which reduces the volume of undesirable material but does not necessarily increase reliability.

How can you know what to trust from the Internet? The Internet creates a situation of "user beware," so be alert! Look for sources—or ask for them in group discussions or news postings. And above all understand that the best test for reliability of a source comes from data in other sources.

As you widen your research, keep in mind that the best help in evaluating the reliability of any source, printed as well as electronic, comes from data in other sources. Look for overlapping information, and be skeptical about information that varies significantly from the norm. Exceptions could be extremely reliable and important, of course, but they merit careful examination.

EXERCISES

A. Answer the following questions about the materials available in your college library:

1. Is the catalog of books automated?

2. Does the library have automated access to one or more periodical indexes? To an index for newspaper articles?

3. Are reference tools available on CD-ROM? What about reference materials such as encyclopedias or collections of articles? List three CD-ROMs that look potentially useful for your research paper.

4. What online information services does your library provide? Can you get into the Internet from your library?

5. If you have Internet access where you live or in some college facility other than the library, can you access the automated data bases for books and periodicals in your library through the Internet?

B. On 26 February 1993, a large bomb went off in the parking garage of the World Trade Center in New York City. Two days later investigators got lucky and found a small piece of twisted, charred metal that quickly led to an arrest of a suspect in the bombing. *Time* magazine ran an article that discussed this piece of luck.

1. What is the title of the *Time* article?

2. What is the full date of the *Time* issue that includes the article?

3. On what page does the article begin?

4. How did investigators locate the suspect?

5. How did you go about finding this article?

C. Other magazines and journals also included articles about the bombing of the World Trade Center. Find three periodical articles about the event. With each article title, provide the name of the reference tool in which you found the article listed.

D. In December 1989, the *New York Times* reported that deposed Romanian (or Rumanian) leader Nicolae Ceauşescu had been held captive in a moving armored vehicle for several days prior to his trial and execution. Use library resources to answer the following:

1. How many days was he imprisoned in the moving armored car?

2. Who was held prisoner with him?

3. What issue of the *New York Times* carried the article?

4. In what section and on what page did the article appear?

5. What library reference tool did you use to answer these questions?

E. In September 1994, the United States sent a peacekeeping force into Haiti. Use library reference tools to do the following:

1. List three articles, each in a different periodical, on the subject. Use at least two different reference tools to find the articles. With each article title, provide the name of the reference tool in which you found the article listed.

2. List the name, date, and page number of a national newspaper article that treated the subject. Also name the reference tool in which you found the listing.

3. List the name, date, and page number of a local newspaper article that treated the subject. How did you find this article?

F. In 1989, *Defense and Foreign Affairs* published an article by Carleton A. Conant about Libyan chemical weapon developments.

1. What was the name of the article?

2. Which national government was alleging that the Libyans were developing a chemical weapon manufacturing capability?

3. In what issue did the article appear, and on what page?

4. What reference tool did you use to find the article?

G. If you have Internet access, locate the World Wide Web site for the U.S. Internal Revenue Service (IRS). Answer the following questions:

1. What is the URL for the IRS web site?

2. If you want to obtain a copy of Publication 17, *Your Federal Income Tax*, from the IRS Web site, what URL do you move to?

3. If you want to download a copy of Publication 17, the IRS offers it in five formats, one of which is pdf. What are the other four formats?

4. What is the file transfer protocol (ftp) URL to download Publication 17 in pdf format?

H. The URL for the Smithsonian Institution's home page is <http://www.si. edu/newstart.htm>. If you have Internet access, go to the Smithsonian's Web site to answer the following questions:

1. The Smithsonian Institution was started because of a bequest to the people of the United States in Englishman James Smithson's will. However, if Smithson's nephew had had heirs, the money would have gone to them instead. What is the name of the nephew of James Smithson who died without heirs, allowing the inheritance to go to the United States?

2. What mineral was named for James Smithson, and what is the mineral composed of?

3. In 1838, Richard Rush, formerly U.S. minister to Great Britain, physically brought Smithson's bequest to the United States in the form of eleven boxes of gold sovereigns. When this gold was melted and recoined into U.S. money, what was it worth?

CHAPTER 21
Taking and Organizing Notes

Let's review for a moment: When you prepare to write a long paper, first you settle on a general topic and then narrow it as much as you reasonably can. Your preliminary reading helps you focus the topic and at the same time reassures you that sources are available for you to draw on for support material. For example, let's say you're interested in those prehistoric people who left their homes on the Asian continent, found their way to the North and South American continents, and developed new lives here. You realize that *prehistoric Indians* is too large a topic, so you reduce it to *prehistoric Indians in North America*, to *the new way of life in America*. That, you decide, is still too broad, but it's a place to start with your preliminary reading. This preliminary exploration of the topic leads you to a new, interesting idea: Contrary to the popular belief you've heard for years that the prehistoric Indians wandered across North America struggling to survive, relatively recent evidence suggests that the prehistoric Indians adapted well and produced sophisticated cultures.

Using the computerized listings of books and periodicals from your library's reference section, you find that available sources appear adequate to support your research. You have in hand a list of sources that look promising. Now what? Here's where the work begins.

You obviously can't remember every fact or idea you find as you read those sources. You could keep all the books and magazines piled up around you and flip through them to find a bit of support when you need it, but that's the hard way. Most researchers develop some systematic way to organize their research reading. This organization is different from ordering ideas and support for writing your paper. The organization here involves keeping track of the research information you find as you work through your potential sources.

This chapter shows you two methods for noting specific ideas and facts and keeping them organized. The most commonly taught system for keeping track of research information involves taking notes on note cards. This system, which we'll call "the traditional system," has proved its value to thousands of researchers. The second system we'll call "the copying-machine system" because it relies heavily on a stack of coins and a copying machine. It offers a shortcut in the notetaking process by eliminating the need to write down notes.

THE TRADITIONAL SYSTEM

Both the traditional and the copying-machine systems involve keeping track of *two* kinds of information. The first kind is information about the sources you use; the second kind is the information you find in those sources.

The traditional system employs two sets of index cards—one set for each kind of information. Some researchers prefer two sizes of index cards (for example, three-by-five-inch cards for sources and four-by-six-inch or five-by-eight-inch cards for notes from the sources); others use the same size cards for both kinds of information. No matter what size of index cards you choose, here's the traditional notetaking process.

Bibliography Cards

For Books

Pick the most likely looking book and check the table of contents or index to see which parts of the book apply. (It's just not sensible to read the entire book if only Chapter 2 deals with prehistoric Native Americans.)

If the book has nothing useful, put it aside to return to the library as soon as you can. Someone else may need it.

When you find a book that has useful information, make out a *bibliography card*. Record only one book on each card and be careful to include all the necessary data about the book. Chapter 25, "Works Cited," explains in detail the information you'll need and shows the various formats for presenting that information for your final paper. For now, be sure your bibliography card mentions the following items that apply to the book you're recording:

- author(s) or group responsible
- title and subtitle of book (and volume title if part of a multivolume set)
- title of part of the book (if you're using only a piece of the book, such as an essay in a collection)
- translator(s)
- editor(s)
- edition. Don't worry about the number of "printings," but do note the edition if the book is other than the first edition.
- volume number and number of volumes in a multivolume set
- series (if the work is part of a series, such as "Studies in Anthropology, No. 5")

- place of publication (the first one listed if there are several)
- publisher
- date of publication (latest copyright date, not date of printing)
- inclusive page numbers of a part of the book (if you're using only a piece of the book, such as an essay in a collection)

You can save yourself time later by putting all the items in correct bibliographic format for your paper's Works Cited pages (Chapter 25 shows formats). Here's a sample bibliography card with the necessary information in the form required for its Works Cited entry:

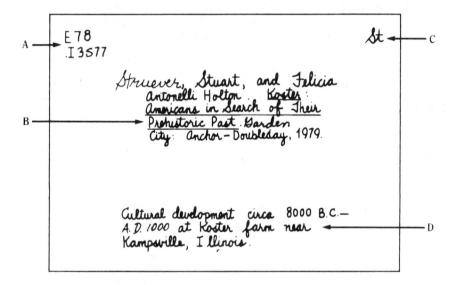

Note the following about the bibliography card:

A. Always include the *library call number* for books; it will save you time if you have to go back to recheck a quotation or find information you forgot to copy down.

B. Provide the Works Cited entry for the source.

C. Add your own *bibliography code*. We use the first two letters of the first author's last name. But you may use any consistent system—numbering, small letters, Roman numerals. The coding system will save you time as you take notes and as you write drafts of your paper.

D. *Optional.* As a reminder, add a brief note about what the book contains.

With your first bibliography card, you've begun to compile your paper's working bibliography. As you consult the books and articles you've found, prepare a separate card for each one.

For Articles in Periodicals

For magazines, journals, and newspapers, be sure your bibliography card has all the following items that apply to the article you're recording:

- author(s). Articles may be unsigned, and sometimes you'll find only initials for the author.
- title of article
- type of article (for letters to the editor and reviews)
- name of periodical
- series number (such as "old" or "new")
- newspaper edition (if the newspaper publishes more than one edition per day)
- volume and/or issue number(s)
- date of publication
- inclusive page numbers for the article

Also note whether the periodical is paginated continuously throughout a volume or independently by issue. For example, if issue 2 of a volume ends with page 563 and issue 3 of the same volume begins with page 564, the publication paginates continuously throughout a volume. If each issue starts with page 1, the issues are paginated independently. This distinction won't matter for your research, but it will help you decide which format to use when you write your entries for the Works Cited pages of your final paper.

For Portable Electronic Sources

Portable electronic sources include CD-ROMs, diskettes, and magnetic tapes, with CD-ROMs being the most commonly available. A portable electronic source may contain material already published in another form (in a book or periodical article, for example), material that has no printed counterpart, or a mixture. You'll need to keep track of not only bibliographic information about the individual portion or portions of the source you actually use, but also information about the portable electronic source itself. The sample Works Cited entries for these types of sources in Chapter 25 show what data you need to record about your sources. As with all other source types, getting the Works Cited format in final form as you record data could save you countless headaches later in the research paper process.

For Online Electronic Sources

Online electronic sources, such as articles from information services or information you glean from sites on the Internet's World Wide Web, cause particular documentation problems. If you plan to use online sources, we recommend strongly that you read about them in Chapter 25 before you begin compiling your sources and taking notes. If you wait until the last minute to see how to record these sources, you may find that you've failed to keep track of vital information. Moreover, because material online is changeable, you also may not be able to find later exactly what you find today!

In particular be aware that you need to record the electronic location—the Uniform Resource Locator (URL), E-mail address, or command path that gets you to the source online. In addition, because online material may change over time, be sure to register the date you access the information. We recommend that, whenever possible, you print a copy of online material you find that appears promising as source material for your research paper. *Indeed, some instructors may require that you be able to provide a printed copy of online source material if they need to review your sources.* Be sure to check with your instructor about this possible requirement.

For Other Source Types

Besides books, articles in periodicals, and portable or online electronic sources, your sources may include speeches; lectures; class handouts; reference works, such as encyclopedias or *Who's Who;* unpublished theses, dissertations, or letters; manuscripts or typescripts; interviews; maps or charts; cartoons; films, filmstrips, slide programs, or video recordings; radio or television programs; sound recordings; performances; musical compositions; art works; or legal records or documents. The bits of information you'll need to record now so you can document these varied sources later differ greatly from type to type. Check the Works Cited formats in Chapter 25 to see what data you need to keep track of. And, as with the other source types, understand that recording the source information in the proper Works Cited format during research ensures that you have the appropriate information you'll need when you finalize your research paper.

Note Cards

When you come across a fact or idea you think you can use, make a *note card.* Put only one fact or idea on each card. When you are ready to use the information for your draft, you can move the information more freely if you have only one idea on each card.

Now read the following passage from page 244 of the Struever and Holton book about the archaeological diggings at the Koster farm near Kampsville, Illinois. ("Horizon 11" is the designation for a level of human occupation dating to about 6400 B.C.)

> Traditionally, archaeologists have assumed that Archaic people went through a long, slow, gradual process in learning how to cope with their environment and how to extract a decent living from it. They thought it took the aborigines several thousand years, from Paleo-Indian times (circa 12000–8000 B.C.) to 2500 B.C., to learn about various foods in eastern North America and how to exploit them.

This is simply not true. The Koster people knew their food resources intimately and did a superb job of feeding their communities. During the occupation of Horizon 11, Early Archaic people had developed a highly selective exploitation pattern of subsistence. They were not just taking foods randomly from the landscape. Rather, they calculated how to provide the community with the most nutritious foods possible while expending the least effort. In addition to deer and smaller mammals, they ate large quantities of fish, freshwater mussels, and nuts. Fish and nuts—in addition to being available each year, and easy to take in large quantities—are highly complementary components of a nutritious diet. Nuts contain fat for high energy, which many freshwater fish lack. The kind of input-output analysis which was taking place was worthy of the most sophisticated culture.

Quotation Note Cards

Here's a sample note card for a *quotation* of an important portion of that passage:

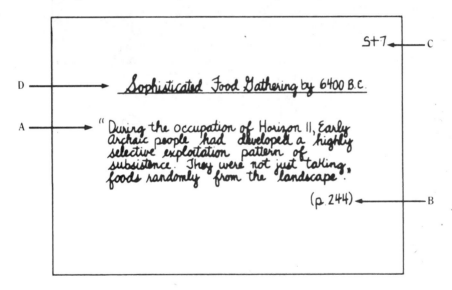

Include the following on a quotation note card:

A. Put *quotation marks* around quoted material.

B. Put the *page number* (here, p. 244) in parentheses. If you are using a book that is part of a multivolume set but doesn't have a separate title, include the volume number followed by the page number: (3:172).

C. The *code number* shows that this is the seventh card made from the Struever and Holton book. Using the bibliography code (St) from the bibliography card makes it unnecessary to put complete bibliographic information on each note card, and the number added (to make St7) provides a code that distinguishes this note card from others from the same book. In Chapter 22 we'll show you another way to use the code number. For now, keep all note cards from the same work together.

D. *Optional.* Use keyword headings that might help you later to arrange the facts and ideas and to make sure you have enough support.

Summary Note Cards

If you had *summarized* the entire passage, condensing the original material into a shorter version in your own words, the card would look like this:

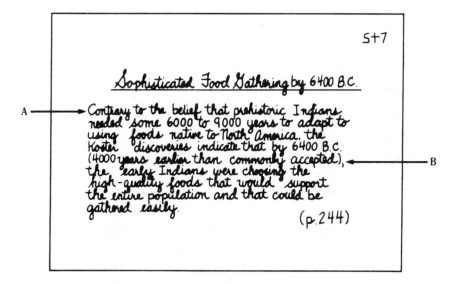

What's different about a summary note card?

A. *No quotation marks.* Of course, even though you don't borrow the exact words, you do borrow the idea, and you must give credit for it (more about this in Chapter 23).

B. *Your own words, but the author's ideas.* More important than reducing the length of the original, with a summary you mentally "process" the material, capturing the idea or facts and making yourself more knowledgeable about your topic. Notice that the comment in parentheses within the summary above is an *interpretation* of the evidence in the original, demonstrating that the writer of the note card has processed the passage.

Paraphrase Note Cards

A *paraphrase,* too, is a retelling of the original in your own words, but a paraphrase is different from a summary: the paraphrase tends to follow the sentence-by-sentence pattern of the original more closely and also is about the same length as the original. Use paraphrase note cards sparingly. If you're going to take notes that follow the original so closely, why not quote instead? Then you'll have the exact words in case you decide to quote all or part of the passage in your paper. Still, a paraphrase is useful when the original is technical or complex or when it isn't worded well—then the paraphrase can help simplify or "interpret" the original. If we paraphrase the two sentences quoted in the sample quotation note card on page 231, the paraphrase would look like this:

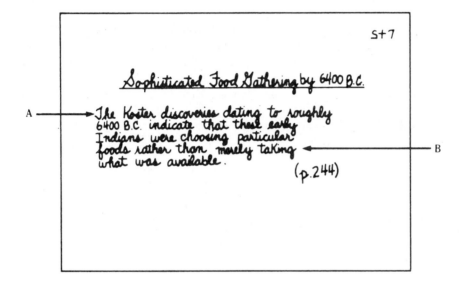

What distinguishes the paraphrase note card?

A. *Your own words,* so it uses no quotation marks. Of course, a paraphrase (or a summary) could include *some* exact words from the original, and those words would go in quotation marks. Yet, the paraphrase as a whole is not a quotation. Even so, it is a borrowing and you must give credit for it (more on that in Chapter 23).

B. *An interpretation of the original,* especially complex or technical wording. "During the occupation of Horizon 11" has become "dating roughly to 6400 B.C.," and "highly selective exploitation pattern of subsistence" has been simplified to "choosing particular foods."

Plagiarism

Research papers use borrowed material, but academic integrity requires that the writer of the paper properly credit the borrowing. Failure to credit your sources is dishonest, a form of cheating called *plagiarism.* Plagiarism is presenting someone else's words or ideas as if they were your own. The word *plagiarism* comes from the Latin for "kidnapping," which raises an interesting comparison. If you plagiarize—by failing to give proper credit for material you take from your sources—you're performing an act of "academic kidnapping," and your act will be scorned and punished if you are caught.

On the other hand, borrowing material is perfectly acceptable because you give credit for words and ideas to the original writer. In fact, one mark of accomplished writers is their ability to integrate borrowed material smoothly into their own writing—to introduce the borrowed material, to incorporate the borrowing into the flow of their ideas, and to give proper credit when and where it is due. Never, however, would accomplished writers present the borrowings as if they were their own.

Students who intend to steal material from others and present it as if it were their own generally know exactly what they're doing. But what about the majority who have no intention of cheating? Can they plagiarize? Well, they certainly can create circumstances that appear to prove wrongdoing; that is, extreme clumsiness at presenting borrowed material can look exactly like intentional cheating.

So how—exactly—can you avoid being accused of wrongdoing? Here are the errors you want to avoid:

- Presenting someone else's idea but not documenting it (so the idea seems to be yours).
- Presenting someone else's words without documenting them (so they seem to be part of your writing).
- Quoting someone else's words—perhaps even documenting them—but failing to use quotation marks to identify what is borrowed (making the words seem to be your own).

If you're careful to keep track of your sources' words and ideas when you take notes, and if you're also careful when you work the material into your paper, you're not likely to be guilty of any of those errors.

Most of the problems with taking notes come with paraphrases and summaries. If you're putting the original into your own words and you want to retain wording from the original, you must use quotation marks. What if a student writes something like this?

> For many years archaeologists have assumed that the prehistoric Indians needed several thousand years to discover how to exploit the various foods in eastern North America, but the Koster Indians had learned to be highly selective in their food choices rather than just taking foods randomly from the landscape (Struever and Holton 244).

This looks like a paraphrase or summary, right? It looks like one, but it's an unacknowledged, loose quotation. The writer has borrowed key words when he seems to be borrowing only ideas. Even giving the source credit through the parenthetical documentation at the end of the passage doesn't solve the problem. With the necessary quotation marks, the passage would look like this:

For many years "archaeologists have assumed" that the prehistoric Indians needed "several thousand years" to discover "how to exploit" the "various foods in eastern North America," but the Koster Indians had learned to be "highly selective" in their food choices rather than "just taking foods randomly from the landscape" (Struever and Holton 244).

Of course, that passage looks peculiar. No thought has been given to choosing portions of the original for a quotation—rather, the use of key words from the original appears to be accidental.

You can mix quotation with summary and paraphrase, but be selective in the quotation part. And keep this rule in mind: *Whenever you use another author's words, put them in quotation marks.* Failure to do so is dishonest.

Electronic Notetaking

When you take notes from electronic sources—an online article or a CD-ROM, for example—the medium provides a shortcut. Most computerized sources allow you to take notes directly into your own data file. You can summarize or paraphrase as you read, or you can copy directly from the original into your electronic notes. For quoting, copying electronically from the original means you can get the material down exactly as written without risk of misquoting.

But wait! This shortcut also provides a quick trip to plagiarism unless you're careful!

When you copy material from the original directly into your own data file, nothing automatically puts quotation marks around what you borrowed. You have to remember to take care of that step. Make it your practice to always mark the direct borrowings with quotation marks as you copy them. Failure to do so as you copy the material electronically could lead to serious problems later.

THE COPY-MACHINE SYSTEM

As you can see, the traditional system requires considerable writing, and that can slow you down, interrupting your train of thought during research. The copy-machine system offers an alternative.

- Use a copy machine to make a copy when you find a portion of a book or an article that looks worthwhile.
- Write the complete bibliographic information on the copy (just as you would on a bibliography card in the traditional system).
- Use a *highlighting* pen to mark anything you want to be able to refer to later (the equivalent of writing down quotations in the traditional sys-

tem). Please do not highlight material in library copies of books and periodicals.

WHICH SYSTEM SHOULD YOU USE?

The traditional system takes time but offers two distinct advantages:

- As you take notes, you are actively involved with the material, so you will understand it better than if you had only glanced through it.
- Note cards offer flexibility: you can rearrange them to match your outline or even place them in the rough draft to save time during the writing stage.

At the same time, though, the traditional system can be tedious. Nevertheless, for many researchers the benefits of the painstaking process outweigh the cost.

For others, the pain of notetaking outweighs the benefits. If you are one of these, consider the copy-machine system. You won't be able to shuffle note cards. Moreover, you'll still have to spend time processing the material you've highlighted on the copies—turning the original material from your sources into quotations, summaries, and paraphrases to integrate with your own writing. However, you'll do that processing as you write the draft of your paper, so you'll choose the form for presentation to fit your needs as you write. That offers flexibility not possible with the traditional system.

Choose the system that fits your personality. Either system can work well. What won't work is having no system at all: random reading combined with mistaken confidence in your ability to remember details from research when the time comes to write your paper.

EXERCISES

A. The passage below is from page 46 of *The First Americans*. The passage concerns the gradual transition in the American Southwest from nomadic to settled life among prehistoric Native Americans. The book was written by the editors of Time-Life Books. It was published in 1992 by Time-Life Books of Alexandria, Virginia. Its library call number is E61.F56 1992.

   Working the land was not necessarily any easier or healthier than the ancient nomadic regime had been. Indeed, during peak seasons the early farmers of the Southwest, wielding wooden implements, probably had to labor two or three times as many hours as they would have if they had been subsisting by means of hunting and gathering, and the resulting diet was no more nutritious. The combined pressures of increasing population and dwindling wild resources, however, left the region's inhabitants little choice but to devote more energy to agriculture. And gradually, Indians working the fields devised ways of maximizing the harvest and preserving it for longer periods of time, thus affording growing communities a modicum of security.

1. Make a bibliography card for the book.

2. Select a significant point from the passage and prepare a note card that quotes directly from it.

3. Prepare a second note card that paraphrases the lines you quoted in Exercise A2.

4. Prepare a note card that summarizes the entire passage; use no more than two sentences of your own words for the summary.

5. A final check.

   • Did you put a bibliography code on the bibliography card?
   • Did you use that code on the note cards?
   • Is the library call number on the bibliography card?
   • Did you use quotation marks where needed?

B. In the periodicals in the library you find an article in *MHQ: The Quarterly Journal of Military History* about the prisoner-of-war camps in the North that held Confederates during the American Civil War. *MHQ* is a quarterly journal that paginates each issue independently. The article, by Philip Burnham, is titled "The Andersonvilles of the North." It appears on pages 46 to 55 of the autumn 1997 issue of *MHQ;* this issue is volume 10, number 1, of the journal. The following passage is from page 46:

New York's prisoner-of-war camp—nicknamed "Helmira"—was only the most infamous of dozens of Northern prisons where hunger, exposure, brutality, and disease were everyday hazards. Yet Elmira remains something of a military secret, while the 30,000 Union soldiers who perished in places like Georgia's Andersonville Prison and Libby Prison in Richmond are the stuff of national legend. The numbers belie such a discrepancy. Some 26,000 rebels died in what was called "Yankee captivity"—six times the number of Confederate dead listed for the battle of Gettysburg; twice that for the dead of Antietam, Chickamauga, Chancellorsville, Seven Days, Shiloh, and Second Manassas combined.

1. Make a bibliography card for the article.

2. Select a significant point from the passage and prepare a note card that quotes directly from it.

3. Prepare a second note card that paraphrases the lines you quoted in Exercise B2.

4. Prepare a note card that summarizes the entire passage; use no more than two sentences of your own words for the summary.

5. A final check.

   • Did you put a bibliography code on the bibliography card?
   • Did you use that code on the note cards?
   • Did you use quotation marks where needed?

Chapter 22
Organizing Your Thoughts and Support

In the previous chapter we discussed organizing your research material so that you know which supporting ideas and facts are from which sources. Now we need to look at organization in a different way—this time ordering ideas and their support so that you can write your paper.

Outlining

Of course, you don't need to wait until you've finished taking notes to begin organizing that new knowledge. You'll do well to develop an outline early and revise and expand it as you learn more. A working outline helps you discover gaps in your support that suggest areas for continued research. In other words, you need to work back and forth between notetaking and outlining—each influences the other.

A Working Outline

How do you begin organizing support material? By thinking. Jot down the *key* ideas you've discovered about your topic—just the key words. Now look for patterns:

- Do certain ideas seem to fall logically into clusters? Look for points that fit into groups with other points.
- Do you see a pattern of thought that relates those clusters of ideas to each other? Would chronological order work? How about cause and effect or one of the other patterns of development you studied in Part 4?

Once you recognize the basic arrangement that will work to bring order to the ideas and supporting facts for your topic, fill in a simple working outline such as the following:

Basic Working Outline

Introduction—working thesis
I.   First major topic:
   A. Support idea:
   B. Support idea:
   C. Support idea:
II. Second major topic:
   A. Support idea:
   B. Support idea:
   C. Support idea:
III. Third major topic:
   A. Support idea:
   B. Support idea:
   C. Support idea:
Conclusion—restated working thesis

Does the working outline form look familiar? It should. It's the same basic pattern you've been working with from the beginning of this book, expanded to handle more ideas than you needed for shorter papers. Of course, you may not need exactly three major topics with three support ideas for each. This is just a model.

An outline reduces a large quantity of information to its bare skeleton—just the main ideas and key support. It's a tool to show logically and clearly the relationships among the main points of your paper.

As you conduct your research, the working outline can help you see gaps in your support. Moreover, trying to fit the pieces together as you go along can help you discover new areas you may want to examine—new directions for your research.

A Final Outline

When you've worked out fully the major ideas, supporting ideas, *and* specific support for your paper, you'll have its complete skeletal organization. That skeleton provides the framework for your writing. It ensures that you follow a logical structure as you write.

Outline Numbering and Lettering Scheme

I.
II.
   A.
   B.

```
    1.
    2.
       a)
       b)
          (1)
          (2)
             (a)
             (b)
III.
```

- If you have a *I*, there should be a *II*; if you have an *A*, there should be a *B*; and so on.
- Outlines rarely should go beyond the fourth level—the *a* and *b*.

The final outline you prepare to guide your writing could be a topic outline or a sentence outline. A *topic outline* lists key points as ideas but does not show complete thoughts. Each entry begins with a capital letter, but the entry has no punctuation at the end since it isn't a complete sentence.

Partial Topic Outline

Here's a topic outline for the first major idea of the sample research paper in Chapter 19:

I. Grant's strategy
    A. Scott's Anaconda Plan preceded Grant
        1. Emphasis on territory—naval blockade, opening Mississippi, and capturing Richmond
        2. By 1864, blockade and open Mississippi, but Richmond not taken and Confederate armies in field
    B. Grant's strategy added to Scott's in 1864
        1. Objection to Confederate's ability to reinforce across theaters because Union operations uncoordinated
        2. Emphasis on destroying armies through coordinated converging operations
    C. Five armies in Grant's plan
        1. Banks against Mobile to prevent reinforcement of Johnston
        2. Sherman against Johnston
        3. Meade, with Grant, against Lee
        4. Butler against Richmond to prevent reinforcement of Lee
        5. Siegel in Shenandoah Valley to prevent reinforcement of Lee
    D. Only Sherman and Meade parts successful
        1. Banks bogged down in Louisiana, allowing reinforcement of Johnston

2. Butler pinned to Bermuda Hundred, allowing reinforcement of Lee
3. Siegel defeated at New Market, allowing reinforcement of Lee
4. No reinforcement between Johnston and Lee

The key points of a topic outline are adequate for someone familiar with the material summarized in the topic entries. Thus, a topic outline can work well as a guide for writing. It may be all you need to prepare before you begin writing the first draft of your research paper.

However, because the entries in the topic outline don't provide complete thoughts, the outline usually doesn't communicate well to anyone besides the person who wrote it. In particular, the unity and coherence of the points within the topic blocks may not be obvious in a topic outline.

For this reason, many instructors require their students to submit sentence outlines for their research papers—either before writing a draft or with the final paper. A sentence outline more clearly demonstrates the links among points within the outline—so unity and coherence become more clear. As a practical matter, the sentence outline is the outline type that someone besides the writer—such as an instructor—can read and understand.

In a *sentence outline,* each entry begins with a capital letter and ends with the punctuation appropriate for the sentence. Following is the sentence outline for the sample research paper in Chapter 19. It's formatted to be handed in with the research paper; for that reason its pagination begins with the page number following the Works Cited page of the sample paper. If your instructor wants the outline to come at the beginning, use the same format but change the page numbers to lowercase Roman numerals (i, ii, etc.—*Henderson i,* for example).

Henderson 14

Thesis: Grant had reason to imagine that an assault on the morning of 3 June 1864 might prove successful, though errors in timing, lack of planning, and poor execution brought disaster instead.

I. Examination of the strategy Grant was pursuing contributes to an understanding of what he hoped to achieve in the assault.
   A. The Union military strategy prior to Grant's becoming general-in-chief was General Winfield Scott's Anaconda Plan.
      1. That plan required a naval blockade, opening the Mississippi River, and capturing Richmond—emphasizing territory.
      2. By 1864 there was an adequate blockade and the Mississippi was open, but Richmond had not been taken and the Confederacy had large armies in the field.
   B. Grant added his own military strategy to the Anaconda Plan when he became general-in-chief in 1864.
      1. Grant objected to the Confederates' ability to reinforce armies because Union operations were uncoordinated between theaters.
      2. Grant wanted coordinated converging operations among theaters—emphasizing destroying Southern armies in the field.
   C. Grant's strategic plan involved five Union armies.
      1. General Banks was to threaten Mobile to prevent reinforcement of General Johnston.
      2. General Sherman was to destroy General Johnston's army.
      3. General Meade and the Army of the Potomac, accompanied by Grant, were to destroy General Lee's Army of Northern Virginia.
      4. General Butler was to threaten Richmond from the east, preventing reinforcement of General Lee.
      5. General Siegel was to operate in the Shenandoah Valley, preventing reinforcement of General Lee.

Henderson 15

D. Only the Sherman and Meade parts of Grant's strategy
   worked.
   1. Banks bogged down in Louisiana, allowing reinforce-
      ment of Johnston.
   2. Butler was pinned down in the Bermuda Hundred,
      allowing reinforcement of Lee.
   3. Siegel was defeated at New Market, allowing rein-
      forcement of Lee.
   4. Grant's strategy still worked because Johnston and Lee
      could not reinforce each other.
II. Examination of how far Grant would push warfare also con-
    tributes to an understanding of why Grant ordered the 3 June
    1864 assault.
    A. Technology changed lethal aspects of combat for the
       American Civil War.
       1. Rifled muskets and rifled artillery were more lethal at
          longer ranges, making Napoleonic tactics obsolete.
       2. Soldiers learned to entrench for protection.
       3. Effective offensive tactics against entrenchments were
          not developed until late in World War I.
       4. Grant expected his armies to sustain heavy losses.
       5. Grant learned after Shiloh that "complete conquest"
          rather than a single decisive battle would be required
          for the Union to win the war.
       6. Grant added destroying the South's resource base to his
          emphasis on destroying armies in the field—an order he
          added to Sherman's instructions in early 1864.
    B. Grant expected his campaign to destroy Lee's Army of
       Northern Virginia to result in heavy losses for the Army of
       the Potomac.
       1. Grant felt that the Army of the Potomac lacked "self-
          confidence" because of too great a focus on failure.
       2. Grant accepted severe losses as a necessity of the
          upcoming campaign, which would require continuous
          pounding of Lee's army.
       3. By Cold Harbor, Lee's soldiers knew Grant's intent was
          to hammer them until their army was worn away.

Henderson 16

III. The progress of the Wilderness Campaign set up the 3 June 1864 assault.
   A. Grant's and Meade's problem was to cross the Northern Virginia rivers and pull Lee out of his defenses into an open battle the Union could win.
      1. Going around Lee's left flank would have provided better terrain.
      2. Going to the left, around Lee's right flank, became the campaign pattern because of protection of the Union's supply lines and proximity to Butler's forces east of Richmond.
   B. The Battle of the Wilderness resulted in 2:1 Union-to-Confederate losses through fighting Grant had hoped to avoid.
   C. The Battle of Spotsylvania Court House resulted in greater losses but offered hope of successfully breaching Confederate entrenchments.
      1. Spotsylvania Court House was critical geographically for threatening Lee's supply lines, which could have forced Lee into battle.
      2. Although the Confederates built the most formidable entrenchments to date, the Union army tried offensive tactics that seemed to offer promise of success.
      3. Losses at Spotsylvania remained at 2:1, Union-to-Confederate, a pattern for the Wilderness Campaign, because the Union had to assault entrenchments.
   D. North Anna and crossing the Pamunkey consumed maneuvering space.
      1. Lee's entrenchments at North Anna were so strong and well positioned that Grant chose not to assault them.
      2. Lee told General Early that the South had either to destroy Grant's army or be caught in a siege in Richmond, which Lee could not win.
   E. Cold Harbor became the last critical point before both sides had to accept a siege of Richmond.
      1. Lee saw that a corps reinforcing Grant could outflank him at Cold Harbor.

Henderson 17

    2. The Union held Cold Harbor at first and attacked Lee's unfinished trenches successfully on 1 June, opening an opportunity for a major assault on 2 June.

IV. Timing errors, lack of planning, and poor execution of the 3 June assault brought heavy Union losses rapidly.

    A. The Union army was 24 hours late getting prepared to assault because of delays in moving one corps and an ammunition shortage in another.

    B. The 24-hour delay allowed Lee's army to build truly deadly defenses that did not appear overwhelming.

    C. Meade formed no overall assault plan and corps-level reconnaissance was not performed.

    D. As a result, the three corps attacked on different approaches, allowing both frontal fire and crossfires to rip the Union lines apart.

V. Grant's ordering of the assault was based on geography plus his mode of operating throughout the Wilderness Campaign.

    A. Because he could not get Lee to fight in the open, attacking temporary field entrenchments was Grant's only option, with Cold Harbor the last place for such an attack before the siege of Richmond.

    B. Grant's mode of operating in the Wilderness Campaign was to hammer Lee's army, and Cold Harbor was no different than other battles.

    C. Besides, no one at the time knew any better way to assault entrenchments, because technology had created a situation for which adequate tactics had not been developed.

    D. Grant's expression of regret about the 3 June 1864 assault was not because of the heavy losses themselves, but because they brought no Union advantage.

Conclusion: Having noted that the 3 June assault temporarily benefited the Confederates and having accepted the blame, Grant dealt with the crisis by focusing on the upcoming operations to besiege Richmond and to cut off Lee's supplies.

Outlining and the Computer

Computer programs can be a big help with outlining. With some programs, in fact, the outline on the computer serves as a direct step toward establishing headings within the paper that you write on the computer.

Several computer programs are designed primarily to assist with organizing thinking. Their output, as you might expect, is an outline. These programs are intended to assist with brainstorming and to convert the disorganized results of brainstorming into the organized pattern of an outline. The programs allow rapid clustering of points and easy movement of blocks of material among the various subordination levels that make up the outline.

Some of the programs permit users to "hide" (save in a hidden mode) notes, paragraphs, and even graphics under an entry in the outline. With this type of capability you can write a rough version of a piece of your paper as you think about it, while you're organizing your material. You then tuck it away behind its outline point. As you write your paper, you reveal the hidden text and incorporate it into your draft.

Many computer word processing programs have some of these same features for outlining. They have built-in formats that set up the standard letter–number system of an outline, and they allow you to move material easily from one level of subordination to another within the outline. If the word processing program operates with a split-screen or multiwindow mode, you can review the outline on screen as you write the paper's draft in another part of the screen. Some word processing programs even are set up to convert parts of an outline into particular levels of headings in the text of a document.

HEADINGS FOR LARGE PAPERS

Just as the points in an outline guide you through the research paper, headings—which equate to major points in an outline for a paper—guide readers through the material they read. In Chapter 10 we showed you a good way to make headings—using initial capital letters and starting on the left margin. But because research papers can get fairly long, you may need more than one type of heading (to show more levels of subordination). Here are two types we suggest:

TWO HEADING STYLES

xxxxxxxx xxxxx xxxxxxxxx xxxx xxxxxxxx xxxx xxxxx xxxxxx
xxxxx xxxx xxxxxxxxx xxxx xxxxxxx

THIS IS A MAJOR HEADING

XXXXXXXX XXXXX XXXXXXXXX XXXX XXXXXXXX XXXXXXXX XXXXX XXXXX
XXXX XXXXXXXXX XXXX

This Is a Minor Heading

XXXXXXXX XXXXX XXXXXXXXX XXXX XXXXXXXX XXXX XXXXXXXXXX XXXXX
XXXX XXXXXXXXX XXXX

This Is Another Minor Heading

XXXXXXXX XXXXX XXXXXXXXX XXXX XXXXXXXX XXXX XXXXX XXX XXXXX
XXXX XXXXXXXXX XXXX XXXXXXXXXX

THIS IS ANOTHER MAJOR HEADING

XXXXXXXX XXXXX XXXXXXXXX XXXX XXXXXXXX XXXXXXXX XXXXX XXXXX
XXXX XXXXXXXXX XXXX

If you have a computer, you can get much fancier, of course. In fact, you could have headings in different sizes and typefaces:

HEADINGS USING A COMPUTER

XXX XXXXXXXX XXXXX XXXXXXXXX XXXX XXXXXXXX XXXX XXXXX XXXXX
XXXX XXXXXXXXX XXXX XXXXXXXXX XXXXX

THIS IS A MAJOR HEADING

XXX XXXXXXXX XXXXX XXXXXXXXX XXXX XXXXXXXX XXXX XXXXX XXXXX
XXXX XXXXXXXXX XXXX XXXXXXXXX XXXXX

This Is a Minor Heading

XXX XXXXXXXX XXXXX XXXXXXXXX XXXX XXXXXXXX XXXX XXXXX XXXXX
XXXX XXXXXXXXX XXXX XXXXXXXXX XXXXX

This Is Another Minor Heading

XXX XXXXXXXX XXXXX XXXXXXXXX XXXX XXXXXXXX XXXX XXXXX XXXXX
XXXX XXXXXXXXX XXXX XXXXXXXXX XXXXX

THIS IS ANOTHER MAJOR HEADING

xxx xxxxxxxx xxxxx xxxxxxxxx xxxx xxxxxxxx xxxx xxxxxx xxxxx xxxx xxxxxxxxx xxxx xxxxxxxxxx xxxxxx

---

Whichever way you make headings, be sure the major heading stands out more on the page than the minor heading does.

A Practical Point about Outlines and Headings

Outlines rarely need to go beyond four levels of subordination, and headings shouldn't go even that far. Levels of headings equate to outline levels, of course, but you have to be wary of the complexity you try to portray with levels of headings. For assignments the length of a research paper, two levels of headings will work well.

Even writers of books only occasionally go beyond two levels of headings. (You can find third- and even a few fourth-level headings in Chapter 25 of this book, for example, because the complex material there is easier to follow with the extra heading levels.)

Why not provide headings to match every item in an outline? Writing with excessive headings appears choppy. Moreover, readers become confused when writers try to portray three and four levels of subordination throughout a document.

A smart writer, then, uses headings to highlight important points of a paper's organization—but only the most important points.

A TIME-SAVER IN WRITING

Once you've prepared an outline, you're ready to assemble your detailed support. Arrange your notes (note cards or highlighted photocopy pages, depending on the research system you chose) to follow your outline. Use the floor, your desktop, your bed, whatever you need to spread the notes out so you can see how they fill out the outline's skeleton.

Don't let your outline keep you from moving notes around. That outline is not engraved in bronze; you can alter it as you need to. But laying out your notes will help you see where the outline may be incomplete or where you need more information. You may have more notes than you can use. Don't throw any away; you may find a place for them later.

When you are satisfied with the outline and its support, start writing. You may begin at the beginning with an introduction, then move on to the first major topic, then the second, and so on. Many writers do it this way, and it may work for you. Another choice is to start with the first major topic, go on to the next topics, and finish writing with the conclusion—and then the introduction. Many other writers do it this way.

The reason is simple: Frequently you're not sure what you're going to say until you've said it. You actually discover that you think as you write because the ideas take over and lead you to new discoveries. If you have already written the introduction, you may find it has little relationship to what you finally say.

Regardless of where you start writing, you'll have to use some of your notes. If you're quoting and if you've used the traditional system with note cards, here's a trick that can save you some work: In writing your draft, when you come to a place for a quotation, don't copy it again. Just paper-clip or tape the quotation note card in place or leave room in your draft and write in the code number for the note card (remember the code number *St7* we used on page 231). Doing this will save you writing and will keep the quotations accurate, no matter how many drafts you go through.

A caution: This trick isn't intended for use with summaries and paraphrases; those notes already are in your own words, and you should be weaving the ideas and facts into the fabric of your writing in the paper's draft.

Working those quotations, summaries, and paraphrases of the material you borrow from your sources into your writing is one of the skills you need to develop for writing a research paper. We'll discuss skillful use of borrowed material in the next chapter.

ABSTRACT

Many teachers of English and other academic subjects require students to submit an abstract with the final paper. An abstract is a brief summary of a piece of writing. Clearly, then, you should not try to write the abstract for your paper until you've finished writing the paper itself. Even though you write it last, the abstract normally appears at the beginning of a paper, like an executive summary, between the title page and the body of the paper. This type of summary is intended to tell readers what they'll find in the paper itself, letting them judge whether they need to read the full paper. (Your instructor, of course, will read your research paper regardless of the quality of the abstract you write.)

You may be asked to write either a descriptive or an informative abstract. Descriptive abstracts are common in library reference tools, but informative abstracts are preferable when the abstract accompanies the paper itself.

Descriptive Abstract

A descriptive abstract tells readers what is covered in the study. It resembles a narrative form of a table of contents or topic outline: *it reveals topics but not what they mean.* We still have to read the report to find out what the author has to say about the subject—what conclusions the writer comes to. A descriptive abstract, then, usually is useful only for alerting readers that the report contains topics of interest to them. Here's a descriptive abstract of a research paper about minimum competency testing in American schools:

> This report discusses the effects of minimum competency examinations on the education of students who are subject to the tests. It examines the social and educational causes for adoption of minimum competency testing. Next it discusses the problems for education that the tests themselves generate. Finally, it looks at the overall long-term effects of the testing on students who undergo the education and testing programs.

Informative Abstract

This kind of abstract—the one we recommend—is more useful and complete. An informative abstract does more than merely name the topics in a report: *it tells the key ideas, summarizes basic facts, and reports major conclusions or decisions.* Because it summarizes the report, an informative abstract can serve as an executive summary at the beginning of a study. Compare the above descriptive abstract to the following informative abstract for the same research paper:

> Minimum competency tests are of questionable value for students; they hold at risk the quality of education of all students—not just those who fail one or more times—making them hostages to the testing system. The tests were a response to a need for simple measures of quality to restore public confidence in American education. What resulted were standardized examinations of development of minimal skills—primarily in reading, writing, and mathematics—that were linked to serious consequences. Unfortunately, the tests lead to three major drawbacks in education: class time lost to coaching, narrowing or trivialization in the curriculum, and deflection of the curriculum away from areas of value. Thus, even though minimum competency test scores have increased, these improvements are a natural result of the high stakes connected to the tests. With the tests defining both curriculum content and teacher success or failure, true education is at risk, even though no evidence connects the tests to success in life.

The informative abstract corresponds closely to the sentence outline for the same research paper. Both abstracts highlight the major points of a research paper, though in different ways. A hint: Pay attention to your sentence outline as you structure your informative abstract.

EXERCISE

Reexamine the full-sentence outline on page 243–46. Notice also the partial topic outline on page 241–42 for the first major block of the same paper. Using the format on the next page, finish the topic outline for the sample research paper. We've supplied the major headings from the sample paper as the Roman-numeral-level entries in the outline.

II. Grant's frame of mind

   A.

      1.

      2.

      3.

      4.

      5.

      6.

   B.

      1.

      2.

      3.

III. Progress of the Wilderness Campaign

   A.

      1.

      2.

   B.

   C.

      1.

      2.

      3.

   D.

      1.

      2.

   E.

      1.

      2.

IV. 3 June at Cold Harbor

   A.

   B.

   C.

   D.

V. "I have always regretted . . ."

   A.

   B.

   C.

   D.

CHAPTER 23

Using Borrowed Material in Your Paper

Skilled use of borrowed material is one mark of an accomplished writer. You can't expect just to sprinkle it on the paper in the hope it will magically create an argument for you. Good arguments with borrowed material to support them don't just happen; they come from careful work. To make sure your borrowed material helps your argument, you must consider two key questions: whether to quote or not, and from what to quote. Answers to these questions are closely related and depend on the paper you're writing.

CHOOSING THE TYPE OF PRESENTATION

In Chapter 21 you studied three types of note cards: quotations, paraphrases, and summaries. Let's consider now why you might prefer to use one of those types of presentation of borrowed material rather than the others.

Writers have three basic reasons for choosing to quote from a source:

- A passage is worded particularly well, providing facts or opinions phrased effectively.
- A passage is written so clearly that paraphrasing or summarizing would provide a poor substitute.
- A passage provides the words of an authority (not necessarily someone famous, just someone in a position to know).

Paraphrases restate original source material in your own words. You interpret the technical or complex wording, but you retain the flow of the thought from the source. Thus, choose a paraphrase when the way a source presents an argument works well but the words themselves need adjustment for your purposes.

Summaries extract information from sources. They capture facts and opinions from the original but use neither the original words nor the original thought pattern. Choose a summary when you want only the data from a source.

We also can evaluate the three presentation types in relation to the two types of source material we discussed in Chapter 20—primary and secondary sources.

Because a primary source is the origin of facts or opinions on your subject, material from it is likely to fit one or more of the criteria for quoting. For example, the excerpt from Grant's writing about the Vicksburg campaign (page 219) provides clear, effective wording. More important, it provides the words of an authority on Grant's thinking at the time of the campaign. If you were examining the successes and failures of military planners at Vicksburg, for instance, you'd be more likely to quote Grant than to paraphrase or summarize the passage.

Secondary sources select, filter, and analyze material from primary and other secondary sources. Therefore, the material itself already is pointed toward summaries. Material in secondary sources sometimes meets a criterion for quoting. As a general rule, though, you'll find fewer reasons to quote from secondary sources and more reasons to summarize or paraphrase. By no means is that an absolute rule, however.

But whether you use primary or secondary sources, whether you quote or summarize or paraphrase, you must follow three steps to use borrowed material effectively:

- *Introduce* the borrowed material.
- *Present* it.
- *Credit* the source.

INTRODUCING BORROWED MATERIAL

Perhaps the most neglected step in using borrowed material is the first one—introducing it. In this step you mention the author or title of the source before presenting the material, to signal to your readers that you are beginning the borrowed material. Here are some sample introductions:

As Grant explained in his *Memoirs* . . .

According to the press secretary, the president decided that . . .

Reverend Jackson was right when he said . . .

In his essay "Here's HUD in Your Eye," Larry McMurtry reveals . . .

The variety of introductions is almost endless, but all of them identify your source, often helping your readers judge whether the source you're citing is reputable. Without an introduction, the borrowed material seems just spliced in; look for such an example in the following paragraph:

Washington's victory at Yorktown was precarious almost up to the moment of the British surrender. What really defeated the British was the inability of Lord Cornwallis to move his forces away from Yorktown. "The secret of the British failure there was either the ministry's neglect in immediately securing absolute naval supremacy on this coast . . . or the over-confidence or carelessness of the admirals in command. It is the British naval administration that is to be charged with the Yorktown catastrophe" (Johnston 101). The British under Cornwallis were occupying Yorktown because it was the best available naval station, and retreat by sea would have been possible had not the French fleet kept the British fleet away from the battle area.

Readers will recognize where the borrowing begins and ends because of the quotation marks, but they will wonder who Johnston is and where the quotation comes from. Annoying, isn't it? Don't annoy your readers; don't even leave them slightly frustrated from wondering about who said what. Introduce the material:

Washington's victory at Yorktown was precarious almost up to the moment of the British surrender. What really defeated the British was the inability of Lord Cornwallis to move his forces away from Yorktown. In *The Yorktown Campaign and the Surrender of Cornwallis,* historian Henry P. Johnston blames the British navy: "The secret of the British failure there was either the ministry's neglect in immediately securing absolute naval supremacy on this coast . . . or the over-confidence or carelessness of the admirals in command. It is the British naval administration that is to be charged with the Yorktown catastrophe" (101). The British under Cornwallis were occupying Yorktown because it was the best available naval station, and retreat by sea would have been possible had not the French fleet kept the British fleet away from the battle area.

This tells readers who wrote what you've quoted and where you found it. The parenthetical documentation reference, used in conjunction with the research paper's Works Cited list, gives all the information interested readers need to find the source reference if they desire to look for it.

An introduction is even more important for a summary or paraphrase than it is for a direct quotation. Quotation marks show where a quotation begins and ends. But where does the paraphrase begin here?

Washington's victory at Yorktown was precarious almost up to the moment of the British surrender. What really defeated the British was the inability of Lord Cornwallis to move his forces away from Yorktown. The British failed because the navy did not control the sea off the American coast or because the British admirals blundered. The British navy should be blamed for the Yorktown defeat (Johnston 101). The British under Cornwallis were occupying Yorktown because it was the best available naval station, and retreat by sea would have been possible had not the French fleet kept the British fleet away from the battle area.

How many of the ideas come from Johnston's book? Does the paraphrase begin at the first word of the paragraph, or is it only the sentence ending with the parenthetical documentation reference? Who knows? When you introduce the paraphrase, everyone will know:

> Washington's victory at Yorktown was precarious almost up to the moment of the British surrender. What really defeated the British was the inability of Lord Cornwallis to move his forces away from Yorktown. In *The Yorktown Campaign and the Surrender of Cornwallis,* historian Henry P. Johnston asserts that the British failed because the navy did not control the sea off the American coast or because the British admirals blundered. The British navy should be blamed for the Yorktown defeat (101). The British under Cornwallis were occupying Yorktown because it was the best available naval station, and retreat by sea would have been possible had not the French fleet kept the British fleet away from the battle area.

With that simple introduction readers know where the paraphrasing begins. Be sure to introduce your summaries as well.

PRESENTING BORROWED MATERIAL

Paraphrases and summaries, no matter what their length, should be fully integrated with your own writing. Introduce them when appropriate, of course, and always credit the source, usually with a parenthetical reference, as we'll discuss later, but no special formatting is required for the presentation. Quotations require special presentation techniques.

Presenting Prose Quotations in Your Final Paper

Format a short prose quotation—*four or fewer lines of typing in your paper*—in the following way:

- Type the quotation along with your own writing, without special indentation or spacing.
- Use double quotation marks (" ") to enclose your source's exact words and punctuation; if the quoted material itself includes quotation marks, use single quotation marks (' ') to enclose the interior quotation.
- Place a parenthetical reference, if required, after the quoted material and closing quotation mark but before the punctuation mark, if any, that ends the sentence, clause, or phrase with the material the reference documents. ("Placement in Text," in Chapter 24, provides a thorough explanation about placing parenthetical references in the text of your paper.)

Format a long prose quotation—*more than four lines of typing*—in a paper with double-spaced text as follows:

- Begin the quotation on a new line.
- Double space before, within, and after the quotation.
- Do *not* use quotation marks for the quotation; however, if the quoted material itself includes quotation marks, use double quotation marks (" ") to enclose that interior quotation.
- Indent the entire block quotation one inch from the left margin, but retain the normal right margin. If you quote all or part of one paragraph, show no extra paragraph indentation. However, if you quote two or more paragraphs, show each paragraph opening as an additional one-fourth-inch indentation in your block quotation. If you begin within a paragraph, do not use an extra indentation for the first line of the block quotation.
- For the parenthetical reference, if required, skip one space after the punctuation that ends the quotation, provide the parenthetical reference, and put no punctuation after the closing parenthesis of the reference.

Here's a sample showing double-spaced text followed by a long prose quotation:

> In his novel *Santa Evita,* which freely mixes historical fact and fiction, Thomás Eloy Martínez comments on the literary aspects of history and historical sources:
>
> > For historians and biographers, sources are always a headache. They are not self-sufficient. If a dubious source wants to enjoy the right to appear in print, it must be confirmed by another and that one in turn by a third. The chain is often endless and often useless, since all the sources taken together may add up to a lie. . . . Why does history have to be a story told by sensible people and not the delirious raving of losers . . . ? If history—as appears to be the case—is just another literary genre, why take away from it the imagination, the foolishness, the indiscretion, the exaggeration, and the defeat that are the raw material without which literature is inconceivable? (126, 129)

Notice that the block indentation of the long quotation substitutes for quotation marks. The indentation indicates that you are quoting.

Remember, like a short quotation, the long one needs an introduction, too. In fact, the introduction to a long quotation often tells readers what you expect them to notice about it, thus giving them the right perspective. In the introduction to the passage from *Santa Evita,* we told you that you would read the novelist's comment about "the literary aspects of history and historical sources."

Presenting Quotations from Poetry and Drama

Poetry. If your quotation is all or part of a *single line of poetry*, include it in your standard body text with quotation marks, just as you would prose. If you quote *two or three lines of poetry*, you still can include the material within your standard body text with a slash (/) to mark the division between lines of the poem:

> In the infamous "mud march," General Ambrose Burnside moved the Army of the Potomac back and forth along the north bank of the Rappahannock River for three days in icy rain and mud. After this hopeless attempt to find a new way around General Lee's army, Confederate soldiers enjoyed a rhyme at Burnside's expense: "Burnside, Burnside, whither doth thou wander? / Up stream, down stream, like a crazy gander."

Block indent *poetry of more than three lines* one inch from the left margin of your paper. Do not use quotation marks; as with quoting prose, the block indentation substitutes for a set of quotation marks. Begin each line of the poem on a new line, double-spacing between lines. If a line of poetry is too long to fit within your margins, wrap the extra material to another line and indent it an extra one-fourth inch. If the poem uses peculiar spacing, try to reproduce the special presentation as accurately as possible. The next-to-last paragraph of the sample research paper in Chapter 19 illustrates a block-indented six-line poem (page 199).

Drama. If you quote from one speech of a single character, present it as you would prose (or poetry for a verse drama). However, if you need to present dialogue for two or more characters, use a block indentation. One inch from your paper's left margin, all in capital letters, give the speaker's name, followed by a period. Then begin his or her speech, wrapping lines as necessary but indenting all lines after the first one an additional one-fourth inch. Present each additional character's speech in the same way, beginning on a new line, of course, for each character.

> Alfred Hitchcock took the name of one of his movies from a revealing comment that Hamlet makes about the focused nature of his madness:

HAMLET: You are welcome. But my uncle-father and aunt-mother are
      deceived.
GUILDENSTERN: In what, my dear lord?
HAMLET: I am but mad north-northwest. When the wind is southerly, I know
      a hawk from a handsaw. (2.2.393-97)

SOME FINE POINTS IN QUOTING

Be careful to quote accurately. If you need to alter a quotation, there are special techniques to show the alteration.

Omitting Words

Sometimes you'll want to omit words from something you're quoting because they're irrelevant or awkward out of their original context. In addition, you may need to alter a passage so that the edited passage fits into the grammar and sense of your own writing. The device you use to show an omission is an ellipsis (. . .)—three spaced periods with a space at the beginning and the end.

When you quote only a sentence fragment, a word or phrase, you don't need to show that material has been left out before or after the quotation; the cutting is obvious. However, when the quotation you have edited appears to be a complete sentence (or complete line of poetry), use the ellipsis to show that you've modified the original, no matter how minor the change. Of course, it's *never* acceptable to edit the original so that you change its meaning (for example, by leaving out *not* or *never*); omissions are acceptable only as a convenience to trim unnecessary words or to fit the quotation into the pattern of your writing.

When the omission occurs *inside a sentence (or line of poetry)*, the remainder will look like this:

"Fish and nuts . . . are highly complementary components of a nutritious diet."

If the omission occurs at the *end of a sentence,* use four spaced periods without a space in front of the first period (a period for the sentence plus the ellipsis):

"The Koster people knew their food resources intimately. . . . They were not just taking foods randomly from the landscape."

An ellipsis at the end of a sentence can represent an omission of the end of that sentence, one or more sentences, or one or more paragraphs. At the end of a line of poetry, it would indicate omission of one or more lines of poetry.

Except for a block-indented quotation, if an omission at the end of a sentence precedes a parenthetical documentation reference, show the ellipsis before the ending quotation mark and parentheses and provide the sentence punctuation after:

> "The Koster people knew their food resources intimately . . ." (Struever and Holton 244).

Notice that there is a space between *intimately* and the ellipsis but not between the ellipsis and the ending quotation mark. If that same sentence ended a block-indented quotation (which would not have quotation marks), it would look like this:

> The Koster people knew their food resources intimately. . . . (Struever and Holton 244)

Now there is no space after *intimately*, but there is a space between the final period and the opening parenthesis of the parenthetical reference.

Within a block-indented quotation of poetry, show the omission of a line or more of the poem with one line of spaced periods that is about the length of a normal line of the poem.

Adding Words

If you need to add an explanation within a quotation so that the quotation will make sense in the context of your writing, use square brackets to separate your words from those you're quoting:

> "During the occupation of Horizon 11 [circa 6400 B.C.], Early Archaic people had developed a highly selective exploitation pattern of subsistence."

Don't use parentheses instead of square brackets. If your typewriter can't make brackets, draw them neatly by hand, using black ink or pencil.

Adding Emphasis

You can emphasize a portion of a quotation by underlining (or italicizing) it. However, to ensure that readers can tell who added the emphasis, provide an explanation at the end of the quotation if the emphasis is yours (no explanation is required if the emphasis is part of the original):

> "The kind of input-output analysis which was taking place was *worthy of the most sophisticated culture*" (emphasis added).

Verifying Quotation Accuracy

If you find an error, or material that may seem to be peculiar, in the quotation you want to use, add "sic" to the quotation—in square brackets if inside the quotation or in parentheses if outside. The word *sic* (Latin for "thus") tells readers you have rendered the quotation faithfully:

> "When the Imperial Air Forces of Japan attacked Pearl Harbor on 7 December 1940 [sic], they demonstrated how vulnerable ships were to surprise air attack."

Altering Capitalization

If you alter the case of the initial word in a quotation, show the change in square brackets. For example, Struever and Holton actually wrote this about the long-held assumptions of archaeologists:

> "They thought it took the aborigines several thousand years . . . to learn about various foods in eastern North America and how to exploit them."

If you choose to begin your quotation and a sentence with the third word (*it*), you'll have to alter the case of that word:

> "[I]t took the aborigines several thousand years . . . to learn about various foods in eastern North America and how to exploit them"—so scientists insisted for many years before recent discoveries proved otherwise.

Of course, recasting the sentence would allow you to retain the original lower-case *it* and avoid introducing the brackets.

However, altering case is most likely to come up *within* a quotation after an ellipsis:

> According to Struever and Holton, the Koster people "calculated how to provide the community with the most nutritious foods possible. . . . [T]hey ate large quantities of fish, freshwater mussels, and nuts."

Altering Final Punctuation

Within a quotation, punctuation must appear as in the original, unless properly modified through use of an ellipsis or an addition in square brackets. Final punctuation, however, will depend on how you integrate the quotation into your own writing. This quotation ends in a period:

> "They were not just taking foods randomly from the landscape."

However, you might change that period to a comma if the quotation became an internal clause in your writing:

> "They were not just taking foods randomly from the landscape," according to authorities Stuart Struever and Felicia Holton.

CREDITING YOUR SOURCE

Whenever you use borrowed material, the third step also is essential: crediting your source. You must identify the printed or spoken source of your information.

Failure to credit your source is dishonest. In Chapter 21 we discussed plagiarism—presenting someone else's words or ideas as if they were your own—in the context of notetaking. Certainly unintentional plagiarism can begin with a failure to keep track of ideas and especially words from your original sources. But plagiarism occurs if you fail to document the words or ideas of others when you use them in your writing. So to avoid plagiarism, you need to understand the mechanics of documentation.

Together, the next two chapters cover documentation. Chapter 24 explains the parenthetical documentation references that you'll place in the text of your research paper. Chapter 25 tells you how to prepare the Works Cited pages, the list of sources for your paper. In combination these in-text references and the Works Cited list make up the parenthetical documentation system.

EXERCISES

A. In volume 2 of his memoirs (*Personal Memoirs of U. S. Grant,* published by Charles L. Webster & Company of New York in 1885), Ulysses S. Grant describes fears in the North about Sherman's army being cut off during its famous march to the sea from Atlanta and Grant's assurances to President Lincoln:

> The Southern papers in commenting upon Sherman's movements pictured him as in the most deplorable condition: stating that his men were starving, that they were demoralized and wandering about almost without object, aiming only to reach the sea coast and get under the protection of our navy. These papers got to the North and had more or less effect upon the minds of the people, causing much distress to all loyal persons—particularly to those who had husbands, sons or brothers with Sherman. Mr. Lincoln seeing these accounts, had a letter written asking me if I could give him anything that he could say to the loyal people that would comfort them. I told him there was not the slightest occasion for alarm; that with 60,000 such men as Sherman had with him, such a commanding officer as he was could not be cut off in the open country. He might possibly be prevented from reaching the point he had started out to reach, but he would get through somewhere and would finally get to his chosen destination: and even if worst came to worst he could return North. I heard afterwards of Mr. Lincoln's saying, to those who would inquire of him as to what he thought about the safety of Sherman's army, that Sherman was all right: "Grant says they are safe with such a general, and that if

they cannot get out where they want to, they can crawl back by the hole they went in at."

1. Does this material represent primary or secondary source material?

2. What would be the advantages or disadvantages of quoting part or all of this material in a research paper about Sherman's march to the sea?

3. Quote at least two sentences from Grant and provide an introduction for the quotation. Be sure to quote accurately; if you alter the original material in any way, use the techniques demonstrated in this chapter to show the alteration. Use (2:366–67) for the parenthetical documentation reference if your introduction contains the name of the author or (Grant 2:366–67) if it doesn't.

B. "Amazons," an article by Adrienne Mayor and Josiah Ober, originally appeared in *MHQ: The Quarterly Journal of Military History* and is one of the articles collected in *Experience of War*, edited by Robert Cowley (New York: Norton, 1992). In the following two paragraphs, Mayor and Ober discuss the possible historical foundation for the Amazons in Greek myths. Page 22 ends with "warlike," while page 23 begins with "nomadic."

What about the Amazons of Greek myth? Must they, too, be seen only as symbolic figures of psychological projection? Until quite recently, most serious historians would have had to answer yes. Yet in the 1950s large-scale Soviet archaeological excavations in the Steppes of the southern Ukraine—exactly where early versions of Amazon legends located the women's homeland—began to uncover remarkable tombs of Sarmatian warriors—warlike, nomadic horsepeople who traded with the ancient Greeks. And the archaeologists found that 20 percent of the fourth-century B.C. graves that contain weapons and armor belonged to women.

Typically, the young women's skeletons are surrounded by large iron lances; brightly painted wooden quivers and bows, and many triple-barbed bronze arrowheads; iron knives, daggers, swords, and spears; metal-plated leather armor; and horse trappings. Clear evidence of battle wounds—severe head injuries, bronze arrowheads embedded in bone—show that Sarmatian women were indeed warriors.

1. Does this passage represent primary or secondary source material?

2. Would you be more likely to quote, summarize, or paraphrase material from this passage in a research paper about Greek mythology?

3. Write a short paragraph of your own in which you summarize or paraphrase material from this passage. Be sure to introduce the

borrowing. For the parenthetical documentation reference, use (22–23), (22), or (23) if your introduction contains the names of the authors; use (Mayor and Ober 22–23), (Mayor and Ober 22), or (Mayor and Ober 23) if it doesn't.

C. In *Red, Hot & Blue: A Smithsonian Salute to the American Musical* (Washington: Smithsonian, 1996), Amy Henderson and Dwight Blocker Bowers reveal some interesting background about the original conception for *West Side Story.* The following is from page 184:

> After *Bells Are Ringing,* Jerome Robbins and Oliver Smith reunited with Bernstein in the landmark 1957 *West Side Story.* This show was the culmination of an idea that had been percolating since January 1949, when Robbins had called Bernstein to suggest that they refashion *Romeo and Juliet* and set it in New York's East Side slums at the time of celebrations for Easter and Passover; in this version, originally called *East Side Story,* the family antagonisms posed against one another were Jewish and Catholic. But both Robbins and Bernstein would be too involved in other projects to focus on this show for years—Robbins, with establishing himself as one of Broadway's leading director-choreographers in such productions as Irving Berlin's *Call Me Madam* (1950) and Rodgers and Hammerstein's *The King and I* (1951); and Bernstein, who aside from conducting, teaching at Brandeis, and riveting audiences with his *Omnibus* telecasts, composed *Trouble in Tahiti* (1952) and *Candide* (1956).
>
> By the time Robbins and Bernstein rekindled the idea of their modern *Romeo* in 1955, the demographics of New York had changed enough to make the Jewish-Catholic antipodes outdated. Now, the newspapers were full of stories about juvenile delinquency and Puerto Rican–Anglo gang warfare on the West Side, and it was decided to refocus on what became *West Side Story.*

1. Does this passage represent primary or secondary source material?

2. Would you be more likely to quote, summarize, or paraphrase material from this passage in a research paper about Leonard Bernstein's theater work?

3. Write a short passage of your own in which you include material from the passage from *Red, Hot & Blue.* Be sure to introduce the borrowing. For the parenthetical reference, use (184) if your introduction names the book's authors or (Henderson and Blocker 184) if it doesn't.

CHAPTER 24

Parenthetical Documentation

Whether you use quotations, paraphrases, or summaries, you must document the sources of your information. In Part 3 you learned a preliminary documentation system that let readers know whenever you were using outside sources for support. This chapter introduces a better system, one that not only tells readers that you are using borrowed material, but also gives them enough information to find the source.

The formats for documentation in this chapter and the next generally follow the fourth edition of the *MLA Handbook for Writers of Research Papers,* published by the Modern Language Association of America. This handbook is an accepted standard for documentation in many academic fields, especially the humanities. Other style guides also exist, of course, and you will notice differences in specific entry and presentation formats from one manual to another. We've chosen to follow MLA on most points because the guidance is thorough, reasonable, and widely accepted.

Differences Among Documentation Style Manuals

Don't be too concerned about these differences. Most of them exist to accommodate the varied needs of differing academic fields. More important, however, most documentation guides differ little on what should go into a specific documentation entry for an article or book. In practical terms, then, if you learn one system well—the one in this book, for example—you can adapt easily to the particular style in another place at another time. You'll know basically what should be included in documentation entries by anybody's standard, so you'll be able to see quickly the peculiarities of any other system you're required to follow.

PARENTHETICAL DOCUMENTATION SYSTEM

The parenthetical documentation system depends on the interaction of material you place in two portions of your research paper:

- *General source listing.* At the end of your research paper you provide an alphabetized listing, called Works Cited, with full publication information about each source document you used. The list provides a general reference to your sources but, of course, doesn't identify the specific portions you used for the quotations, summaries, and paraphrases in the body of the paper.

- *Specific portion reference.* Within the body of your paper, along with each presentation of material borrowed from your sources, you include in parentheses a documentation reference to the specific portion(s) of the source or sources supporting your text. This parenthetical information provides a reference to the data in the Works Cited listing so readers can connect the general and specific documentation portions.

Interaction of References in Text and Works Cited

When readers combine the information in parentheses in the body of your paper with the full publication information in your Works Cited listing, they have the data they need to locate each source and to find the specific portion you used.

Let's say this is a portion of your paper:

In the Indian pottery canteen, form and function came together. Art historians have noted the usefulness of the canteen's shape and the way it was fired. The shape of the canteen allowed it to be carried by a rider on a horse. Because of the way the pottery was fired, it was somewhat porous; as a result, the action of water seeping through to the outside, where it evaporated, cooled and sweetened the water remaining in the canteen (Clark and Ingram 47).

The *specific portion reference* is *(Clark and Ingram 47).*

- *Clark and Ingram* tells readers to look for an entry in the Works Cited listing with those names.
- The *47* indicates that the information came from that specific portion of the work.

In the Works Cited pages—the *general source listing*—readers would find this entry, alphabetized under *Clark:*

Clark, Karen, and Fred Ingram. *Acoma Canteens and Other Pottery Designs.* Washington: Steinman, 1996.

Clearly, then, you want to learn the conventions for both the general source and specific reference portions of the parenthetical documentation system. The next chapter focuses on format conventions for the Works Cited listing (the general source portion of the parenthetical documentation). The rest of this chapter treats the specific portion references that give the system its name: the parenthetical references.

PARENTHETICAL REFERENCES

Basic Content

Parenthetical references in the text of your paper should give your readers the following information:

- *A reference to the opening of the corresponding entry in the Works Cited list.* If the Works Cited entry shows only one author, you'll give that author's last name. The reference also could be two or three last names, one person's name with "et al.," the name of a group, a shortened version of the title, or a name with the title, depending in every case on what information is necessary to identify clearly the *one* work in Works Cited that you are referring to. ("Basic Forms" below details the various possibilities.)
- *Identification of the location within that work of the material you're documenting.* Normally this will be a reference to a single page or several pages. However, when your Works Cited listing gives a multivolume work, the parenthetical reference will require a volume number with the page(s). If the reference is to a one-page article, to an article in an encyclopedia that alphabetizes its articles, or to a source that has no pagination (such as a film or videocassette), there will be no place reference.

Basic Forms

The material required for the parenthetical reference varies somewhat with the nature of the work you refer to from your Works Cited list and how much of it you are citing. (For rules on showing inclusive page numbers, see page 306.)

Work with One Name Listed

When the Works Cited listing begins with only one person's name, use the last name and the page reference: (Brown 281) or (Brown 281–83). If the name has a qualifier such as "ed." or "trans.," you still use only the last name.

Work with Two or Three Names Listed

If the Works Cited entry opens with two or three names, include those names in the parenthetical reference: (Wesson and Jones 117) or (Stockton, Avery, and Beal 63).

Work with One Name and "et al."

If the Works Cited entry begins with a name and "et al.," which means "and others," include the "et al." in your parenthetical reference: (Steinnem et al. 92–93).

Work with Group as Author

Treat the group just like another author: (President's Commission on Energy 315). A reference such as this, of course, could easily interrupt a reader's train of thought; we'll discuss later how to avoid that problem by streamlining the parenthetical references.

Work Listed by Title

If the Works Cited entry begins with a title, use the title, or a reasonable shortened version of it, in the parenthetical reference. Be careful in shortening the title, though, because readers must find the words you give in an alphabetized list; make sure the shortened title includes the word by which the work is alphabetized in your Works Cited listing. A reference to *A Short Study of Linguistics for Beginners* might look like this: (*Short Study of Linguistics* 53). Again, streamlining might be preferable.

Multivolume Work

In reference to a multivolume work, normally you'll give a volume number with the page reference: (Martin 2:65–66). This is a reference to pages 65 to 66 of volume 2 of a multivolume work alphabetized in Works Cited under "Martin." However, if the entry in Works Cited clearly identifies only a single volume of the multivolume work, then the parenthetical reference need not include the volume number.

Multiple Works Listed for the Same Name(s)

When two or more works are alphabetized in Works Cited for the same name(s), include in the parenthetical reference the title, or a shortened version of it, of the specific work you're referring to. If two books are listed for Brian Pierce, a reference to one of them would look like this: (Pierce, *Amateur Golfing* 27). Here's another candidate for streamlining.

Citing an Entire Work

If you need to document a textual reference to an entire work, a page reference is inappropriate, so the parentheses would contain only the author element: (Brown). Streamlining, however, will eliminate the need for any parenthetical reference.

Work with Numbered Paragraphs

A few sources, primarily electronic ones, have numbered paragraphs rather than numbered pages. If your parenthetical reference refers to such a source, begin with the author's name, follow it with a comma, the abbreviation *par.* or *pars.* (for "paragraph" or "paragraphs"), and the appropriate paragraph number(s): (Wilton, par. 27) or (Wilton, pars. 27–29).

Indirect Reference

Although you always should attempt to find the original source for a quotation, sometimes you'll have to quote information from a source that includes the original. If you quote or paraphrase a quotation, add "qtd. in" (for "quoted in") or "paraphrased from" to the parenthetical reference, as here:

> John Harris calls literary critic Edmund Wilson a "pompous, close-minded reader" for his insistence that detective fiction is not worth reading (qtd. in Armstrong 13).

Shouldn't the indirect quotation here have both double and single quotation marks to indicate that we are quoting already quoted material? That depends on the source from which we borrow the material. If the exact words we borrow are within a direct quotation in our source, our presentation should include both types of quotation marks. If our source shows no quotation marks, our borrowing, as here, will have only double quotation marks.

Multiple Works in a Reference

To include two or more works in a single parenthetical reference, list each as you would for itself and use semicolons to separate them: (Jackson 53–54; Morgan 15). Again, streamlining may help reduce the interruption, but if you need to show a long, disruptive list, consider using an actual footnote instead (see the section "Notes with Parenthetical Documentation" below).

Verse Plays, Poetry, and the Bible

For verse plays, use the play's title, or a reasonable shortened form of it, followed by act and scene or by act, scene, and verse—with the parts of the play separated by periods: (*Othello* 4.2) or (*Othello* 4.2.3–4).

For poetry, again use the poem's title, or a reasonable shortened form of it, followed by the line numbers for a poem without divisions or by portions separated by periods for a long poem with major divisions: ("Coming Home" 10–12) or (*Iliad* 9.7–12).

For the Bible, use the book title followed by chapter and verse (with a period separating chapter and verse): (John 3.16). Notice that books of the Bible, like the Bible itself, require neither italics (underlining) nor quotation marks.

Streamlining Parenthetical References

Several times we've mentioned the possibility of streamlining. The idea is to keep the information within the parentheses as short as possible so readers are not distracted. You accomplish this by giving part or all of the needed reference in the introduction to the borrowed material. If the introduction includes the name of a book's author, the parentheses might contain only the page reference.

> Brown notes General Grant's occasional impatience with the progress of the Wilderness Campaign in 1864 (280).

Because Brown's name is in the introduction to the material from his book, the parenthetical reference needs only the page reference.

Especially in the case where your Works Cited list has several works by the same author and you must refer to one of those works, streamlining lessens the interruption of the parenthetical reference. Without streamlining, a reference might look like this:

> Although the Battle of the Crater, for which Union coal miners tunneled under the Confederate fortification lines near Petersburg, captures our imagination today, it has been labeled a bloody tactical blunder because of the cost in lives (Winchester, *Civil War After Gettysburg* 314).

The version below streamlines that long parenthetical reference:

> Although the Battle of the Crater, for which Union coal miners tunneled under the Confederate fortification lines near Petersburg, captures our imagination today, in *The Civil War After Gettysburg* Winchester labels it a bloody tactical blunder because of the cost in lives (314).

Keep in mind that streamlining does not permit omission of required material, but it can reduce the interruption of parenthetical references.

Placement in Text

Place the parenthetical references in the text of your paper so that they interrupt the flow of thought as little as possible. Put the parentheses as close as reasonably possible after the end of the material you're documenting, but always at the end of a clause or phrase so the reference doesn't intrude. Normally, the parenthetical reference can be placed at the end of a sentence. Even with quotations, the reference doesn't have to come *immediately* after the quotation marks:

> Brown asserts that General Grant's "inability to remain patient with the pace of the Wilderness Campaign" led to unnecessarily high Union losses throughout this bloody phase of the Civil War (280).

Of course, don't delay the parenthetical reference until the end of a sentence if readers could be confused about what material the reference documents:

> Although Brown notes Grant's occasional impatience with the progress of the Wilderness Campaign (280), the overall strategy of attrition—Grant against Lee's Army of Northern Virginia and Sherman against the Southern homeland supply base—led to eventual Union victory.

The reference here is in the middle of the sentence because only the first portion is attributable to the source. Note, however, that the parentheses do come at the end of the opening clause so the reference intrudes as little as possible.

Position Relative to Sentence Punctuation

Notice that the parenthetical reference in the first of the two samples above preceded the period at the end of the sentence, and the parentheses in the second sample came before the comma that ended the clause. Place your parenthetical reference before the punctuation mark, if any, that ends the sentence, clause, or phrase with the material you're documenting. If a quotation ends the sentence, clause, or phrase, normally you'll place the parenthetical reference between the ending quotation marks and the punctuation for the sentence, clause, or phrase:

> Heavy Union losses in early 1864 can be attributed to General Grant's "inability to remain patient with the pace of the Wilderness Campaign" (Brown 280).

The exception to this placement guidance is for a long quotation — one that is set off from the left margin of the rest of the paper with a block indentation. For this type of quotation, skip a space after the ending punctuation, provide the parenthetical reference, and put no punctuation after the closing parenthesis of the reference. You can see a sample of this technique in the illustration for presenting a long quotation on page 257.

Notes with Parenthetical Documentation

Parenthetical references will take care of almost all documentation references, but they don't accommodate digressions from the text. Avoid long side arguments, but if you must add notes to support your text, use standard foot-note or endnote entries: That is, use parenthetical references for your normal documentation, but also use notes for the explanatory digressions, such as this:

> [1]Smithson disagrees with Brown about the cause of the Union losses during Grant's Wilderness Campaign (226) but offers little support. See also Winchester 271; Souther 416–18; and Blake 76.

If you use many notes of this type, we recommend collecting them as end-notes at the end of your paper. In that case, you would include a page titled "Notes" between the body of your research paper and the Works Cited pages.

The alternative—particularly important if you have only a few such notes—is to include each as a footnote at the bottom of the page on which its in-text reference number falls. In this case, separate the footnote(s) from the body text by a short line (the equivalent of 20 spaces long) near the bottom of the page, as in this sample:

last line of body text of the page on which footnote reference 1 occurs.

———————

[1]Smithson disagrees with Brown about the cause of the Union losses during Grant's Wilderness Campaign (226) but offers little support. See also Winchester 271; Souther 416–18; and Blake 76.

EXERCISES

A. Given the Works Cited entries below as the general source listing of a research paper, write parenthetical references to show the specific portion references required for the numbered exercise items that follow. (Just show the parentheses and what would go in them. Don't be concerned in this exercise with placing the references into textual passages.)

Backus, Susan B. *The Siegeworks of Petersburg.* New York: Shirlington, 1993. Vol. 3 of *Civil War Engineering.* 4 vols.

Dovberg, Walter, et al. *Under the Gun: Developments in the Use of Engineering in the Army of the Potomac.* New York: Schocken, 1993.

Jameson, F. Fitzroy. *The Letters of a Union Engineering Specialist.* Washington: Steinman, 1994.

McDonald, J. Thomas. *Engineers and Engineering During the American Civil War.* 2 vols. New York: Shirlington, 1994.

Roper, Henry Pleasants, and Sarah Jane Jefferson. "Visiting the Defenses of Washington." *Civil War Battles* 3.4 (1992): 316–32.

1. Page 73 of *Under the Gun: Developments in the Use of Engineering in the Army of the Potomac.*

2. Pages 40 to 41 of *The Siegeworks of Petersburg.*

3. Page 63 of *The Siegeworks of Petersburg* at the end of a sentence that quotes from *The Siegeworks of Petersburg* and credits the material to historian Susan Backus.

4. Page 318 of "Visiting the Defenses of Washington."

5. Pages 54 to 55 of *The Letters of a Union Engineering Specialist.*

6. Page 62 of volume 2 of *Engineers and Engineering During the American Civil War.*

7. A quotation from Cyril Green's "Yankee Defensive Works" that is quoted on page 38 of *Under the Gun: Developments in the Use of Engineering in the Army of the Potomac;* the sentence with the reference credits the quotation to Cyril Green.

8. Page 133 of volume 1 of *Engineers and Engineering During the American Civil War* if another source by Thomas J. McDonald appeared in the same Works Cited listing.

B. Rewrite the following passages to streamline their parenthetical references. In your revisions, be sure to modify the material inside the parentheses to account for information you incorporate into introductions to the research material. And be sure you've followed the rules for punctuation relative to parenthetical references and quotation marks.

1. One historian notes that "the colonial governor of New York gave William Kidd royal commissions both against pirates and as a privateer against the French in 1695" (Beckman, *Privateers and Pirates of Prerevolutionary America* 174), but Captain Kidd became a pirate himself by attacking the ships of other countries off the east coast of Africa.

2. We know "Goyathlay ('One Who Yawns'), of the Mimbreño Apache tribe" (Wallman, "Apache Rebellion" 35), by the name the Mexicans gave him—Geronimo.

CHAPTER 25
Works Cited

As you saw in Chapter 24, parenthetical references in the body of your research paper are possible because they refer to a *general source listing* at the end of the paper. This chapter focuses on that source listing—first on the format of the pages for the list as a whole, then on the formats of the entries that appear in that list, and finally on a few special format rules that affect the appearance of parts of some entries.

WORKS CITED PAGE FORMAT

The usual name for the listing of works at the end of the paper is *Works Cited*. This title assumes that the listing contains all (and only) the works you cite in the text of your paper; it does not include others that you read but that did not account for ideas or data in your paper. Your instructor might ask you to include the other works you read during research, in which case you could change the title to *Works Consulted*.

To create the Works Cited page(s), start the list on a new page, numbering that page in sequence with the rest of your paper. Here's how to set up the page:

- Use the same margins as for the rest of the pages of your research paper.
- Center the title one inch from the top of the page.
- Double-space after the title to find the line on which to begin the first entry.
- Double-space both within and between entries. *Note:* Your instructor may prefer you to single-space within individual entries and double-space only between entries.
- Begin the first line of each entry on the left margin, but for all subsequent lines of an entry indent one-half inch (five spaces on a standard typewriter).
- List entries in alphabetical order.

Richards 9

Works Cited

Clark, Karen, and Fred Ingram. *Acoma Canteens and Other Pottery Designs.*
	Washington: Steinman, 1996.

Donovan, Janet. *Art of Southwest America.* New York: Shirlington, 1994.

Macy, Linda S. *Santa Clara Designs.* New York: Shirlington, 1993. Vol. 2 of
	Pottery of the American Southwest. 5 vols.

Moon, Calvin Roy, et al. *Mimbres Pottery, Decorations, and Symbology.*
	Albuquerque: La Madera, 1994.

WHAT WORKS CITED ENTRIES CONTAIN

It has become commonplace to say that Works Cited documentation entries contain three basic parts: author, title, and publication information. And that's true enough for the most simple citations, which usually make up the majority of entries in a Works Cited list. Unfortunately, there are dozens of exceptions to that basic pattern. We believe that the following six basic groups more accurately describe a documentation entry and will better help you understand the job ahead:

1. Person(s) or group responsible for the piece of material you're documenting
2. The title(s)
3. Amplifying information, to help identify or describe the work precisely
4. Publishing information, or similar information that will help someone find the work
5. Identification of the portion you are citing
6. Supplemental source information (used with *multivolume book* citations only)

Here are three of those groups in a simple three-part citation:

1	2	4

Donovan, Janet. *Art of Southwest America.* New York: Shirlington, 1994.

Group 3 is missing because no amplifying information is necessary to describe the book; group 5 is unnecessary because the entry is for the entire book, not a portion of it; and group 6 is unnecessary because the entry is not for a multi-volume book.

An entry for an essay in a collection of essays published in one volume of a multivolume work, however, has all six basic groups:

$$\underline{\qquad\qquad 1 \qquad\qquad} \quad \underline{\qquad\qquad\qquad\qquad 2 \qquad\qquad\qquad\qquad}$$

McKay, Felix Edgar. "Cocaine Cultivation in Peru." *The Illegal Drug Indus-*
$$\underline{\qquad\qquad\quad} \quad \underline{\qquad\qquad 3 \qquad\qquad} \quad \underline{\qquad\qquad 4 \qquad\qquad}$$

try in Latin America. Vol. 3. Ed. Faith Dixon. New York: Schocken, 1989.
$$\underline{\quad 5 \quad} \quad \underline{\qquad\qquad\qquad 6 \qquad\qquad\qquad}$$

213–65. 4 vols. Gen. ed. Christopher N. Kennedy. 1987–90.

As you can see, documentation entries can be quite complex. Yet, generally, despite complexities, the information falls into the six groups.

ENTRIES FOR BOOKS

General Form: Books

Divided here into the six basic groups are fourteen elements you may need for a book citation. Few entries actually have all fourteen; the simple citation in the previous section has only five elements, whereas the sample complex citation has eleven. Obviously, you include only those elements that are appropriate for the book you're documenting.

(1) Person(s) or Group Responsible for the Piece of Material You're Documenting

- *Name(s) of individual(s) or group.* Usually this is an author, but it can be an editor, translator, or organization. The key is identifying the people *directly responsible* for the particular piece of material you're documenting. Use names as they appear on the title page of the book. Do not include professional or educational titles, such as "M.S." or "Ph.D." If the entry is to begin with a person's name, reverse the name for alphabetizing (last-first-middle instead of first-middle-last).

(2) The Title(s)

- *Title of a part of a book.* You'll need this when you're documenting an essay, a poem, a short story, and so forth, within an anthology, or when you cite a division of a book (such as the Introduction).

- *Title of the book.* If a book has both a title and a subtitle, give both with a colon and a single space between them (omit the colon if the title itself ends with punctuation, such as a question mark). (Special rules beginning on page 303 give guidance for capitalization, quotation marks, and underlining in titles.)

(3) Amplifying Information, to Help Identify or Describe the Work Precisely

- *Translator(s).* One translation is rarely like another, so it's necessary to name the translator(s) of the work.

- *Editor(s).* The order of translator(s) and editor(s) can be reversed; name them in the order in which they appear on the book's title page.

- *Edition.* Readers will assume you're citing the first edition, without revisions, unless you indicate otherwise. Portions of different editions of the same book will be different, so you need to show exactly which one you used.

- *Volume number or number of volumes.* In a citation for a multivolume work, the number of the volume used or the number of volumes in the set can appear before the publication information, depending on how you refer to the material within your paper.

- *Series.* If the work you're citing is part of a series, give the series name and the number of the work in the series (for example, "Archaeological Studies, No. 12").

(4) Publishing Information, or Similar Information That Will Help Someone Find the Work

- *Place of publication.* Look for the place of publication on the title or copyright page or at the back of the book, especially for a book published outside the United States. If several cities are listed, use the one listed first unless you have some reason for using a different one. Give the state along with the city if the city is not likely to be recognized or could be confused with another city with the same name. For cities outside the United States, add an abbreviation for the country if the city is unfamiliar or might be mistaken for one in the United States.

- *Publisher.* You need not name the publisher for a book printed before 1900. For books printed since 1900, use a shortened version of the publisher's name; for example, "Holt" rather than "Holt, Rinehart and Winston." (See page 305 for special rules on dealing with publishers' names and special imprints.)

- *Date of publication.* Again, look for the publication date on the title page, on the copyright page, or at the back of the book. If no publication date appears, give the latest copyright date. Ignore dates for multiple printings; however, if you are citing a work in other than its first edition, use the publication date for the edition you're using, not the original date. For example, if a book in its third edition shows dates of 1990, 1993, and 1998, use 1998.

(5) Identification of the Portion You Are Citing

You'll use this part of an entry only when you're citing a part of a book (for example, an essay or introduction).

- *Page numbers.* Show the *inclusive* page numbers for the portion of the book you're citing. Don't be concerned if you refer to only one or a few of those pages in the text of your paper; those specific page references will be clear in your parenthetical references in the text. Here you must show the pagination for the entire piece. (See page 306 for special rules on showing inclusive page numbers.)

(6) Supplemental Source Information

You'll use this part of an entry only when your citation is for a multivolume work—and even then only part of the time, depending on the complexity of the source information and how you refer to the material within your paper.

- *Number of volumes.* The number of volumes in a multivolume work will appear after publication and specific portion data when the earlier information in the citation is for a single volume of the set.
- *Information for the set of volumes.* Data pertaining to the set of volumes—for example, general editor and span of publication years for the set—may appear at the end of the citation for a multivolume work.

Sample Entries: Books

Following are samples illustrating recommended formats for citations for books. A word of caution: These samples were designed to illustrate particular portions of a book citation. They do not cover every variation you may run across. (A list of samples detailing all the variations would be unbelievably long.) If the book you're citing doesn't quite fit a sample, adapt the format to fit your needs, but be sure to include all the appropriate information you've just read about in the preceding section. *Note:* Because the samples have been listed to demonstrate points about formats, no attempt has been made to alphabetize them, except for entries under "Two or More Books by the Same 'Author(s).' " In your Works Cited pages, of course, you'll list all works in alphabetical order.

One Author

> Jameson, F. Fitzroy. *The Letters of a Union Engineering Specialist.* Washington:
> Steinman, 1994.

Two or Three Authors

Only the name of the person listed first is given in last-first-middle order. All others appear first-middle-last. Be sure to use authors' names as they appear on the book's title page. Do not include professional or educational titles, such as "M.S." or "Ph.D." Names of multiple authors may not be alphabetized on the title page; list them in the order in which they appear.

> Clark, Karen, and Frank Ingram. *Acoma Canteens and Other Pottery Designs.*
> Washington: Steinman, 1996.
> Hyson, Curtis F., G. Randolph Dill, and Jay H. Felmet, Jr. *Magic, Mystery, and
> Medicine.* Nashville: Vanderbilt UP, 1990.

More Than Three Authors

For more than three authors, give the one listed first in the book and follow that with *et al.* (for "and others"). An acceptable alternative is to list all authors if you have a particular reason for providing all the names. List them in the order in which they appear on the title page in the style of an entry for three authors.

> Dovberg, Walter, et al. *Under the Gun: Developments in the Use of Engineering
> in the Army of the Potomac.* New York: Schocken, 1993.

Group as Author

When a group or agency is responsible for a book, treat that group as the author and list its name first, even though the group's name may appear in the book's title or may appear again as publisher. List the group or agency name in normal order. (*GPO* in this entry is the accepted abbreviation for "Government Printing Office," which prints U.S. federal publications. Note that "DC" is omitted.)

> National Commission on Health Care. *Report of the National Commission on
> Health Care.* Washington: GPO, 1994.

Government and International Body Publications

Many government agency publications are simple enough to be treated as books with groups as authors, with the responsible agency serving as author, as in the entry above. Occasionally government publications show a specific person as author; you can begin with that person (as in the second sample below), or you can show the individual author after the title (as in the first sample).

For the *Congressional Record,* you need show only the full date and the inclusive pages for the portion being cited. For other congressional documents, give the government and body, house, committee (if appropriate), document title, number and session of Congress, and type and number of publication, followed by standard publication data. Congressional documents include bills (S 16; HR 63), resolutions (S. Res. 16; H. Res. 63), reports (S. Rept. 16; H. Rept. 63), and documents (S. Doc. 16; H. Doc. 63).

You may also refer to state and local government documents, foreign government documents, and those of international bodies (such as the United Nations). Begin these as you would a U.S. federal publication, naming first the government or international body (for example, "Indiana. Dept. of Revenue" or "United Nations. Committee for Economic Development").

> United States. Dept. of State. *Islamic Developments in Africa.* By Edan Irwin. Washington: GPO, 1989.
> Irwin, Edan. *Islamic Developments in Africa.* U.S. Dept. of State. Washington: GPO, 1989.
> *Cong. Rec.* 21 Sep. 1990: 3143–45.
> United States. Cong. House. Permanent Select Committee on Intelligence. *Technological Transfer Losses in the 1980s.* 101st Cong., 2nd sess. H. Rept. 1122. Washington: GPO, 1990.
> United Nations. Committee for Economic Cooperation. *Resource Development in West Africa.* Elmsford: Pergamon, 1989.

Author Not Given

If no author is given in a book, do not use "Anonymous" or "Anon." Instead, begin the entry with the title. (When you alphabetize the entries for your Works Cited pages, you'll go by the first word in the title other than an article—that is, other than *A, An,* or *The.*) Of course, treat books with groups as authors or government and international body publications as indicated above, even though these books frequently show no individual as author.

> *A Collection of Slavic Stories and Rhymes.* Baltimore: Court, 1995.

Editor(s)

If your use of an edited book, for the most part, is the text of the work itself, then the name(s) of the editor(s) ("ed." or "eds.") should appear after the title, as in the first sample below. However, if the work of the editor(s)—including introductory or other extratextual comments—is being cited, begin the entry with the editor(s), as in the second sample. Moreover, if you are citing an anthology or other collection—rather than a piece within the collection—use the second format below (for a piece in a collection, see "Part of a Collection" below).

> Kemp, Gilbert M. *Narcotics Trafficking and the Caribbean Islands.* Ed. Pamela Hoffman. Madison: U of Wisconsin, 1990.
>
> Hoffman, Pamela, ed. *Narcotics Trafficking and the Caribbean Islands.* By Gilbert M. Kemp. Madison: U of Wisconsin, 1990.

Translator(s)

Normally you'll show the translator(s) of a book after the title, as in the first sample below. However, as with editors, if you are citing primarily commentary by the translator(s), begin with the translator(s), as in the second sample. If the book has both a translator and an editor, show them in the order in which they appear on the book's title page.

> Gatti, Carlo. *Cats of Venice.* Trans. Rachel Hipson. New York: Shirlington, 1989.
>
> Hipson, Rachel, trans. *Cats of Venice.* By Carlo Gatti. New York: Shirlington, 1989.
>
> Della Bella, Mario. *The Shores of the Adriatic.* Trans. Carl Elliot. Ed. Malcom Hawk. Washington: Slay, 1990.

Two or More Books by the Same "Author(s)"

Sometimes two or more entries in your Works Cited listing have *exactly* the same names at the beginning for the person(s) or group responsible for the piece you're documenting. In such a case, give the name(s) only for the first entry; in the following entries type *three hyphens* and a period in place of the name(s). *The three hyphens signify the same name(s),* so if a person named is shown in the first entry as, say, an author and in the next as a translator, you should use the three hyphens for the name in the second entry and follow the hyphens with a comma and "trans." (In the samples below the order is determined by the alphabetical order of the titles because the author block is the same for each.)

> Chin, Lee. *"Hong Kong Tea" and Other Stories.* Arlington: Burning Tree, 1990.
>
> ---, trans. *"The Lagoon" and More.* By Mario Della Bella. New York: Shirlington, 1989.
>
> ---. *Singapore Tales.* Arlington: Burning Tree, 1988.

However, if an entry with a single name is followed by an entry in which the first of multiple authors is that same name, do not use the three hyphens in the second entry. Three hyphens can stand for more than one name, but the name block in each case must be *exactly* the same.

> Gatti, Carlo. *Cats of Venice.* Trans. Rachel Hipson. New York: Shirlington, 1989.

> Gatti, Carlo, and Rachel Hipson, trans. *Carabinieri Parade.* By Luigi Mautone.
> Washington: Luke, 1990.
> ---, trans. *Neapolitan Manners.* By Rosa Valentino. New York: Shirlington, 1989.

Finally, the three hyphens also should be used when groups, governments, or international bodies serve as authors. And because government entries begin with the name of the government and the name of the body or agency sponsoring the work, you may need more than one set of three hyphens. The samples below illustrate the author blocks for several government publications.

> Indiana. Dept. of Health.
> ---. Dept. of Revenue.
> United States. Cong. House.
> ---.---. Senate.
> ---. Dept. of Energy.

Extratextual Material

In citations for such extratextual material as an Introduction or Afterword, give the name of the author of that division of the book, followed by the name of the extratextual piece; the author of the work itself follows the book title. If the author of the extratextual material is also the author of the book, give only the last name after the book title, as in the second sample. Notice that both samples contain inclusive page numbers for the named extratextual section of the book.

> Muñoz, Hector. Introduction. *Protest in the Vietnam War Years.* By David M.
> Ross. Washington: Luke, 1988. v–xxi.
> Readman, Donna L. Afterword. *Vienna Christmas.* By Readman. Washington:
> Spinnaker, 1990. 224–32.

Part of a Collection

For parts of anthologies, collections of articles, and casebooks, the title of the piece precedes the title of the work. Normally the title of the piece will appear in quotation marks; however, if it was published originally as a book, italicize (or underline) it instead. Notice that as for an extratextual piece of a book discussed above, the inclusive pages for the piece of the collection end the citation.

> Sacco, Franco. "Umberto Eco's Labyrinth." *Contemporary European Fiction.* Ed.
> Victoria Wood. Boston: Liberty, 1990. 175–98.

Cross-References

If you're documenting multiple pieces from the same collection, you have a choice. You can treat each piece as a part of a collection, giving full data for the collection itself each time. Or you can give one entry for the collection and then simplify the citations for the pieces by referring to the entry for the collection. Keep in mind, however, that each specific piece of the collection that you refer to in the text of your paper requires its own entry in the Works Cited section. Thus, with cross-referencing you save repeating some information in each of the citations for a piece of the collection, but you then must add an entry for the collection itself.

Fisher, Jill M. "Milan Kundera: Far From Unbearable." Wood 142–74.
Sacco, Franco. "Umberto Eco's Labyrinth." Wood 175–98.
Wood, Victoria, ed. *Contemporary European Fiction.* Boston: Liberty, 1996.

Republished Books

If you use a republished book (a new publication of an out-of-print book or a paperback version of a book originally published in hardcover), show the original publication date before the new publication information.

Lord, Michele I. *Mapping the Shenandoah Valley for Stonewall Jackson.* 1885.
   Baltimore: Court, 1994.

If the original book is republished under a new title, begin with the publishing information for the republished work as if it were an original book. Follow that information with *Rpt. of* (for "Reprint of"), the original title, and the original publication date.

Ferry, R. Michael. *Can We Save the Rain Forest?* Albuquerque: La Madera, 1997.
   Rpt. of *The Amazonia Rain Forest.* 1973.

Republished Scholarly Article

When a scholarly article is republished as a part of a collection, provide full information for the article as if it were in a journal; you'll learn how to cite journal articles later in "Sample Entries: Articles in Periodicals." Follow that information with *Rpt. in* (for "Reprinted in") and information for the collection, as in "Part of a Collection" above.

Davis, Roberta. "Computerized Special Effects." *Studies in Film* 5 (1995): 115–43.
   Rpt. in *Computers and the Arts.* Ed. Stanley Wickham. Washington: Luke,
   1997. 76–103.

Edition Other Than First

Readers will assume the book is a first edition unless you indicate otherwise, such as second edition ("2nd ed."), alternate edition ("Alt. ed."), revised edition ("Rev. ed."), and so on.

> Doyle, Rachel Marie. *Desktop Publishing Software*. 3d ed. New York:
> Schocken, 1997.

Series

If a book is part of a series, give the series name and the number of the work in the series.

> Mosman, Kristina J. *The Iceman and His World*. Archaeological Studies, No. 33.
> Albuquerque: La Madera, 1994.

Multivolume Work

For a specific page reference to a multivolume work, the parenthetical reference in the text of your paper will include the volume number with the page reference if you need to refer to more than one volume of the set (for example, 2:111–12 for pages 111 to 112 of volume 2). However, if in your paper you never need to document material from more than one volume of the set, you can show the specific volume number in the Works Cited entry—as in the following sample—and give only the page reference in the text of your paper (for example, 111–12 instead of 2:111–12). Notice that the sample ends with the total number of volumes in the multivolume set.

> Hill, Elliot F. *History and Art of the Mayans*. Vol. 2. New York: Schocken, 1990.
> 3 vols.

If the single volume you cite for your paper has its own title, include the specific volume reference between the individual publication data and the multivolume title, as in the samples below. Again, references in the text of your paper would not include the volume number. Notice that the first sample ends with the number of volumes in the set; the second sample adds inclusive years of publication for the set because not all volumes were published in the same year.

> Backus, Susan B. *The Siegeworks of Petersburg*. New York: Shirlington, 1993. Vol.
> 3 of *Civil War Engineering*. 4 vols.
> Moore, Donald. *Oriental Patterns in European Porcelains*. Bloomington: Indiana
> UP, 1988. Vol. 3 of *European Porcelain Manufacture*. 4 vols. 1985–90.

If your paper requires references to two or more volumes, use the more general multivolume citation in your Works Cited listing (as below) and include the volume number with each parenthetical reference in the text of your paper.

> Hill, Elliot F. *History and Art of the Mayans*. 3 vols. New York: Schocken, 1990.

If the multiple volumes of the set were published over a period of years, the publication date portion shows the first and last years of the set:

> Moore, Donald. *European Porcelain Manufacture.* 4 vols. Bloomington: Indiana UP, 1985–90.

If the multivolume set has not been completed, include "to date" with the number of volumes and follow the publication date of the first volume with a hyphen and a space before the ending period.

> King, Chester N. *European Chamber Music and Its Composers.* 3 vols. to date. Baltimore: Court, 1987– .

When you cite a piece in a multivolume collection of pieces, show the volume number before the publication data and both the inclusive pages for the piece and the number of volumes in the set at the end of the entry.

> Haynes, Clinton R. "Athapaskan Descendants." *Indians of the Americas.* Ed. Kimberly L. Dawson. Vol. 1. Austin: U of Texas P, 1989. 718–42. 3 vols.

Depending on the factors applicable to a multivolume work, the Works Cited entry can become quite complex. The following example shows a piece in a volume of a multivolume set; the volume has one editor and the multivolume set has a general editor; the volumes of the set were published over a period of years.

> McKay, Felix Edgar. "Cocaine Cultivation in Peru." *The Illegal Drug Industry in Latin America.* Vol. 3. Ed. Faith Dixon. New York: Schocken, 1989. 213–65. 4 vols. Gen ed. Christopher N. Kennedy. 1987–90.

Multiple Publishers

If a book's title page shows multiple publishers, include all of them in the order shown. Put a semicolon after each publisher except the last one. *Note:* Do not confuse multiple publishers with the more common multiple office locations for the same publisher.

> Rowe, Jennifer. *Traditional Irish Dance.* Dublin: Aubry; Washington: Steinman, 1997.

The Bible

In the Works Cited listing, give the title and the version, but omit all publishing information. Remember that you use neither italics (underlining) nor quotation marks for the Bible and its books.

> The Bible. New International Version.

Published Conference Proceedings

If the book title doesn't include information about the conference, provide amplifying information after the title.

> *The Child '94: The Legacy of Mental, Physical, and Sexual Abuse.* Proc. of a Conference of the Association of Social Workers and Child Care Specialists. 23–25 May 1994. Minneapolis: U of Minnesota P, 1994.

If you need to cite an individual presentation from the published proceedings of a conference, treat the presentation as if it were an essay in a collection. That is, put the author (if known) and the title of the presentation before information about the conference, and end the citation with the inclusive page numbers for the presentation within the published proceedings.

> Adams, Tommie. "Generational Relationships and Sexual Abuse." *The Child '94: The Legacy of Mental, Physical, and Sexual Abuse.* Proc. of a Conference of the Association of Social Workers and Child Care Specialists. 23–25 May 1994. Minneapolis: U of Minnesota P, 1994. 210–23.

Pamphlet

Treat pamphlets as books.

> Enos, Bernard B. *Choosing a Hard Disk.* Baltimore: Court, 1990.

Book in Language Other Than English

Treat a book in a language other than English as you would any other book. Cite author, title, and publication information as the book shows them. You can, if you believe it will be useful, provide a translation of the title within square brackets after the original. Name foreign cities in the original language if your readers are likely to recognize the name (for example, Napoli for Naples). If your readers are unlikely to recognize the name in its original language, you can provide the city in the original language, followed by the name in English within square brackets (as in the example below)—or you can simply provide the English name for the city.

> Pauwels, Phillippe, ed. *Alte Kunst [Old Masters].* Brüssel [Brussels]: Königliche Museen für Schöne Künste von Belgien, 1995.

Missing Publishing or Pagination Data

Use the following abbreviations for missing publication or pagination information:

no place of publication: n.p.

no publisher: n.p.

no date: n.d.

no pagination: n. pag.

The abbreviations for "no place" and "no publisher" are the same, but their positions left or right of the colon will allow readers to tell the difference. When a book has no pagination indicated, your Works Cited entry needs to contain "N. pag." so that readers will understand why parenthetical references in the text of your paper do not show page numbers.

Newsletter Design and Desktop Publishing. N.p.: N.p., 1996. N. pag.

ENTRIES FOR ARTICLES IN PERIODICALS

Periodicals are publications that are issued periodically on some sort of schedule—quarterly, bimonthly, weekly, daily, and so forth. Authorities group periodicals into three classes: journals, magazines, and newspapers. Newspapers are easy to recognize, but there isn't an absolute distinction between journals and magazines.

Many journals lack the word *journal* in their titles, and not all periodicals with *journal* in their titles are considered journals for documentation. Nevertheless, some differentiation is necessary because the data required after the publisher information in a Works Cited entry differ for the various types of periodicals. Fortunately, we don't need a scholarly distinction; instead we can make fairly simple divisions based on how the periodicals paginate their issues and on how frequently they publish issues. Therefore, the sample formats for periodicals can be distinguished on the following bases:

- *A periodical paged continuously throughout a volume is treated as a "journal, with continuous pagination."* (If, for example, the first issue of a particular volume ends with page 171 and the next issue begins with page 172, the periodical uses continuous pagination.)

- *When each issue of the periodical is paginated independently it is treated as a "journal, with issues paged independently" if it is published less frequently than every two months.* (If each issue of a periodical begins with page 1, the issues are paginated independently.)

- *All other periodicals are distinguished by frequency of publication.*

General Form: Articles in Periodicals

(1) Person(s) or Group Responsible for the Piece of Material You're Documenting

- *Author(s)*. If an article is signed, the name(s) (sometimes only initials) will appear at either the beginning or the end of the article. Treat multiple authors as you would for book entries.

(2) The Title(s)

- *Title of article.* (See pages 303–305 for guidance on capitalization, quotation marks, and underlining in titles.)

(3) Amplifying Information to Help Identify or Describe the Work Precisely

- *Type of article.* You'll need this only for editorials, letters to the editor, and reviews.

(4) Publishing Information, or Similar Information That Will Help Someone Find the Work

- *Name of periodical.* The name of the periodical itself is all the publishing information that is necessary. Drop any introductory article from the title. If readers aren't likely to recognize the title by itself, insert after the title the name of the institution or, particularly for newspapers, the city; enclose the name in brackets.

(5) Identification of the Portion You Are Citing

- *Series number.* If a journal has been published in more than one series (for example, old and new), indicate the applicable one. Otherwise readers may have difficulty determining where to find the article you used.
- *Newspaper edition.* If a newspaper has both morning and evening or special editions, you may need to show which you used; check the masthead of the newspaper when you read it. The same article often will appear in more than one edition, but not necessarily in the same place in each.
- *Volume and/or issue number(s).* For journals, you'll include the volume and/or issue number for the issue you used.
- *Date.* All entries will include at least the year, but whether year only, month and year, or complete date depends on the type of periodical.
- *Page number(s).* Generally this will be the inclusive page numbers for the article. (See page 306 for guidance on showing inclusive page numbers.) However, if the article does not appear on consecutive pages (for example, it begins with pages 16 to 24, then goes to page 37, and then to page 46), show only the first page number followed by a plus sign (for this example, "16+").

Sample Entries: Articles in Periodicals

As with the samples for books, the following entries were designed to illustrate particular portions of documentation entries. You may need to adapt the formats to fit your needs, but be sure to include all pertinent information listed in the preceding discussion of general form. *Note:* The three-hyphen form for repeated authors (see "Two or More Books by the Same 'Author(s)' " on pages 281–282) applies to entries for articles in periodicals as well, but is not repeated below.

Journal, with Continuous Pagination

This type of entry includes the volume number followed by the year in parentheses, a colon, and then inclusive page numbers for the article.

> Myers, Georgia. "Tellem Cliff Dwellings of Mali." *African Studies* 25 (1990): 373–92.

Journal, with Issues Paged Independently

After the volume number, add a period and the issue number.

> Roper, Henry Pleasants, and Sarah Jane Jefferson. "Visiting the Defenses of Washington." *Civil War Battles* 3.4 (1992): 316–32.

Journal, with Issue Numbers Only

If a journal does not use volume numbers, use the issue number as if it were a volume number.

> Bishop, Quinn T. "Progression in Regressive Pueblos in New Mexico and Colorado." *American Science* 43 (1990): 37–51.

Journal, with Series

If a journal has been published in more than one series, precede the volume number with the series. Use a numerical designator such as "4th ser." or "ns" and "os" for "new series" and "original series."

> Lambert, Byron. "Draining the Aral Sea." *World Science* ns 12 (1988): 612–34.

Monthly or Bimonthly Periodical

Instead of volume and/or issue, use the month(s) and year.

> Kinard, Mary Wayne. "Optical Disk Storage." *Computers at Home* May 1990: 63–78.

Weekly or Biweekly Periodical

Whether a magazine or a newspaper, for a periodical published weekly or every two weeks, give the complete date rather than volume and issue numbers.

> Weinert, Garfield P. "Barbettes and Embrasures: Artillery Fortifications in the Civil War." *Museum News* 18 June 1994: 17+.

Daily Newspaper

Show the newspaper's name as it appears at the top of the first page, omitting any beginning article (*The Washington Post* becomes *Washington Post*). If the newspaper title doesn't name the city, give the city and state in brackets after the title, as in the first sample below. The first sample also illustrates how to indicate the edition for a newspaper that prints more than one edition a day (again, check the masthead on the first page to see if an edition is given).

For inclusive page numbers, check the pagination system of the newspaper carefully. If the newspaper doesn't have sections or if it numbers continuously through the edition, you'll need only the page number(s) after the date (8 Oct. 1994: 38). If the newspaper includes the section number with the page number(s), the appropriate section-number combination can follow the date (8 Oct. 1994: A12–A13). But if the section designator is not combined with the page number(s), show the section designator between the date and the page number(s) (8 Oct. 1994, sec. 3: 12). Of course, if the article is not on consecutive pages, use only the first page number and a plus sign (8 Oct. 1994: A12+).

> Carey, Kelly. "What's Become of the Gulags?" *Star-Herald* [St. Louis, MO] 8 Oct. 1990, early morning ed.: A12–A13.
> Sumner, Rachel. "UN Peacekeeping Efforts Flounder." *Washington Post* 21 May 1994: A5.

Author Unknown

Whatever the type of periodical, if no author is given, begin with the article's title. The format for the rest of the entry, of course, depends on the type of periodical in which the article appears; the sample below is for a monthly magazine.

> "Prehistoric Skywatchers Charted the Heavens." *Ancient History* May 1989: 53–67.

Editorial

Begin with the author if named, otherwise with the editorial's title, and follow the title with "Editorial." The rest of the entry depends on the source; our sample uses a daily newspaper.

> "Is Washington a 'District of Colombia'?" Editorial. *Washington Post* 17 Sep. 1989: A15.

Letter to the Editor/Reply

Because letters to editors can appear in any type of periodical, the portion after the title depends on the type of publication in which the letter appears. We show a journal (with continuous pagination).

> Im, Lee. Letter. *Journal of Antiquity* 15 (1990): 276.

For a published response to a letter to the editor, label the item "Reply to the letter of . . ." Do not use quotation marks, italics, or underlining for this label.

> McCallum, Ben. Reply to the letter of Lee Im. *Journal of Antiquity* 15 (1990): 276–77.

Review

Reviews may be signed or unsigned and titled or untitled, and they may appear in any type of periodical. For a signed review, use the name(s) of the reviewer(s), the review title (if there is one), and then "Rev. of . . ." For an unsigned review, give the title (if there is one); if not, begin with "Rev. of . . ." The first entry below shows a signed and titled review in a monthly magazine; the second sample is for an unsigned, untitled review in a daily newspaper.

> Neal, Carla. "Playing and Working on the Internet." Rev. of *A Practical Guide to the Internet,* by Andrew Hight. *Computers at Home* Feb. 1994: 46–49.
> Rev. of *Mr. Lincoln's Generals,* by Charles Barnard. *Austin Gazette* 10 Mar. 1994, sec. 4:3.

Serialized Article

For a serialized article or a series of related articles run in more than one issue of a periodical, combine all of the installments in one citation if all the pieces have the same author and title. The first entry below shows a serialized article appearing in a journal with continuous pagination, so the parts of the series appear as separate sets of inclusive pages. The second entry, however, is for a series in a monthly publication; a semicolon separates the portion information for each part of the series.

> Odland, Jessica B. "Ratings of Health Management Organizations by Region." *Journal of American Health Care* 12 (1997): 96–99, 146–48, 183–87.
> Hill, Gloria Grayson. "Low-Fat/No-Fat Substitutes for Conventional Ingredients." *Cooking Today* Apr. 1996: 17–23; June 1996: 35–38.

When related parts of a series have different titles, provide each part as a separate citation. However, you can include at the end of each entry a brief description of its place in the series.

> Fuller, Pierre. "Overcoming Denial." *Washington Post* 5 Oct. 1997: C2+. Pt. 1 of a series, Coping with Life-Threatening Illnesses.

Microform Collection

To document articles compiled on microfiche or microfilm, begin with the citation you would use if you were documenting the original source. To this add information about the microform collection you used: the title of the microform source, italicized (or underlined); the volume number, if available; the year the microform source was released; and identification of the particular part you used (for example, "fiche 16, grids 1–3").

> Collier, Tracy. "NASA Gathers Geological History of Mars." *American Science* 130 (1997): 43–49. *Science Studies for Secondary Schools* 8 (1997): fiche 16, grids 1–3.

Loose-Leaf Collection

Some information services select articles from periodicals and produce them in loose-leaf volumes. Begin with the entry you would use if you were documenting the original source. To this add information about the loose-leaf product: title, italicized (or underlined); name of editor, if applicable; volume number, if applicable; city of publication, publisher, and year of publication; and article number.

> Lucas, Anthony. "Is Stealth Technology Worth the Price Tag?" Editorial. *Philadelphia Gazette* 1 Oct. 1997: 32. *Military Technology Today.* Gen ed. Phyllis Rutland. Vol. 4. St. Paul: Myrine, 1997. Art. 6.

ENTRIES FOR PORTABLE ELECTRONIC SOURCES

General Form: Portable Electronic Sources

Portable electronic sources include CD-ROMs, diskettes, and magnetic tapes. The material released on them may already have been published in some printed form, or it may be material that has no apparent printed counterpart. The portable source may be released at the same time as the printed publication it mirrors. It may compile a number of already printed works. Or it may aggregate both printed works and material with no apparent printed counterpart. Whatever the contents of the portable electronic source, you can treat it with the following general form:

(1) Identification of the Portion of the Source You're Documenting

- *If the material has a printed counterpart, provide the full Works Cited entry you would for the printed source*—see entries for books, articles in periodicals, and other sources. The portable electronic source may not provide all the needed information about the printed work. Include all the parts of the entry you can and omit the others. Remember that you can use *n.p.* for "no place of publication" and for "no publisher" and *n.d.* for "no date." Also, some portable electronic sources that reproduce already printed material maintain the pagination from the original, some show the page number for the first page only, and some show no pagination. Again, provide what you can, but do not leave pagination information blank if something is called for. For example, use *n. pag.* if the source lacks pagination information.

- *If the material has no apparent printed counterpart, provide the following*—author, if known; title of the material you used, in quotation marks; and, if available, the date of the material.

(2) Publishing Information for the Portable Electronic Source

- *Title of the portable electronic source.*
- *Edition, release identification, or version number.* This can be particularly important for portable electronic sources that are issued without a planned periodic replacement schedule. For others, particularly for material replaced on a periodic schedule, this information may not be shown, because the release date would be more important. If the information does not appear on the source, simply omit it.
- *Medium.* This would be "CD-ROM," "Diskette," or "Magnetic Tape."
- *City of publication.*
- *Name of publisher or vendor.*
- *Date of electronic publication.* Usually this will be the release year, but it could be a month and year for a portable electronic source replaced on a periodic schedule (quarterly, for example).

Sample Entries: Portable Electronic Sources

Standalone Publication with Printed Counterpart

The first sample is a printed book from a CD-ROM collection of similar books. This CD-ROM showed no version information. The second sample is for a full-length play from another CD-ROM collection; the vendor for this CD-ROM provided no publication information about the sources for the collected works (except to indicate that they were from the public domain).

Collello, Thomas, et al. *Lebanon, A Country Study.* N.p.: Dept. of the Army, 1987. *Countries of the World on CD-ROM.* CD-ROM. Parsippany, NJ: Bureau of Development, 1991.

Shakespeare, William. *A Midsummer Night's Dream.* N.p.: n.p., n.d. *The Complete Works of William Shakespeare: His Plays and Poetry.* 1992 ed. CD-ROM. Portland: Creative Multimedia, 1992.

Periodical Article with Printed Counterpart

The *Time* CD-ROM collection shows the opening pages for articles, so the sample uses "36+" to show inclusive pages for the article cited.

Stengel, Richard. "The Birth of a Leader." *Time* 9 May 1997: 36+. *The 1995 Time Magazine Compact Almanac.* Multimedia ed. for Macintosh. CD-ROM. Cambridge: SoftKey, 1995.

Material without Apparent Printed Counterpart

The first sample is for an entry in a CD-ROM encyclopedia. Works Cited documentation for articles in standard reference works that alphabetize entries, as you'll see later in "Sample Entries: Other Sources," requires only the author (if the article is signed), title, encyclopedia title, and edition. The second sample is for a CD-ROM version of an exhibition from 1994; the CD-ROM provides individual credits but does not indicate authors of many of the specific portions of the contents, so the sample begins with the portion title.

Wagley, Charles. "Folklore." *The Academic American Encyclopedia.* 1998 ed. *The 1998 Grolier Multimedia Encyclopedia.* Deluxe ed., vers. 10.0.0. CD-ROM. Danbury: Grolier, 1997.

"Jazz." 1994. *Smithsonian America: An Interactive Exhibition of American History and Culture.* Vers. 1.1 for Macintosh. CD-ROM. Portland: Creative Multimedia, 1994.

Computer Software

A source of this type may not have either author or title information. That is, you would be citing only the publishing information for the portable electronic source itself.

Filefolder Data Base Management. Vers. 2.5.1. Diskette. Palo Alto: Scienobyte, 1997.

ENTRIES FOR ONLINE ELECTRONIC SOURCES

Online electronic sources cause problems for individuals accustomed to documenting books and articles in periodicals. For one thing, the online sources exist in cyberspace, and just try handing a piece of cyberspace to your instructor! In addition to lacking the physical form of a book or journal article, many online electronic sources are modified frequently, so what you find at a particular site on one day may differ greatly from what others find if they look for your sources. Indeed, because of the continuing expense of providing material on the Internet, some useful sources could cease to exist after you access them, while others may change location on the Internet as their providers find lower cost server arrangements for their material. For these reasons, where you find the online material and the date you access it are particularly important portions of documentation for online electronic sources.

Some scholars have noted that the Works Cited forms for online sources in the fourth edition of the *MLA Handbook for Writers of Research Papers* fail to adequately cover the sources available. For this reason, the entries here for documenting online electronic sources generally follow the forms in the *MLA Handbook* but have been expanded, and have some format elements modified, to incorporate useful points in the following online Internet papers:

> Walker, Janice R. "MLA-Style Citations of Electronic Sources." Vers. 1.1, Aug. 1996. Online. Internet. Available <http://www.cas.usf.edu/english/walker/mla.html> (28 Sep. 1997).
>
> Harnack, Andrew, and Gene Kleppinger. "Beyond the MLA Handbook: Documenting Electronic Sources on the Internet." 25 Nov. 1996. Online. Internet. Available <http://falcon.eku.edu/honors/beyond-mla/#contents> (28 Sep. 1997).

Showing Electronic Source Locations

Works Cited entries for online sources require an electronic address, which can be a command sequence path someone would follow to locate an item electronically, a Uniform Resource Locator (URL), or an electronic mail (E-mail) address. Following the reasoning that Andrew Harnack and Gene Kleppinger present, instructions that follow for citing online electronic sources call for portions of command sequence paths to be separated by spaces, while URLs and E-mail addresses will be enclosed in angle brackets (< >), a convention that has become popular on the Internet and in documents discussing it. E-mail addresses and URLs cannot have blank spaces, and URLs, in particular, often are quite long. Using angle brackets to enclose a URL or E-mail address will allow you to show it on more than one line, if necessary, in a Works Cited entry: You can break a URL where necessary to fit the margins for your research paper and continue the URL on the following line. By convention, the angle brackets indicate that everything within them is to be reproduced exactly as shown and without blank spaces, so readers will know that your line ending does not indicate a blank space.

A related point: when you copy a URL or E-mail address, reproduce the capitalization and punctuation exactly as you find them. Sometimes the case of letters and numbers matters and sometimes it doesn't—but always showing the case as you find it will ensure that any browser on any computer network can use the electronic address. Similarly, the punctuation may not make sense to you, but reproducing it exactly is necessary if anyone is to locate the material you found using the electronic address you provide.

General Form: Online Electronic Sources

The primary parts of the general form for online electronic sources are the same as those for the general form of portable electronic sources.

(1) Identification of the Portion of the Source You're Documenting

- *If the material has a printed counterpart, provide the full Works Cited entry that you would use for the printed source*—see entries for books, articles, and other sources. The online source may not provide all the needed information that would be available for a printed work. Include the parts you can and omit the others. Remember, though, that you can use *n.p.* for "no place of publication" and "no publisher" and *n.d.* for "no date." Pagination information also generally is lacking for online electronic sources; use *n. pag.* for "no pagination" rather than simply omitting pagination data.
- *If the material has no apparent printed counterpart, provide the following*—author, if known; title of the material you used, in quotation marks; and, if available, version number and/or publication date or date of latest revision.

(2) Publishing Information for the Online Electronic Source

- *Publication medium.* This always will be *Online.*
- *Name of computer network or service.* This could be a computer network, such as the Internet, or a computer service, such as DIALOG, Data-Star, NEXIS, or ProQuest.
- *Type of communication.* For synchronous communications, communication types would include group discussion and personal interview. For E-mail the types would include personal E-mail, distribution list, and office communication. For other types of Works Cited entries, this item is not applicable and should be omitted.
- *Command sequence path, URL, E-mail address, or accession number.* Begin this portion with *Available.*
- *Access date (in parentheses).*

Sample Entries: Online Electronic Sources

Material from a Computer Information Service

Computer information services provide printed materials in online forms. Your university library may have one or more of these services available for your use, but they generally are not available via personal computers. Notice that this entry shows the accession number the computer information service applies to track the article.

> Asker, James R. "U.S./Russian Satellite Maps Worst Antarctic Ozone Hole." *Aviation Week & Space Technology* 25 Oct. 1993: 72. Online. ProQuest. Available 00775829 (12 July 1994).

Material from a File Transfer Protocol (FTP) Site

Provide a URL, in angle brackets, or a command sequence path for a file downloaded using a file transfer protocol; this sample shows a URL.

> Erbe, Jan R. "The History of a Dinosaur Sale." Oct. 1997. Online. Internet. Available <ftp://ftp.wvc.edu/docs/mkt> (14 Oct. 1997).

Material from World Wide Web (WWW) Site

Provide a URL, in angle brackets, for the information you use.

> Peagram, William. "American Civil War Ordnance." 1996. Online. Internet. Available <http://www.geoglobe.com/users/~rausch/acw_docs/ord1.html> (10 Feb. 1997).

Material Accessed via Telnet Protocol

Provide the command sequence path to access the material using the telnet protocol.

> Wolfe, Randolph. "Exploring the Universe." Mar. 1997. Online. Internet. Available telnet spacelink.nsea.gov 3016, help, press 5 (15 Aug. 1997).

Material Acquired via Synchronous Communications

Synchronous communications allow for one-on-one or group discussions, so be sure to include the type of communication used for your material: personal interview or group discussion. For information about the discussion, begin with the individual interviewed or the speaker, if known, whose information you used from a group discussion. If a group discussion concerned a particular topic, name it.

> Slowik, Mark. Personal interview. 7 Nov. 1996. Online. Internet. Available telnet
> world.geolat.net 8300 (7 Nov. 1996).

Material Acquired via Gopher Search Protocol

For the location at which the material is available, provide either a command
sequence path or a URL. The sample shows a URL.

> Dorman, George. "Report to the Territorial Governor Regarding Land Sales."
> 1872. Online. Internet. Available <gopher://wiretap.spies.com/11/Gov/
> US-History/ter_doc> (13 Dec. 1996).

Material Accessed via Usenet Newsgroup

For material from a Usenet newsgroup posting, provide the author's name, if
available; the E-mail address, in angle brackets, used for the posting; the subject, in quotation marks, shown for the posting; and the posting date.

> Wilkens, Sarah. <sjwilk@erols.com> "RE: North Anna Trenches." 12 Nov. 1997.
> Online. Internet. Available <soc.history.war.us-civil-war> (14 Nov. 1997).

E-mail Messages

Provide the author's name, the subject, and the date sent. Be sure to include the
type of E-mail communication: personal E-mail, distribution list, or office
communication.

> Krueger, Kenneth. "Digital Printing." 17 Apr. 1997. Online. Internet. Personal
> E-mail. Available <jburke7341@aol.com> (18 Apr. 1997).

ENTRIES FOR OTHER SOURCES

General Form: Other Sources

This mixed group of sources lacks a "standard form." Still, the general idea for
documentation entries is the same as for books and articles in periodicals:
(1) person(s) or group responsible for the piece of material you're documenting; (2) the title(s); (3) amplifying information, to help identify or describe the
work precisely; (4) publishing information, or similar information that will
help someone find the work; and (5) identification of the portion you are citing.

Sample Entries: Other Sources

If you can't find a sample that fits your need exactly, adapt entries or create a
format, but keep the general guidelines in mind.

Speech

Follow the speaker's name with the title of the presentation, in quotation marks. Provide the name of the meeting or sponsoring organization, if applicable, and the date. If the presentation has no formal title, use in its place a designator such as *Address, Keynote speech,* or *Lecture* (any of these without quotation marks).

> Binder, Calvin. "Community Action Groups Combat Neighborhood Drug Trafficking." Conference of Law Enforcement Officers. Cincinnati. 10 Sep. 1995.

Class Handout or Lecture

Show class, place, and date; as appropriate and available, give speaker and title.

> "Recognizing and Correcting Passive Voice." English 101 handout. Wolfram State College, 1997.
> Unruh, Michael. Math 210 lecture. Miami U, 17 Oct. 1994.

Reference Work

Entries for items in standard reference works require less information than do basic entries for books. For a signed article (the first entry below), give the author, article title, encyclopedia title, and edition. For an unsigned article (the second sample), begin with the article title. Notice that neither entry includes volume and page information; these data are unnecessary for encyclopedias and dictionaries that alphabetize entries. Do not show a general editor for the reference work, even though the work itself may include one.

If the encyclopedia has separate major divisions, each of which has articles in alphabetical order, include the division title with the encyclopedia title (the third sample). This arrangement would apply as well to yearbooks issued to supplement an encyclopedia or other reference work.

For other standard reference works, such as one of the *Who's Who* series, give only the edition, if applicable, and publication year after the title (for example, 14th ed. 1991–93). However, treat an article in a less common reference work as a piece in a book collection (see "Part of a Collection," page 282), and give full publication information.

See also page 294 for a reference work on CD-ROM.

> Mahan, Jack S. "Balkans." *Funk and Wagnalls New Encyclopedia.* 1996 ed.
> "La Brea Tar Pit." *Encyclopedia Americana.* 1997 ed.
> Edmonds, Gilbert. "Islam." *Encyclopaedia Britannica: Macropaedia.* 1995 ed.

Unpublished Thesis or Dissertation

When a thesis or dissertation has been published, treat it as a book. However, if you use an unpublished form, show the type of work, the institution for which it was prepared, and the year it was accepted. Note that the title appears in quotation marks because the work is unpublished.

> Keifer, Jesse Monroe. "Communist Command Economies and Environmental Destruction in Eastern Europe." Diss. U of Nebraska. 1994.

Unpublished Letter

Treat a published letter as a part of a book collection or as a letter in a periodical. The first entry below shows the format for a letter you yourself have received. The second illustrates an unpublished letter in an archive.

> Acton, Anthony Norton. Letter to the author. 11 Dec. 1997.
> Dean, George B. Letter to Robert James Webb. 17 Mar. 1866. Robert James Webb Collection. Hurley Museum Library, Huntington, SC.

Manuscript or Typescript

Provide the author and title. Whether the title should be in italics (or underlining) or quotation marks depends on whether it represents a work that has been published in a standalone form (book, play, and so on) or as part of another larger work (essay, poem, and so on); the former should have italics (or underlining), and the latter should have quotation marks. If the manuscript or typescript has never been published, its title should have quotation marks. If the work is untitled, use a description such as Notebook (without quotation marks, italics, or underlining). Indicate the type of material with *ms.* for "manuscript" or *ts.* for "typescript," and add an accession number if the institution holding the work has given it a number. End the citation with the name of the institution holding the work and the city for the institution.

> St. Martin, Oliver S. "The Music of Maria Callas." Ts. 21. Baird Library, St. Paul.

Interview

To document an interview you have conducted, begin with the name of the person interviewed, show the type of interview (personal or telephone), and give the date it was held.

> Fishbine, Joshua W. Personal interview. 7 July 1994.

If an interview has been published, treat it as a part of a collection or as an article in a periodical. For an interview broadcast on radio or television, see "Radio or Television Program."

Map or Chart

Begin with the title, followed by an identification of whether the item is a map or a chart.

Chesapeake Bay. Map. New York: Ward, 1996.
Fat Content of Popular Fast Foods. Chart. N.p.: Foodwatchers, 1997.

Cartoon

Follow the cartoonist's name with the title, if available, in quotation marks and Cartoon, without quotation marks, italics, or underlining. The rest of the citation depends on where the cartoon appeared; the sample shows a daily newspaper.

Adams, Scott. "Dilbert." Cartoon. *Washington Post* 14 Oct. 1997: F21.

Film, Video Recording, Filmstrip, or Slide Program

For a film, usually you'll begin with the title, followed by the director, distributor, and year released. Other information (stars, writers, and such) is optional but should be included if it bears on how you discuss the film in your research paper; provide this information as amplification after the director. However, if your paper deals with the work of a particular individual connected with the film, begin with that person. For related media other than a film, provide the medium, without quotation marks, italics, or underlining, before the name of the distributor. Applicable media types are videocassette, videodisc, laser disc, filmstrip, and slide program.

Braving Winter. Dir. Julia Kowalski. Panorama, 1994.
Installing Memory Chips in a PowerMac. Dir. Jill Vantine. Videocassette. Video
    Concepts, 1996.

Radio or Television Program

As a minimum, give the program title, the network that aired it, the local station and city for the broadcast you heard or viewed, and the broadcast date. An episode title, if available, can be shown in quotation marks preceding the program title (as in the first sample), and a series title, with no special markings, can be shown after the program title. Other information may be added for amplification. If your research paper deals with the work of a particular person connected with the broadcast, begin the entry with that individual's name. For a radio or television interview (the second sample), provide the title, if there is one, in quotation marks before the program title. If the interview has no title, use Interview (without quotation marks, italics, or underlining) with the name of the interviewer.

"Hotline." *Weekend Newsline.* ABC. WCAM, Cincinnati. 22 Sep. 1997.
Stone, Oliver. Interview with Ted Koppel. *Nightline.* ABC. WCAM, Cincinnati.
    12 Mar. 1995.

Sound Recording

Begin the entry with the person you want to emphasize (speaker, author, composer, producer); give the title, the artists, and any amplifying information that is relevant to your research paper. End with the manufacturer and the release year. If the recording is anything other than a compact disc, provide the medium (audiocassette, audiotape, or LP), without quotation marks, italics, or underlining, in front of the manufacturer's name.

> Gatti, Carlo. *Cats of Venice.* Read by Veronica Erno. Audiocassette. Recorded Books, 1989.

Performance

Give the title, author, director, and key performers, followed by the place of the performance—normally theater and city—and the performance date. If your research paper deals with the work of a particular person related to the performance, begin your citation with that individual.

> *A Midsummer Night's Dream.* By William Shakespeare. Dir. James T. Brady. Perf. Milton Jennings and Rose-Marie Krainik. Acton Theater, St. Louis. 12 June 1996.

Musical Composition

Give the composer and title (first sample). If you identify the music only by form, number, or key, don't use quotation marks, italics, or underlining (second sample). However, if your citation is for a published score, capitalize *no.* and *op.* and use italics (or underlining) for the identification of the music (third sample).

> Joplin, Scott. *Maple Leaf Rag.*
> Beethoven, Ludwig van. Symphony no. 8 in D minor, op. 125.
> Beethoven, Ludwig van. *Symphony No. 8 in D Minor, Op. 125.* New York: Ward, 1996.

Artwork

Provide the artist's name, followed by the title of the painting or sculpture. If the work is held by an institution, give its name and city. If the work is held by a private collector, give the owner's name and city.

> Benzino, Guido. *St. Jerome.* Private collection of Rudolph Street, Baltimore.
> Romero, Salvatore. *The Church.* Barry Museum, Detroit.

If you used a photograph rather than the original work of art, provide complete publication information as well, and end the citation with the page number or the slide, figure, or plate number, as appropriate.

> Rowe, Stuart. *Boat with Shells*. Private collection of Natalie Griffith, Spokane.
> *American Still Lifes*. By Leo Stein. Baltimore: Court, 1996. Plate 34.

Legal Citation

Complex legal citations are beyond the scope of this book. Consult the Harvard Law Review Association's *A Uniform System of Citation* for help. The sample entries below are for federal statutory material; both use section references rather than page references. Use similar entries for state constitutions and statutes.

> 5 US Code. Sec. 522a. 1974.
> US Const. Art. 3, sec. 1.

Citations for law cases show the names of first plaintiff and first defendant, the volume of the report being cited, the name of the report, the name of the court where the case was decided, and the year decided.

> Jefferson v. Sommers. 153 AS 613. Ind. Ct. App. 1978.

SPECIAL RULES FOR TITLES

Capitalization

Do use capital letters for the *first letters* of the following types of words in titles:

- each important word in the title (see below for "unimportant" words)
- the first word in a title ("*A House on Tatum Hill*")
- the first word after a colon that joins a title and a subtitle ("Faulkner's 'Delta Autumn': The Fall of Idealism")
- parts of compound words that would be capitalized if they appeared by themselves ("School Declares All-Out War on Misspelling")

Don't use capital letters for the following "unimportant" words:

- the articles *a, an,* and *the*
- all prepositions

- the conjunctions *and, as, but, for, if, nor, or, so, yet*
- the infinitive *to*
- the second element of a compound numeral ("Twenty-*five* Years of Tyranny")

Neither Quotation Marks nor Italics (Underlining)

Don't use either quotation marks or italics (or underlining) for the following:

- the Bible, the books of the Bible, and other sacred works such as the Talmud or the Koran
- legal references (such as acts, laws, and court cases)
- extratextual material in a book (such as the Introduction or Foreword)

Italics (Underlining)

Printers usually use italics, and you should as well if your typing system, such as a word processor, has this capability (use underlining if it doesn't) for certain types of titles. Italicize the title of works published separately—such as novels and poems that are entire books or pamphlets—and the titles of periodicals (magazines, journals, and newspapers). Also italicize the titles of movies and radio or television programs.

Quotation Marks

Use quotation marks to enclose titles of works published as parts of other works—such as short stories, most poems, and essays. Also, enclose titles of speeches and class lectures in quotation marks.

If, however, a work that has been published separately appears as part of a larger work—such as a novel as part of an anthology—italicize the title. For example, italicize Voltaire's *Candide* even when it is a part of an anthology titled *Great Works of World Literature*.

Mixed Quotation Marks and Italicizing (Underlining)

You have to adapt the rules somewhat when one title appears within another. The following samples illustrate the markings for the four possible combinations of titles with quotation marks and titles with italics (or underlining):

- "Faulkner's 'Delta Autumn': The Fall of Idealism" (a short-story title within an essay title: each title without the other would have double quotation marks, but here the title within a title has single quotation marks)

- *Faulkner's "Delta Autumn" and the Myth of the Wilderness* (a short-story title within a book title: each title has its normal markings)
- "Laertes as Foil in *Hamlet*" (a play title within an essay title: each title has its normal markings)
- *Shakespeare's "Hamlet": Action versus Contemplation* (a play title within a book title: the title within a title, which by itself would be italicized, here has double quotation marks)

SPECIAL RULES FOR PUBLISHERS' NAMES

Shortening

Follow these rules in shortening publishers' names for your Works Cited entries:

- Omit the articles *a, an,* and *the.*
- Omit business designators such as *Co., Inc.,* or *Ltd.*
- Omit labels such as *Books, Press,* or *Publishers. Note:* University presses create an exception. Because both universities and their presses may publish independently, use *P* for *Press* when the publisher is a university press (thus, *Indiana U* is distinct from *Indiana UP*).
- If the publisher's name includes the name of one person, use only the last name (*Alfred A. Knopf, Inc.* becomes *Knopf*).
- If the name includes several people, use only the first name (*Holt, Rinehart and Winston* becomes *Holt*).
- Use the following standard abbreviations: *ALA* for the American Library Association, *CAL* for the Center for Applied Linguistics, *ERIC* for Educational Resources Information Center, *GPO* for Government Printing Office, *HMSO* for Her (His) Majesty's Stationery Office, *MLA* for the Modern Language Association of America, *NAL* for the New American Library, *NCTE* for National Council of Teachers of English, *NEA* for the National Education Association, *UMI* for University Microfilms International, and *UP* for University Press.

Imprints

When the title page or copyright page of a book shows a publisher's special imprint, combine the imprint with a shortened version of the publisher's name: for example, a Sentry Edition published by Houghton Mifflin Company becomes Sentry-Houghton; a Mentor Book published by The New American Library becomes Mentor-NAL.

SPECIAL RULES FOR
INCLUSIVE PAGE NUMBERS

When you indicate inclusive page references, often you can shorten the second number. Up to 100, show all digits (for example 3–4, 54–55). Thereafter, reduce the second number of a set to two digits (for example 253–54, 304–05, 2614–15) *unless* the hundredth or thousandth digit changes (for example 499–501, 2998–3002).

EXERCISE

Prepare a Works Cited page to include entries for the works below.

1. A book by Clara Hardin and Norma C. Tanner titled "People of the Desert" and subtitled "Hohokam Farmers and Craftsmen." This book was published in 1996 by the La Madera Press of Albuquerque, New Mexico.

2. An article titled "Potters of the Rio Grande," by Thomas Cochran, that was published on pages 221 to 246 of volume 4 of the *Journal of American Arts in the Southwest*. Volume 4 was published in 1997, and this journal paginates continuously throughout each volume.

3. A book titled "Southwest American Ruins." It is the third edition and was published in 1996 by Court Press of Baltimore, Maryland. The Association of American Archaeologists prepared the book.

4. A videocassette titled "Taming the Stars." It was directed by Chip Du Plain and was produced in 1995 by Video Arts, Inc., of Sacramento, California.

5. Material on the Internet's World Wide Web by Donna Simpson. The title is "Desert Designs: Art in the Southwest," and it is dated 1997. The URL is <http://www.designworld.com/files7/desert.html> and it was accessed on 14 October 1997.

6. A book of essays titled "Essays on Rio Grande Pueblo Potters," edited by Robin Knudson. It was published on 12 May 1997 by Burning Tree Press of Arlington, Virginia.

7. Material on a CD-ROM titled "Native American Arts and Crafts," which was published in 1996 by Steinman Publishers of Washington,

DC. The material actually used from the CD-ROM is "Jobs versus Preservation," an article by Carole Dickenson that was published originally in a monthly magazine called "American Indian Arts"; the article appeared on pages 15 to 26 of the January 1996 issue of the magazine. The CD-ROM itself is version 1.1.

8. Material posted as "Mimbres Shapes" by Hector Hernandez on the Usenet group <rec.arts.pottery> on 21 August 1997. It was accessed on 22 August 1997. The E-mail address for Mr. Hernandez is <hec2710@prince.com>.

9. A two-volume book set titled "Anasazi Pueblo Architecture," by Edith Barnes. Both volumes were published in 1994 by Shirlington Press of New York City.

10. An article by Lisa Kitt titled "Pot Robbers." It appeared on pages 117 to 128 of a book titled "Conservation of America's Prehistoric Ruins." The book was edited by David Foster and was published in January 1995 by Slay Press of Washington, DC.

11. An article titled "Mimbres Animal Figures" that was published in a monthly magazine called "Native American Arts Today" in June 1997. The article was by Jan McNally and appeared on pages 37 to 44 of the magazine.

SECTION III

Improving Your Punctuation and Expression

PART 6

Punctuation

There's more to good writing than just getting commas and apostrophes in the right places—yet those commas and apostrophes are important, too. We don't try to cover everything about punctuation in this part of the book—just those rules we think will be especially helpful for you.

CHAPTER 26

Definitions

Why begin studying punctuation with a review of grammar? If you understand the terms in this chapter, learning to punctuate a sentence will be easy, for punctuation is not really mysterious. In fact, once you understand these terms, you probably will be surprised just how easy punctuation can be. The catch (and, of course, there is a catch) is that you must work hard to understand them.

A Pep Talk

Skimming this chapter once, or even reading it through carefully once, will not suffice. You will have to memorize a few terms. All of this material is essential in later chapters, however, so please spend some time with it now.

1. Clause. *A clause is a group of words containing a subject (S) and a verb (V).*

         S   V

Clause: Sharon ran in the New York Marathon.

Sometimes people are fooled into believing a group of words is a clause simply because it contains something like a verb.

Not a clause: Running in a marathon.

The above group of words cannot be a clause for two reasons: (1) it has no subject; (2) it has no verb. Words that end in *-ing* and seem like verbs are actually *verbals*. Just remember that an *-ing* word can never function by itself as a verb, and you will stay out of trouble. To be a verb, the *-ing* word must have a helper:

     S   V

Rosemary is running along the beach.

The word *is* is a helping verb. Because we have added a subject and a helping verb to the *-ing* word, we now have a clause.

Clauses are either *independent* or *dependent*.

> **2. Independent clause (IC).** *An independent clause is a clause that makes a complete statement and therefore may stand alone as a sentence.*

Independent clauses:

> S   V
> The monkey is brown.

> S   V
> The automobile runs smoothly.

> S   V
> Marilyn knows her.

> S   V
> (You) Close the door.

In the final example above, *you* is an unstated but understood subject. That is, readers understand the subject to be present in the sentence, even though it isn't actually there. Such understood subjects are common in imperative sentences—sentences that give commands or directions.

> **3. Dependent clause (DC).** *A dependent clause is a clause that makes an incomplete statement and therefore may not stand alone as a sentence.*

Dependent clauses:

> S   V
> *Although* the monkey is brown. . . .

> S   V
> *If* the automobile runs smoothly. . . .

> S   V
> . . . *whom* Marilyn knows.

> S   V
> *After* you close the door. . . .

Dependent Clause

Notice that a dependent clause is not a sentence by itself. That is why it is dependent—it depends on an independent clause to make a complete, or even an intelligible, statement. By itself, a dependent clause doesn't make any sense.

This definition and the one above for independent clauses—though fairly standard—may not satisfy you. Fortunately, we can offer another definition that works almost all the time (and you don't need to worry about the exceptions). A *dependent clause* almost always contains a subordinating conjunction or a relative pronoun (both covered later in this chapter); we've italicized them in the examples of dependent clauses above so you can see where they are. The subordinating conjunctions and relative pronouns are like red flags signaling dependent clauses. You can recognize an *independent clause,* then, because it contains no subordinating conjunction or relative pronoun.

4. **Sentence.** *A sentence is a group of words that contains at least one independent clause.*

Sentences (independent clauses) are underlined once:

<u>Marilyn knows her.</u>

Although Marilyn knows her, <u>she does not know Marilyn.</u>

After you close the door, <u>Susan will turn on the record player,</u> and <u>Sally will get the potato chips.</u>

5. **Phrase (P).** *A phrase is a group of two or more related words that does not contain both a subject and a verb.*

Phrases: in the submarine

running along the beach

Remember, *-ing* words are not verbs.

6. **Subordinating conjunction (SC).** *A subordinating conjunction is a kind of word that begins a* dependent *clause.*

You should memorize the italicized words (which are quite common) in the following list of subordinating conjunctions.

after	how	though
although	*if*	unless
as	in order that	until
as if	inasmuch as	*when*
as long as	now that	whenever
as much as	provided that	where
as though	*since*	wherever
because	so that	whether
before	than	while

Here are examples of subordinating conjunctions beginning dependent clauses (the dependent clauses are underlined twice):

SC
Because your horse is properly registered, it may run in the race.

SC
The race will be canceled if the rain falls.

SC
Sign up for the trip to Memphis while vacancies still exist.

7. **Relative pronoun (RP).** *A relative pronoun is a kind of word that marks a* dependent *clause.*

However, unlike a subordinating conjunction, a relative pronoun doesn't always come at the beginning of the dependent clause, although it usually does. You should memorize these five common relative pronouns:

who, whose, whom, which, that

Here are examples of relative pronouns in dependent clauses (the dependent clauses are underlined twice):

RP
The woman who runs the bank is registering her horse.

RP
The man whose car lights are on is in the grocery store.

RP
The woman whom I met is in the broker's office.

RP
The schedule with which I was familiar is now obsolete.

RP
The schedule that I knew is now obsolete.

Sometimes, unfortunately, these same five words can function as other than relative pronouns, in which case they *do not* mark dependent clauses:

Not relative pronouns: *Who* is that masked man?

Whose golf club is this?

Whom do you wish to see?

Which car is yours?

That car is mine.

As a general rule, unless they are part of a question, the four words in our list that begin with *w (who, whose, whom,* and *which)* are relative pronouns. The other word, *that,* is trickier, but we can generally say that unless it is pointing out something, it is a relative pronoun. In "That car is mine," *that* points out a car, so it is not a relative pronoun.

8. **Conjunctive adverb (CA).** *A conjunctive adverb is a kind of word that marks an* independent *clause.*

Many students make punctuation errors because they confuse subordinating conjunctions (which mark dependent clauses) with conjunctive adverbs (which mark independent clauses). You should memorize the italicized words (which are quite common) in the list of conjunctive adverbs below:

accordingly	*however*	next
as a result	indeed	nonetheless
consequently	in fact	otherwise
first	instead	second
for example	likewise	still
for instance	meanwhile	*therefore*
furthermore	moreover	thus
hence	*nevertheless*	unfortunately

Transition Words

You may remember seeing some of these words in Chapter 5, "Coherence." A conjunctive adverb serves as a *transition,* showing the relationship between the independent clause it is in and the independent clause that preceded it.

A conjunctive adverb may not seem to mark an independent clause, but it does. The following examples are perfectly correct as sentences because they are independent clauses:

CA

Therefore, I am the winner.

CA

However, the car is red.

Often a conjunctive adverb begins the second independent clause in a sentence because that clause is closely related in meaning to the first independent clause:

CA

I finished in first place; therefore, I am the winner.

CA

You thought your new car would be blue; however, the car is metallic brown.

Sometimes a conjunctive adverb appears in the middle or even at the end of a clause (that clause, of course, is still independent):

CA

I finished in first place; I am, therefore, the winner.

CA

I finished in first place; I am the winner, therefore.

9. Coordinating conjunction (CC). *A coordinating conjunction is a word that joins two or more units that are grammatically alike.*

You should learn these seven coordinating conjunctions:

and	*nor*	*so*
but	*or*	*yet*
for		

A helpful learning aid is that the coordinating conjunctions are all two or three letters long. A coordinating conjunction can do the following:

CC

Join two or more words: Bill and Mary

CC

Join two or more phrases: in the car and beside the horse

CC

Join two or more dependent clauses: after the dance was over but before the party began

Join two or more independent clauses: He won the Philadelphia

CC

Marathon, for he had been practicing several months.

Remember: Unlike subordinating conjunctions, relative pronouns, and conjunctive adverbs, the coordinating conjunction is not a marker for either an independent clause or a dependent clause. It simply joins two or more like items.

EXERCISES

A. In the sentences below, underline each independent clause once and each dependent clause twice. Label each subordinating conjunction (SC), relative pronoun (RP), conjunctive adverb (CA), and coordinating conjunction (CC).

1. Kleenex was developed during World War I as a substitute for cotton surgical gauze.

2. Although it had been developed for medical use, Kleenex was marketed commercially in 1919.

3. Advertisers presented Kleenex as a "sanitary" means to remove makeup, but buyers found many additional uses for the product.

4. A Kleenex tissue was disposable; consequently, many people felt it was more sanitary than a reusable pocket handkerchief.

5. When it was established, the Mason-Dixon Line had no connection to Northern or Southern sentiments.

6. In 1750 the English Court of Chancery ordered the line to be drawn because the court wanted to settle border disputes between the Penns (of Pennsylvania) and the Calverts (of Maryland).

7. The Penns and Calverts hired two surveyors from England; they wanted surveyors who would not be biased toward either family.

8. After Charles Mason and Jeremiah Dixon worked between 1763 and 1767, they established a line that you still can recognize on maps of the United States today.

9. Even though the Mason-Dixon Line itself separates only Pennsylvania and Maryland, the line also was used as the north-south boundary limiting the spread of slavery in the Missouri Compromise of 1820.

10. Thus, a line that began as a surveyed boundary became the symbolic division between North and South after it was associated with the limits of slavery.

B. In the sentences below, underline each independent clause once and each dependent clause twice. Label each subordinating conjunction (SC), relative pronoun (RP), conjunctive adverb (CA), and coordinating conjunction (CC).

1. Fannie Farmer standardized measurements in recipes in her first cookbook in 1896; to her we owe the concept of a level teaspoon.

2. Thousands of miles of wooden roads were laid in several American states in the 1840s and 1850s; most were replaced by gravel roads, however, when the wooden planks began to rot.

3. Richard Lawrence, who was the first person to attempt to assassinate a U.S. president, fired two pistols at Andrew Jackson at point-blank range.

4. Although both weapons were properly loaded and although later tests proved both pistols functional, both misfired.

5. Lawrence was charged with simple assault, which was a misdemeanor in those days, because there was no legal precedent for dealing with a failed assassination attempt.

6. Because the prosecutor (Washington District Attorney Francis Scott Key) agreed with the defense that Lawrence was mad, Lawrence was freed on a plea of insanity and spent the rest of his life in asylums.

7. Milton Hershey began building his fortune by making caramels, and he produced chocolate formed as cigarettes and dominoes as a novelty.

8. Because chocolate would retain the impression of his name in hot weather, Hershey began to focus on chocolates.

9. David Rice Atchison became president of the United States for one day when Zachary Taylor delayed taking the oath of office for a day because Inauguration Day fell on Sunday.

10. Although he died before taking the new seat, ex-President John Tyler was elected to the Confederate House of Representatives, so the Confederates buried him with honors in Richmond while the Union ignored his death.

11. Ray Kroc was impressed by the clean, efficient, and high-volume operations in a drive-in restaurant that the McDonald brothers owned in San Bernardino, California.

12. Kroc persuaded the McDonald brothers to let him create a franchise of their system; part of the agreement, however, retained the original McDonald's name.

13. Kroc opened his first franchise drive-in in Des Plaines, Illinois, in 1955; in 5 years there were 228 franchise operations marketing some $40 million of fast food annually.

14. Antonio López de Santa Anna, Mexican leader at the Alamo, brought to New York in 1869 a lump of chicle, the sap of the sapodilla tree; he hoped that inventor Thomas Adams could create a rubber substitute from the chicle.

15. Adams failed at inventing a rubber substitute from refined chicle; however, after seeing a girl buy paraffin to chew, he used the chicle to create chewing gum.

CHAPTER 27

Sentence Fragment

A sentence fragment is an error involving punctuation.

Sentence fragment (frag). *A sentence fragment is a group of words punctuated like a sentence but lacking an independent clause.*

Because it lacks an independent clause, a sentence fragment is just a piece of a sentence. Here are some examples:

Sentence fragments: Running along the beach.

Even though the movie won an Oscar.

These so-called sentences are actually frauds: they begin with a capital letter and end with a period, but they lack an independent clause.

Usually a sentence fragment relates closely to the sentence that preceded it. The two examples above might have appeared in the following contexts:

Sentence fragments: I finally found that stray mutt. Running along the beach.

Marie absolutely refused to go to the theater. Even though the movie had won an Oscar.

To correct a sentence fragment, either connect it to an independent clause or add a subject and a verb to convert it to an independent clause.

Fragments connected to independent clauses:

I finally found that stray mutt running along the beach.

Marie absolutely refused to go to the theater even though the movie had won an Oscar.

Fragments converted to independent clauses:

I finally found that stray mutt. It was running along the beach.

Marie absolutely refused to go to the theater. The movie had won an Oscar.

Of the two types of changes above, most readers would prefer the connection of the fragment to an independent clause. That solution provides smoother writing, avoiding the choppiness that results from converting each fragment to its own independent clause. More important, however, the first solution increases coherence: connecting the fragment to an independent clause links the thought of the fragment to the thought of the independent clause.

Are fragments always wrong? No, of course not. Fragments are common in speech and appear in all types of writing. You'll find examples in this book because the writing was designed to communicate to you directly, as if the authors were speaking to you. Because fragments break the conventional pattern of writing, they can create a useful effect. For example, the second "sentence" of this paragraph—really a fragment—communicates the desired thought more directly and simply than would this sentence combination: "Are fragments always wrong? No, of course fragments are not always wrong." And because the fragment answers the question in the first sentence, the meaning is clear.

Cautions

- Fragments are never acceptable if they destroy coherence.
- Be aware of your probable readers. Some may never find fragments acceptable.
- Use fragments sparingly for good effect.

EXERCISES

A. Indicate whether each "sentence" below is a complete sentence or only a fragment.

1. The American South being called "Dixie Land" during the Civil War.

2. The name "Dixie" originally was a nickname for New Orleans.

3. The nickname for New Orleans coming from a ten-dollar note issued by a local bank, each note showing *Dix*, French for "10," on both sides.

4. Both Tony Curtis and Jack Lemmon appeared in drag in the film classic *Some Like It Hot.*

5. *Narcissism* being the psychiatric term for "self-love."

6. In 1933 Fleischer Studios introduced a sailor named Popeye in an animated cartoon starring Betty Boop.

7. A five-thousand-year-old ear of popping corn found in a cave in New Mexico.

8. Although based on ancient games, the modern Olympics, founded by Baron Pierre de Coubertin.

9. Dancer Bill Robinson's nickname was Mr. Bojangles.

10. Was it Robert Frost who wrote that "Good fences make good neighbors"?

11. Known as Minnesota Fats, Willie Mosconi, considered the world's greatest pool player, once sunk 526 balls in a row.

12. Even though each player has eight pawns at the beginning of a game of chess.

13. The headless horseman chasing frightened Ichabod Crane in "The Legend of Sleepy Hollow."

14. Finding the Great Lakes, early explorers were so impressed with the vastness of the water that they thought they had found the passage to the Orient.

15. America's Great Plains were at first thought to be unfit for agriculture.

B. Correct each of the following sentence-fragment combinations in two ways.

1. M&Ms were introduced in 1941 as part of Army C-rations. Providing American soldiers bite-sized pieces of energy-producing chocolate covered with a candy coating.

2. The Puritans fled England to seek religious freedom. But proved intolerant of other religions in America.

3. The term *private eye* comes from the logo of Allan Pinkerton's National Detective Agency. An open eye with the words "We never sleep."

4. Thomas "Boston" Corbett, of the 16th New York Cavalry, claimed to have shot John Wilkes Booth with an Army carbine. Even though the autopsy showed Booth died from a pistol bullet.

5. Herman Melville planned *Moby Dick* to be a sea adventure, like his previous two novels. But Ahab's obsession with the white whale taking the book along symbolic paths examining the nature of good and evil.

C. Correct the following sentence fragments.

1. On August 6, 1930, Judge Joseph Force Crater dined with friends, entered a taxi to go to a Broadway show, and disappeared. After hearing testimony from almost one hundred witnesses, a grand jury finding it had no idea what had happened to Judge Crater.

2. A popular graffiti message becoming "Judge Crater, call your office."

3. The saying "buyer beware" applies to an early Sears catalog advertisement. Because it offered a sewing machine for one dollar but the buyer received only a needle and thread.

4. Although he was never in a battle, Stephen Crane wrote "The Red Badge of Courage" about a soldier's struggle with fear during combat. His description being so vivid and realistic that many Civil War veterans insisted the battle described was one they had fought in.

5. The U.S. purchase of Alaska for $7.2 million in 1867 was not a widely popular move. It being called "Seward's Folly" and gaining U.S. Senate approval by only one vote.

6. C. W. Post marketed a wheat flake cereal originally named "Elijah's Manna" but changed that name to "Post Toasties." Because religious groups created a storm of protest over the use of the religious name.

7. *The Last of the Mohicans* created controversy when it was published in 1826. The reason being its sympathetic portrayal of Native Americans.

8. Until late in the nineteenth century there was no such thing as standard time throughout the United States. The railroads, needing a

dependable timetable for efficient operations, dividing the nation into four time zones in 1863.

9. The Internet beginning in 1969 when the Department of Defense established a computer network linking a number of universities and military facilities in a system resistant to attack because it had no central computer.

10. The hit of the 1893 World's Columbian Exposition in Chicago was a revolving steel wheel, invented by engineer George Washington Ferris, that carried passengers in glass-enclosed cars twenty stories into the air. Whereas today's Ferris wheels usually take passengers up only about forty feet.

CHAPTER 28

Comma Splice and Fused Sentence

Comma splices and fused sentences are sentences that are punctuated incorrectly.

> Comma splice (CS). *A comma splice occurs when two independent clauses are joined by only a comma.*

In other words, two independent clauses are "spliced" together with only a comma. Using *IC* for independent clause, we can express the comma splice as follows:

Comma splice: IC, IC.

Here are some comma splice errors:

Wrong: We hiked for three days, we were very tired.

Wrong: The television is too loud, the picture is fuzzy.

Correcting Comma Splices

There are five ways to correct a comma splice.

1. Change the comma to a period and capitalize the next word. (IC. IC.)
   Correct: We hiked for three days. We were very tired.
2. Change the comma to a semicolon. (IC; IC.)
   Correct: We hiked for three days; we were very tired.
3. Change the comma to a semicolon and add a conjunctive adverb.
   (IC; CA, IC.)

> Correct: We hiked for three days; hence, we were very tired.

4. Add a coordinating conjunction before the second independent clause. (IC, CC IC.)

> Correct: We hiked for three days, so we were very tired.

5. Change one independent clause to a dependent clause. (DC, IC.)

> Correct: Because we hiked for three days, we were very tired.

An extremely common form of comma splice occurs when only a comma precedes a conjunctive adverb at the beginning of the second independent clause in a sentence.

> Wrong: Mount Rainier is beautiful, however, it is also forbidding.

The best way to correct this kind of comma splice is to change the first comma to a semicolon. (IC; CA, IC.)

> Correct: Mount Rainier is beautiful; however, it is also forbidding.

Another form of comma splice occurs when two independent clauses are separated by a dependent clause but the strongest mark of punctuation is still only a comma.

> Wrong: The artist is selling the portrait, because he does not have enough money, he has run out of paint.

How would you correct the sentence above? Does the writer mean that the artist is selling the portrait because he does not have enough money? Or does the writer mean the artist has run out of paint because he does not have enough money? Here is one instance in which correct punctuation is essential to meaning. One of several ways to correct the sentence is to place a period on the appropriate side of the dependent clause, depending on the meaning you wish to express. (IC DC. IC.) or (IC. DC, IC.)

> Correct: The artist is selling the portrait because he does not have enough money. He has run out of paint.

> Correct: The artist is selling the portrait. Because he does not have enough money, he has run out of paint.

Fused sentence (FS). *A fused sentence occurs when two independent clauses are joined without punctuation or a coordinating conjunction.*

In other words, a fused sentence is a comma splice without the comma.

Fused sentence: IC IC.

Here are some fused-sentence errors:

Wrong: We hiked for three days we were very tired.

Wrong: The television is too loud the picture is fuzzy.

Correcting Fused Sentences

Correct a fused sentence with essentially the same methods you used to correct a comma splice:

1. Add a period after the first independent clause and capitalize the next word. (IC. IC.)

   Correct: The television is too loud. The picture is fuzzy.

2. Add a semicolon after the first independent clause. (IC; IC.)

   Correct: The television is too loud; the picture is fuzzy.

3. Add a semicolon and a conjunctive adverb after the first independent clause. (IC; CA, IC.)

   Correct: The television is too loud; furthermore, the picture is fuzzy.

4. Add a comma and a coordinating conjunction after the first independent clause. (IC, CC IC.)

   Correct: The television is too loud, and the picture is fuzzy.

5. Change one independent clause to a dependent clause. (DC, IC.)

   Correct: Whenever the television is too loud, the picture is fuzzy.

EXERCISES

A. Correct the following comma splice in five different ways.

   Clara Barton became famous for her work in hospitals during the Civil War, she founded the American Red Cross in 1881.

B. Correct the following fused sentence in five different ways.

   Baseball cards began as incentives to buy products they appeared as bonuses in packs of cigarettes in the 1880s and with chewing gum in the 1930s.

C. For each sentence below, write *CS* if the sentence is a comma splice, *FS* if it is a fused sentence, or *Correct* if it is correct.

1. ____ Sequoya created the Cherokee alphabet, the first written alphabet for a Native American tribe, he believed that written letters were the key to the white man's power.

2. ____ Alfred Butts invented a game named Lexico (later Scrabble) during the Depression he covered a checkerboard with paper and ruled a 225-square grid on the paper.

3. ____ Railway-station agent Richard Sears and watchmaker Alvah Roebuck began the mail-order business in 1893; their 538-page catalog offered rural people merchandise without a trip to a town or city.

4. ____ Workmen in New York City in 1931 erected a sixteen-foot Christmas tree among the rubble of their building site they were working on the future Rockefeller Center.

5. ____ They used tin cans, paper, and tinsel for decorations, two years later seven hundred blue and white lights adorned the first official Christmas tree at Rockefeller Center.

6. ____ *The Andy Griffith Show* demonstrated that a small town and its values could be the makings of a successful sit-com the show's Mayberry, North Carolina, lacked crime but was filled with eccentric characters.

7. ____ Novelist Dashiell Hammett drew on his eight years as a Pinkerton detective for background for his detective novels; his most famous fictional detective was Sam Spade, in the *Maltese Falcon*.

8. ____ The famous painting of George Washington and his army crossing the Delaware on Christmas night in 1776 was painted in Germany in 1851 the boats, flag, clothing, and ice are not accurate.

9. ____ Nathan Hale was hanged for spying against the British during the American Revolution, according to accounts of British eyewitnesses, Hale's last words were not "I regret that I have but one life to lose for my country."

10. ____ Former Teamsters Union president Jimmy Hoffa disappeared from a restaurant parking lot outside Detroit in 1975; the Mafia has often been suspected of causing the disappearance.

11. ____ In the mid-nineteenth century, paying postage on a letter got the mail to the addressee's post office to get the letter the recipient had to pay an additional fee.

12. ____ When the Whig Party nominated Zachary Taylor for president in 1848, they notified him by mail, Taylor didn't know he was nominated because he would not pay to receive the letter.

13. ____ After the First and Second Battles of Bull Run devastated his home and land, Wilmer McLean moved his family to Appomattox Court House, Virginia, there his home was used in 1865 for surrender talks between Generals Lee and Grant.

14. ____ George Eastman brought photography to the common man with his Kodak camera in 1888; with his lighter, cheaper Brownie camera in 1900 he ensured the availability of handheld cameras for the masses.

15. ____ K-rations ensured that American soldiers could carry with them three "meals" packaged together in cardboard, the *K* comes from the name of the designer, Ansel Keys.

16. ____ In 1874 billions of Rocky Mountain locusts arrived in the Great Plains and ravaged farms for several years a swarm would settle in an area, eat everything in sight, including clothes and curtains, and then move on.

17. ____ People hit the locusts, set out smudge pots to drive them off, burned fields where they had settled, and even fired guns at them, nothing worked.

18. ____ The Rocky Mountain locust was extinct by 1902; no reason for its extinction has been discovered.

19. ____ Many people today think the Edsel failed because of the design of its grill; in truth, the car failed because it was a full-sized car that hit the market just when the public was demanding smaller, more economical cars.

20. ____ A visit to Monument Valley Navajo Tribal Park would take most of us to magnificent views we've already seen the red sandstone buttes and pinnacles of Monument Valley have appeared in dozens of Westerns and many advertisements for automobiles, especially for all-terrain vehicles.

D. Choose three sentences with comma splices and three fused sentences from Exercise C and rewrite them correctly.

CHAPTER 29

Comma

This chapter presents the nine most important uses of the comma (,).

1. Use a comma after every item in a series except the last item.

> Example: The ethics of contemporary surgery are often a problem for the patient, the doctor, and the patient's family.

You probably already knew to put a comma after the first item (*patient* in this case), but why do you need one after the next-to-last item (*doctor*)? Consider this example:

> Example: The ethics of contemporary surgery are often a problem for the patient, the doctor and the hospital board, and the patient's family.

Each comma tells your reader that you are moving to the next item in a series. If you omit a comma, you imply that you're still in the same item—a compound item, as in the example above. However, if readers find only the end of your sentence, they have to reread to confirm the substance of your series. Providing the final comma helps readers understand where they are in a series so they don't have to reread.

Is the Final Comma Necessary?

Some magazines apply the editorial policy that the final comma in a series isn't really necessary because readers can identify the final item in a series from context. In many cases this policy works well. However, as we've shown, the final comma ensures that readers don't have to reread a sentence to verify the parts of the series. Forcing rereading is a hazard if you omit the final comma. For this reason, many authorities agree that using the final comma benefits efficient communications.

Whichever editorial policy you choose to follow, *be consistent.* Omitting the final comma on some occasions but using it on others will throw readers off course completely because they can find no recognizable pattern. Inconsistency requires readers to recheck all your series.

2. **Use a comma before a coordinating conjunction that joins two independent clauses. (IC, CC IC.)**

Examples: I never liked parsnips, but my mother made me eat them.

$$\overbrace{\hspace{4cm}}^{IC} \quad CC \quad \overbrace{\hspace{4cm}}^{IC}$$

She thought they were great, and she thought they would make me grow taller.

Note: Do not confuse a coordinating conjunction that joins two verbs with a coordinating conjunction that joins two independent clauses.

   S   V   CC   V

The parsnips tasted awful and looked like paste.

No comma precedes the coordinating conjunction because it connects only the two verbs *tasted* and *looked.*

3. **Use a comma after a dependent clause that begins a sentence. (DC, IC.)**

Examples: Although Harriet tried as hard as she could, she could not win even a fun-run.

Because she couldn't run fast enough, she couldn't have the free T-shirt for the first two hundred runners crossing the finish line.

**4. Use a comma after a long phrase that begins a sentence.
(Long phrase, IC.)**

The word *long* is rather vague, of course, but usually you will wish to place a comma after an introductory phrase of three or more words.

Long Phrase

Examples: Even after a grueling night of writing, I couldn't finish the paper.

Long Phrase

Running to my next class, I tried to think of an excuse to give my professor.

5. Use commas to set off any word, phrase, or clause that interrupts the flow of the sentence.

In other words, if you could set off a word or group of words with parentheses or dashes but do not wish to, set off that word or group of words with commas.

Examples: My first excuse, wild as it was, didn't sound convincing.

I had thought of several good excuses for not finishing my paper, such as a computer error deleted my only draft.

The excuse I settled on was quite good, especially the part about the dog in the dormitory.

The class, together with the professor, turned their heads as I plowed into the classroom.

The professor ignored me as he finished his lecture, "Freshman English for Nonconformists."

Notice that interrupters in the middle of sentences have commas on *both* sides. You'll learn more about setting off interrupters with commas, parentheses, and dashes in Chapter 32.

6. Use commas to set off nonrestrictive clauses.

This rule is actually an expansion of rule 5, because all nonrestrictive clauses are interrupters. You may wonder, however, just what restrictive and nonrestrictive clauses are.

A *restrictive clause* is essential to defining whatever it modifies. If you have only one brother, you could say, "My brother is meaner than I am." Because you have only one brother, no modifier is necessary to distinguish which brother you mean. But what if you have several brothers? Now you need to include a modifier that will restrict the meaning of *brother* to a particular brother.

My brother who is wearing a red motorcycle helmet is meaner than I am.

The restrictive clause *(who is wearing a red motorcycle helmet)* is essential to defining *brother*, limiting any brother to the one wearing the helmet. You probably noticed that a restrictive clause is not an interrupter and, therefore, is not set off with commas.

A *nonrestrictive clause* is not essential to defining whatever it modifies—it just supplies additional information. Because it is not essential, you could omit it and everybody would still know who (or what) you are talking about. Thus, if you have only one brother, you could write this:

My brother, who is wearing a red motorcycle helmet, is meaner than I am.

Because you have only one brother, readers could omit the nonrestrictive clause *(who is wearing a red motorcycle helmet)* and still know who you are referring to. The word modified—*brother*—is not limited in any way by the clause; it is only described in more detail. You'll notice that we set off nonrestrictive clauses with commas (or parentheses or dashes), just as we do other interrupters.

Thus, the presence or absence of commas with modifying clauses becomes quite important for how readers interpret what you write. For example, consider this statement:

Authorities say that truckers who drive unsafe rigs cause most of the accidents on the Beltway.

Who causes most of the accidents? All truckers? No, the absence of commas tells us that the blame falls on "truckers who drive unsafe rigs." *Who drive unsafe rigs* is a restrictive clause limiting *all truckers* to that portion with unsafe equipment.

Now consider this example:

The board members are not likely to question the Research Department's recommendations, which are generally well prepared.

A comma sets off *which are generally well prepared,* the nonrestrictive clause that provides additional detail—in this case one possible explanation for why the board members almost always accept recommendations from the Research Department. Is this essential information? No, the punctuation within the sentence indicates that the board members almost always accept recommendations from this particular department; why they do so remains speculation.

7. Use commas to set off a conjunctive adverb. (CA, IC.), (IC, CA.), (IC; CA, IC.), or (IC; IC, CA.).

This rule applies no matter where the conjunctive adverb appears within the sentence. If, as in the next-to-last example, the conjunctive adverb is in the middle of the independent clause, it will have commas on *both* sides of it.

IC   CA

Examples: The beautiful young princess kissed the frog. However, his lily

IC

pad started sinking when she stepped on it.

IC   CA

The beautiful young princess kissed the frog; however, his lily pad started

IC

sinking when she stepped on it.

IC   CA

The beautiful young princess kissed the frog; his lily pad, however,

IC

started sinking when she stepped on it.

IC   IC

The beautiful young princess kissed the frog; his lily pad started sinking

CA

when she stepped on it, however.

8. Use a comma between coordinate adjectives unless they are joined by "and."

Coordinate adjectives are sets of adjectives that independently modify a noun.

Example: The bulldog is noted for its wrinkled, flattened face.

Both *wrinkled* and *flattened* modify *face* independently. That is not the case with cumulative adjectives. When an adjective's modification is cumulative, it modifies not only the noun but also the whole adjective-noun phrase it precedes.

Example: Alicia wore a red felt hat.

Here *red* modifies not just *hat* but the phrase *felt hat*. Notice that no comma is used with cumulative adjectives.

Coordinate and Cumulative Adjectives

Distinguishing between coordinate and cumulative adjectives isn't always simple. However, because of the independence of coordinate adjectives, you can check for two characteristics that help identify them.

- Coordinate adjectives are reversible, whereas cumulative adjectives aren't. That is, *flattened, wrinkled face* works as well as *wrinkled, flattened face*. On the other hand, *felt red hat* just sounds foolish.
- *And* fits naturally between coordinate adjectives, but not between cumulative adjectives. Thus, you could write *wrinkled and flattened face* but not *red and felt hat*.

Of course, modifier chains can include both coordinate and cumulative adjectives.

Example: The stands were full for the homecoming game even though it was a cold, rainy autumn day.

Cold and *rainy* are coordinate and are separated by a comma. However, both modify *autumn day* rather than just *day*, so there is no comma after *rainy*.

9. Use a comma to set off words in direct address.

Words in direct address normally are names but can be phrases used in place of names.

Examples: Kristina, have you washed the dishes?

Where are you going now, little sister?

You look charming, Alicia, wearing that red felt hat.

Notice that the word in direct address in the last example has commas on *both* sides because it occurs in the middle of the sentence.

EXERCISES

A. For each pair of sentences below, answer the accompanying question.

1. Which sentence implies that only part of the hamburgers are spoiled?

    a. Don't eat the hamburgers that are spoiled.

    b. Don't eat the hamburgers, which are spoiled.

2. Which sentence implies that only one emergency board meeting has occurred?

    a. The emergency board meeting, which was held last Wednesday, resulted in the resignation of the company's president.

    b. The emergency board meeting that was held last Wednesday resulted in the resignation of the company's president.

3. Which sentence implies that not all tourists show proper respect?

    a. Tourists who show proper respect are welcome in the churches of Italy.

    b. Tourists, who show proper respect, are welcome in the churches of Italy.

B. Writing a nonrestrictive modifier as if it were a restrictive one can make your writing seem foolish. That's the cause of the logical problem in this sentence:

The 1996 death of chief editor Jonathan Quinlan caused a change in the newspaper's editorial policies.

    a. What is the illogical implication in this sentence?

    b. Rewrite the sentence to correct the problem.

C. Add commas where necessary in the following sentences.

    1. A weather vane has a practical purpose indicating a shift in wind direction but many weather vanes also are noteworthy as art objects.

    2. Wood carvers and metal workers have created weather vanes that advertise a trade support a particular cause or just demonstrate a sense of humor.

    3. During Prohibition which started with the 18th Amendment and ended with its repeal it was illegal to make sell or transport liquor in the United States yet drinking liquor was not against the law.

4. As we know from books and movies about the Prohibition years public drinking moved to speakeasies but drinking also became popular at home a new habit for Americans.

5. California's wine makers produced a legal grape juice that easily became a thirty-proof wine after sixty days of home fermentation.

6. Beer makers made wort which was a half-brewed beer without alcohol; likewise home fermentation would produce an alcoholic beer.

7. Information on making a home still was readily available in books and magazines and the federal government even offered a pamphlet on home brewing.

8. Rudolph which is farther south—Minneapolis Indianapolis or Chicago?

9. Even when he played a disreputable character John Wayne's movies were marked with his drawl his swagger and his strong code of ethics.

10. John Wayne Maureen served as the ideal male for many young people in America.

11. The helmet law that was passed in 1995 requires even tricycle riders to wear protective helmets. [Punctuate to imply the existence of other helmet laws with other provisions.]

12. The helmet law which was passed in 1995 requires even tricycle riders to wear protective helmets. [Punctuate to imply the passage of only one helmet law.]

13. Although he had achieved success as a newspaper writer Mark Twain wanted to be published in a magazine so he was delighted when his "Forty-three Days in an Open Boat" appeared in *Harper's New Monthly Magazine.*

14. Unfortunately because *Harper's* editors had trouble reading Twain's handwriting his story appeared with the author shown as Mike Swain.

15. The Batman television series and movies featured the Riddler the Joker and the Penguin.

16. Teflon is the trade name for tetrafluoroethylene a plastic that is not affected by other chemicals and that is extremely slippery.

17. Teflon is used to make pans that prevent foods from sticking to line tubes and to coat conveyor belts.

18. The word *teflon* also is used to indicate someone who is not affected by criticism—a "teflon politician" for example.

19. As its name implies bone china is porcelain that includes the calcium phosphate ash from burned bones.

20. In addition to its use in ceramics bone ash is also used as a fertilizer and in cleaning and polishing compounds.

21. The teddy bear inspired by a cartoon that showed President Theodore Roosevelt sparing the life of a bear cub became a hit at a toy fair in Germany in 1903 and later the toy bears became popular in the United States.

22. Atlantic City merchants began the Miss America pageant in 1921 as a gimmick to keep tourists there after Labor Day and the first Miss America a sixteen-year-old schoolgirl won a golden statue of a mermaid.

23. When Tennessee passed a law forbidding the teaching of evolution the American Civil Liberties Union offered to defend anyone willing to test the law's prohibition of free speech.

24. John Scopes who taught science in a Tennessee high school was recruited to be the defendant starting the so-called "Monkey Trial" which matched William Jennings Bryan for the prosecution against Clarence Darrow for the defense.

25. Scopes told *Life* magazine after the trial that he had only substituted in the biology class and that he doubted he had really taught evolution because he knew little about it.

26. Noah Webster began the separation of American English from British English creating the situation that punsters call "two nations separated by a common language."

27. Webster deliberately modified the British spelling of words such as *honour* based spelling and usage on common speech and set forth a "new language" for a new nation.

28. Webster also invented a new way to teach spelling the spelling bee a teaching device that is still popular today.

29. Although she wanted to be known for the support she gave the feminist struggle newspaper editor Amelia Jenks Bloomer is remembered for "bloomers" the adaptation of Turkish pantaloons she popularized.

30. Joseph Stalin who led the Soviet Union through World War II was *Time*'s "Man of the Year" for both 1939 and 1942.

CHAPTER 30
Semicolon

The semicolon (;) is stronger than a comma but weaker than a period. This chapter presents the three most important uses of the semicolon.

1. **Use a semicolon between two independent clauses closely related in meaning but not joined by a coordinating conjunction. (IC; IC.)**

                       IC   IC

   Examples: Lee won some battles; Grant won the war.

                  IC   IC

   The pale sun rose over the frozen land; the arctic fox gazed quietly

   at the sky.

2. **Use a semicolon between two independent clauses when the second independent clause is joined to the first with a conjunctive adverb. (IC; CA, IC.)**

                         IC   CA

   Examples: Auto theft is a major national crime; however, people keep

              IC

   leaving their cars unlocked.

             IC   CA   IC

   Most stolen cars are recovered; unfortunately, many have been vandalized.

Note: If a conjunctive adverb is moved from the beginning of the second independent clause into the middle of it, the conjunctive adverb is then preceded by a comma instead of a semicolon; the semicolon, however, remains between the independent clauses.

$$\overbrace{\hspace{4cm}}^{IC} \qquad \underline{CA} \quad \underline{IC}$$

Example: Most stolen cars are recovered; many, unfortunately, have been

vandalized.

3. **When commas occur within one or more of the items in a series, use semicolons rather than commas to separate the items in the series.**

Commas normally separate the items, with the commas clearly indicating where each portion of the series begins and ends. When any portion needs its own commas, however, readers may become confused if commas separate the portions of the series.

> Confusing: Key air routes include Lisbon, Portugal, Rome, Italy, Frankfurt, Germany, and Istanbul, Turkey.

Readers with a good sense of world geography probably would understand this sample. However, you can make the readers' job easier by using semicolons to separate the major items in the series.

> Better: Key air routes include Lisbon, Portugal; Rome, Italy; Frankfurt, Germany; and Istanbul, Turkey.

This way readers won't have to reread to understand the structure of the series.

EXERCISES

In the following sentences, add semicolons and commas where necessary.

1. Try as it might the U.S. government could not convict Al Capone for his notorious crimes instead the government imprisoned him in 1931 for income-tax evasion.

2. Throughout the world there are numerous ways of portraying Santa Claus the rotund red-cheeked man most Americans know as Santa Claus comes from his portrayal by cartoonist Thomas Nast.

3. *Citrus paradisi* is the name for the grapefruit tree whoever named it must not have been thinking of the acid pulp of the fruit of the tree.

4. The Dust Bowl of the 1930s was centered on the area where Colorado New Mexico Texas and Oklahoma meet in all the Dust Bowl equaled an area more than twice the size of Pennsylvania.

5. The 1920s brought prosperity to the area and millions of acres of land were plowed and planted however when drought came in 1931 crop failures left nothing to hold the loose soil in place as winds swept the region.

6. In January 1933 the first great dust storm blew through the region winds blew away an estimated 850 million tons of topsoil in 1935 alone.

7. Unfortunately the natural conditions that led to the Dust Bowl still exist in the Southwest indeed only careful soil management and conservation keep the disaster of the 1930s from reoccurring.

8. Even though it features the trouble and misery of Dust Bowl farmers John Steinbeck's classic *The Grapes of Wrath* became a best-seller when it appeared during the Depression it spoke to the misfortunes everyone was suffering and portrayed Americans as strong enough to endure.

9. In Boston in January 1919 a steel tank filled with more than two million gallons of molasses popped its rivets as the tank flew apart the first wave of molasses was some thirty feet high.

10. The wave of molasses swept away people and animals and crushed buildings the disaster killed twenty-one people and injured more than fifty others.

11. After the wave subsided some streets were left with molasses up to three feet deep for weeks people tracked molasses all over Boston they stuck to things they touched or sat on and the odor of molasses hung over the city.

12. In the early 1900s archaeologists were finding so few undisturbed areas among the royal tombs in Egypt that most concluded grave robbers had taken everything of value then in November 1992 Howard Carter opened the tomb of Tutankhamen the boy-pharaoh and found its contents nearly intact.

13. The statues and particularly the golden objects recovered from the tomb of Tutankhamen caught the attention of the world even today many people have heard of King Tut.

14. Charles Willson Peale painted a tall rectangular canvas with two of his sons climbing the stairs after he mounted the canvas in a doorway and put a real step on the bottom the illusion was so effective that George Washington bowed a greeting to the boys.

15. The Empire State Building originally was planned to be only 4 feet taller than the 1,046-foot Chrysler Building but builders added a 200-foot mooring mast for dirigibles when they realized how dangerous a dirigible mast could be builders converted it into a tower with an observation deck making the building 1,250 feet tall.

16. The battle between the *Monitor* and the *Merrimack* was the first battle between two ironclad ships though their battle was inconclusive it spelled the end of the prominence of wooden ships.

17. When England refused to accept Germany's conquests in continental Europe Hitler ordered Operation Sea Lion a plan for a massive invasion of England however Germany could afford to invade England only after gaining air superiority over landing sites there.

18. Germany's air war against England had three stages: first German planes tested Britain's air defenses with attacks against coastal towns and shipping second Germany flew major raids against Royal Air Force installations in an attempt to destroy Britain's air defenses on the ground finally the air war escalated to attacks on Britain's major cities.

19. In August 1940 the German Air Force accidentally bombed London Winston Churchill ordered the Royal Air Force to respond with attacks on Berlin which angered Hitler so much that he ordered the attacks on Britain's major cities.

20. The shift of German air raids from Royal Air Force installations to Britain's cities may have ended Germany's hopes to invade England though German attacks on cities were devastating for the British people they allowed the Royal Air Force to rebuild and Germany could not gain the air superiority it needed for an invasion.

CHAPTER 31
Colon

The English language has many rules for the colon, several of them relatively obscure. But there is one important rule you should know:

> **Use a colon after the last independent clause in a sentence to point to some more useful information about what you just said.**

Virtually any grammatical unit can follow the colon:

- a word or phrase
- a series of words or phrases
- a dependent clause
- an independent clause (or sentence)
- even a series of independent clauses or sentences

Examples:

> The used car had one large defect: no engine.

> The used car had three large defects: no tires, no brakes, no engine.

> She sold the car for good reason: because it had no engine.

> She sold the car for good reason: it had no engine.

> She sold the car for three good reasons: It had no tires. It had no brakes. It had no engine.

When you have one entire sentence after the colon, should you capitalize the first letter of that sentence? There's no real standard: some style manuals do and some don't. (*Or* There's no real standard: *Some* style manuals do and some don't.) Authorities agree, though, that when you have a *series of sentences* after the colon you should begin each with a capital letter.

The rule in this chapter says to put a colon after an independent clause. Although there are sometimes reasons to put colons after words, phrases, or dependent clauses, we suggest that first you learn and apply the one simple rule we have given you: it can do wonderful things for your writing.

You should avoid unnecessary colons, however. But how can you tell whether a colon is necessary? The rule we've given you says that the colon points to additional useful information about what you've just written. You may find it useful to think of the colon as a sort of equal sign. After something that comes before it, the colon points to a sort of equivalency for what came before: something that equals that earlier thought. For example, colons frequently precede lists when what comes before the colon announces the list, as in this example:

> He bought four items: two bicycle tires, a bicycle pump, and a tire
>   repair kit.

Before the colon is *four items,* announcing the list; after the colon follow the four items the colon points to. Here's a more sophisticated example of the same type:

> Germany's air war against Great Britain had three phases: first, raids
>   against coastal targets to test defenses; second, attacks against air
>   defense installations; and third, attacks on major cities.

(You'll also notice that this series uses semicolons because items in the series have interior commas, one of the lessons in the previous chapter.)

Do these examples mean, then, that lists always have a colon before them? No, only if some sort of announcement of the list precedes the colon. In the following sentence the colon is unnecessary because nothing before it points to the list after it:

> Wrong: He bought: two bicycle tires, a bicycle pump, and a tire repair kit.

Notice that the last three examples—all indented to set them off—were preceded by colons. Colons are the most common punctuation mark to come before an indented list, a long quotation, and the like. You also can see that before the colons preceding those three examples were words pointing to the information following the colons: *as in this example, a more sophisticated example of the same type,* and *In the following sentence.* All of those pointers are obvious. In the final example for this chapter the relationship between the material before the colon and that after it is more subtle, but notice that *intriguing start* points to the independent clause following the colon:

The mail-order business got an intriguing start in 1886 when railway-station agent Richard Sears was stuck with a shipment of gold-filled watches: Sears bought the watches himself and telegraphed along the rail line for buyers, selling the watches quickly and demonstrating that he could sell merchandise without an actual store.

EXERCISES

A. Write five sentences using a colon correctly. Follow the colon with these grammatical units (using a different grammatical unit for each of the five sentences):

- a word or phrase
- a series of words or phrases
- a dependent clause
- an independent clause (or sentence)
- a series of independent clauses or sentences

B. Describe the different effects these two sentences produce:

As the two players stared at each other across the net, each communicated the same message: she was going to win.

As the two players stared at each other across the net, each communicated the message that she was going to win.

C. Add colons where appropriate in the following sentences:

1. Since its publication in 1945, one book has been the chief guide for rearing children in America Dr. Benjamin Spock's *The Common Sense Book of Baby and Child Care.*

2. Since its publication in 1945, the book that has been the chief guide for rearing children in America has been Dr. Benjamin Spock's *The Common Sense Book of Baby and Child Care.*

3. At the beginning of the American Civil War many of the uniforms varied from the standard blue and gray that would predominate later a New York regiment in plaid kilts, regiments on both sides in colorful pantaloons and bright jackets of the French Zouaves, and even a Confederate unit with former prisoners in striped pants.

4. Many units in the Civil War comprised recruits, and the fancy uniforms had a special purpose their flair generated local pride and encouraged recruitment.

5. President Ronald Reagan appointed Sandra Day O'Connor as the first female Supreme Court justice.

6. In the fourteenth century, Europe, Africa, and Asia were all ravaged by the same disease the Black Plague.

7. As the first of the Confederate column of troops reached the Union Army command element at Appomattox, Union Major General Joshua Chamberlain gave an unusual order he directed his soldiers to salute the Confederates as a sign of respect and peace.

8. The availability of movies in videocassettes created a booming business video rental stores.

9. In the 1980s many Americans discovered a way to challenge death bungee jumping.

10. In the 1980s many Americans discovered they could challenge death by bungee jumping.

CHAPTER 32
Dash

Years ago people considered the dash too informal for most writing other than letters home. Today, though, the dash has come into its own—it's an extremely handy mark if you want to give a slightly more personal feeling to your writing. If you want to close the gap between you and your readers, use dashes. If you want to widen the gap, don't.

We'll discuss two common rules for the dash. Notice that the first rule we discuss is identical to the one we gave you for the colon (but—yes—the dash gives a more personal feeling).

1. Use a dash after the last independent clause in a sentence to point to some more useful information about what you just said.

Virtually any grammatical unit can follow the dash (though not normally a series of independent clauses):

- a word or phrase
- a series of words or phrases
- a dependent clause
- an independent clause (or sentence)

Examples:

The used car had one large defect—no engine.

The used car had three large defects—no tires, no brakes, no engine.

She sold the car for good reason—because it had no engine.

She sold the car for good reason—it had no engine.

2. Use dashes instead of parentheses to set off useful information in the middle of a sentence.

In the following sentences notice these points:

- The dashes emphasize the words they set off.
- The parentheses remove emphasis from the words they set off and make them seem like a whispered aside.
- The commas provide standard emphasis.

With dashes: The store—the one around the corner—was robbed again.

With parentheses: The store (the one around the corner) was robbed again.

With commas: The store, the one around the corner, was robbed again.

Note: A dash (—) is longer than a hyphen (-). Most word processing and page-layout applications offer dashes as special or optional characters. If your computer application doesn't offer one or if you have only a standard typewriter, you can make a dash in one of three ways:

- You can make a dash - which isn't on a typewriter - by using a hyphen with spaces on each side, as in this sentence.
- You can make a dash--this way--with two hyphens in a row (and no spaces at all on either side).
- Or you can make a dash -- this way -- with two hyphens in a row and a space before and after each set of hyphens.

EXERCISES

A. Write four sentences that use a dash correctly. Follow the dash with these grammatical units (using a different grammatical unit for each of the four sentences):

- a word or phrase
- a series of words or phrases
- a dependent clause
- an independent clause (or sentence)

B. Write four sentences, with dashes, that have useful information in the middle of the sentence. For topics, write about four different places you'd like to visit on a vacation.

C. What different effects do the following sentences have?

Through high school and college she had one goal—marriage.

Through high school and college she had one goal: marriage.

Through high school and college her one goal was marriage.

D. What different effects do the following sentences have?

The applause—amazingly loud—made all the practice seem worthwhile.

The applause (amazingly loud) made all the practice seem worthwhile.

E. Add dashes where appropriate in the following sentences.

1. Travis worked all weekend for one reason money.

2. For the death of Sergeant Elias in Oliver Stone's *Platoon,* the music adapted from Samuel Barber's *Adagio for Strings* adds poignancy to the loss of Elias.

3. For the death of Sergeant Elias in Oliver Stone's *Platoon,* the adaptation of classical music Samuel Barber's *Adagio for Strings* adds poignancy to the loss of Elias.

4. Alfred Hitchcock's *North by Northwest* the title based on Hamlet's statement on his own madness has insanity as an underlying theme.

5. The GI Bill of Rights enabling more than half the American veterans of World War II to attend college or technical school began a boom in the education business.

6. On the evening of Election Day, 1948, many Americans went to bed believing that Thomas E. Dewey would be the next president and awoke to find something different Harry Truman had been reelected.

7. *Geheime Staatspolizei* (or "secret state police") was shortened into an infamous contraction Gestapo.

8. In the early 1900s, rural Americans looked to the two mail-order giants Sears and Montgomery Ward for their every need.

9. The Galapagos Islands known for their endangered species belong to Ecuador.

10. The October breeze surprisingly chilly made spring seem far away.

CHAPTER 33

Apostrophe

The apostrophe (') is, for good reason, one of the most neglected marks of punctuation. Unlike other punctuation marks, the apostrophe can usually be omitted without any loss of meaning. Because it is still an accepted convention of our language, however, we should know its two important uses.

1. Use an apostrophe to show possession.

Examples: Sara's silver Honda

the dog's fleas

Note A: To form the possessive, follow these general rules:

(1) If the word does not end in an *s,* add an apostrophe and an *s:*

Base word: carpet

Possessive: carpet's design

(2) If the word ends in an *s,* add only an apostrophe (though adding an apostrophe and an *s* sometimes is correct, too):

Base word: dolls

Possessive: three dolls' dresses

Notice that if the word is singular, you simply apply these rules. If the word is to be plural, however, you make the word plural first, and then apply the rules.

Examples: dog (singular)

a dog's fleas (singular possessive)

two dogs (plural)

two dogs' fleas (plural possessive)

Note B: Some words—particularly those expressing units of time—may not seem possessive but still require an apostrophe:

Examples: a day's work

seven minutes' delay

a month's pay

Note C: Do not use an apostrophe to show possession for personal pronouns *(yours, his, hers, its, ours, theirs).*

Wrong: It's shell is broken.

Correct: Its shell is broken.

2. Use an apostrophe to show that letters have been left out of a word.

Examples: *cannot* becomes *can't*

do not becomes *don't*

does not becomes *doesn't*

I will becomes *I'll*

let us becomes *let's*

it is becomes *it's*

Note D: The word *it's,* by the way, has only two meanings: "it is" or "it has."

EXERCISES

A.   Form the singular and plural possessives of these words:

	singular possessive	plural possessive
year	_____	_____
hero	_____	_____
chairman	_____	_____
elephant	_____	_____
terra-cotta	_____	_____
week	_____	_____
potato	_____	_____
scissors	_____	_____
engine	_____	_____
train	_____	_____

B. Add the necessary apostrophes to these sentences:

1. Oliver Stones movie *Philadelphia* tells the story of a lawyer with AIDS who is fired by his law firm when his superiors feel theyre threatened by his disease.

2. As we watch Tennessee Williams *A Streetcar Named Desire*, weve little doubt about wholl win the confrontation between realist Stanley Kowalski and dreamer Blanche DuBois, but we come to realize whats lost when Blanche fails.

3. The song "John Browns Body" isnt about the John Brown who raided the federal arsenal at Harpers Ferry; instead, the songs John Brown was a sergeant in a Massachusetts volunteer regiment, whose friends made up the song to taunt him.

4. No matter how hard Ive tried to keep the dogs toys in its box, the dog has tried harder to keep its toys wherever it wants.

5. J. D. Salingers *The Catcher in the Rye* details two days of antihero Holden Caulfields sixteen-year-old life.

6. Salingers story is peppered with Holdens feelings about lifes phoniness and corruption.

7. For a time combination car-planes were being developed in the United States; however, they didnt fly as well as an airplane or cruise as well as an automobile, and the markets interest in them didnt last long.

8. Rose Greenhow, considered one of Washingtons most alluring hostesses, provided the Confederates one of the Civil Wars most important secrets—warning of when the Union Army was moving toward Manassas, Virginia, for the wars first battle.

9. Dr. Kings "I have a dream" speech has inspired millions of Americans.

10. In the early 1960s a military aid effort in Vietnam escalated to become Americas war; nevertheless, by the end of the decade, as the wars costs mounted, increasing numbers of Americans wanted out.

11. *Life* magazines success was built on photojournalism, as millions of Americans waited eagerly each week for its next group of pictures.

12. Many of Jack Londons stories were set in Alaskas frozen wilderness and showed an individuals ability to struggle against a brutal world.

13. Although we may not have seen the film classic *On the Waterfront*, many of us are familiar with the words of Marlon Brandos character, Terry Malloy: "I coulda had class. I coulda been a contenda."

14. Jesse Owens four gold medals in the 1936 Berlin Olympics made a mockery of Adolf Hitlers contention of Aryan supremacy.

15. Louisa May Alcotts *Little Women* tells of the March sisters struggle to make ends meet while they await their fathers recovery and return from a Civil War hospital.

CHAPTER 34
Quotation Marks

This chapter presents the two important uses of quotation marks (" ") and three rules for using other punctuation within quotation marks.

1. **Use quotation marks to enclose the exact words written or spoken by someone else.**

   Example: Irving Knoke stated, "If someone is looking for an easy way to commit suicide, all he needs to do is stick his thumb out on any road."

2. **Use quotation marks to enclose the title of a poem, short story, magazine article, or newspaper article.**

In other words, use quotation marks to enclose the title of a work that is published as part of another work. Poems and short stories are rarely published separately; rather, they are usually part of a book that includes other poems or stories. Similarly, magazine articles appear as part of a magazine, and newspaper articles appear as part of a newspaper.

Note: The book, magazine, or newspaper title—that is, the title of the larger work containing the poem, short story, or article—should be italicized (or underlined).

Examples: "The Lottery," *Learning Fiction* (a short story in a collection of fiction)

"The Love Song of J. Alfred Prufrock," *Poetry for First Graders* (a poem in a collection of poetry)

"The Problems of Bigamy," *Gentlemen's Weekly Journal* (an article in a magazine)

"Mayor Silvers Wins Again!" *Cripple Creek News* (an article in a newspaper)

The following rules explain how to use other punctuation with quotation marks:

1. Always place periods and commas inside quotation marks.

Examples: I enjoyed reading "The Lottery."

I just read "The Lottery," a strange story by Shirley Jackson.

2. Always place semicolons and colons outside quotation marks.

Examples: I just read "The Lottery"; it is weird.

Three really interesting characters appear in "The Lottery":
Mrs. Hutchinson, Old Man Warner, and Mr. Summers.

3A. Place question marks and exclamation points inside quotation marks if the quotation is a question or an exclamation.

Examples: Tessie Hutchinson yelled, "That's not fair!"

The crowd answered, "Why do you say that, Tessie?"

Note: This rule applies even if the sentence is also a question or an exclamation.

Example: Was the crowd afraid of something when it asked Tessie, "Why do you say that, Tessie?"

3B. Place question marks and exclamation points outside quotation marks if the sentence is a question or an exclamation but the quotation is not.

Examples: Who just said, "Steak fries are good"?

I can't believe you said, "Steak fries are better than noodles"!

EXERCISES

Add the necessary quotation marks in these sentences. Be careful to place quotation marks clearly inside or outside any other punctuation.

1. In H. H. Munro's short story Tobermory, the main character is the house cat of Sir Wilfrid and Lady Blemley; a guest at their house party has taught the cat to talk.

2. After looking for Tobermory to give a demonstration, Sir Wilfrid returns to his guests saying this about Tobermory: by Gad! he drawled out in a most horribly natural voice, that he'd come when he dashed well pleased! I nearly jumped out of my skin!

3. Mavis Pellington makes the mistake of asking Tobermory this: What do you think of human intelligence?

4. When Mavis makes clear she is asking about her own intelligence, Tobermory replies, Sir Wilfrid protested that you were the most brainless woman of his acquaintance, and that there was a wide distinction between hospitality and the care of the feeble-minded.

5. Why does Major Barfield try to change the subject by asking, How about your carryings-on with the tortoise-shell puss up at the stables, eh?

6. Tobermory causes general panic at the house party when he answers, From a slight observation of your ways since you've been in the house I should imagine you'd find it inconvenient if I were to shift the conversation on to your own little affairs.

7. Can you blame Sir Wilfrid when he announces, We can put some strychnine in the scraps he always gets at dinner-time?

8. Like the story Tobermory, Mrs. Packeltide's Tiger is also a satire about life among the English gentry.

9. I'm particularly fond of three short stories: Stephen Crane's The Blue Hotel, Ernest Hemingway's The Killers, and Robert Louis Stevenson's Markheim.

10. In The Blue Hotel, the Swede, who sees everyone's actions as if they were occurring in a dime novel of the Old West, says to the men playing cards, Oh, I see you are all against me.

11. The cowboy cries out in reply, say, what are you gittin' at, hey?

12. Why does the Swede jump up and shout, I don't want to fight!?

13. Why does the cowboy reply, Well, who the hell thought you did?

14. Why does the cowboy later say of the Swede, It's my opinion . . . he's some kind of a Dutchman?

15. What Keats poem contains the statement: Beauty is truth, truth beauty?

PART 7

Expression

Your writing style is how you express yourself. Basic to that style are principles of punctuation (such as those you studied in Part 6) and of grammar—both part of the way we communicate with each other in writing.

This section presents some grammar "do's" and "don't's" to help you deal with expression problems common in the writing of college students. It also demonstrates techniques that will help you advance your style beyond the basics so that you express yourself skillfully.

CHAPTER 35

Subordination

You probably know what *in*subordination is, but subordination, particularly in writing, is something else altogether. When you first learned to read and write, almost every sentence was an independent clause: "Jane, see Spot." Every idea—small as it was—had exactly the same emphasis as every other idea. Of course, nobody in college writes like that, but too often college students have not progressed far enough from that grade-school style.

Your challenge is to combine related ideas into one sentence, giving them just the right emphasis. To succeed, you must learn *subordination—making less-important ideas part of more important ideas.*

We all know that a subordinate is someone who ranks lower than someone else. Parts of a sentence have a rank structure, too.

RANK IN A SENTENCE

Independent Clause	More Important
Dependent Clause	↑
Phrase	↓
Word	Less Important

Ideas expressed in an independent clause naturally seem more important than ideas expressed with only a word. Subordination, then, reduces the emphasis of an idea by lowering its position on the rank structure. To subordinate an idea originally in an independent clause, we might place it in a dependent clause, a phrase, or—sometimes—even a word. For example:

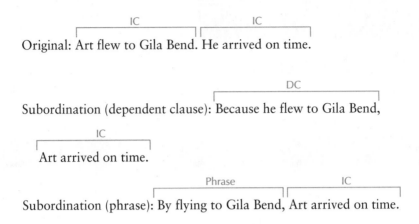

Notice that subordination here has two effects:

- It shows what the writer considers the important idea: Art's arriving on time (expressed in the independent clause).

- It shows the relationship between the two ideas: The words *because* in the first revision and *by* in the second revision serve as road signs. They tell readers to be ready for a cause-effect relationship. (Because something happened, something else resulted: "Because he flew to Gila Bend, Art arrived on time.") These road signs make the readers' task much easier.

Subordination beyond the Sentence Level

This chapter focuses on subordination at the sentence level. But subordination also is important elsewhere in the writing process—especially in prewriting when you cluster related ideas and when you develop topic sentences and a thesis statement. As you study the essay and research paper models in the first five parts of this book, you see subordination in an outline form:

- In a one-paragraph essay, related specific support ideas are clustered and subordinated to a topic sentence idea.

- In a five-paragraph essay, related central paragraphs are clustered and subordinated to a thesis idea.

- In a research paper, related main ideas are clustered and subordinated to the research paper's thesis idea.

The relationships among the ideas vary with the patterns of development. However, for all of these increasingly complex levels of organization, the *effects of subordination* are the same as those within a sentence: *showing what the writer wishes to emphasize as most important and showing relationships among ideas.*

Now let's return to our sentence example. We could have subordinated the second independent clause if we had decided that Art's flying to Gila Bend was more important than the idea that he arrived on time.

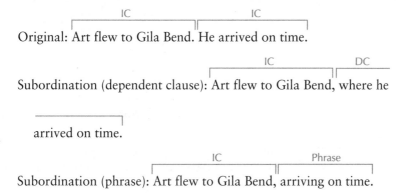

Original: Art flew to Gila Bend. He arrived on time.

Subordination (dependent clause): Art flew to Gila Bend, where he

arrived on time.

Subordination (phrase): Art flew to Gila Bend, arriving on time.

When you write, therefore, you must decide which ideas you wish to emphasize and which you wish to subordinate.

"But," you might protest, "I use subordination all the time." Sure you do—though probably not enough. Let's express some ideas in grade-school style, early college style, and a more sophisticated style.

■ Degrees of Subordination

Grade-school style: The girl is playing tennis. Her name is Sally. She is a beginner. She is taking lessons. Karen is teaching her. Karen is a professional. Karen teaches at the Andromeda Club. Karen teaches every Tuesday morning.

Early college style: Sally is playing tennis. She is taking beginning lessons from Karen. Karen is a professional, and she teaches at the Andromeda Club every Tuesday morning.

Improved style: Sally is taking beginning tennis lessons from Karen, a professional who teaches at the Andromeda Club every Tuesday morning.

The last revision certainly is easier to read than either of the other versions. Why? Subordination pushes the unimportant ideas to the side so the readers can easily see the most important idea, the independent clause.

Apply Subordination during Editing

Here's a final tip to help you with subordination. On a first draft, you're naturally too busy thinking of ideas and how they relate to each other to worry about subordination at the sentence level. When you edit the draft—during the rewriting phase—pay attention to how you piece ideas together *within sentences.* Depending on the time you have available, you may even want to make a trip through your paper, beginning to end, just working on the best way to combine ideas into better sentences. The results will be worth the effort.

Remember, your effort as you write makes your readers' work much easier. Subordination lets readers see which main ideas you consider important. And, after you finish school, that's the main reason you will write.

EXERCISES

A. Combine these simple sentences in two different ways, emphasizing a different idea each time.

1. The Continental Congress passed a resolution for independence on July 2, 1776. It signed the Declaration of Independence on July 4.

    a. _____

    b. _____

2. Nat "King" Cole's voice had only a two-octave range. His breathy, purring style made him a star as a singer.

    a. _____

    b. _____

3. The Goodyear company is known for its blimps. It launched its first blimp, the *Pilgrim,* in 1925.

    a. _____

    b. _____

4. The U.S. government promised Nez Percé Chief Joseph that his people could return to their Oregon homelands. Instead, the government sent them to Oklahoma.

    a. _____

    b. _____

5. Walt Disney pioneered animated feature films. His first full-length production was *Snow White and the Seven Dwarfs.*

a._____

b._____

B. For each numbered exercise below, combine all of the ideas into one good sentence.

1. Thousands of miles of wooden roads were laid in several U.S. states.

   The roads were laid in the 1840s and 1850s.

   Gravel roads replaced most of the wooden roads.

   The wooden planks began to rot.

   _____

   _____

   _____

2. A prairie schooner was boat-shaped.

   It was pulled by three yoke of oxen.

   It could carry up to three thousand pounds of possessions and supplies.

   Flour was an essential supply.

   Bacon was an essential.

   Coffee also was an important supply.

   _____

   _____

   _____

3. Richard Lawrence fired two pistols at Andrew Jackson.

   He fired the pistols at point-blank range.

   Both pistols misfired.

The weather probably affected the powder.

The weather was damp.

_____

_____

_____

4. Cowboys prospered for twenty years after the Civil War.

    They made large profits from cattle drives.

    They moved large herds of cattle from Texas to Missouri.

    Sometimes they moved large herds of cattle from Texas to Kansas.

    Fences ended the days of open range.

    This ended the years of profitable cattle drives.

    _____

    _____

    _____

5. At age seventy-six "Grandma" Moses began painting.

    Her full name was Anna Mary Robertson "Grandma" Moses.

    She began painting when arthritis made needlework too difficult.

    She painted colorful scenes of country life.

    "Grandma" Moses was famous as a folk artist.

    _____

    _____

    _____

CHAPTER 36
Sentence Variety

After studying the preceding chapter, you may suspect that "good" writing consists of one complicated sentence after another. Not so; you'd lose the readers after a couple of pages. On the other hand, how would you like to read sentence after sentence in grade-school or early college style?

Well, then, is the solution a compromise of all medium-length sentences? No, not really. Good writing has a mixture of:

- varied sentence lengths
- varied sentence structures

Although experienced writers avoid varying sentences just for the sake of variety, good sentence variety is important for good coherence—the smooth flow from one idea to the next. If you find yourself writing many short sentences in a row, or beginning many sentences with the subject of the independent clause, ask yourself, "Do my sentence patterns help my ideas flow smoothly? Or do they make my ideas seem fragmented, choppy?"

This chapter will give you some tips on how to vary your sentences to achieve better coherence.

SENTENCE LENGTH

Actually, not very many beginning writers have poor sentence variety from writing only long sentences. The problem is usually a series of short sentences:

> The new governor was sworn in today. He is a Democrat. Ten thousand people attended the ceremony. The governor gave a brief inaugural address. The governor promised to end unemployment. He said he would reduce inflation. He also promised to improve the environment. The audience gave him a standing ovation.

Pretty dismal, right? The average sentence length is only 6.25 words, and all of the sentences except the second are either 6 or 7 words long—not overwhelming variety. Let's use the technique of subordination we learned in the previous chapter to come up with something better:

> The new Democratic governor was sworn in today. At a ceremony ten thousand people attended, he gave a brief inaugural address, promising to end unemployment, reduce inflation, and improve the environment. The audience gave him a standing ovation.

This version is certainly much easier to read, mainly because we've eliminated choppiness and subordinated some unimportant ideas. The average sentence is now thirteen words long, within the desirable goal of twelve to twenty words per sentence.

PRACTICAL WRITING: THE PROBLEM OF COMPLEX SENTENCES

Although beginning writers tend toward short, choppy sentences, writers in business, industry, and government sometimes tend the other way. Some even believe that writing long, complex sentences is a mark of their educational competence. They think their superiors *expect* them to write long sentences, and they aim to please.

Here's a sample of the type of writing that results:

> Whether the terrorists style themselves as separatists, anarchists, dissidents, nationalists, Marxist revolutionaries, or religious true believers, what marks them as terrorists is that they direct their violence against noncombatants with the goal of terrorizing a wider audience than the immediate victims, thereby attempting to gain political influence over the larger audience. In one variant of terrorism, organizational terrorism, represented by such groups as the Red Army Faction in Germany, the Red Brigades in Italy, Direct Action in France, and 17 November in Greece, small, tightly knit, politically homogeneous organizations that are incapable of developing popular support for their radical positions resort to terrorism to gain influence. In a second variant of terrorism, that conducted within the context of ethnic separatist or countrywide insurgencies, such as in the Philippines, El Salvador, and Colombia, groups conducting paramilitary or guerrilla operations against the established government turn to attacks on the populace at large to undermine the government's credibility, legitimacy, and public support.

These three sentences, all roughly the same length, average fifty-four words each. You can understand what they say, of course—if you read very carefully.

Yet, today, successful writers—and the people they work for—are insisting on something else. They're demanding simpler writing so that busy readers don't have to struggle with the material they need to understand. Sentence averages in the twelve- to twenty-word range simply communicate more effectively.

SENTENCE STRUCTURE

Let's look again at the bad example that began the discussion on sentence length. Notice how many sentences begin with the subject (and its modifiers) of an independent clause:

The new governor was sworn in today. He is a Democrat. Ten thousand

people attended the ceremony. The governor gave a brief inaugural

address. The governor promised to end unemployment. He said he would

reduce inflation. He also promised to improve the environment. The audi-

ence gave him a standing ovation.

Every sentence begins with the subject of an independent clause, which makes it hard for readers to move from idea to idea. To make this paragraph easier to read, some of the sentences should begin with dependent clauses, others with phrases, and still others with transitional words. For example, look again at the revision:

> The new Democratic governor was sworn in today. *At a ceremony ten thousand people attended,* he gave a brief inaugural address, promising to end unemployment, reduce inflation, and improve the environment. The audience gave him a standing ovation.

The introduction to the second sentence provides nice relief.

Many sentences, of course, should begin with the subject of an independent clause; still, they should not all look alike. They could end with a dependent clause, they could contain a couple of independent clauses, or they could contain a series of parallel phrases or clauses (see Chapter 37). The sentences in the paragraph you are now reading, for example, all begin with the subject of an independent clause, but after that beginning, their structures vary considerably.

Apply Sentence Variety during Editing

You may think *you* would never begin a lot of sentences all the same way. And surely you'd never string together all short, choppy sentences or long, overly complex ones. Yet, in our first draft many of us write with just those patterns.

We think of an idea and write it down: "subject—verb"; we think of another idea and write it down: "subject—verb"; and so on. Similarly, we become comfortable writing sentences with much the same lengths— short ones or long ones, whichever way we're used to writing. If we don't take the time to rewrite the draft, our sentences look much the same. Check your last few pages to see if you've fallen into this bad habit.

Good writing is not an automatic process, a flow of uninterrupted inspiration flowing forth onto the page. Good writing results from a painstaking and very conscious process. Don't just hope sentence variety will happen in your writing. After you write a draft, ask yourself these questions:

- Are my sentences different lengths?
- Do my sentences begin in a variety of ways?
- Do the sentences that begin with the subject of an independent clause have a variety of structures?

If the answers are "no," edit your paper for sentence variety. Be careful, though, not to sacrifice clarity for the sake of variety. And don't create grotesque, unnatural sentences. Variety is a means to achieve good writing—not the goal itself.

EXERCISES

A. Revise these paragraphs for better sentence variety. In both the original and your revision, circle the subject of the first independent clause in every sentence. Compute the average number of words in each sentence (count all the words in the paragraph and divide by the number of sentences).

1. Original: Two larger-than-life heroes of American folklore are Paul Bunyan and Pecos Bill. They belong partly to legend. They also belong partly to literature. Paul Bunyan is a superhuman lumberjack. He may be based on oral tradition. There were tales of him among French lumberjacks in Canada. There also were tales of Paul Bunyan among Irish lumberjacks in Canada. Paul Bunyan's legend grew largest when he was popularized in an advertising booklet in 1914. The booklet advertised the Red River Lumber Company of Minneapolis. Advertising agent W. B. Langhead wrote the booklet. He used a collection of tales of Paul Bunyan's feats to establish Paul as the symbol of the Minnesota lumber company. Langhead also named Paul's companion. His

companion is Babe, the giant blue ox. A story of Paul Bunyan credits him with forming the Grand Canyon. Paul did it when he accidentally dragged a spiked lumberjack pole behind him. Babe is made responsible for forming the Mississippi River. The river formed when Babe's water bowl sprung a leak. Pecos Bill was a legendary cowboy. He also is credited with forming the Grand Canyon. In addition, he is credited with forming the Rio Grande River. In one tale Pecos Bill rides a cyclone bareback. The cyclone tries to throw him. As it does this, it rains so much that it washes out the Grand Canyon. Pecos Bill finally returns to earth in California. His landing creates Death Valley. Pecos Bill appears in numerous folk tales. He actually was created by Edward O'Reilly. O'Reilly introduced Pecos Bill in *The Century Magazine* in 1923. Both Paul Bunyan and Pecos Bill serve as popular symbols. They symbolize American strength and energy.

Average number of words per sentence: _____

Your revision: _____

_____

_____

_____

_____

_____

_____

_____

_____

_____

Average number of words per sentence: _____

2.   Original: The Whiskey Rebellion was in 1794. It was one of the greatest threats to the authority of the U.S. federal government prior to the Civil War. It began as a test of the government's ability to collect taxes. Farmers in western Pennsylvania had surplus corn. They distilled whiskey from the corn. The liquor was cheaper to transport. It also served as currency in barter for necessities. In 1791 Secretary of the Treasury Alexander Hamilton imposed a tax on

stills and distilled liquors. America needed the income to pay off war debts. Many Pennsylvania farmers refused to pay the tax. They compared it to England's Stamp Act. By 1794 tax collectors in western Pennsylvania faced violent resistance. Frequently they were met with tar and feathers. In August, 5,000 armed farmers gathered at Pittsburgh. They came to protest the tax. They also talked of secession. President Washington called out the militia. He sent a force of 13,000 men to suppress the insurrection. Major General Henry Lee led the militia. The militia advanced into western Pennsylvania. The resistance collapsed. The federal government had demonstrated its power.

Average number of words per sentence: _____

Your revision: _____

_____

_____

_____

_____

_____

_____

_____

_____

Average number of words per sentence: _____

3.   Original: During the Civil War, the North blockaded Southern ports. The Confederate navy wanted to break the blockade. The Confederates developed submersibles to attack Union ships. The *H. L. Hunley* was a submarine. A submarine is a true submersible. This submersible had forward dive planes. It also had a propeller at the stern. The propeller received its power from eight crew members inside. They turned a crude hand crank. The *Hunley* was fashioned from a 25-foot-long boiler cylinder. The *Hunley* was built at Mobile, Alabama. It also was tested there. Then it was shipped by rail to South Carolina. The *Hunley* was tested in Charleston harbor. It sank twice there because of human error. The first time five of eight crew members were killed. The

second time all eight were killed. Captain Horace L. Hunley died in the second accident. The submarine was named for him. The *Hunley* was designed to tow a floating torpedo. The *Hunley* would tow the torpedo toward a target ship. Then the submarine would dive. It would resurface beyond the target ship. In this way it would pull its torpedo into the target vessel. This system was tested in Mobile Bay. The *Hunley* pulled its torpedo perfectly in that test. The *Hunley's* torpedo towing also was tested in Charleston harbor. There the torpedo tended to move too close to the submarine. The Confederates fitted an explosive charge on a spar. They mounted the spar to the *Hunley's* bow. During the night of February 17, 1864, the *Hunley* rammed its torpedo against the *USS Housatonic*. The *Housatonic* was a wooden blockade ship. It was anchored outside Charleston harbor. The *Housatonic's* stern disintegrated. The *Housatonic* sank quickly. The *Hunley* never returned. Many thought the *Hunley* had been sunk by the same charge that sank the *Housatonic*. However, the *Hunley's* commander had promised to show signal lights after completing his mission. Observers on shore saw signal lights flash after the attack. A survivor from the *Housatonic* also saw a signal light. The light he saw was directly in the path of a Union ship. It was rushing to aid the *Housatonic*. These reports suggest that the *Hunley* was not destroyed by its own explosive charge. It probably was hit or swamped by a rescue ship instead.

Average number of words per sentence: _____

Your revision: _____

_____

_____

_____

_____

_____

_____

_____

_____

_____

_____

Average number of words per sentence: _____

B. Revise the three sentences in the section called "Practical Writing: The Problem of Complex Sentences" on page 370 for better sentence variety. Those three sentences have fifty-one, fifty-five, and fifty-four words, for an average of fifty-four words per sentence. The average number of words per sentence in your revision should fall in the twelve- to twenty-word range. Although the primary purpose of this exercise is to reduce the average sentence length, be sure your revision also demonstrates a variety of sentence structures.

Average number of words per sentence: _____

Your revision: _____

_____

_____

_____

_____

_____

_____

_____

_____

_____

Average number of words per sentence: _____

CHAPTER 37
Parallelism

Now that you've studied sentence variety, you may be afraid of writing sentences that repeat simple patterns. Don't be. Some ideas work best in sentences that clearly show a pattern. When you analyze an idea, you take pains to discover similarities and differences among its parts. Whether you intend to compare or contrast those elements, you want readers to see how the parts are alike or different. Parallelism is the key.

The principle of parallel construction is simple: *be sure ideas that are similar in content and function look the same.* Parallelism works because the similarity of the appearance of the items shows clearly the pattern of the thought. The principle of parallelism applies most often to the following:

- two or more items in a series (usually with a coordinating conjunction)
- a pair of items with correlative conjunctions—a special type of series and conjunctions we'll explain later in this chapter

ITEMS IN A SERIES

The principle of parallelism requires that all items in a series must be grammatically alike. That is, all words in a series must be the same type of word, all phrases the same type of phrase, and all clauses the same type of clause. Grammatical likeness also applies to sentences in a series: each item in the series must be a *complete* sentence—not a fragment—and, therefore, the same "type" of sentence. However, the structures within these complete sentences can vary, so the patterns within the sentences may appear somewhat different, as we'll see later in this section.

Coordinating Conjunctions with a Series

Two or more items in a series within a single sentence normally use a coordinating conjunction (CC)—*and, but, or, nor, for, so,* or *yet*—before the final item.
Thus, the series looks like this:

item CC item

or this:

item, item, CC item

A series of complete sentences, however, usually will not include a coordinating conjunction before the final item.

Here are sentences with parallel constructions:

Words in series: I saw John and Mary.

I saw John, Bill, and Mary.

Phrases in series: I see him going to work and coming home.

I plan to eat in a restaurant and to see a movie.

Dependent clauses in series: The phone rang when I reached the motel

but before I unpacked my suitcases.

Independent clauses in series: I liked the parrot, so I bought it for my

mother.

Complete sentences in series: She sold the car for three good reasons:

It had no tires. It had no brakes. It had no engine.

Notice that each item—word, phrase, clause, or sentence—in a series has the same form as the other items in the same series.

A Reminder: Use Commas and Semicolons with Items in a Series

As you saw in Chapters 29 and 30, commas and sometimes semicolons mark the division of items in a series within a sentence. Commas are the most common dividers:

> The ethics of contemporary surgery are often a problem for the patient, the doctor, and the patient's family.

When commas occur within one or more of the items in a series, semicolons mark the divisions between the items:

> Key air routes include Lisbon, Portugal; Rome, Italy; Frankfurt, Germany; and Istanbul, Turkey.

Words in a Series

The words in a series of words seldom present special problems. However, the articles that appear with the series can create a minor parallelism problem.

Articles with Words in a Series

Articles are *a, an,* and *the.* When articles appear with words in a series, be sure the articles fall in one of these two patterns:

> *article* word, word, CC word
> *article* word, *article* word, CC *article* word

Notice the placement of the articles in these sample sentences:

> Wrong: I bought food for *the* dog, cat, and *the* horse.

> Correct: I bought food for *the* dog, cat, and horse.

> Correct: I bought food for *the* dog, *the* cat, and *the* horse.

The correct sentences have either an article before the entire series or an article before every item in the series.

Phrases in a Series

Unlike words in a series, phrases often cause problems. Many times students mix types of phrases. Be sure that *-ing* phrases fit with other *-ing* phrases, *to* phrases with *to* phrases, and so forth.

> Wrong: I like *swimming in the pond, cycling down the lane,* and *to ride horses in the pasture.*

> Correct: I like *swimming in the pond, cycling down the lane,* and *riding horses in the pasture.*

> Correct: I like *to swim in the pond, to cycle down the lane,* and *to ride horses in the pasture.*

> Wrong: I plan *to study hard, doing well on my exams,* and *to graduate with honors.*

> Correct: I plan *to study hard, to do well on my exams,* and *to graduate with honors.*

> Correct: I plan on *studying hard, doing well on my exams,* and *graduating with honors.*

Clauses in a Series

Clauses in a series seldom cause major problems. However, if the series contains dependent clauses, you can help your readers by signaling the beginning of each dependent clause. Consider this sentence:

> I expect to be entertained if I'm going to pay nine dollars to get in a theater and I'm going to sit there for two hours.

What does the *and* join? Does it join the two independent clauses?

item

I expect to be entertained if I'm going to pay nine dollars to get in a

CC   item

theater and I'm going to sit there for two hours.

Or does it join two dependent clauses?

item

I expect to be entertained if I'm going to pay nine dollars to get in a

CC   item

theater and I'm going to sit there for two hours.

The intended meaning is probably the second one: the *and* joins two dependent clauses. Readers will see the separation of the items more easily if the writer repeats the word that signals the beginning of the clauses:

```
                                        item
                              |_____|
I expect to be entertained if I'm going to pay nine dollars to get in a

      CC              item
|____||_____|
theater and if I'm going to sit there for two hours.
```

Now the meaning is clear. Here's another sample:

> "I can see that you don't like the meal and that you'd rather not be here," she pouted.

Notice that the repetition of *that* (which signals the beginning of dependent clauses) makes the parallel construction clear.

Like Grammatical Units in a Series within a Sentence

In addition to having like words, like phrases, and like clauses in a series within a sentence, be sure that the items in the series are the same type of grammatical unit. Do not, for instance, mix phrases and clauses in a series, as in this sentence:

```
                           item    CC        item
                         |_____|      |_____|
Wrong: My roommate likes to sleep in bed and when he's in class.
```

The sentence is awkward because the writer has joined a phrase *(in bed)* with a clause *(when he's in class)*. Here's what the writer should have written:

> Correct: My roommate likes to sleep when he's in bed and when he's in class.

Now a clause fits with a clause. (Notice also that the sentence repeats *when*, the word that signals the beginning of each dependent clause.)

Complete Sentences in a Series

In the earlier sample of full sentences in a series, all of the sentences are quite short, and their internal structures are exactly alike: "It had no tires. It had no brakes. It had no engine." Clearly, this is a technique you have to apply sparingly. This type of series could provide a punchy variation if it were mixed in with longer sentences. Too much of it, though, could create the type of choppy, repetitive writing you learned to avoid when you studied sentence variety in the last chapter.

However, complete sentences in a series don't have to be so much alike. Here's another sample, this time with some variation within the sentences.

> My great-grandfather wrote that Abraham Lincoln's appearance at the caucus was striking: Lincoln's beard was short and neatly trimmed. His suit was of a dark cloth that gave him a somber but dignified air and seemed to hang on his lank frame. In his hand he loosely held a black stovepipe hat.

These sentences are of varied lengths: seven, twenty-three, and ten words, respectively. Obviously their internal structures are not exactly alike. Are they parallel? Well, yes, they are. In the simplest sense, they have grammatical similarity, as each is a complete sentence. More important, each provides the same type of information—a quick, descriptive example—that answers the same question: How was Lincoln's appearance striking? And even though the sentence structures are not exactly alike, their basic idea patterns are similar: his beard was . . . ; his suit was . . . ; his hand held . . .

Parallelism in Headings and Indented Lists

In Chapter 10 you learned about layout techniques that can make your writing look better. Two of those techniques—headings and indented lists—depend on parallelism. Here are the headings that were added to the sample paper about the humorous things children do as they grow up:

Learning to Speak
Discovering Objects Aren't Human
Imitating Others around Them

Notice that the headings are parallel phrases, each the same type of phrase: learning . . . , discovering . . . , imitating . . .

Parallelism is even more important when you use indented lists. Their purpose is to *emphasize a pattern* of organization, and that is also the reason for using parallel construction. Here's a sample list without parallelism:

Desktop publishing offers our department three benefits:

• product more professional
• Production time will be cut.
• saves money

This list a jumble of styles that reminds us of the result of brainstorming, where we're interested in jotting down ideas quickly without worrying about how well they communicate. Readers will get the point—if they take

the time to apply the organization that the writer has left out. Notice the difference that parallel construction makes in this revision:
Desktop publishing offers our department three benefits:

- a more professional-looking product
- reduced production time
- cost savings

PAIRS OF ITEMS WITH CORRELATIVE CONJUNCTIONS

Correlative conjunctions mate pairs of related items. The rule for parallelism with correlative conjunctions is simple: the grammatical units following each of the correlative conjunctions must be alike.

Correlative Pairs

Common correlative conjunctions are these: *either . . . or; neither . . . nor; not (only) . . . but (also)*; and *whether . . . or.*
Items mated by correlative conjunctions (CorC) will look like this: CorC item CorC item . . .

Here are sentences with such pairs:

I don't like either his appearance or his manners.

Neither my aunt nor my cousin will speak to me.

Can you find the problem in this sentence?

Wrong: *Either* I go to bed early *or* get up late.

This sentence demonstrates the most common failure to maintain parallelism with correlative conjunctions: *either* precedes the subject of the sentence *(I)*, but *or* precedes the second verb *(get)*. You have two options for dealing with the problem:

Correct: I *either* go to bed early *or* get up late.

Correct: *Either* I go to bed early *or* I get up late.

The first solution moves *either* so that both correlative conjunctions precede verbs (*go* and *get*). The second solution places *either* and *or* before subjects of clauses (*I* and *I*). In both corrections, the grammatical units following each correlative conjunction are alike.

All of this may seem complicated, but it's not. You wouldn't try to compare apples and automobiles, because they're not alike. Similarly, you can't expect your readers to accept a comparison of items that appear dissimilar. The principle of parallelism requires only that you make like items *look* alike so readers can see the similarity.

EXERCISES

A. Improve the parallelism in each of the following sentences:

1. Michael likes cycling, to ride horses, and swimming in the summer.

2. To work on the project, Alice wanted a computer, page-layout application, and a laser printer.

3. Whether he studied his notes for days or cramming several hours before class, Hector never felt prepared for a chemistry test.

4. Carlo bought a shirt, a pair of suspenders, tie, and cap.

5. The policy change concerned not only the workers but also those who supervised them.

6. Marla's stomach was queasy before going onstage and she heard the applause as the moderator introduced her.

7. When she was home from school, Rachel both wanted to shop with her mother and sister and to eat home-cooked meals.

8. Julio prefers swimming, hiking, and to skate both with ice-skates on ice and on pavement with rollerblades.

9. After I revised my English paper and testing in calculus, I still had to study for a midterm in statistics.

10. The boat seemed certain to capsize as it was tossed about by high waves and with strong winds hammering it.

11. Maria didn't go to the concert because she didn't have the time, the energy to leave her room, and she didn't care for the band.

12. After he talked to a lawyer, a judge, and to his senator, Mr. Sims was sure he had done all he could to settle the issue.

13. At Thanksgiving we like to bring all of the family together and eating turkey with dressing.

14. Franco went to the party for the food, the entertainment, and to meet with his friends.

15. After I drive in rush hour traffic or reading about crime in the city, I long to live in the country.

B. Revise the following sentences to improve the parallelism in each one.

1. In the early 1950s, U.S. civil defense officials advised Americans to take measures to survive a nuclear attack; these measures included stockpiling food and water, to plan escape routes, and to build fallout shelters in their backyards.

2. The Social Security Act, passed in 1935, was noteworthy for establishing welfare payments and it established insurance for the unemployed, the disabled, and old people.

3. President Roosevelt believed that federal administrations of the future would have a hard time changing the social security system if it was based on funding not only from employers but also included money from the employees.

4. The tomb of China's emperor Qin Shi Huangdi was protected not only by an army of more than six thousand terra-cotta soldiers but there were real drawn crossbows set to shoot intruders who set off their triggers.

5. Despite having a secret agreement with Stalin and even though every general on his military staff advised against it, Hitler attacked the USSR in 1941 because he was convinced that Stalin's government would collapse quickly if Germany invaded with sufficient force.

6. Germany's invasion of the USSR faltered because Hitler had underestimated the determination of the Russian people to resist, the sheer enormity of the territory to be conquered and held, and especially because Hitler did not appreciate the severity of winter in Russia.

7. The French defeat at Dien Bien Phu in 1954 led to Geneva Accords that same year that dismantled French Indochina—granting independence to Cambodia and Laos and divided Vietnam in half, with a

communist government in the north and a noncommunist government in the south.

8. Greek temples for the god of medicine, Asklepios, not only were places of worship but also to heal.

9. Three related advances in electronics were crucial for the devices we use today, particularly for home computers: miniature transistors replaced bulky vacuum tubes, transistors were devised to fit on wafers of silicon crystal, and development of integrated circuits.

10. The Romans constructed their baths by elevating the floors on brick pillars, enclosing the pillars and rooms to control the air circulation, and then they installed furnaces to circulate hot air.

C. In the following exercises, revise the indented lists to make the items parallel.

1. Winter weather was one of the chief opponents of the German army that invaded the USSR in 1941; temperatures that reached as low as forty degrees below zero caused problems that the German army was not prepared to deal with:

   - Frozen tank and truck batteries.
   - When gun oil solidified, machine guns jammed.
   - The hobnails in the boots of the German soldiers passed the cold to the soldiers' feet, causing frostbitten feet that turned gangrenous and had to be amputated.

2. In his war with the Celtic tribes of Gaul in 52 B.C., Julius Caesar encircled the Gauls with a field of hazards:

   - The field facing the Gauls had pits with sharp stakes at the bottom—all covered with brush to hide the traps.
   - A thicket of pointed branches angled toward the Gauls.
   - Two trenches, one filled with water, came after the thicket.
   - A steep wall with towers from which Caesar's soldiers could throw spears.

3. Through his short stories and novels, Dashiell Hammett, creator of Sam Spade, Nick Charles, and other detectives, developed the typical "hard-boiled" detective:

   - Crime was taken out of the drawing room of the quaint English detective story and put into the streets.

- His dialogue captured the style and rhythm of street talk.
- Tough-guy detective who lived by a code of honor of his own making.

4. Television programming in the early 1970s developed a social consciousness that was remarkable for its time:

- *All in the Family* introduced a sitcom with real-life situations treating formerly taboo subjects such as racism, rape, and sexuality.
- Portrayal of the life and life problems of a single career woman on *The Mary Tyler Moore Show*.
- *Saturday Night Live,* with its Not Ready for Prime-Time Players, satirized the great of America and the icons of life that most Americans held sacred.

5. Greek health-care centers, called *asklepieia*, offered a variety of services to the ill and infirm:

- Facilities for bathing and ritual exercise.
- There were pavilions in which patients could sleep and be visited by the god of healing, Asklepios.
- Temples for worship of Asklepios and for handling dogs and snakes, which were associated with Asklepios, also were available.
- Operating theaters where temple physicians performed surgery.

CHAPTER 38

Misused Modifiers

Dangling participle! Nothing—not even "split infinitive"—can strike such terror in the heart of an English student. But don't be afraid. Behind the fancy name is a simple concept you'll understand after studying this chapter. You won't learn the differences between dangling participles, dangling gerunds, and dangling infinitives, because the differences aren't really important for what we're studying: we'll group them together and treat them as *dangling modifiers*. In addition to the special type of modifier problem, you'll also study *misplaced modifiers*.

What Is a Modifier?

Modifiers are words, phrases, or clauses that limit or provide additional information about other words. In the phrase "I never saw a purple cow," the modifier *purple* limits the discussion from all cows to only purple cows. (As you saw in the discussion of comma usage in Chapter 29, modifiers that limit the definition of other words are *restrictive modifiers*.)

In "Standing on the bridge, the captain watched his ship move slowly through the channel," the modifier *standing on the bridge* provides additional information about the captain—but it in no way limits the definition. (Modifiers that provide information but do not limit definition are *nonrestrictive modifiers*.)

This chapter focuses on placement of modifiers within a sentence. Because placement problems can occur with both types of modifiers, restrictive and nonrestrictive, we do not distinguish between them. However, if you study the examples carefully, you'll see that the most commom problems are with placing nonrestrictive modifiers. Why? Because a nonrestrictive modifier is less essential to the point of the sentence, a writer is less likely to notice that the modifier is misplaced.

As you've seen in earlier chapters, modifiers allow you to combine several ideas into one sentence. You might write this:

Jonathan ate the doughnut. It was the only doughnut.

However, you save time and space by reducing the second sentence to a modifier:

Jonathan ate the *only* doughnut.

Still, there is a catch: word order in an English sentence often determines meaning; therefore, different word arrangements may yield different meanings. Let's see what happens if we place *only* in every possible position in "Jonathan ate the doughnut."

Only Jonathan ate the doughnut.	(No one else ate it.)
Jonathan *only* ate the doughnut.	(He didn't do anything else to it.)
Jonathan ate *only* the doughnut.	(He ate nothing else.)
Jonathan ate the *only* doughnut.	(There were no other doughnuts.)
Jonathan ate the doughnut *only*.	(He ate nothing else.)

Five combinations yield four distinctly different meanings. Play this game with other sentences and such words as *almost, every, just, merely, most, nearly, only, primarily,* and *principally.*

The game's implication is obvious, isn't it? Unless you carefully place the modifiers in your sentences, you may not write what you really mean. Modifiers are terrific savers of time and space in your writing—but they also can obscure or distort your meaning, sometimes making your writing appear ridiculous.

MISPLACED MODIFIERS

Placing a modifier in a sentence requires good judgment and careful editing. No particular place in a sentence is always right for a modifier, but this much is true: *A modifier tends to modify what it is close to.* "Close to" may be before or after the thing modified, so long as the sentence makes sense.

These sentences make little sense:

A jeep ran over the soldier *that had muddy tires.*

People stared in amazement *on the sidewalk.*

The accident left *neatly pressed* tire marks on the soldier's shirt.

In these sentences something comes between the modifiers and the things modified. As a result, the modifiers appear to refer to the things they are closest to: *that had muddy tires* seems to modify *soldier; on the sidewalk* seems to refer to *amazement;* and *neatly pressed* appears to modify *tire marks*.

Let's move the modifiers so they modify what they should.

A jeep *that had muddy tires* ran over the soldier.

On the sidewalk, people stared in amazement.

or

People *on the sidewalk* stared in amazement.

The accident left tire marks on the soldier's *neatly pressed* shirt.

Notice that *on the sidewalk* works before or after *people,* whereas *that had muddy tires* works only after *jeep* and *neatly pressed* works only before *shirt.* What matters, then, is that the modifier must be close enough to the thing it modifies to complete the thought logically.

A second type of placement problem occurs when you write strings of modifiers. Consider this example:

A man *with red hair in a green suit* crossed the street.

Both *with red hair* and *in a green suit* should modify *man,* but instead *in a green suit* seems to refer to *hair.*

One solution is to put one modifier before and another after the thing modified:

A *red-haired* man *in a green suit* crossed the street.

or

Wearing a green suit, a man *with red hair* crossed the street.

A second solution is to combine the modifiers with a coordinating conjunction:

A man *with red hair and a green suit* crossed the street.

Again, the exact position of the modifier doesn't matter if the result makes sense.

DANGLING MODIFIERS

Dangling modifiers can occur anywhere in a sentence, but the most common problem is at the beginning. A modifier that *begins* a sentence must refer to something that follows. Because of convention, readers expect an introductory word or phrase modifier to refer to the subject of the sentence.

Walking along the beach, Mary found a sand dollar.

Because we expect the opening phrase *(walking along the beach)* to modify the subject of the sentence *(Mary),* we know that Mary, not the sand dollar, was walking along the beach. But what if the sentence reads this way?

Walking along the beach, a sand dollar was found by Mary.

Again we expect the introductory phrase to modify the subject of the sentence, but sand dollars don't walk. Because the modifier cannot logically modify the subject of the sentence, we say that the modifier "dangles." The following sentences contain dangling modifiers:

Enthusiastic, the hour seemed to pass quickly.

Finishing the game, the crowd loudly booed the home team.

After examining the data, the steam engine appeared to be the best choice.

To enjoy surfing, the waves must be high.

When only nine, John's mother took him to a circus.

Was the hour enthusiastic? Did the crowd actually finish the game? Did the steam engine examine the data? Can waves enjoy surfing? Do you really believe that John had a mother who was only nine years old? Because the modifiers above have no logical connection to the subjects of the sentences, we say the modifiers dangle.

You have two options to correct dangling modifiers:

- The first, the most obvious, is to recast the sentence so the subject matches the modifier.

Enthusiastic, we thought the hour passed quickly.

Finishing the game, the home team heard loud booing from the crowd.

After examining the data, we concluded that the steam engine was the best choice.

To enjoy surfing, you need high waves.

When only nine, John went to the circus with his mother.

- The second method is to change the word or phrase modifier into a clause.

Because we were enthusiastic, the hour seemed to pass quickly.

As the game ended, the crowd loudly booed the home team.

After we examined the data, the steam engine appeared to be the best choice.

If you want to enjoy surfing, the waves must be high.

When John was only nine, his mother took him to a circus.

The Bottom Line

You can avoid *both* types of problem modifiers—misplaced as well as dangling—if you keep in mind the essential relationship between modifiers and the things they modify:

- A modifier tends to modify what it is close to.
- A modifier should be close to what it must modify.

EXERCISES

A. 1. Write one sentence with a misplaced modifier and one with a dangling modifier.

   a._____

   b._____

   2. Now correct your sentences.

   a._____

   b._____

B. The game at the beginning of the chapter isn't just an amusing pastime. It demonstrates a real and common modifier problem in business and technical writing. Here are the possible variations of a sentence, based on placement of *only*, that could appear in a report that evaluates the effectiveness of military operations of a coalition of several nations against another nation, a common situation in our times:

  a. Only coalition attacks damaged the communications.

  b. Coalition only attacks damaged the communications.

  c. Coalition attacks only damaged the communications.

  d. Coalition attacks damaged only the communications.

  e. Coalition attacks damaged the only communications.

  f. Coalition attacks damaged the communications only.

Placing *only* in every possible position among the other five words yields six variations. Disregard the second sentence (b), which is nonsensical; no one would really write that variation.

  1. How many different meanings do the remaining five variations present?

  2. Which variation should an author use to indicate that the attacks damaged but didn't destroy the communications?

  3. Which variation should a writer use to suggest that the attacks were successful because they damaged all the communications available in the opposing country?

  4. Which variation indicates that damage was limited to the communications?

C. Rewrite the following sentences to eliminate the modifier problems.

  1. The cat ate the food with black and white spots.

  2. Billy's mother packed an apple in his lunch that was rotten.

  3. Before boiling dry, you need to refill the kettle.

  4. A man driving a pickup with a large sombrero bought the pig that won first place.

  5. She was only a child a mother could love.

6. Put an *x* in the box if you want to receive a replacement at the bottom of the form.

7. Feeling the ropes loosen, the kidnap victim's struggle to get free was nearing success.

8. Marta adjusted the hat on her head that she had bought at the thrift store.

9. Who was the man who told you where to leave the package in the yellow windbreaker?

10. A young girl in a pink jacket with a Girl Scout uniform was selling cookies outside the west entrance of the mall.

11. Driving through the park, the bears came right up to the car.

12. On Wednesday the butcher thought he had nearly cut apart two hundred chickens.

13. When thawed, salt should be rubbed on the roast.

14. Jason began repairing the church window with a song in his heart.

15. Adjusting his large red nose, the announcer introduced the clown.

16. Bleating piteously, Mary allowed the lamb to follow her to school.

17. A girl carrying a pie with a shy smile approached the table.

18. After reaching a rolling boil, skim the fat from the surface of the soup.

19. Patty almost seemed angry after the selection.

20. Opening the garage door, the snow outside came almost to Henry's waist.

21. To ensure they arrive by Christmas, packages should be mailed by the middle of November.

22. Letitia began the drive to the beach without a care in the world.

23. The dog walked through the door with its tail between its legs.

24. The government is only interested in eliminating illegal drug production.

25. With winter storms on the way, the success of the operations appeared in doubt.

CHAPTER 39

Subject-Verb Agreement

One of the most common grammar problems for students is agreement between subjects and verbs. The rule itself is quite simple: *A verb must agree in number with its subject.* If the subject is singular, the verb must be singular; if the subject is plural, the verb must be plural.

Singular and Plural Verbs

Usually the verb itself doesn't cause trouble. In fact, the forms for many singular and plural verbs are identical, so they can't cause a mistake in agreement. Yet, English verbs retain one peculiarity that some students find troublesome.

You know that an *-s* or *-es* ending on a noun makes the noun plural: car, car*s*; tomato, tomato*es*. Although the same would seem to be true for verbs, it isn't. An *-s* or *-es* ending on a verb makes the verb singular:

Plural	Singular
They run.	He run*s*.
They go.	She *goes*.
They jump.	It jump*s*.

If you understand this difference between verbs and nouns, verbs themselves are not likely to cause you agreement problems. The problems stem from the subjects of the verbs.

Most errors in agreement occur because of some difficulty related to the subject of a sentence, particularly in:

- identifying the subject
- recognizing the subject's number

IDENTIFYING THE SUBJECT

greement problems result from difficulties in finding the subject of a sentence. Two sentence structures make identifying the subject particularly troublesome:

- when the subject is delayed—so it isn't where we expect it to be
- when a phrase comes between the subject and the verb—confusing us about the subject's identity

Delayed Subject

We usually can find the subject if it comes in its ordinary place—just before the verb—but we may have trouble if it follows the verb. Watch for sentences that open with *there* or *here*. These words delay the subject so that it appears after the verb. You'll have to think through such a sentence because you won't know whether the verb should be singular or plural until you get beyond it to the subject.

        V   S

There *are* three *sailboats* at the dock.

        V   S

There *is* the *sailboat* with the sail on upside down.

      V   S

Here *are* the *supplies* you ordered.

      V   S

Here *is* the *box* you wanted first.

Phrase between Subject and Verb

Sometimes, even when the subject comes before the verb where we expect to see it, it is still hard to identify because of a phrase between the subject and verb. Because of the intervening phrase:

- We may think a word in the phrase is the subject.
- We may think the phrase is part of the subject, making it plural.

Let's look first at an example in which a word in the phrase might seem to be the subject:

                            S   V

Wrong: One of the Coyne *boys have climbed* the water tower.

Here the word *boys* is so close to the verb that the writer thought it was the subject, but that is incorrect. *Boys* is simply part of a phrase that comes between the subject and the verb. The real subject is *one:*

     S   V

Correct: *One* of the Coyne boys *has climbed* the water tower.

Now let's look at a phrase that might seem to be part of the subject:

          S   V

Wrong: *Martha, as well as her sisters, work* in the fields regularly.

As well as her sisters seems to be part of the subject. It seems to be equivalent to *and her sisters.* But it isn't.

Confusing Prepositional Phrases

The words here are merely prepositions; they begin phrases that have nothing to do with determining the agreement between a subject and its verb:

as well as	including
accompanied by	like
along with	together with
in addition to	with

How can we find the subject in our example above? Mentally eliminate the entire phrase:

     S   V

Correct: *Martha* ~~(as well as her sisters)~~ *works* in the fields regularly.

The subject is now clear.

RECOGNIZING THE SUBJECT'S NUMBER

The problems we just looked at occur because the subject isn't where we expect it. Sometimes, though, we can find the subject and still not know whether it is singular or plural. These rules will help you:

- **Two or more subjects joined by** *and* **are almost always plural. The** *and* **joins the items—singular, plural, or mixed—into one plural unit.**

S   S   V

Charlotte and her *brothers drive* the metallic brown dune buggy.

S   S   V

That *woman* and her *husband look* a lot alike.

- **If *or* or *nor* joins subjects, the verb agrees with whichever subject is closer to the verb.**

S   S   V

Either *Beverly* or my other *aunts have* my thanks.

Here, because *aunts* is closer to the verb than is *Beverly,* the verb is plural. What if we reverse the subjects?

S   S   V

Either my other *aunts* or *Beverly has* my thanks.

Now *Beverly* is closer, so the verb is singular.

A Tip on Word Order

Does "Either my other aunts or Beverly has my thanks" seem awkward to you? It's technically correct. However, many readers feel uncomfortable when the singular subject (*Beverly* in this case) of a mixed singular-plural set forces use of a singular verb (*has* in this case). The better choice is to put the plural portion of the set closer to the verb so the verb will be plural.

The rule still applies if both items are singular or if both items are plural. If both are singular, naturally a singular subject will be next to the verb, so the verb is singular. Likewise, if both subjects are plural, a plural subject will be next to the verb, so the verb is plural.

- ***Some, all, most, part, half* (and other fractions) may be either singular or plural, depending on the phrase that follows them.**

We told you in the first part of the chapter not to let a phrase between the subject and the verb influence subject-verb agreement. However, as happens in English grammar, that rule has an exception; here it is:

Many times the words in the previous list are followed by a phrase beginning with *of* ("All *of* the jurors. . . ." "Some *of* the tea . . . "). If the main word in the *of*-phrase is plural, the verb should be plural. However, if the main word is singular or just can't be counted (we wouldn't say "one *milk*" or "thirteen *tea*," for example), the verb should be singular.

S   V
Some of the grapes *are* still on the table. (*Grapes* is plural, so the verb is plural.)

S   V
Some of the milk *is dripping* on the floor. (*Milk* cannot be counted, so the verb is singular.)

- **Relative pronouns** *(who, whose, whom, which,* **and** *that)* **may be singular or plural, depending on the word they refer to.**

Usually the relative pronoun refers to the word just before it:

S   V
Jeannette is one of the children *who love* to read. (*Who* is a pronoun replacing *children*. Not just one child but all the children love to read.)

Again, here comes an exception. What if Jeannette is the *only one* in the group who loves to read? Then the pronoun *who* refers to the word *one*, not the word *children*:

S   V
Jeannette is the only one of the children *who loves* to read.

The exception, then, is that in the phrase *the only one . . . who/that*, the relative pronoun refers to the word *one*, so the verb must be singular (after all, what can be more singular than *one*?).

- **A collective noun as subject requires a singular verb when the group acts as a unit but a plural verb when the members of the group act as separate persons or things.**

A collective noun names a group: *audience, class, committee, family, jury, orchestra, team,* and so forth. The key is to determine whether the parts of the group are acting as a single body or as separate entities (that are doing the same thing).

S   V
The *jury has been sequestered*. (The members of the collective group have been separated from the public as a single body, so the verb is singular.)

S V
The *jury are* unable to agree on a verdict. (Clearly, the members of the collective group are acting as separate individuals—because they cannot agree as a unit—so the verb is plural.)

A. Use one of the following verbs when completing this exercise:

Singular verbs: *throws, goes, misses, takes*

Plural verbs: *throw, go, miss, take*

Do not use other forms of these verbs (such as *threw, had thrown,* or the like).

1. a. Write a sentence with the subject following the verb. Use a singular verb.

   _____

   b. Now use a plural verb.

   _____

2. Write a sentence with a singular subject and the phrase *as well as (fill in a word)* between the subject and the verb.

   _____

3. Write a sentence that has two subjects joined by *and.*

   _____

4. a. Write a sentence with two plural subjects joined by *or.*

   _____

   b. Write a sentence with two singular subjects joined by *or.*

   _____

   c. Write a sentence with a singular and a plural subject joined by *or.*

   _____

   d. Rewrite sentence *c* but reverse the order of the subjects.

   _____

5. Write a sentence with *all* as the subject and a phrase beginning with *of* between it and the verb.

   _____

6. Write a sentence that contains a relative pronoun as a subject and draw an arrow to the word it refers to.

   _____

7. a. Write a sentence with a collective noun as the subject and with a singular verb.

   _____

   b. Write another sentence with the same collective noun as the subject and with a plural verb.

   _____

B. Circle the correct verb in each set of choices below.

1. The family (has, have) decided to start construction on the garage immediately.

2. There (is, are) the peanuts you bought to feed the elephants.

3. One of the lawyers or Tracy (is, are) going to join us when we get to court.

4. Michele is the only one of the editors who (has, have) finished her publication.

5. Two alternatives to settle the disagreement (has, have) been suggested, yet so far neither (is, are) acceptable.

6. The committee (is, are) bringing objects from their personal collections for the display.

7. Some of the jury (is, are) waiting for the defendant to explain what she was thinking.

8. Jenifer is the only one of the graduate students who (has, have) started her dissertation.

9. There (was, were), according to reliable witnesses, at least one shot fired.

10. The rest of her pictures, though, along with the ones of the apes and orangutans, (was, were) worth keeping.

11. Half of the suckers (is, are) for the younger children; the rest (is, are) for Hilde's party favors.

12. Several swimmers from our club (is, are) going to compete in the meet next Saturday.

13. The committee (is, are) not likely to agree on how to discipline the doctor.

14. Physical abuse of the elderly is one of today's social problems that (is, are) beginning to receive attention.

15. Is it clear that Marilyn and her friends (realizes, realize) their error?

16. The pace of the last two chapters of the novel (was, were) too slow.

17. A mixture of ballads and show tunes (was, were) on the program.

18. The audience (was, were) quiet as the actor spoke the opening lines of the play.

19. Neither the rookies nor their instructor (wants, want) to run the obstacle course today.

20. Those compact discs, particularly that one with Glenn Miller's "In the Mood," (is, are) going into the pile of my favorites.

21. The speed of the CD-ROM drives that man bought for his employees (is, are) a generation behind what (is, are) available in the marketplace.

22. There (is, are) only a dresser and three chairs left to load into the van.

23. By the time the police arrived, there (was, were) heated arguments and a few punches being thrown.

24. Neither the birds nor the bees (has, have) to be told about people.

25. Nina is one of those dogs that (follows, follow) you wherever you go.

26. All of the grapes (has, have) spoiled.

27. Part of the liquid (has, have) been spilled from the beaker.

28. Each of the workers (complains, complain) about the quality of the air in the building.

29. Laura together with her friends (is, are) playing Crazy Eights.

30. Religion (is, are) a dangerous subject to discuss because everyone (has, have) a belief he or she holds sacred.

CHAPTER 40

Pronoun Agreement

This chapter deals with another agreement problem—agreement between pronouns and the things they refer to.

Pronouns and Antecedents

Pronouns replace nouns or other pronouns in sentences. A pronoun must have something to refer to—called the *antecedent* of the pronoun. Look for the antecedent for *his* in this sentence:

The boy found his dog.

Clearly, *his* refers to *boy,* so boy is the antecedent for *his*.

The grammar rule that students often find troublesome is this: *A pronoun must agree in number with its antecedent.* If the antecedent is singular, the pronoun must be singular; if the antecedent is plural, the pronoun must be plural.

Because the pronoun's number depends on the antecedent, our attention should be on problem antecedents. When the antecedent is simple, making the pronoun agree is a simple task. You wouldn't write this:

The *boys* looked for *his* books. (Assume all the boys are missing books.)

Boys is a plural antecedent, so you'd write this:

The *boys* looked for *their* books.

Yet, special problems do arise with two types of antecedents:

- indefinite pronoun antecedents
- compound antecedents

INDEFINITE PRONOUN ANTECEDENTS

The biggest headache connected with pronoun agreement occurs when the antecedent is an indefinite pronoun such as *everyone* or *nobody*. We needn't be concerned here with all indefinite pronouns, but we must look at one problem group.

Singular Indefinite Pronouns

The following indefinite pronouns are singular and always require singular pronoun references:

each	everyone	everybody
either	someone	somebody
neither	anyone	anybody
another	no one	nobody
one		

The words formed from *-one* (such as *everyone*) and from *-body* (such as *everybody*) often seem plural, but they're not. Try thinking of them as if they had the word *single* in the middle, like this: *every-single-one* or *every-single-body*. Now they seem to be singular.

An unusual mental block is associated with the indefinite pronouns above. Few people would write this:

Everyone *have* a coat.

Have just doesn't sound right following *everyone*. And for good reason. *Have* is plural, but *everyone* is singular.

Yet, often the same people who recognize *everyone* as a singular subject have trouble recognizing *everyone* as a singular antecedent. Far too often they write this:

Everyone *has their* coat.

Has, of course, is correct: the singular verb agrees with the singular subject. But plural *their* cannot refer to singular *everyone*. As illogical as this problem seems, it is still common.

Study these samples:

Wrong: Everyone wore *their* coat.

Correct: Everyone wore *his* coat.

Wrong: Nobody looked at *their* books.

Correct: Nobody looked at *his* books.

Avoiding Sexist References

You may be uneasy with the "correct" revisions above: often the *everyone* you are talking about refers to a mixed group of men and women, so *his* may seem inappropriate. You're right, of course.

Usage is changing, though in formal English the conventional use of *his* to refer to both sexes is still common. On the other extreme, some writers—particularly advertisers—are matching *their* with indefinite pronouns such as *everyone*. Unfortunately, that solution would return us to the illogical agreement issue we just discussed.

So what's the solution? Fortunately we have several options for avoiding the sexist tone that comes from using only masculine pronouns—without having to match plural pronouns with singular antecedents.

Here are four techniques to avoid sexist pronoun references:

- **You can use *his or her*, as in these sentences:**

No one can read his or her assignment.

Everybody brought his or her book instead.

This technique works well for occasional references, but it will grow awkward and tiresome and attract attention to itself if you use it frequently.

- **You can alternate between *his* and *her*, so that readers perceive a balance in your treatment of the sexes.**

No one can read his assignment.

Everyone wore her coat.

Set together like this, the sentences seem silly, don't they? This technique is useful only in long works, where the writer can use masculine references in some passages and feminine references in others—but not close together. (We've occasionally employed this technique in this textbook.)

- **You can avoid the problem altogether by omitting the pronouns whenever possible.**

Instead of this:	Everyone wore his coat.
Better:	Everyone wore a coat.

Instead of this:	Each of the voters cast her ballot.
Better:	Each of the voters cast a ballot.

- **You also can avoid the problem by changing both antecedents and pronoun references to plural forms.**

Instead of this:	Everyone wore his coat.
Better:	All wore their coats.
Instead of this:	Each of the voters cast her ballot.
Better:	All of the voters cast their ballots.

For most writing, the last two methods are the techniques of choice. Considerate writers will avoid implying that the world has only masculine or only feminine members (by avoiding such statements as "man's best friend is his dog"). They also will avoid implying that specific groups (such as teachers, lawyers, nurses, vice presidents, and so forth) have members of only one sex. A significant part of avoiding such gender-specific language is avoiding sexist pronoun references.

Similar problems occur with words such as *each, either, neither, another,* and *one.* Usually, however, these pronouns are followed by a phrase that begins with *of* and ends with a plural noun, like these:

Each of the girls . . .

Either of the students . . .

Don't be fooled. The singular indefinite pronoun, not the word in the *of*-phrase, is the antecedent for a pronoun in the rest of the sentence.

Wrong: Each of the girls gave me *their* money.

Correct: Each of the girls gave me *her* money.

The pronoun refers to *each,* not to girls.

Wrong: Either of the students may bring *their* books.

Correct: Either of the students may bring *his or her* books.

His or her refers to *either,* not to *students.*

Better: Either of the students may bring the books.

COMPOUND ANTECEDENTS

Compound antecedents may be joined with *and, or,* or *nor.* And the ante-cedents themselves may be all singular, all plural, or a mixture of singular and plural. The rules for agreement depend on the various combinations of these factors.

> • **Two or more antecedents joined by *and* require a plural pronoun.**

Whether the antecedents are singular, plural, or mixed makes no difference: the *and* makes the compound antecedent plural.

> John and the other boy found *their* seats.

> John and the other boys found *their* seats.

> • **Plural antecedents joined by *or* or *nor* require a plural pronoun.**

Either the boys or the girls will clean *their* rooms first.

Neither the boys nor the girls want to clean *their* rooms.

> • **Singular pronouns joined by *or* or *nor* require a singular pronoun.**

Either the dog or the cat will get *its* food first.

Neither the dog nor the cat will eat *its* food.

> • **When *or* or *nor* joins a singular antecedent and a plural antecedent, the pronoun agrees with whichever antecedent it is closer to.**

Neither Freddy nor the other boys like *their* jobs. (The pronoun *their* agrees with *boys.*)

Neither the other boys nor Freddy likes *his* job. (*His* agrees with *Freddy.*)

A Reminder about Word Order and Agreement

"Neither the other boys nor Freddy likes his job" is technically correct, but it may seem awkward. The problem—as well as the solution—is the same as you saw with subject-verb agreement in the previous chapter. The better choice is to put the plural portion of a singular-plural subject/ antecedent set closer to both the verb and the pronoun reference: "Nei-ther Freddy nor the other boys like their jobs."

EXERCISES

A. Circle the correct pronoun in each set of choices below.

1. Another of the women qualified for (his, her, his or her, their) license today.

2. Transistors and vacuum tubes differed greatly in (its, their) size and power consumption.

3. If Angela or her coworkers find an error, (she, they) will want to correct it.

4. Everybody wants to know what (his, her, his or her, their) present will be.

5. Each snowmobile that we want to use for the mission must have (its, their) belts checked for wear and replacement if (it, they) are badly worn.

6. Everyone expected that when Hector and his son arrived, (he, they) would bring (his, her, his or her, their) tools.

7. Alan and his sister found (his, her, his or her, their) seats in the new stadium.

8. Either Pat or one of the other waiters will find you an empty table in (his, her, his or her, their) section.

9. The family is looking for a way to express (its, their) appreciation.

10. Neither Val nor Tiffany could get (her, their) car unstuck after the snow in the parking lot thawed and refroze.

11. Kristina and Travis moved into (his, her, his or her, their) new townhouse last month.

12. Members of the jury will be able to discuss (his, her, his or her, their) views of the evidence when they enter the jury room.

13. Everyone indicated that (he, she, he or she, they) wanted the vendor to be replaced.

14. No one wants to nominate (himself, herself, himself or herself, themselves) to chair the committee.

15. One of the men discovered that somebody had scratched the paint on (his, her, his or her, their) car.

B. Correct errors in pronoun agreement in the following sentences.

1. Neither Nancy nor Edgar liked their new assignment.

2. When the working group stopped for lunch, I telephoned my office, but neither Albert nor Carlos could remember their phone number.

3. After both boys crawled out of the overturned vehicle, each showed the sheriff the cuts and bruises on their foreheads.

4. High water and mud filled the lower levels of all the stores on Main Street, but none of the women appeared to let it discourage them from reopening after the cleanup.

5. Some will want to know what they can do to help.

6. Low prices and good food may have built the restaurant's clientele base, but its quality today won't bring in new customers.

7. Each of the jury members understood their responsibilities, but no one wanted to see himself or herself responsible for convicting the young mother.

8. Either of the men should be able to find their briefcase.

9. April and Elizabeth remembered her lines, but neither thought to bring their costume for the rehearsal.

10. The Committee to Restore Downtown is looking for contributors for their fund-raiser.

C. Revise the following sentences to eliminate the gender-specific language.

1. Someone is bound to volunteer himself to lead the discussion.

2. Another of the plumbers tested for his license today.

3. A corporate executive today expects to find himself involved in helping downsize his company.

4. Each pilot is responsible for the safety of his aircraft.

5. I hope you remembered to thank each of the secretaries for her help with your project.

6. Every vice president in this company would sacrifice his seat in the executive dining room if that would increase profits.

7. A good officer understands the need for his personal attention to the needs of his troops.

8. Did everyone catch his bus on time?

9. None of the nurses who took care of her was present when Carrie brought a basket of fruit to thank each of them for her kind attention.

10. One of the teachers tried to use her influence to convince the principal to revise his ruling.

CHAPTER 41
Passive Voice

Do you ever find yourself struggling with a passage you're reading, even though you know all the words? Does the phrasing seem wordy and sort of backwards? Chances are the passage is loaded with passive voice. Like most readers, you've come to expect sentences in the active voice, perhaps without even knowing what active and passive voice are.

Active and Passive Voice

"Voice" is a grammatical term for a particular form of a verb; it refers specifically to the relationship between the subject of a sentence and the *action* of the verb. The natural order of the English sentence—actor-action-acted upon—requires *active voice,* as in the following:

> *Adam*   *ate*   the *apple*
> (actor)   (action)   (acted upon)

The subject of the sentence is the actor, the one doing the eating.

Passive voice reverses this normal, expected order. The subject is no longer the actor; the new subject is acted upon, as in this *passive voice* sentence:

> The *apple*   *was eaten*   by *Adam*
> (acted upon)   (action)   (actor)

Notice that the actor now appears after the verb, in a "by" prepositional phrase.

However, a passive voice sentence may not even name the actor, as in this version:

> The *apple*   *was eaten.*
> (acted upon)   (action)

The subject still is acted upon, but we no longer know the identity of the actor.

Comparing even the simple active and passive sentences above allows us to see some of the disadvantages of passive voice:

- A passive construction is *wordier* than an active one.
- Because it reverses the normal order of an action, passive voice is *indirect*.
- As its name implies, a "passive" verb *lacks the vigor* inherent in an active verb.
- And if the writer doesn't include the actor, the passive construction *may be vague*.

Passive Voice in Business and Technical Writing

Passive voice is one of the less desirable features of "bureaucratic writing" or "governmentese." Moreover, some business writers, particularly in technical fields, have developed the notion that eliminating the actor from a sentence—which often results in passive voice—will make their writing more objective. Don't be fooled. Passive constructions have a function, as we'll see later in this chapter, but usually passive voice does more harm than good.

Why? In addition to the disadvantages of passive voice listed above, *passive constructions generate other awkward writing*. For example, passive voice frequently is associated with misplaced modifiers. Moreover, wordy sentences, such as ones beginning with *It is* and *There are* often include passive voice.

Professional editors know to look for certain wording patterns when they attack an awkward passage. They know that addressing one or two easily recognizable structures is a quick way to get at the rest of the problems in a complex passage. Of course, passive voice is chief among those structures.

Let's look at an awkward piece of bureaucratic writing and see how an editor would work with it:

There has been very little effort made by overextended police forces to attempt interdiction of drug shipments and processing laboratory destruction operations.

Although we might be tempted to start by revising the overly complex wording, an efficient editor will first solve simple problems such as faulty sentence structure. The beginning of the sentence combines a passive construction (*has been . . . effort made by . . . forces*) with a *There are* type of opening. Revising to eliminate the passive construction fixes both voice and wordiness problems:

> *Overextended police forces have done little* to attempt interdiction of drug shipments and processing laboratory destruction operations.

Now the editor can focus on the wordiness and lack of parallelism in the rest of the sentence:

> Overextended police forces have done little *to interdict drug shipments and destroy processing laboratories.*

The revision is simpler and certainly more clear. Remember to attack the simple problems in a sentence first; revising passive voice is an easy place to begin once you know how to recognize passive voice and deal with it.

RECOGNIZING PASSIVE VOICE

Identifying passive voice is really quite simple. Only a passive sentence will receive "yes" answers in all of the following tests:

- **Is the subject of the sentence acted upon?**

In our sample sentence, *apple,* the subject of the sentence, is acted upon (eaten) by Adam.

- **Does the sentence use a form of the verb *to be* followed by the kind of main verb that almost always ends in *-ed* or *-en?***

The simple forms of *to be* are these: *is, am, are, was,* and *were.* Compound forms of *to be* use *be, being,* or *been* (for example, *will be, is being, has been*). Thus, passive verbs look like these: *is divided, was beaten,* and *will have been destroyed.* In our sample passive sentence, *was eaten* is the passive verb form.

- **If the actor appears in the sentence, is the actor in the prepositional phrase *by someone or something?* Or if the actor doesn't appear in the sentence, does the sense of the sentence imply *by someone or something?***

"The apple was eaten by Adam" ends with *by Adam,* whereas "The apple was eaten" implies *by someone.*

Passive Voice and Past Tense

Don't confuse passive voice and past tense. They sound alike, but there is no essential connection between them. Both active and passive verb forms can appear in any number of tenses, as this sample shows:

Tense	Active Voice	Passive Voice
present	takes	is being taken
past	took	was taken
future	will take	will be taken

USING PASSIVE VOICE

You may have decided by now that passive voice was created (by someone) merely to entrap you. Not so. In fact, passive constructions have legitimate uses:

- **Passive voice is useful when the object of the action is more important than the actor.**

Residents of Sandstone, Nevada, are afraid that a lethal gas manufactured in nearby Cactus Flower may someday poison them. They fear, for example, that the *lethal gas may be released* by a defective valve or a worn gasket.

The emphasis in the last sentence is clearly on the lethal gas. That is, the context of the passage makes the gas more important than the parts that might allow a leak. Only passive voice will allow the object of the action (lethal gas) to gain emphasis by appearing first in the sentence.

- **Because passive voice can hide the actor, it is useful when the actor is obvious, unimportant, or uncertain.**

For example, if we didn't know who dropped a canister of gas, we might write this:

When a canister *was dropped,* a lethal gas enveloped the laboratory workers.

Passive Voice and Evasiveness

A strong warning is necessary here. Passive voice makes it all too easy for a writer to omit the "by" part of a thought; this evasiveness in particular is a mark of "bureaucratic writing." Imagine being told this:

Leave your application in the box. If you *are found* acceptable, you *will be notified.*

"By whom?" you want to demand. Omissions of the responsible individuals in statements like this frustrate and irritate readers.

Deciding when passive voice is a good choice requires some thought. You can stretch the justifications for its use to cover most sentences if you try hard enough. Therefore, keep in mind this general rule: *Write with the active voice unless you have an excellent reason for using the passive.*

ACTIVATING THE PASSIVE

Far too often writers use passive voice because they can't think how to write the sentence in the active voice; in such cases, the passive is more accidental than intentional. You can prevent this lack of control in your own writing by learning the following three methods to convert passive voice into active:

- **Reverse the object and the subject.**

Passive: An example *is shown* in Figure 3.

Active: Figure 3 *shows* an example.

- **Delete the main verb, leaving the sentence with a form of *to be* as the only verb.**

Passive: Your cousin *is seen* as the best candidate.

Active: Your cousin *is* the best candidate.

- **Change the verb.**

Passive: Jonathan *was given* a new book.

Active: Jonathan *received* a new book.

If you learn to recognize passive voice and determine to use active voice instead whenever you can, these three methods will provide you with the tools you need to write simple, direct, and vigorous active sentences.

EXERCISES

A. Rewrite the following sentences to eliminate passive voice. For some you may need to supply actors.

1. Fifteen sets of bells were rung during the ceremony.

2. The last Americans were evacuated from Saigon in 1975.

3. Florida is located in the southern United States.

4. The second alternative is seen as the better option.

5. The most economical service is offered by long-haul communications.

6. A keynote address will be delivered by the company's chief executive officer.

7. Until the building collapsed, the cracks in the foundation were not viewed as a problem.

8. Jack was notified that he was seen as the most likely to be selected for the promotion.

9. The party is made up of several factions.

10. Silicon crystal wafers are commonly used for integrated circuits.

11. The red switch should be pushed if the machine functions are stopped.

12. The door is secure when the hook is placed inside the eye.

13. After the pants were washed three times, a dull red stain was left on the left leg.

14. Construction can be begun Thursday if the building materials are delivered on time.

15. Southern California is favored for making films because the weather is mild and labor can be obtained at a reasonable cost.

16. Thousands of new jobs are expected to be created if the Zydeco Company is lured into the county.

17. When the first stage of the missile has been separated, the second-stage rockets can be ignited.

18. The charity carnival was canceled when the funds to cover cleanup costs could not be guaranteed by the sponsor.

19. A van filled with high-explosives was driven into the underground parking garage by a man who was dressed in dark blue coveralls and a red baseball cap.

20. The shaft is made of steel.

21. Worldwide as many as 27 million people were killed by influenza in 1918.

22. We are no longer surprised by the news that a child has been killed by stray bullets during a drive-by shooting.

23. The conflict in *West Side Story* originally was conceived as being between American Catholics and Jews.

24. During the McCarthy hearings in the 1950s, the loyalty of thousands of Americans was questioned.

25. The effectiveness of a polio vaccine that had been developed by Dr. Jonas Salk was tested in a major study in 1954 that involved almost 2 million American children.

B. Each of the following sentences contains a number of writing problems that need to be corrected. Those problems include at least one passive construction per sentence. Revise the passive voice first and then see what else you can do to improve the sentences.

1. Numerous important agreements between Russia and Ukraine were agreed to at the talks.

2. The use of the same pistol in each attack may be the method used by the gang in order to authenticate its responsibilities for attacks to the authorities.

3. The number of small boats operating in the region is numerous, in the thousands, and many are used by smugglers to carry their goods.

4. At the same time that global threats were diminished in number, there also was an upsurge in regional threats.

5. The commander is faced with the issue of where the line is to be drawn between operational and tactical objectives.

6. The plan was designed to expand the country's agricultural base with priority being placed on the coffee-growing and forestry segments of the economy.

7. Until an indigenous capability to produce high-technology components is attained, the nation's electronics industry will remain backward in technology.

8. The organization of the supply system is deficient in great measure because it has been severely affected by corruption in the government and also in the industries as well.

9. Drug trafficking, as well as other illegal activities that are related to the trafficking, will continue in the district until an effective permanent governmental presence can be maintained there.

10. Nontraditional machining processes can be differentiated from traditional cutting and grinding processes because the nontraditional machining processes are characterized by higher power consumption and lower material removal rates than conventional machining methods.

CHAPTER 42
Word Choice

The French have a phrase that could be the title of this chapter. The phrase is *le mot juste,* and it means—roughly—"the right word." *Le mot juste* is often the difference between an A paper and an ordinary C paper—not just one good word, of course, but a lot of them. This chapter covers some basic and advanced techniques for finding those good words.

BASIC TECHNIQUES

Use Precise Words

What is a good word? Is it something really impressive, a big word that proves how educated we are? No, usually it's a word we all know. Unfortunately, even though it's a common word, it's one we rarely use because we choose an even more common word instead. *See* is one of those more general words we might slap down in a rough draft. But think of all the more precise synonyms that might work better: *glimpse, gaze, stare, peer, spot,* and *witness.*

Let's take a longer example. Suppose you are reading a paragraph and run across these words:

The man walked into the room.

The words are so general they could fit into a number of strikingly different contexts:

The policeman, hidden behind a parked car, watched as *the man walked into the room.*

or

The Capitol guard smiled as *the man walked into the room.*

or

The class quieted somewhat as *the man walked into the room.*

or

The patients gasped as *the man walked into the room.*

"What a great clause!" you say. "I can use it anywhere." The truth is, it's a lousy clause—you can use it anywhere. All of the words are general, the kind of words that pop into your mind in a second.

Let's try to make the words more exact. Here are some possibilities:

man: *thief, senator, English teacher, Dr. Rodney*
walked: *sneaked, hurried, sauntered, reeled*
room: *motel room, antechamber, classroom, office*

Now let's rewrite that all-purpose clause using more specific words:

The policeman, hidden behind a parked car, watched as *the thief sneaked into my motel room.*

or

The Capitol guard smiled as the *senator hurried into the antechamber.*

or

The class quieted somewhat as *the English teacher sauntered into the classroom.*

or

The patients gasped as *Dr. Rodney reeled into his office.*

Each clause is better—and certainly more interesting—because the writer took the time to come up with just the right words. Try it yourself. Look for the dull, general words in your own writing and make them more specific. This technique is one of the best ways to improve your writing dramatically.

Beware of Peculiar Words

Don't become so obsessed with the idea of seeking different words that you choose them just because they're unusual. *Perambulate*, for example, means "to walk through," so we could write this:

> The senator perambulated the antechamber.

Readers probably will notice the peculiarity of *perambulated* rather than its preciseness. Your goal is to get the right words—not just the unusual ones.

Use Modifiers

The second basic technique, in addition to using the right word, is to use modifiers. Sometimes nouns and verbs don't tell the whole story. To be really precise, you need to add some adjectives and adverbs. Let's work with one of the sentences we improved in the previous section:

> The policeman, hidden behind a parked car, watched as the thief sneaked into my motel room.

From the clause we revised *(the thief sneaked into my motel room)*, we can modify *thief*, *sneaked*, and *motel room*. Here are just a few possibilities:

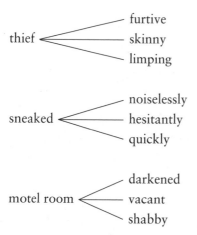

```
                    ┌─ furtive
        thief  ─────┼── skinny
                    └─ limping


                    ┌─ noiselessly
       sneaked ─────┼── hesitantly
                    └─ quickly


                    ┌─ darkened
     motel room ────┼── vacant
                    └─ shabby
```

We don't want to overload the sentence with modifiers, so let's just modify *thief* and *sneaked*:

> The policeman, hidden behind a parked car, watched as the furtive thief sneaked noiselessly into my motel room.

We've come a long way from "The man walked into the room," haven't we?

Beware of Piling On

If you watch football, you've seen teams penalized for "piling on"—when players jump onto a pile of tacklers and the ball carrier after the referee has blown the whistle and the play is dead. Similarly, you need to beware of piling on modifier after modifier. You have to restrain your use of modifiers to what is relevant to accomplish your purpose—and no more. Only the writer and the child's mother could love this sentence:

The diminutive, chunky, azure-eyed, eighteen-month-old baby boy toddled to his rocking horse.

ADVANCED TECHNIQUES

Use Comparisons

If you really want to get your readers' attention, use a comparison. It may be the most memorable part of your theme. Remember when we said transitions are like road signs? And when we said the blueprint for your paper is like the architect's design for the structure he plans to build? These and other comparisons help readers understand an idea.

Comparisons have one drawback: they can be hard to think of, particularly good comparisons. We all can think of bad ones. The familiar phrases that come to mind almost automatically are *clichés*, and they can doom writing as effectively as original comparisons can save it. Consider this sentence:

Although he was *blind as a bat,* Herman remained *cool as a cucumber* when he entered the arena.

See how clichés attract the wrong kind of attention to themselves? Hearing a cliché is like hearing a comedian go through the same routine time after time. After a while, nobody listens.

A good rule is that if you have heard a comparison before, don't use it. But do use original comparisons. Be daring. Try one in your next theme.

Replace General Ideas with Specific Samples

Here's something else to try in your next theme: When you want to use a general word that stands for an entire class of items—such as *toys* or *vehicles* or *books*—use just one item from that class instead. Let the specific stand for the general. Consider this sentence:

Inflation means that most Americans can hardly afford to eat, but some congressmen don't seem to care how much *food* costs.

Let's make the sentence a little more interesting by replacing the word *food* (an entire class of items) with *a loaf of bread* (one item from that class):

> Inflation means that most Americans can hardly afford to eat, but some congressmen don't seem to care how much *a loaf of bread* costs.

Here's another example:

> As a photographer she is limited. She may be able to take pictures of *nature,* but she can't take good pictures of people.

We can make the second sentence more interesting by changing the word *nature* to something more specific:

> As a photographer she is limited. She may be able to take pictures of *trees,* but she can't take good pictures of people.

See how the detail instead of the generality makes the sentence livelier?

Most college students neglect both of the advanced techniques in this section. And few of them get A's. If you want to learn how to write an A paper, you might start by occasionally using a comparison or a specific word instead of a general one.

EXERCISES

A. Rewrite the following sentences two different ways. Replace the underlined general words with more precise words.

Example: <u>The official</u> <u>talked to</u> <u>the man</u>.

a. The district attorney grilled the arsonist.

b. The manager congratulated the pitcher.

1. <u>The animal</u> <u>ate</u> <u>the food.</u>

    a._____

    b._____

2. <u>The audience</u> <u>liked</u> <u>the show.</u>

    a._____

    b._____

3. <u>The worker</u> dropped <u>the tool.</u>

    a._____

    b._____

4. <u>The speaker</u> <u>spoke</u> about the value of a good <u>thing.</u>

    a._____

    b._____

5. <u>The scientist</u> <u>talked about</u> <u>the invention.</u>

    a._____

    b._____

B. In each sentence below write a modifier in the blank. Make the modifier as colorful and specific as you can, but fit it into the context of the sentence.

Example: The _____ policeman arrested the mayor.

Words such as *short* and *young* may not help much. On the other hand, try these choices:

The <u>rookie</u> policeman arrested the mayor.

or

The <u>bitter</u> policeman arrested the mayor.

1. Just when the _____ explosives expert was about to touch the fuse, a nearby truck backfired.

2. The _____ tiger stalked the gazelle.

3. His parents were _____ when they saw the decorations in Oliver's room.

4. Florence was shocked to find a/an _____ worm on the remains of her apple.

5. Seventeen of us piled into the _____ van.

6. The _____ woman flinched when the balloon popped.

7. The drunk staggered _____ through the museum.

8. As the parade passed by, the children cried out
_____.

9. The _____ juror was startled when the prosecutor stopped pacing in front of her.

10. The class laughed _____ when the novice instructor dropped his notes.

C. We use comparisons every day, but too many of them are clichés, such as "nervous as a cat on a hot tin roof" or "scared as a rabbit." For this exercise write one original comparison on any topic. (If you have trouble thinking of a topic, consider blind dates, a hobby, a famous person.)

D. List three clichés other than the ones we've used as examples. (Remember, clichés are bad as bad can be: avoid them like the plague.)

1. _____

2. _____

3. _____

E. Improve the sentences below by changing each italicized generalization to something more specific.

Example: Small movie houses that show film classics are going out of business. After all, who wants to pay *good money* to see *an old movie*?

Revision: Small movie houses that show film classics are going out of business. After all, who wants to pay *eight dollars* to see *Humphrey Bogart*?

1. As we *moved* through the crowd, we bumped into *some people* and their *things*.

moved: _____

some people: _____

things:_____

2. Opponents of colorizing movies question whether adding color to *a classic black-and-white* movie will improve or cheapen it.

   a classic black-and-white movie: _____

3. Couch potatoes spend their days watching *situation comedies* and *sports programs.*

   situation comedies: _____

   sports programs: _____

4. *A publication* reported that *things we eat* cause *a disease.*

   A publication: _____

   things we eat: _____

   a disease: _____

5. As I drive to work, all I hear on the radio is *music* and *people talking.*

   music: _____

   people talking: _____

SECTION

Sample
Student
Essays

Introduction to Section Four

Over the years, we've gathered sample papers from our students, from the students of other instructors, and from others throughout the country. These papers give you an idea how people have applied the various models we've presented in the book.

Some samples follow our models exactly. For example, some sample five-paragraph essays have introductions, central paragraphs, and conclusions that have all the subparts of the model:

- introductions with a motivator, a thesis statement, and a blueprint
- topic sentences with a transition, a reminder of the thesis statement, and a statement of the main idea of the paragraph
- and so forth

Other samples vary from the model—perhaps leaving out the blueprint, or having a conclusion that doesn't explicitly restate the thesis. Usually these examples succeed—showing that the models make excellent starting points for your writing, but they don't have to be artificially constraining.

The Stage I Paragraph

Renoir: And Now for the Rest of the Story . . .

by Victoria Eugenie Boot

Knowing the story of a painting can help us appreciate it even more. For example, Renoir's *Luncheon of the Boating Party,* one of the most famous paintings in the world, has a bit of humor in it. The painting shows attractive men and women having lunch by the river, the men in shirtsleeves and the women formally dressed in long dresses and hats. Everyone seems attractive, and the dozen or so people are generally paired off and seem engaged in flirtatious activity. But the woman most in the foreground is an exception: instead of flirting with the man beside her, she is snuggling up to a puppy. And the man beside her is staring off in the distance, as though his conversation has gotten nowhere. The humor? The woman in the foreground is Renoir's fiancee—and apparently Renoir didn't want any man in the scene to be making any progress with her! So a little knowledge about a painting can help us enjoy it.

Fall

by Laura Rosenfeld

As I sit looking out of my bedroom window, I am reminded why fall is my favorite time of year. The once-green trees have just begun turning the vibrant colors of the season: reds, oranges, yellows, and unlimited combinations of each. Their beauty is breathtaking, and I cannot stop admiring them. The weather has also changed from the heat of endless summer to a rejuvenating cool, and I no longer dread working in the yard or going for my daily walk. This change of season also signals the start of the holidays. Halloween is just around the corner, followed by Thanksgiving, Hanukkah, and New Year's. In my family, these holidays mean wonderful celebrations of tradition and togetherness that bring the year to a satisfying close. As I continue gazing out the window, I am filled with the anticipation as once again fall is upon us.

The Joy of Writing

by Rob Jacobs

Writing on a regular basis has made an unexpected difference in my life. Like many people, I used to dread putting pen to paper because it seemed like such a tedious task. Once I began doing it on a daily basis, however, I discovered the many benefits of writing. I find that I can work through problems more efficiently when I write them down. I've learned many new things about myself as I explore my past and present while writing. I also learned that writing is a relaxing time for me, and it helps me to unwind at the end of a busy day. Despite the dread many people feel when faced with a writing task, I have found writing to be a wonderful activity.

Switzerland Is Breathtakingly Switzerland: The Postcards Tell the Truth

by Edward Hiller

Switzerland is breathtakingly beautiful. A small town named Grindelwald, for example, lies at the foot of two of the most famous mountains in the world—the Eiger and the Jungfrau. These rugged, snowy mountains tower above the grassy alpine meadows, the cows with their melodic bells around their necks, and the tidy little chalets with their red geraniums on the window sills. But Switzerland has more than mountains: the lovely town of Geneva lies at the end of a beautiful lake. In the middle of the lake is a famous fountain, shooting its spray high into the air; just beyond the lake lie the hilly vineyards with row upon perfect row of grapes. For a visit to a land of postcard beauty, you can't go wrong with Switzerland.

An Embarrassing Moment

by Christine Holt

One of my most embarrassing moments occurred while I was meeting my husband's parents for the first time. Jim's father was well known for his dry humor, and Jim had warned me about the "masked comedian," but in my nervous state, Dad's apparently stern presence was terribly intimidating. We were standing in the living room when he turned and pointed to a picture on the wall. He told me his sister Marge had given it to him and then asked me what I thought of it. Of course I replied that I thought it was very nice. He glared at me and said, "I think it's a shame such an ugly thing has to hang on our wall." I was paralyzed. I had no idea that Aunt Marge's gifts to the family were a continuous source for jokes. That was the fact I learned, to my great relief, as Dad and Jim burst out laughing. It was a moment I have never forgotten and undoubtedly one of my most embarrassing.

My Uncle Joe

by Allan Jackson

One of my relatives, an uncle named Joe, has the most amazing resolve that I have ever seen. Even though he is seventy-two years old, Joe has never been dependent on anyone in his entire life. He is from an era when a person had to know how to survive, or didn't. And Uncle Joe has never forgotten the lesson life taught him. He has been on farms all of his life, lives on one now, and still does all the work necessary to keep it going. He rides horses, milks the cows, and tends the chickens, pigs, goats, and other animals without any outside help. When Joe's only son decided not to take over the family farm, Joe sold a few acres to achieve a farm the size he could maintain alone, and did it! I've never seen or known anyone like my Uncle Joe.

Computers Earn Their Wings

by Brooke Pleasants

Although the computer isn't going to replace teachers anytime soon, it has taken a significant step in that direction with its primary role in training airline pilots. One way the computer trains pilots is by teaching them the classroom knowledge they need to know through computer-based training—well-designed multimedia presentations let the pilots learn complex material at their own pace. A second way computers train pilots is by controlling the ground simulators pilots sit in and learn to "fly" the new airplane. In fact, the simulators are amazingly like the real airplane, actually moving on various axes and simulating the sounds and vibrations of the real thing. Computers may not be able to fly, but they do a great job training the pilots who can.

The Robot and the Orange

by Debbie Stewart

Once fully developed, the best technological wonder of the South will be the robotic orange picker. University of Florida researchers are working on a prototype that can locate fruit among leaves and branches with the help of a television camera, a filter that sharpens contrast, and a computer that scans the image for bright objects. These researchers are confident that once the robot hand is perfected, the robot will be able to harvest an orange every two seconds, which is twice the rate that a human worker would be able to sustain. Furthermore, the robot could pick at night. Imagine the impact this development would have on the citrus industry!

The Virtuoso Shopper

by Karen Eisenhauer

I am convinced that anything that can be bought can be bought at a discount. I have become a virtuoso sale shopper over the years by carefully watching and waiting for some of my favorite stores to have sales. I have been known to call the store and ask when the next sale will start, what items will be featured, and what type of discount will be offered. I have also found that it is possible to save as much as 50 percent on certain major items such as furniture, electronics, china, and even jewelry by ordering them from places that deal exclusively in those items. If there is one thing I hate to do, it is waste money, and my bargain hunting techniques have really paid off.

QUESTIONS

Identify the topic sentence in each of the preceding essays. Then identity the type of support. Determine the unity. Does each sentence in the essay in some way support the topic sentence? Now determine the coherence of each essay. What explanations of the support, reminders of the opinion in the topic sentence, and transitions are used? Are they adequate? Does each essay have a concluding sentence that is a literal or strongly implied rewording of the topic sentence?

The Stage II Paragraph

Sailing Alone: Not for the Fainthearted

by Tippy Sophster

Sailing the oceans alone doesn't get much press today, but it was a death defying act a little more than a century ago. One reason it was death defying is that pirates and others of malicious intent were a real threat. In *Sailing Alone Around the World,* Joshua Slocum recounts sailing around Cape Horn and being followed by some savage looking, primitive people. At night, Slocum ingeniously threw sharply pointed carpet tacks around the deck. One night he heard men come aboard aiming, without doubt, to murder him. The tacks worked perfectly! In his typical low-key style, Slocum says, "They jumped pell-mell, some into their canoes and some into the sea, to cool off, I suppose, and there was a deal of free language over it as they went. . . . I turned in again, feeling sure I should not be disturbed any more by people in so great a hurry" (p. 103). Of course people weren't the main threat to his life: the ocean was. Sailing single-handedly, Slocum had only his own (considerable) resources to draw on. Storms came and went, but a single, rogue wave almost finished him. He tells of "a tremendous wave, the culmination, it seemed, of many waves, rolled down upon her [his ship, *Spray*] in a storm, roaring as it came. . . . I saw the mighty crest towering masthead-high above me. The mountain of water submerged my vessel" (pp. 81–82). Slocum survived that wave and the entire trip, becoming famous throughout the world for his feat that took place from 1895 to 1898. Yet even such a famous mariner was not invulnerable to danger, succumbing to the sea a few years later.

Mountain Climbing

by Gary Coyne

Mountain climbing is especially dangerous for people who are inexperienced. One reason it's dangerous is that inexperienced climbers often misjudge the weather—they think the weather at the foot of the mountain is like the weather at the top. But that can be deceptive. New Hampshire's Mount Washington, for example, is known for its freezing temperatures and extraordinarily strong winds in every month of the year—including July. Yet every summer, inexperienced climbers head for the top wearing only shorts and T-shirts. And every summer, some are hurt or even killed as a result. A second reason climbing is dangerous for the inexperienced is that climbing *up* is easier than climbing *down*. New climbers scrambling up rocky ravines and cliffs sometimes reach a place that they can barely climb up. They do it—and then reach a place they simply can't climb up. Then they're trapped. They can't go up; they can't go back down. Yet they often try one direction or the other, usually with disastrous results. A particularly awful cliff in Colorado known as Longfellow has claimed many lives over the years with just that scenario. And almost inevitably, the climbers have been inexperienced. So mountain climbing, despite the ropes and other good equipment now available, often isn't safe—especially for the inexperienced.

The Mouse That People Like

by Amy Fisher

There's one mouse that lots of people today consider useful around the house and office: the mouse on a computer. One reason a mouse (a small gadget that positions the cursor on the computer screen) is useful is that it can move much faster than the arrow keys. In this paragraph, for example, suppose you want to move the cursor from the first word of the paragraph to the one at the end of this sentence. You'd have to press the down arrow several times and the right arrow several times. But with a mouse, you simply move the pointer directly to the word you want. Secondly, the mouse is useful for drawing on the screen. Graphics programs let artists and would-be artists create freehand designs. Imagine trying to draw the moon over a lake with arrow keys! But with a mouse, you simply move your hand the same way you would move it in drawing the moon and the lake on paper—the mouse makes such drawings simpler. So don't worry about having this mouse around—it's useful and eats no cheese!

Woodworking

by Bonnie Banks

I spend my spare time working at various hobbies, but no hobby gives me more enjoyment than working with wood. For example, there is the pleasure I receive when I build for family or friends. A hat rack that I built for Karen, my sister, this past Christmas meant more to her and me than any gift I could have purchased. Also, in 1982 when my friend Maureen graduated from West Point, I enjoyed building a nameplate holder for her desk as a graduation present. Another satisfaction of my woodworking hobby is being able to build things I need. I built an oak captain's bed and bookcase set. To relieve an overcrowded room, I designed the bed to be mounted on top of the bookcase set. Likewise, when I acquired too many woodworking tools to fit my old tool box, I enjoyed building a larger tool box. Finally, the amount of joy I receive from this hobby cannot be measured. When I view the finished products, such as my captain's bed, I feel a sense of triumph. I find redeeming qualities in all my hobbies, but the gratification I feel when I work with wood cannot be matched.

Callaway Gardens

by Karen Eisenhauer

Callaway Gardens in Pine Mountain, Georgia, is a wonderful place for a family vacation. There is such a great variety of activities for children and adults that it is possible to be more tired at the end of the vacation than at the beginning. For the children there are planned activities everyday from 9:00 A.M. until 3:00 P.M. that are well supervised and well run. These activities include outdoor games, arts and crafts, miniature golf, and circus activities, to name a few. For adults there are hikes, golf, tennis, water-skiing, arts and crafts, workshops, and tours, and many more. The accommodations are well suited for families. The cottages have fully equipped kitchens, plenty of space, and are completely furnished. Callaway Gardens is located in a scenic area of rolling hills and forests. And it has continually improved the properties, making it a pleasure to look almost anywhere. A vacation at Callaway Gardens is a vacation I would recommend to anyone.

Short Fuse

by Tom Carroll

Although I may seem good-natured, my temper has a short fuse. This character trait tends to come to the surface whenever I participate in sports competition. Whether the activity is football, basketball, or baseball, the official's opinion usually infuriates me. Often during competitive play, my opponents have been known to incite an uncontrollable outburst. For me the most irritating aspect of playing sports is not winning. Losing truly brings out the worst in me. Another time I must deal with my short fuse is when I am driving through the city traffic. Often I find myself fuming. Ignorant people behind the wheel are the biggest cause of my affliction. There is nothing like a driver blocking the passing lane to make me explode. I just don't understand how half of the drivers on the road ever passed the road test to get a license! Loud and offensive people also steam me up. It doesn't take long for a big mouth at a movie theater to get me going. If someone cuts in front of me in a snack line, I am sure to verbally abuse the intruder. And I can't help but say something if I find myself listening to loud drunks arguing at a bar. I really am a good-natured fellow who tries to remain calm, but when my short fuse is lit, my temper erupts like a volcano!

My Love for Music

by Christine Holt

Music may or may not "hath charms to soothe the savage breast," but it certainly plays an important part in my life. When my children or I need a pick-me-up, music lifts our spirits. When I am feeling sad, a favorite song will brighten my day. When my children get bored, I turn on the radio and dance while we all clap hands and sing along. When I feel the need to relax, I always find solace in music. If I find myself in heavy traffic, soothing music from the car radio always helps to ease the tension. I like to play the same relaxing music on my radio at the office because it helps to keep the frustration level low. Music can also provide me with an escape when I have had a busy day. Once my school or work day is finished, I go home, kick off my shoes, lie back in the recliner, and close my eyes. The next thing I know, I am floating far above the world of people and their problems. When my kids' demands become overwhelming, I take my radio to my favorite spot at the beach, and the world of diapers, teething pains, and two-year-old frustrations fades away. My love for music makes it easier to handle the little ups and downs of everyday life.

QUESTIONS

Analyze each essay by identifying its topic sentence. Then identify the subtopic sentences. Finally, determine how each writer linked the subtopic sentences to the topic idea. Do the subtopic sentences answer the questions "How?" "When?" or "Why?"

The Five-Paragraph Essay

My Hearing-Impaired Sister

by Zach Stimus

My younger sister, Tanya, is hearing impaired. When she was eleven years old she lost her hearing after a severe illness that affected her nervous system. In the eight years my sister has learned to cope and adapt with her sudden hearing loss, I have become aware of three important ways that we should treat those with impairments.

First, we should always try to be sure those with impairments are included in the activities that are going on around them. We take so much for granted, and it's important that we be aware as to how this affects the person with disabilities. For example, Tanya and I love going to baseball games, but a lot of important information is relayed via the announcer. After the announcer has spoken, I always tell Tanya (using sign language) what the announcer has said. This helps her to stay involved with the crowd and to understand why those around us may be laughing, booing, clapping, etc.

Second, those with impairments are still contributing members of our society, and they should be treated with the same respect. Because those with disabilities may appear slow, it does not mean they are. It may require more time and patience to interact with persons with disabilities, but that does not make them any less worthy of our time and attention. Even though Tanya can no longer hear, she is still a person with a heart and mind and soul. Her deafness doesn't mean she no longer feels, no longer thinks, no longer wants to belong. Although Tanya's disability makes her different from others, it does not mean she is a less loving, giving, contributing member of society.

Third, it is important that we don't shy away from those who have special needs or impairments. I have become aware of how our society fears those who are not "perfect." It is understandable that we fear that which we do not understand, but how do we overcome that fear unless we learn about it? So often, those with disabilities in our society are ignored, made fun of, or treated as inferiors, and nothing could be further from the truth. As Tanya began to immerse herself in a new world of those who are hearing impaired, my family found itself immersed in this world, too. We have since met the most wonderful people who have enriched our lives and, sadly, people we would never have taken the time to know unless Tanya had not bravely tackled her hearing impairment.

My sister, Tanya, continues to be an inspiration to me. She has not let her disability slow her down as she attends college and has a boyfriend and a wealth of friends (both hearing and hearing impaired). I am proud of my sister and am grateful for the lessons I have learned through her struggles and triumphs.

Leaving Home: Freedom or . . .

by Laura M. Godar

Although moving out of your parents' home into your own place can be very exciting, living on your own is not as simple as it may seem. I thought living away from my parents would be wonderful—I could do anything I wanted! No one would be able to tell me what to do or what time to come home, and I would finally have complete privacy. But when I moved out, I realized I had to do my own cooking, cleaning, and bill-paying—and that wasn't so wonderful.

Probably the hardest thing about living away from home was feeding myself. My not knowing how to cook led to various kitchen disasters. The first time I used the gas oven in my apartment I nearly asphyxiated myself! After that harrowing experience, I lived solely off of McDonald's Big Macs, Kellogg's Corn Flakes, and Domino's pepperoni and mushroom pizza. Soon I found myself missing Mom's cooking—I even missed her famous "Killer Taco Casserole." However, worse than missing Mom's gastrointestinal upsetting casseroles was the problem of me gaining weight . . . since I moved, I had gained twenty pounds! Fortunately, before I had to grease my doorways so I could fit through, my dad bought me a microwave, a box full of microwave meals (Weight Watchers, of course!), and a fire extinguisher.

I also discovered that keeping *my* home clean, even though it was just an apartment, was considerably more work than helping Mom clean hers. I thought it would be great not to have Mom nagging, "Laura, clean your room this instant—it looks like a pig pen!" But it wasn't great when my room, along with the rest of the apartment, looked *worse* than a pig pen. At Mom's when I dropped my coat by the door, it magically hung itself in the closet; at my apartment, it just sat where I dropped it. The dirty laundry was also uncooperative. At my parents' the laundry cleaned, folded, and put itself away—instead of lying all over the furniture like it did at my place! The bathroom was the worst to clean. When I would blow dry my hair, the all-white walls would attract so much loose hair, they looked like they needed to be shaved. Cleaning was far more involved than I ever imagined.

Another misconception I held about living on my own was that keeping a budget was simple. Before I moved out, I carefully planned my expenses on paper: rent, car, utilities, food, and—most important—fun money. It was soon apparent that making ends meet on paper was a lot easier than actually doing it. For example, it cost thirty dollars a month to have my hair done, something I never thought to add into my budget. Food, especially fast food, became extremely expensive! The utilities were never even considered: phone deposit, power deposit, cable TV, water bill, gas for my car, laundry money, and stamps for all the bills. By far the worst expense was the household items: laundry detergent, toilet paper, soap, shampoo, window cleaner, bathroom cleaner, dish washing detergent, light bulbs, etc. . . . None of these items were ever considered when I listed expenses, yet I needed every one of them. I can still remember how crushed I was the first time my friends asked, "Hey, Laura, you want to go downtown tonight?" and I had to respond, "No, I only have twenty bucks and I need toilet paper, soap, and deodorant." Then, just when I would get my bills under control, something that cost lots of money to repair—like my car—would break!

I can't honestly say living on your own is no fun, because it is fun, but it's also a lot of work. As I learned from feeding myself, cleaning my messes, and paying my bills—living on your own is not easy.

My Two "Boys"

by Maggie Mendoza

I have been "blessed" with the task of raising my two-year-old son, Daniel, and my three-month-old kitten, Sam, both at the same time. One morning as I raced to grab one of them from the top of the curtains and the other from inside the garbage can, I came to realize how very similar these two youngsters were.

First, they both need constant supervision. Just when I think I can take my eyes off these two ruffians for half a second, one (or both) is into something he shoudn't. Whether it is digging in the dirt of my potted plants or pulling all the toilet paper off its roll, no home is safe with these two on the loose! Just the other day, while I had Daniel secure in his highchair eating lunch and Sam curled up on the couch napping (or so I thought), I walked three yards away to put clothes in the dryer. In that short time, Sam had climbed up onto the tray of Daniel's highchair and began helping himself to Daniel's lunch! Much to Daniel's delight, he began petting Sam with his goo-covered hands and the mess they created was disgusting!

Second, they both need the constant presence of their mother (or substitute mother in Sam's case). While this is understandable with most youngsters, it would be nice to be able to go to the bathroom without seeing five little fingers and five little toes wiggling under the door, trying to pry it open. It would be nice to sit and read the newspaper without one of the two whacking the paper as I hold it up in front of me, as he tries to get my attention. Just the other day, after I put Daniel down for his nap (hoping Sam would do the same), I sat down for what I hoped would be a couple of hours of study time. No such luck! Daniel began crying because a police siren scared him, and Sam joined right in, wanting to be cuddled right along with Daniel! So much for my study time!

Third, both of my boys give unconditional love. Despite all the demands and hard work these little monsters require, they remind me everyday what it means to love without expecting in return. Just the other day, Daniel unexpectedly grabbed me around the neck and gave me a kiss! And Sam shows the same kind of unconditional love when he climbs on my pillow at night, gently licking my face, and purring softly until he falls asleep.

While everyone told me I was crazy taking in a stray kitten with a toddler in the house, I can honestly say I have enjoyed the chaos that this unlikely combination brings! While Sam will grow quickly into an adult cat leaving Daniel behind, raising these two boys together has been an unforgettable experience!

Troubleshooter for Computer Problems

by Deirdre W. Browne

Being a troubleshooter in an office automation support group can, at times, be a thankless job. Contributing factors are job repetition, impolite users, and a lack of recognition from management.

Troubleshooting over the phone can be thankless when the same user asks the same question time and again. This happens quite frequently. A user will call and say, "I know I've asked this a hundred times before, but can you tell me AGAIN how I paginate a document in DisplayWrite 4?" So, mustering as much patience as I can, I reply, "Sure. No problem. Just press F2, choose option 4 from the menu, and take it from there." The person calling usually replies, "Oh, you're so great. Thanks a million." I usually hang up the phone and say, "Can't these people remember anything?" But, then again, job security is everything!

Then there are the impolite people who call and make my life miserable and make me want to quit my job! Sometimes I can go through a whole day without encountering a rude, impatient, or nasty person. On those days, it's usually my counterpart who has to deal with them. It seems neither of us can get away from impolite people. Recently, a person called and the answering machine picked up. (This happens when my counterpart and I are both on the phone helping other people.) His message was as follows: "This 4357 extension is supposed to be the Help Desk and nobody is answering it? This is Smith on extension 7365, and somebody better call me back and fast!" Did we quickly call him back? No, not quickly, but eventually we did.

Another thankless part of troubleshooting is the lack of recognition from management. Referring to the person in the previous paragraph who left the unfriendly message, I forwarded the message to my boss. He, in turn, sent it to his boss, Susan. When I heard the message had been forwarded up the ranks, I was pleased. I figured Mr. Smith would be called back by Susan and told we won't help him if he was going to leave nasty messages. Instead, Susan called me and asked if the call had come in during working hours. I said it had. So her next question was why Mr. Smith had gotten the answering machine. I proceeded to explain that my counterpart and I were each on a help call when Mr. Smith called, and that's why the answering machine picked up. I couldn't believe I had to explain this fact. Susan knew we had an answering machine for that purpose. Needless to say, she never called Mr. Smith back. Her feeling was that since we are in a service area, we should expect these types of calls. My manager and I totally disagreed with her reasoning and told her so. Why should we have to take verbal abuse from people who call? Unfortunately, our feelings didn't make a difference.

So, as you can see, troubleshooting can be a thankless job. Job repetition, impolite users, and lack of recognition from management are only some of the reasons. The objective is not to take it too personally. If you do, the job will wear you out very quickly.

To Smoke or Not to Smoke

by Andrew Dunn

I searched frantically for my cigarettes—"ARRRGH! They're all gone!" Doesn't that always happen? You can never find a cigarette when you NEED one. I, like many other people in the country, became dependent on a small stick of tobacco to calm my nerves. I gave up smoking several years ago and have realized some things that make me glad I did. If you're a smoker, my advice to you is to quit. You don't have to look hard to find some good reasons—like they're bad for your health, they make you smell bad, and they're expensive.

The most important reason for quitting smoking is obviously your health. If you're like I was, you'll ignore all the warnings from your friends, family, newspapers, magazines, TV, and even the cigarette packs themselves. I never cared about cancer, heart disease, or ulcers—they didn't apply to me. I noticed the effect it had on me when I used to go on long runs with a friend of mine. I smoked—he didn't. It wouldn't be long before I had to stop, slow down, or throw up, but he kept going. It didn't strike me at the time that it was due to smoking.

Another reason to quit is the smell. Even though you don't notice, people around you—especially non-smokers—sense its obnoxious odor. One time while I was in a computer class, I was sitting next to a nice looking girl named Linda. She was a knock-out—what I remember most about her, besides her looks, was her perfume: it smelled beautiful, and accented her looks perfectly. We took a short break and as we walked outside, Linda lit up a cigarette. I didn't think any lower of her, because I used to smoke, too. We talked about the class and the teacher and then meandered back to class. The first thing I noticed when we were back inside was the overpowering stench that mixed with her perfume and created a sickening combination of smoke and flowers. Needless to say, I paid more attention to the teacher after the break.

Even though the two previous reasons are good reasons to quit smoking, the cost is what finally made me do it. When I was in boarding school during my high school days, I kept finding myself short of money. I had to budget myself and cut back on a lot of things like candy, fast food, and presents for girls. I noticed most of my money—what little I had—was going for cigarettes. I decided then that I liked candy, fast food, and girls more than I did cigarettes, so I quit and found myself with a lot more money to waste on things I didn't need.

Quit smoking before you get sick, start to smell bad, or become broke. Now that I don't NEED a cigarette anymore, I don't crave one, either. About the only things I search for frantically now are my wallet and keys. Doesn't that always happen? You can never find your keys when you NEED them.

Passing on Values to the Children

by Vicky Ahmed

When I was a child, my father tried to instill some of his values in me. He did this for one simple reason: he wanted me to grow up with the values he stressed. He stressed that a human being should have a good character, be proud of the freedom he has, and always be honest. Now, as if it's inborn in me, I strongly believe that it is the duty of parents and schools to teach these to children: the essence of character, freedom, and honesty.

Character

During the process of maturation, children form standards of right and wrong. Some educators purposely avoid questions of right and wrong or remain neutral about them. Parents have to involve themselves with their children's lives to foster moral literacy. Respecting the law, respecting one's elders, helping the weak, not stealing, keeping away from drugs, and having persistence and faithfulness help build a good character. Children have to learn these characteristics from the home and school environment. Literature and history are helpful in teaching these values. *A Christmas Carol*, *The Diary of Anne Frank*, and, later on, *King Lear* teach about kindness and compassion. Telling the story of King Midas helps children recognize the outcome of greed. The story of Abraham Lincoln during the Civil War teaches persistence in the face of adversity. The story about the Wright Brothers and the story of one man's discovery of the polio vaccine teach how hard work pays off. Great stories of the Bible teach of virtue and vice. In this manner, the parents and teachers can help children determine what is right and wrong.

Freedom

Besides character, I believe it is the duty of parents and schools to teach children the value of freedom. History and social science books should stress civil and political rights, such as freedom of speech, movement, voting, and the value of the Declaration of Independence. Freedom is not for abusing. Teaching children and reminding them of the freedom our forefathers fought for so vigorously, and many sacrificing their lives for their lands, is an important duty. Freedom is for appreciating, and the perpetuation of our free government must be nurtured in our schools, churches, and families.

Honesty

The seed of honesty has to be sowed in childhood, so as to bear its fruit later in adulthood. Parents have to set an example of honesty if they want their children to be honest. Anecdotes of experiences can be narrated to create a visual effect. History and literature again assist in the learning process. Teaching about Abraham Lincoln, who walked three miles to return six cents, and about Aesops' shepherd boy who cried wolf emphasize the need to tell the truth. Honesty beautifies a reputation. Parents and teachers should be the models and mentors for the children.

I believe that character, freedom, and honesty have to be taught by parents and schools so as to prepare the children to become responsible citizens. They have the future of the country in their hands. Therefore, we must teach our children to love the things we love and to respect and honor the things we respect and honor—nothing short of this will do.

A Modern Wonder: The Computer

by Kevin Hotton

During the last twenty-five years the computer undoubtedly must be considered one of our greatest inventions. Its rapid development and proliferation of use throughout the world have been remarkable. Certainly, the power of the computer has irreversibly changed the way work is done and the speed of progress in written communications, in finance, and in science.

Computers have taken much of the drudgery out of writing. With the advent of word processors, mistakes can be corrected and editing can be done on papers without the need to rewrite or retype the entire paper. The computer in the word processor possesses the power to remember all that has been written and can even consult an internally stored dictionary to check and correct spelling. It also has the ability to do things that done manually would be nearly impossible: for example, it can set margins and maintain them (by slightly expanding or compressing the letters in the line) so that the need to hyphenate words is eliminated, and perfectly straight margins on the left and right sides of the page are achieved. Relatively inexpensive machines are now available that are even able to generate large, stylized type for headings and even illustrations so that it is possible today to produce a fully ready-to-be-printed book. The printing press might have been the first invention to have a profound impact on the written word, but it was not the last. The computer is changing the way we write today.

The computer has also ushered in remarkable changes in the financial world. Take, for example, the use of the computer in banking and the way banks handle money. Today banks have maintained their traditional working hours of operation, but our money is available to us twenty-four hours a day, seven days a week. Why? It is all because the computer has made possible the automatic teller machines that are placed all over any given city, and as a result, our dollars are closer to us and always available. Banks also keep track of our balances and transactions with the help of computers. In the past this had to be done manually; today the speed of computers can accomplish the same thing in a fraction of the time and at a much lower cost. Computers, additionally, rarely make mathematical errors, and so our chances of being "shortchanged" are less today.

The computer has also been a boost to the scientific community, and with its help scientists are making great advances in our knowledge of the world. Just one small example of this is in the science of weather forecasting. The computer's "number-crunching" power has enabled weather forecasters to do something impossible before: store models of the entire atmosphere of the earth in powerful computers. For these models to work, the computer must execute billions of operations per second. Computer power today is capable of this, and the models help make forecasts more reliable and long-range trends predictable. The models can also be used today to evaluate the impact of acid rain or the unthinkable aftermath of a nuclear exchange.

The computer's power is so vast and its impact so far-reaching that I have been able to touch on only a few of the ways it is changing our world. The computer is here to stay, and I welcome it. It is truly a wonder of our modern world.

College: A New Experience

by Joan Ippolito

College is a new and different experience for me. I'm away from home, so I have many things to adjust to. Being on my own, talking with friendly people, and having Fridays off—these are just some things I like about college.

Living at college, first of all, gives me a sense of responsibility, of being on my own. My parents aren't around to say, "No, you're not going out tonight" or "Did you finish your homework?" Everything I do has to be my decision, and that gives me the responsibility of handling my own life. During the second week I was at college, I had to go out and look for a bank where I could open an account. Before that I looked in the phone book since I had no clue about any banks around here or where they were located. Someone told me about a good bank: Continental Federal Savings. I went to the bank and made decisions for myself—whether to have a checking or savings account and whether or not to get a MOST card. That was one example of having responsibility now that I'm on my own and of making my own decisions.

Friendly people: that's another aspect I like about college. On my first day (and even now) people were nice to me. I came to Marymount University here in Virginia from New York and—even though I'd been here before—I was a bit confused about where I was going. My mom and I drove in, not knowing the building we were supposed to go to, and the guard was especially nice: with a smile, he told us what building we were looking for and where we could park our car. My room was on the first floor of New Gerard, and I knew I had to go through some glass doors—but my mom and I didn't know which ones. Some upperclassmen saw me and asked, "Are you a new student?" When they found out I was looking for New Gerard, one said, "Oh, just follow us; that's where we're going." Even now I feel comfortable in the dorm because there are friendly people around to talk with.

Finally—to add to my likes of college—I love having Fridays off; I wouldn't be able to cope with five days of classes in a row. Also, I love to sleep in. One

Thursday night, my roommate and I and the people across the hall went to George-town. We got in rather early the next morning, and my roommate (Juanita) and I decided to sleep in—something I couldn't do in high school.

I do like things about college—being on my own, talking with friendly people, having Fridays off—but this doesn't mean I don't think about things at home. Although I like college, I can still get homesick: New York is a pretty good place, too.

The Negative Effects of Technology

by Laura Eckenroth

Many times my grandmother has given me the advice to "take the good along with the bad." Little did I realize how often I would remind myself of that advice as I tried to set up my new stereo system. The instructions were presented in such a strange way that I thought I was reading a foreign language. It took over four hours to set up the stereo, once I was able to decipher the instructions. All of the trouble I experienced while putting together that stereo showed me that technology, the good, brings along with it a lot of negative effects, the bad. Those negative effects are evident in that the products are more costly, more complicated to operate, and inferior in craftsmanship.

One adverse effect technology has produced is apparent in the increased price of many products. As I waited in line for the computer to total grocery purchases, I read in a magazine that the average price of a new car rose 12% over the last three years. This was due to the technological advances made on the engines in them. The cost increase is not only seen in the price of cars, but household appliances as well. For instance, refrigerators have become a necessity in the home. The base price of a refrigerator that just keeps food cold is approximately $250.00. From there, depending on how much technology you want in the refrigerator, the price can reach over $1,000.00. Ironically, the more hi-tech the appliance, the more costly it becomes.

Even with these technological "advances," understanding how to use the product has become more complicated. Two years ago I had bought the most technological stereo made at that time. When I brought it home, I couldn't figure out how to operate the radio station buttons. Fortunately, or so I thought, the company supplied a detailed owner's manual. This only served to confuse me even further. It was then that I wished I could return to those bygone days of turning a crank to listen to the record player. Not only are the instructions more difficult, but the accessories have become so minute that I was unable to find the appropriate buttons to push because they were the size of a pin head and were concealed behind a panel. Unlike the obvious crank on the old phonograph, electronic technology tends to obscure the vital parts that are necessary to make the product work.

Lastly, the craftsmanship of products has declined because of technology. This is obvious with new toys. All new toys are made out of plastic pieces that are easily broken. This is due in part to the automation of toy production. Technology has made it possible with robotics to have machinery that is capable of doing the work of dozens of toy craftsmen. No longer can you find a toy maker to carve or make toys by hand that could last generation to generation. Toys are now manufactured in a factory with machines that are programmed to assemble pieces of flimsy plastic parts into "toys."

There have been many times I have bought a product that was technologically advanced compared to its predecessors. Once I'd brought it home, I would be so disappointed with its improvements that I would try to find one made that "old-fashioned way." Technology has proven to make products more costly, more complicated, and of inferior quality.

Love That Attitude

by Jennifer Johnson

It was yet another Monday morning. Rolling out of bed, exhausted from a long night of waiting tables, I knew it was going to be another one of my "bad attitude" days. Of course, most people have an attitude on Mondays, but I tend to overdo it a bit. I work as a waitress, and since waitresses are always supposed to be cheerful and smiling, I cherish my days with my bad attitude. Those days always seem to relieve any stress I have for three main reasons: I can always yell at anyone, everyone stays out of my way, and no one asks me to do anything.

After coming to work with a bad attitude, I can basically get away with anything I want. For instance, I can yell at whomever I want, even my boss. All I have to do is blame it on a small tip from rude customers on a slow night. Then, I can yell about my hair, my car, my boyfriend, all the important things. When I am all done yelling, I can quietly shut the door and return to work with a very artificial smile on my face.

Once my co-workers see a plastered smile on my face, they know to stay out of my way. I hear them whispering things like, "Maybe it's PMS" or "You tell her that her food is up!" All the extra "space" is fine with me. Besides this, I always get my drink orders first, and my salads are, conveniently, already made for me. Also, the cooks do not ring the bell a thousand times when my food is ready, and not one waitress would dare to steal my order of french fries.

Although it is nice to have all my french fry orders ready on time, perhaps the best advantage of having a bad attitude is that no one asks me to do anything. No one is going to ask a "grump" to help them. They know the person will yell at them, ignore them, or do a really bad job. People do not even want to talk to a "grump" much less ask a favor of one. They will ask the waitress who just got a twenty dollar tip and has not broken a nail all day long. The only thing they are going to ask me to do at the end of the day is to go home, and that suits me just fine!

By now, it should be obvious how beneficial a bad attitude can be. Whenever I am feeling "rotten" or just want to be left alone, the best thing for me to do is to develop an attitude. Everyone will forgive me tomorrow. Besides, we all have bad days, so why not make the most of them?

New York

by Michelle Brutto

New York loves me so much that it always seems to call me back. The simplest explanation for this is that I lived there for fourteen years and ever since I moved to Florida, I haven't been able to adjust to the different atmosphere. The things that are calling me back are the things I miss most: snow, the city, and friends and family.

The snow made every winter in New York both beautiful and fun. I will never forget the sight of sparkling, white snow as it covers roofs, trees, grass, fences, roads, and cars. The most beautiful sights of all are the mountain peaks and hills after enough snow falls to cover them and eventually turn into ice. There are so many ways to enjoy the snow. My brothers, sister, and I would pack a snowball out of the cold, wet snow and roll it up and down the hills in our yard until the ball was large enough to make a life-sized snowman. We would also have snowball fights, slide down our steep driveway on a snow shovel, toboggan, sleigh ride, and play in the snow in many other ways. To me, winter was always the best season of the year.

I have found New York City to be enjoyable because there is always something to do or see. There are so many places to go! For example, I would go and see the Empire State Building, Twin Towers, Statue of Liberty, Radio City Music Hall, Madison Square Garden, and the Museum of Natural History. As I would walk the streets, I would see people rushing to and from work, vendors selling hot pretzels and sodas on the sidewalks, and taxis, subways, and buses. The scent of freshly baked bagels, pizza, and pretzels would travel through the air. I especially enjoyed going to China Town because there are many little shops and restaurants to go to. During Christmastime, I couldn't wait to go to Rockefeller Center to catch a glimpse of the enormous Christmas tree and outdoor ice-skating rink. It would be fascinating to go to all the little stores that had nativity sets and Christmas decorations in the windows, while the holiday spirit filled the air. I don't think anybody could ever get bored while visiting New York City.

Finally, I feel that my family and friends are calling me back to New York. I definitely miss the holidays spent with relatives. One Thanksgiving, my parents, brothers, sister, grandma, aunt, uncle, and cousins gathered around the dining room table as we admired all of the delicious food, including an enormous turkey, smooth white mashed potatoes, stuffing, juicy corn, Italian bread, and many other mouthwatering dishes which took hours to prepare. I also miss all my friends, most of whom I grew up with. We would all go to the movies, the mall, or someone's house. Even though I keep in touch with all of them by calling or writing, they all wish I were "back home."

In conclusion, if I had the chance to go back to New York and stay, I would go in a second. I can't wait for the day when I can have the things back that I miss most: snow, the city, and friends and family.

There Is Nothing to Fear

by Larry Fitch

There is nothing in my life that invokes a stronger feeling from me than the first time I was hospitalized. I was twenty-four years old and had never been seriously ill. And of all the feelings I had then, fear was the strongest.

There were many things to help invoke the feelings of fear I had. To begin with, the hospital was a large, dark place with hallways that seemed to whisper with the sounds of lost souls. The wards were large and impersonal, with people lined up in rows like items on display in some medical grocery store. And always there were the sounds that were barely audible, causing me to pull the covers even tighter up around me. At night the more seriously ill would cry out in pain, sending shivers that seemed to cut through me like knives. The darkness at night was absolute, save for the signs which marked the exits. These signs showered the darkness with an eerie blood-red glow that seemed to pulsate with the beat of my own heart.

Another factor leading to my fear was the smells that I encountered. No matter how clean it might have been, a smell of decay seemed to permeate. At times it became so stifling that I was forced to rush to the balcony for fear of being consumed by it. There was also an antiseptic smell that reminded me of dissecting animals in my biology class in high school. I remember hoping that I didn't end up inside a bell jar, looking composed, yet very much dead.

The other patients I encountered also helped to establish and maintain my fear. For instance, I saw a man so ill his entire body was emaciated to the point that I could have easily counted his ribs. He stared back at me through sightless orbs sunk deep into his head, all the while crying out in pain. Next, I watched a man as he calmly and casually injected himself with a needle. The result brought a strange expression to his face that caused me to cut short my investigation. Eventually, I witnessed a man changing the dressing from his recent abdominal surgery. The sweat rolled from his brow in a steady stream as he attempted to loosen the soiled bandage, eventually screaming in pain as it at last came free. His cry brought him the attention of a nurse in the ward, who quickly hurried me away.

Everything and everyone help to contribute to one's fears when he is facing the unknown. Consequently, all the things I have described have left me with an apprehension of hospitals. Five years after the fact, I still pause at the threshold of any medical facility. In the blink of an eye, I am transported back to that time and place where I first came eye to eye with the true meaning of fear.

Effective Products

by Heather Winter

As I sit in front of the television, I am bombarded with advertisements to try new products. It can be extremely frustrating and money consuming when a product does not function properly. However, most products do measure up to the claims of their advertisements. From past experience, I've learned that various cleaning products have proven to be as effective as their advertisements claim.

Advertisements for carpet cleaners are constantly being viewed on the television screen. Various products claim they can take out the toughest stains, including the dreaded grape juice stain. One such product that is effective is Resolve Carpet Cleaner. After viewing the advertisement, one would have to actually use it to believe its results. I remember using this product on a light tan carpet that my brother had put skid marks on from a remote-control car. I panicked because I knew my mother would not be pleased at the sight of a stained carpet. I never thought the black grease stain would come out, but after a few minutes of being scrubbed with Resolve, the stain disappeared. Resolve is a carpet cleaner that proved to get the job done.

Window cleaners are also among the many cleaning products advertised on television. Many of these products claim they can effectively clean windows without leaving streaks. One day while working in the pharmacy, I volunteered to clean the windows surrounding the department. Because the windows were excessively dirty, I needed a product that would work. The first cleaner I tried left a dull, streaky film on the windows. Next, I tried Windex, which has the claim of leaving no streaks. Not only had I seen the advertisement, but the claim was printed on the bottle as well. Without a doubt, the Windex measured up to its claim, and the windows were streakless.

Finally, products for cleaning laundry are commonly advertised on television. Nobody likes to wear dirty clothes, so these products are essential. Sometimes stains don't always come clean in a regular washing, so pre-wash stain removers are used in addition to the regular wash cycle. They claim to aid in the removal of the stain. One such product is Clorox Pre-Wash Stain Remover. The first time I tried this product was when I was trying to get a dirty soccer uniform clean. The uniform was covered with grass and mud stains that looked nearly impossible to wash out. I squirted the stained areas with the stain remover and threw the uniform in the machine with hopes that it would eventually come clean. After I took the uniform out of the machine, I was amazed with the results. Therefore, the Clorox Pre-Wash Stain Remover proved its claim.

Now as I sit in front of the television, I am still bombarded with advertisements. The only difference is that I am not doubtful of the various products that appear on the screen. Therefore, many products do measure up to the claims of their advertisements.

QUESTIONS

Can you identify the main parts of the five-paragraph essays? Look especially for the thesis statement, the blueprint, and the topic sentences. You'll notice that some essays don't have a blueprint, while others either imply the topic sentences or start them a sentence or two into the paragraph. These minor variations are all part of adjusting your content to the model. Do you think the essays improve by varying from the model?

Did you notice that one of the essays used headings? Do headings make the layout more appealing? Do they make the organization of the essay easier to see?

COMMENT

The essays in the next set only roughly follow the model for a five-paragraph essay. But they all do have introductions followed by clearly identifiable sections, just as the five-paragraph essay does. They also use the techniques of layout we discussed: headings, lists, and short paragraphs.

PVCs: What Are They ?

by Glorianne M. Langan

Have you ever watched a medical program and heard someone say "The patient is throwing PVCs" and been confused? Maybe you have thought, "What is a PVC? How do you throw one?" This paper is going to discuss:

- What is a PVC?
- What causes PVCs?
- How do you treat them?

Let's look further at these questions.

What is a PVC?

A PVC is a premature ventricular contraction. More simply, it is an early unexpected squeeze of the bottom part of the heart. Let me give you an example.

When I get irritable and someone bugs me, I snap back a response. The same thing can occur in the ventricles (the bottom part of the heart). When they get irritable, they can snap out unexpected beats. The problem is that they upset the natural rhythm of the heart and cause it to become an inefficient pump. Let me elaborate with a second example.

When people play golf, it is important to be quiet. This helps to maintain concentration so that they can swing the club evenly and efficiently to make the ball travel far. When something breaks the concentration, the golfer's swing becomes choppy and inefficient, and the ball doesn't travel very well. Normally your heart beats evenly and efficiently to make your blood travel all over your body. But a PVC breaks that rhythm, and your heartbeat becomes choppy. Your heart becomes an inefficient pump, and, as a result, your blood doesn't travel very well.

As for the term "throwing," it is simply medical slang for the word "having."

What causes PVCs?

There are numerous reasons for a person to have PVCs, but I will highlight the most common ones.

- *Heart muscle stress.* A person who has not been exercising regularly decides to participate in a 10K run. The heart is not used to this level of activity, so it can get irritable and have PVCs.
- *Heart muscle damage.* This is known as a heart attack. Again, the heart can react to this damage by being irritable, causing PVCs.
- *Chemical imbalance.* This can be caused by a variety of factors such as dehydration. When the body is denied its basic nutrients, it can set up a stress chain reaction. Once again, the heart's response to this stress can be PVCs.

How do you treat them?

The best way to treat PVCs is to eliminate the underlying cause. If that is not possible or is ineffective, medications are available to stop the PVCs. The basic feeling is to try to avoid giving someone an extra medication if you can fix the problem another way. Let's look at possible treatments for the causes we discussed earlier.

- *Heart muscle stress.* The best treatment here would be rest with a gradual return to exercise. This allows the heart to build up its tolerance to stress.
- *Heart muscle damage.* The most acute period is the first twenty-four to forty-eight hours of the heart attack. That is the time when PVCs are most likely to occur. Occasional PVCs (one to four per minute) may be tolerated at this time. If, however, the number increases or the patient becomes symptomatic, medications may be necessary.
- *Chemical imbalance.* The best treatment here is to replace the lost nutrients. This restores the body to its normal equilibrium and removes the stress causing the PVCs.

I hope that this discussion helps you to understand about PVCs so that the next time you hear the term you won't be confused.

Lobbying: What Is It?

by Carol J. Byers

Every day, many of us are confronted with the term "lobbying." We see it in the newspaper, and we hear it on radio newscasts.

What is lobbying?

Lobbying is the effort by an individual or group to influence someone's position on a specific issue.

Whether you know it or not, we're all master lobbyists. From the moment we leave the womb, we negotiate our wants and needs. As infants, we cry when we want to be fed, held, or changed. When we are children, we might cry, whine, beg, or throw a tantrum to get something we want. As we get a little older and know how to use the faculty of speech to our benefit, we use language skills and persuasion to get our way.

As we progress through adolescence, we become aware that we can use these skills to get what we want; we realize everything we want is negotiable. If we want to use the car, then we have to get good grades. If we want to go out on Saturday night with a few extra bucks, we have to do some chores around the house and help out with younger siblings. If we want more time to study for a final exam, we try to convince our professors to defer the test for one more week. And so it goes.

How can we use these lobbying tools as adults?

As adult lobbyists, we can use successful negotiating tools to get these things and many more:

- *A college education.* You must lobby a professor if you want to get into a class after it is full.
- *A job.* It is usually necessary to lobby a prospective employer to get a job, requiring communication by phone, by letter, and in person.
- *A spouse.* This is when your lobbying skills are put to work on a daily basis.
- *A promotion.* In your job every day, you work hard to be worthy of a promotion; sometimes you need to lobby your supervisor when raises are being considered.
- *A house.* When buying a house through a real estate agency, you will be in frequent touch with your agent in setting up dates and times to look at available properties; and when you find a suitable house, closing the deal requires more lobbying skills.

I could go on, but I'm sure you get the picture. Most of us have abilities to get what we want in life. We have to know what we want and then lobby to get it.

Marketing Myopia: A Close Look

by Patricia A. Robilotta

What is marketing myopia? Marketing myopia is the narrow or shortsighted view a company may have in defining its purpose or what business it is in.

In other words, the company is too specific in its definition and future planning. It doesn't see the opportunities that a broad definition could bring to the company and thus limits itself.

Common beliefs held by a myopic company

A myopic company makes a mistake of believing:

- A growing population will buy more of its products. The company thinks market share (or how many people buy the product) will grow as the population increases.

- There is no apparent competitive substitute. The company thinks no other industry or company makes a product or service that can replace what it offers.
- It has to improve on what it is already doing. The company tries to improve existing products rather than trying to develop new ones.

These beliefs prevent the company from doing research and development while other nonmyopic companies are getting a head start on the competition with new products or services.

The railroad stays on the tracks

The railroad industry is an example of myopic companies.

The railroad industry decided a long time ago it was in the railroad business—passenger and freight transport by rail. What it did was specifically define its business and limit its possibilities.

Because it chose not to use a broad label like transportation, the railroad industry missed out on the opportunity to develop new modes of passenger and freight transport (cars, trucks, airplanes). Instead, other industries developed and began to produce them.

What other reasons caused the railroad to miss out? The industry believed:

- As America expanded and new towns and cities developed, the number of people using the railroad would increase.
- None of those developments could ever replace the railroad in cross-country travel or shipment.
- If it improved railway service and conditions, it would continue to hold customers. It didn't need to look at or get involved in new product development.

The railroad shows how being myopic can be very costly. Had the railroad defined itself as in the transportation business, it would probably be one of the most powerful industries today.

When planning for the future, a company should think broadly. It will leave the door open for opportunities the company may otherwise miss.

Patient Acuity: How Sick Is Sick?

by Toni R. Ardabell

I will define the term "patient acuity." I believe this term is truly not understood by the public. In very simple terms, patient acuity means "how sick the patient is," but let me explain in greater detail.

What is patient acuity?

Let me give you an example of patient acuity. Let's say you are a patient in the hospital, and you have just had open heart surgery. You realize you are very sick. You are in a critical care unit and have a nurse taking care of just you.

Now think of yourself being in the hospital to have your appendix taken out. You would be on a regular nursing unit, and your nurse may have four to five other patients to take care of. Both examples involve a surgical procedure, but can you see how much sicker the open heart surgical patient is compared to the patient that had his appendix taken out?

The nursing profession over the years began referring to this difference as patient acuity. Even thirty-six patients on the same nursing unit will have different levels of acuity. Patients who are chronically ill but need a lot of nursing care (such as needing someone to give them a bath, needing to be fed, needing dressing changes, needing intravenous medication, etc.) may be referred to as a patient with a high acuity. It's important to understand that the word *acuity* does not equal the word *acute*. The term *acute* refers to the onset of the illness, not to how sick someone is.

How is patient acuity measured?

I have given you some examples of sicker patients in comparison to less sick patients. But how can we objectively measure how sick someone is? There are several objective evaluation tools on the market that hospitals use. The tools are referred to as "patient classification tools." The tools vary from national use down to hospital-developed tools.

One national patient classification tool I have used in several hospitals is Medicus. This tool is filled out once a day by the nurse taking care of the patient. It is computerized and has a reliability of 90%. The hospital has the option of charging patients by acuity with this tool. There are thirty-seven indicators measured for each patient classified. The Medicus tool uses indicators that demonstrate the patient's dependency needs. For example: total bath, bath with assist, or self bath. One of the three would be marked.

Medicus has five acuity types with a type 1 patient being the least sick and the type 5 the most sick. Now if you will recall the open heart example, that patient will classify as a type 5. The appendectomy patient will probably classify as a type 3 the day of the surgery and probably a type 1 within twenty-four hours.

Why is measuring patient acuity important?

Patient acuity is important for the following reasons:

- Nursing can measure workload in a way that we can determine staffing needs on a shift-by-shift basis.
- Patients can be billed according to the amount of care they received.
- Data collected allows for budget planning for the following year based not only on volume (census), but also on acuity.
- Hospitals using national tools become part of a national data base. This provides us with comparative information.
- Acuity systems meet regulatory agencies' mandates that staffing is done in an objective measurable way.

As you can see, the term *acuity* may have nuances even for health care providers, but in its simplest operational sense, it means how sick your patients are today and how many nurses you need to take care of them.

Supercomputers

by Linda L. Brown

Ever heard of a supercomputer? Probably—because a supercomputer is the most powerful computer available.

A supercomputer can process and do calculations on large amounts of data very rapidly. How rapidly? If you multiply two numbers on your calculator, the process takes about two seconds. A supercomputer can complete at least TWO MILLION of these calculations in the same time!

Questions probably come to mind, such as:

- Why would you use a supercomputer?
- Where is a supercomputer made?
- Why doesn't everyone have a supercomputer?

Why would you use a supercomputer?

You would NOT use a supercomputer to type your term paper. A supercomputer is a very complex piece of equipment, and users need specialized training. Supercomputer applications include:

- *Forecasting weather.* The National Center for Atmospheric Research and other weather bureaus use these machines to make medium- and long-range weather predictions.
- *Making cars.* Most of the major car manufacturers use supercomputers to develop new car models. Have you ever seen a car test-crashed against a wall? Supercomputers can simulate these crashes safer and cheaper.
- *Designing yachts.* Engineers used a supercomputer to redesign the hull of the yacht *Stars and Stripes.* This boat raced in the 1986–87 America's Cup competition—and won!
- *Making movies.* All of the spacecraft battles in the movie *The Last Starfighter* were created using a supercomputer.

Who makes supercomputers?

Only two countries, the United States and Japan, make supercomputers. The United States is the leader, however, and its only manufacturer is Cray Research Corporation. Cray's headquarters is in a small town in Wisconsin, and it employs approximately three thousand people. Each machine is hand-assembled and takes about three months to build.

Why doesn't everyone have a supercomputer?

The main reasons that supercomputers aren't as common as PCs are:

- *Usage.* Not everyone needs the power and capability of a supercomputer. It's not practical to use this machine for balancing your checkbook or keeping track of your investments.
- *Cost.* Supercomputers range from $1 million dollars (for a used machine) to Cray's latest model at $14 million dollars.
- *Weight.* Because they're made mostly of copper, these machines weigh almost two tons.
- *Space.* A Cray with its accessories takes up five times as much space as our classroom.

Not everyone uses supercomputers, but they affect our lives daily. The next time you see a weather forecaster on TV, ask yourself, "Did a supercomputer help him with his weather predictions?" The answer is probably, "Yes."

Comparison and Contrast

Growing Up in England and the United States

by Laura Rosenfeld

As a military child, I had the unique opportunity of growing up in both England and the United States. Despite the many similarities between these two countries, there are also many differences. The three differences that stand out most in my mind are:

- England has a slower pace of life than the United States does.
- England has a better public transportation system than that of the United States.
- There is more sense of community in England than in the United States.

The pace of life in England is much slower than it is in the U.S. This became most evident to me when I first moved to England and wanted to go to a store at 7:00 at night. Until just recently, stores in England closed at 6:00 P.M., and no store stayed open twenty-four hours as they do in the U.S. Much of the shopping was done on a daily basis at the local corner shop, or you waited until Saturday to go down to the Town Centre—which was as much a time of visiting with friends as it was for shopping. For my family, these early store closings meant that we were always home together in the evenings because there were no malls or stores open late to entice us away from home.

Secondly, the public transportation system is much better in England than in the U.S. With the use of buses and trains (and the underground in London), it is possible to travel all over the United Kingdom. You can get almost anywhere using public transportation, no matter how small the town or village you want to reach. This freedom of travel is much more difficult in the U.S., and, unless you live in a big city, there is usually only a limited public transportation system. While we do have buses and trains, they stop only in major cities or have limited routes. England's public transportation system allowed me to travel all over England, taking day-trips to London and skiing in Scotland, for example.

Finally, there is more of a sense of community in England because the country is so small and because each community has its own local pub. In a small country, it is much easier for everyone to stay connected to the same traditions, to hear the same news, and to participate in the same fads. The U.S. is so big that each state is more like its own separate country, and it is sometimes difficult for us to unite. The local pubs in England also contribute to this sense of community because each is a gathering place for people in a neighborhood. People get to know one another and stay in touch as they gather on a daily or weekly basis to share a drink. In the U.S., we don't have such gathering places that draw as wide a variety of people as English pubs. U.S. bars don't have the same feeling of community and tradition as pubs, and we tend not to know our neighbors as they do in England.

Having lived in both the United States and England, I had the opportunity of experiencing two different cultures. While England and the United States are alike in many ways, they are also very different in unique and wonderful ways.

Jessica and Jordan

by Karen Eisenhauer

Although two children may have the same mother and father and be raised in the same environment, they may grow to be vastly different from one another. Such is the case with my own two daughters. They are only nineteen months apart in age, but in appearance, habit, and personality they are worlds apart.

My older child, whose name is Jessica, has long, straight, medium brown hair. Nearly everything about Jessica is long and straight, from her hair to her feet. She grows taller, but never any wider. She can still wear shorts that I bought for her three years ago. Jessica tends to be restless and fidgety. She likes to keep on the move. We used to tell her that she wiggled so much she burned up her dinner before she finished it. Jordan, my younger daughter, has thick, wavy blond hair. She weighs exactly the same as Jessica although she is two inches shorter. Sometimes she thinks she is fat when she compares herself to her sister, but she is not. She is just softer and rounder. Jordan is also more content to sit and work on one thing at a time and has delighted me with her ability to play quietly by herself for long periods.

Jessica, with her quickness and restlessness, has never been very neat. She doesn't just drop things when she is finished with them—she tosses them. Her possessions scatter far and wide. At age eight and one-half, she still has to be reminded constantly to keep her fingers out of her food and to hold her fork properly. Jordan has held a fork properly since the day she first picked one up. She is a fastidious eater and hates to get any food on her fingers or face. She also hates to lose anything and consequently is self-motivated to put her things where she knows she will be able to find them later.

The two also differ in their cautiousness and their willingness to try new things. But it is not as one would expect. It is my overactive, exuberant Jessica who must be encouraged to attempt something new, and my quiet Jordan who enjoys the adventure. A few years ago my husband and I took the girls on the Great Thunder Mountain Railroad ride at Walt Disney World. Five-year-old Jessica buried her face in her father's side and cried. When it was all over, she asked why we had taken her on such a terrible ride. Four-year-old Jordan laughed during the entire time and jumped off, asking if we could do it again. I would expect the same reaction today.

At times, these differences in my children drive me to distraction. I feel like a split personality myself, trying to understand and deal with each girl. What works for one child usually does not work for the other. And although they need to be treated differently, they tend to see this as unfair. But most of the time, their differences are fascinating to watch, and I would not change them a bit.

My Mother, Myself

by Julia Waterbury

It has been said that in order to determine what a girl will be like as she gets older, one need only to look at her mother. It is indeed true that many girls perhaps unwittingly model themselves after their mothers. Though at times I hate to admit it, in behavior and attitude, my mother and I are very much alike.

There are times when I realize the full extent to which my behavior resembles that of my mother. I am very domineering in my relationships with others. Looking back, I see that in my parents' marriage, it was my mother who exercised the most control. I seem to be following suit with my boyfriend. I like to call the shots. The resemblance between our behavior is also evident in our mutual love of cooking—and eating. My mother can turn almost anything into a delicious meal. Now that I have my own kitchen, I spend much of my free time cooking elaborate meals and then devouring them. I also share my mother's introverted nature. She always taught me that the quality of friendship far exceeds the importance of quantity. While neither of us engages in active social lives, we do have a few special friends.

As an adult, I have grown to emulate many of my mother's attitudes toward life. When I was a little girl, she was actively involved in the women's movement. Consequently, I have come to share her ardent belief in the need for equality between men and women. My mother has always had a strong need for achievement. She has fulfilled this need by owning a successful restaurant. I also have a strong desire to reach my goals and hope to fully realize them someday. Lastly, my mother harbors many insecurities about herself, such as her appearance. She is constantly worried about her weight. I see the same insecurity in myself. In fact, my mother and I often share diet secrets as well as low-calorie recipes.

It is only natural that a girl use her mother as a role model. It's a sign of a good relationship when a daughter can look up to her mother and respect her attributes. While I appreciate some of the resemblances in attitudes and behavior between my mother and me, I wish that I could have avoided some of her more negative qualities. I guess that's where mothers-in-law get their reputations!

Conformity and Independence

by Jenifer Powell

Both Nathaniel Hawthorne's *The Scarlet Letter* and Arthur Miller's *The Crucible* have settings in Puritan society, but the authors use these settings to get across two very different ideas. Each of the authors values individual thinking differently. These views demonstrate each author's concerns with what he saw as disturbing events during the period in which he wrote.

In *The Scarlet Letter,* Nathaniel Hawthorne expresses the view that the structures of institutions, while not perfect, are necessary to keep society ordered and running smoothly. He felt that institutions keep people from having "dangerous" radical thoughts that might destroy essential order. Although Hawthorne presents Puritan society as rather harsh, he shows that once Hester Prynne is denied its structure, she turns to "dangerous" independence of thought while never really repenting. She never truly repents because she is willing to commit her sin again. Hawthorne comments on Hester's independence of thought and separation from social norms: "But Hester Prynne . . . for so long a period not merely estranged, but outlawed, from society, had habituated herself to such latitude of speculation as was altogether foreign to the clergyman" (Nathaniel Hawthorne, *The Scarlet Letter,* p. 210). The scarlet letter, though causing her to be ostracized by society, "was her passport into regions where other women dared not tread. Shame, Despair. Solitude! These had been her teachers—stern and wild ones—and they had made her strong but taught her much amiss" (Hawthorne, p. 210).

In *The Crucible,* Arthur Miller uses the Puritans to show that too much conformity of thought can lead to hysteria like that during the Salem witch trials. He portrays the Puritan society as not only imperfect, as in *The Scarlet Letter,* but itself dangerous. *The Crucible* shows a few silly girls leading the majority of a town to witch hunting. Miller presents innocent, respectable people who are arrested and some who even lose their lives. John Proctor emerges as the tragic hero, one of the few who retain their independence of thought and see through the farce. Proctor says to Deputy Governor Danforth, one of his judges, "For them that quail to bring men out of ignorance, as I have quailed, and as you quail now when you know in all your black hearts that this be fraud—God damns our kind especially, and we will burn, we will burn together" (Arthur Miller, *The Crucible,* p. 120). Through Proctor's heroic, defiant death, other townspeople begin to realize that the trials have led to the deaths of innocent citizens. Thus, instead of showing a restrictive society as a necessary evil, as Hawthorne does, Miller presents it as a threat to mankind.

One reason for this strong difference of opinion is the period in which each author wrote. Hawthorne published *The Scarlet Letter* in 1850, only two years after the women's convention at Seneca Falls. Hawthorne greatly distrusted the women's movement because it threatened social institutions and traditional values. He says in *The Scarlet Letter* that to change the view of women in society, society itself has to be changed. Hawthorne voices the concern that a woman might lose "the ethereal essence" (p. 172) that actually makes her a woman: "If she be all tenderness, she will die. If she survive, the tenderness will either be crushed out of her, or—and the outward semblance is the same—crushed so deeply into her heart that it can never show itself more" (p. 170). His example of such a changed woman is Hester Prynne, who, estranged from society, has lost the quality that makes her a woman.

Just as events of this time influenced Hawthorne's view of individualism, events of Arthur Miller's time affected his view of individuals and society—but Miller's view is opposite that of Hawthorne's. Arthur Miller wrote *The Crucible* in the 1950s, in reaction to the McCarthy era. Miller feared the hysteria of the Red scare, which resulted in blacklistings of many innocent people. He chose to protest by presenting a similar hysteria, the Puritan witch trials. Miller urges people to retain their independence of thought and to realize the danger of the scare.

Although both Hawthorne and Miller use the Puritan society in their works, each author's purpose is different. Moreover, even though both were protesting events in their times, their views on the value of individualism were directly opposite. Hawthorne tries to show that too much individualism will destroy society and the souls of the individuals themselves. Miller, on the other hand, tries to show that individualism is necessary and must be protected from the conformity and hysteria of society.

Cause and Effect

Successful Marriages

by Christine Holt

Sometimes I think that successful marriages are an endangered societal species. It seems as though every time I turn around, another couple I know is getting divorced. It's a shame because marriage is very important. I believe that if people put more effort into making their marriages work, there would be fewer divorces. Marriage takes certain qualities to make it a success. Partners must be unselfish, have a sense of humor, and be able to communicate. One way to make a marriage work is by being unselfish. My husband, Jim, is probably the most unselfish man I know. He makes me want to do things for him because of his generous nature. He often cleans the house and takes care of the children without my having to ask him to do those things. I know there are many times he would rather be reading, relaxing, or working on the car, but he only does something for himself when all the household chores are done and the kids have been taken care of. In return, I bake him all his favorite homemade cakes and cookies and try to go out of my way to do special things for him. I feel very fortunate to have married him.

Another way to make a marriage last is to have a good sense of humor. The other day Jim and I were both tired after being up with the kids all night, and everything seemed to be going wrong. The clothes dryer broke, we had a flood in the bathroom, and Jason, our son, was being very "terrible two-ish" that day. We were both irritable, and soon we started snapping at each other. We were getting more and more angry over some really trivial matters, but then we just looked at each other and started laughing.

I don't know why, but it felt good and helped relieve the tension. We never did have that impending fight, and it was a fun way to avoid it.

Being able to communicate is very important for a successful marriage as well. Jim is my best friend, with whom I share most of my thoughts. We find it easy to talk about most things, so we don't have very many secrets from each other. When my mother makes him upset, he tells me about it. Things like that are easier to deal with when they're out in the open than when they're kept inside. Thus, we have a very open, comfortable relationship.

I'm glad that Jim and I have learned to deal with our problems and have made our marriage a success. It has taken a lot of work, but it is definitely worth it. I look forward to sharing my life with Jim and to our growing old together.

What Price Utopia?

by Tom Eagle

Ursula K. Le Guin's short story, "The Ones Who Walk Away from Omelas," explores the idea that one must feel compassion for the less fortunate individuals of our society and not ignore the sorrow evident all around us or use that sorrow and misery to establish personal comfort. Ms. Le Guin develops this idea by writing of a utopian community, describing the misery hidden in the community, and personal rejection of the community. This idea is a direct commentary on present society and is relevant to all individuals. It is obvious that the author perceives the many injustices present in our world and uses the short story to state that people must examine their surroundings and deal with the misery and sorrow that exists in society in order to truly make strides to bring about a real "utopia." This theme is a valid social commentary.

Le Guin describes a utopian society in her story. Omelas represents the society that people strive to make. This community is joyous, beautiful, and full of the delights that people adore. It is an epicurean dream. Le Guin develops her theme by firmly establishing this as an idyllic community, and her description causes the reader to believe that in this environment there could only be personal happiness.

However, undergirding this "perfect" community is the misery hidden beneath the city, misery borne by one person in order for the Omelian society to exist. Here the author uses the character of an innocent child, forcing the reader to feel compassion for the child because of the graphic terms used to describe its condition. Lying in its own excrement, the child is a symbol of misery and sorrow. All the citizens of the community know of its existence and observe the child occasionally but do not allow it to benefit from the abundance of pleasure in the society, for if they do, Omelas, as they know it, would be destroyed.

Thus, Le Guin establishes the basis of her theme by these two developments. The outcome of these developments is that one must reject the complacency of utopia. The author further develops this idea by writing of the people who leave the city.

These are the people who observe the miserable child and reject the city of Omelas literally for what it stands on. In essence the author seems to say that one must reject the fantasy of personal happiness and deal with the reality of misery and sorrow before a real utopia can be founded.

Le Guin's short story is a commentary on society. The author accomplishes this by establishing an ideal community, depicting the hidden sorrow that is the foundation of the community, and describing the manner by which some individuals reject the utopia. Her theme is that one should not—no, cannot—ignore the misery that exists in our world.

An Addition to Murphy's Law

by Karen Eisenhauer

Whenever I have scrubbed and waxed my kitchen floor, I have always been amazed at how quickly the evidence of my labor is obliterated. Within hours, the floor will look almost as bad as it did after having gone unwashed for two months. I used to think it was coincidence and poor luck on my part, but lately, I have realized that it is no accident and should be included as one of Murphy's Laws: a clean kitchen floor attracts dirt.

Evidence of the effect abounds. For instance, the last time I scrubbed my kitchen floor, my husband decided to change oil in his car, something he has been doing with no problem for years. But on this particular day, he somehow managed to drop oil onto his pants leg and shoe, which went unnoticed until tracked across my just-cleaned floor from garage door to kitchen sink. Within the next hour, my children came in from playing with two friends and wanted a cold drink; all of the children had coal black feet, and my older daughter dropped her plate of spaghetti on the floor at dinner.

But mine is not the only kitchen floor that suffers this problem. My neighbor mopped her floor last Friday evening when her children were in bed. (She thought she would beat the odds that way.) But Saturday morning her husband lost control of the breakfast sausage and a dozen greasy little sausage links rolled their way merrily around the floor leaving grease tracks behind. Her son slipped on the grease, dumping a twelve-ounce glass of orange juice on the floor, which caused her daughter, in a fit of hysterical laughter, to contribute a jar of strawberry jelly to the disaster. In less than two minutes an entire evening's work was wiped out.

Later, as she was telling me the whole sad story, I asked her what she had done about it, how she had cleaned it all up. "Well," she said, "I wiped up the jelly and the juice, and I mopped with soap and water to clean up the grease and the stickiness. But before the floor was dry, I called the kids in out of the sandbox and had them jump up and down all over the floor. I thought that it would look better with sand on it than with food." An interesting idea; I'll have to remember that.

An Answer to Poverty in America?

by Dale Klocksiem

Poverty in the United States is an increasing problem. "The U.S. Census Bureau estimated that in 1982, there were 34.4 million people living below the poverty level in this country." (*Time*, March 5, 1984, p. 14). Clearly, something must be done to help these individuals to be able to make a better living. Some people believe that the guaranteed annual wage is the answer. The idea behind this is that guaranteeing every adult person in the United States a certain amount of income each year would eliminate poverty, eliminate the need for the giant welfare program, and possibly even save the federal government some money. While all this sounds good, there are some problems with the idea of a guaranteed annual wage. It would eliminate the incentive to work for many people, would require a huge sum of money to operate, would create difficult distribution problems, and would probably cause a large migration of people from other countries into the United States.

The first problem with the guaranteed annual wage is that it would, for many people, eliminate the incentive to work. If they were guaranteed a certain amount of money each year, somewhere above the poverty level, they would no longer need to work to support their families and themselves. They could make as much money sitting at home watching television as they did previously working full time. For those people who did still work, a decrease in compensation and benefits would probably occur. Their employers, knowing that they were receiving a large supplement in addition to their wages, would be very reluctant to give them raises or increases in benefits. As a result, those people who still decided to work would not have the incentive to work as hard as they did previously. The guaranteed annual wage would most likely lead to disinterested workers and a decline in worker productivity.

Another problem with the idea of a guaranteed annual wage is that it would require an enormous sum of money to operate. The federal government would somehow have to raise these funds. In all likelihood, it would be through taxation. However, businesses are already bearing a heavy tax burden, and the amount of taxation required to raise the large sums of money needed to pay everyone the guaranteed annual wage would be unbearable to most of them. A similar situation exists with personal taxation. Most individuals would agree that the amount of taxes they pay is high enough already. Therefore, they would unlikely be willing to pay additional taxes to support the guaranteed annual wage program. It seems, then, that there is currently no feasible way for the federal government to raise money to operate the guaranteed annual wage program.

Even if funds could be raised to support this program, it would be an extremely monumental task to get the funds dispersed. A case in point: there are roughly 200 million adult citizens in our country today. If the federal government sent checks out to every adult only once a year, it would require printing checks at the rate of more than half a million every day for the entire year. The cost of the equipment, supplies, and personnel to accomplish such a task would be astronomical. It would be very difficult to get all the funds distributed properly.

Finally, the guaranteed annual wage would lure many people from other countries into the United States. There already is a severe problem of illegal immigration into the country, and the lure of a guaranteed annual wage would only make matters worse. People from other countries who are living below the poverty level would be tempted to come to the United States and seek citizenship. Many places in America are overcrowded already, and this influx of people would cause greater problems in these areas. The lure of immigrants into this country would be another problem caused by the guaranteed annual wage.

The idea of a guaranteed annual wage appears to be a good one at first, but after examining it closer, several problems appear. It certainly would be nice to receive that check in the mail once a year, but the advantages of getting it are greatly overshadowed by the problems it would cause.

Environmental Paybacks for Eastern Bloc Policies[1]

by Jerry Cole

Environmentalists and the news media in the West have made the public aware of environmental damages resulting from acts of greedy corporations and of government policies that have protected industries rather than the environment. Much less publicized, though, have been similar problems in the USSR and the East European nations allied with it. Since World War II, governments in the Eastern Bloc have driven their economic sectors to produce more and more. Rewards for managers of factories, farm cooperatives, and the government agencies overseeing them have come for production successes, not environmental protection. As a result, following the openness begun in the Soviet Union under Gorbachev, today we're learning about environmental disasters among the Eastern Bloc nations.

Air pollution

The push to develop heavy industries after World War II and to build large companies to feed and clothe the population hurt the environment. Chief among the polluters today are steel mills and industries associated with heavy machinery production, power plants and associated fuels industries, chemical plants, and meat packing companies. According to an article in the *New York Times Magazine* ("Eastern Europe: The Polluted Lands," 29 Apr. 1990, pp. 30–35), because factories were built to burn inexpensive lignite and brown coal, air pollution is serious in the industrial region from eastern Germany (formerly East Germany), through Czechoslovakia, to southwest Poland. In this region, home for 15 million people, almost 40 percent of the forests have been damaged by acid rain. In Poland's Silesia industrial region, air pollution has contributed to high rates of cancer, heart disease, and respiratory ailments, especially emphysema. Part of Bilina, Czechoslovakia, has been abandoned because of air pollution from a coke factory and power plant.

Articles on the Soviet Union in the *National Geographic* also provide examples of serious air pollution. A cement factory in Junda, Estonia, blankets the town with

---

[1] This essay was written in 1990, before the Soviet Union and the Eastern Bloc that was allied with it fell apart. References to "today" and to current situations should be read with 1990 in mind. Nevertheless, the environmental issues the essay discusses are real, even though different governments today have to deal with this legacy from the days of Soviet economic and industrial policies.

a dust known as "gray snow," which hardens like mortar where it falls and produces numerous respiratory problems (Priit Vesilind, "The Baltic Nations," 178 [1990], p. 28). And in Norilsk, in Siberia, sulfur dioxide emissions were 2.5 million tons in 1984—3.3 times as severe as the worst air polluter in North America (Mike Edwards, "Siberia: In from the Cold," 177 [1990], p. 34). Most telling, though, is a picture in the *New York Times Magazine* article. It shows a man from Copsa-Mica, Romania, whose exposed skin is blackened as if he had just come from a coal mine. But he hadn't: his skin is discolored from working outside, exposed to soot from nearby factories. Can you imagine what his lungs must look like?

Water pollution

Water pollution, too, has resulted from uncontrolled industries in the East. Recent *National Geographic* articles provide several examples. Swimming is prohibited in the Baltic near Pärnu, Estonia, because of pollution from a slaughterhouse there. Some 100 miles of beach area on the Baltic near Gdansk and Sopot, Poland, are closed because of water pollution that has produced "algae-rich water the consistency of broccoli soup" (Priit Vesilind, "The Baltic: Arena of Power," 175 [1989], pp. 624, 627). Near Kohtia-Järve, Estonia, fish caught in the Baltic have skin ulcers, and rivers are polluted from waste from slaughterhouses and by-products of oil-shale processing ("The Baltic Nations," p. 21). And fishing in the Ob River, in Siberia, has been eliminated because of water pollution from oil operations upriver. The Ob was a source of sturgeon, but those fish feed on the bottom where oil settles ("Siberia: In from the Cold," p. 35).

A case study: the Aral Sea

Probably the most striking example of environmental destruction resulting from governmental decisions in the Eastern Bloc is the case of the Soviet Union's Aral Sea. William Ellis ("A Soviet Sea Lies Dying," *National Geographic* 177 [1990], pp. 70–93) calls it "nothing less than one of the most extraordinary violations of the environment in modern times" (p. 76). In 1918 Soviet leaders decided to make their country self-sufficient in cotton. They succeeded: by 1937 the USSR was a net exporter of cotton. The Soviets built extensive irrigation systems to feed water from the Amu Darya and Syr Darya Rivers into fields for cotton growth. Today the region affected produces 90 percent of the USSR's cotton. However, the region, which supports 35 million people, also is beset by critical environmental problems as a result.

The two rivers feed the Aral Sea, which used to be larger than any of the Great Lakes except Superior. In the 1960s the water diverted for irrigation began to be greater than the water lost from the Aral because of evaporation. From 1926 to 1960, the two rivers delivered to the Aral Sea some 55 million cubic kilometers of water a year; in the late 1980s almost no water reached the sea. As a result, from 1973 to 1989—in only 16 years—the Aral lost volume equal to 1.5 times the volume of Lake Erie. Aral Sea fishing once supported sixty thousand people. Today the sea is dead (because of its salinity), and the Soviets keep a cannery at Muynak operating by shipping in frozen fish from the Barents Sea. The sea bed exposed as the Aral has receded provides airborne salts and silt for numerous dust storms in the region. Upriver from the Aral, the town of Nukus no longer has a water source, so a pipeline is being built to provide water. Also, Nukus has a throat cancer rate five times greater than in 1959, although the population is only 2.5 times greater. Throat cancer rates are high throughout the region, and the infant mortality rate is the highest in the Soviet Union. Although the Soviets are planning to return water to the Aral Sea, they would have to cut cotton production in half to stabilize the Aral Sea today. Estimates are that the sea will end up being less than one-third of its size today, with a salinity four to five times that of the world's oceans.

Prospects for improvement

The process of change that began in the Soviet Union in the late 1980s and swept through Eastern Europe is producing massive reforms and governmental restructuring. Yet, for countries faced with governmental and multiple economic crises, cleaning up the environment will be exceedingly difficult. Environmental groups and issues are becoming increasingly important throughout the Eastern Bloc. However, the nations must deal with environmental disasters resulting from forty-five years of production-driven economies. The paybacks for those years of environmental neglect are severe.

QUESTIONS

What kind of cause-effect essays are these? Do they examine causes, effects, or the entire cause-effect statement of the thesis?

What types of support do the essays provide? Are their theses sufficiently supported?

Classification

Types of Animal Rights Activists

by Zach Stimus

When I became involved in the animal rights movement, I was surprised by the various types of people involved in the movement and the varying types of commitments they possessed. There are three main types of people in the animal rights movement: the supporter, the activist, and the zealot.

The supporter is involved in the animal rights movement on a basic level. The supporter attends local meetings and national conferences, volunteers at a local animal shelter, writes letters of protests and boycotts companies who test on animals, and is likely a vegetarian. The supporter freely speaks to those who will listen about the issues of animal rights, but generally does not participate in protests or demonstrations.

The activist does much the same as the supporter, but also participates in public protests and demonstrations. This type of animal rights activist goes out in public and passes out fliers against buying fur, participates in demonstrations against companies that test on animals, and organizes protest rallies during the national conventions of such groups as the National Rifle Association which promotes hunting. In addition, the activist is likely to be a vegetarian who does not eat meat and dairy products and does not buy any products made from or with animal ingredients (such as leather shoes or gelatin).

The zealot is the activist in the extreme. The zealot is the animal rights activist who will go to any length to get the message across. The zealot is the one who may throw red paint on a person wearing fur, and who is not afraid to participate in an act of civil disobedience (such as chaining himself or herself to the door of a furrier) or an act of not-so-civil disobedience (such as storming the offices of a clothes designer who uses fur). The zealot does all he or she can to be sure there is newspaper and television coverage of all animal rights events. The zealot is definitely a person who does not hesitate to discuss animal rights issues with anyone who will listen.

As with any movement, it takes all kinds of people to make progress, from those who do what they can, to those who are willing to go to the extreme. The animal rights movement is no exception, and I am proud of the work that is done on behalf of animals by each of the various types of people involved in the animal rights movement.

My Favorite Escape: Books

by Tommi Hilts

When I was in the Navy, I was stationed in southern Spain for four years on a Spanish base. There were a few American luxuries I had to do without, such as McDonald's Big Macs, fresh milk, and American television. The one I got along without best was the television. Since I'm an avid reader, I had no problem entertaining myself when I was off duty. Books are actually more entertaining than television because I can use my imagination when I read. I especially enjoy books that provide a sort of sacred haven or "never, never land" for my mind—a place where I can go when I want to relax or forget my problems. The books I enjoy the most are fiction novels because I can escape into the exciting action they provide. My favorite "escape" novels are classical literature, adventurous spy stories, and horror/fantasy stories.

Classical literature is enjoyable because I have to actually think about what I'm reading rather than just skimming the book. Novels like *The Great Gatsby* by F. Scott Fitzgerald and *The Agony and the Ecstasy* by Irving Stone are examples of one type of literature I enjoy. Fitzgerald's novel not only portrays the era in which he lived, but also contains symbolism that adds depth and meaning to the story. Stone's novel is very similar to Fitzgerald's in that it contains symbolism and reflects an era of history; however, Stone writes about actual historical figures and the time in which they lived rather than about his own. *The Agony and the Ecstasy* is the story of Michelangelo's life. Because Stone is so descriptive in his interesting novel, the story almost comes to life. I can easily visualize Michelangelo chipping away at a block of marble that is later to become the marvelous statue of David. Long after I read novels like these, I still think about their themes or hidden meanings. These novels not only enrich my mind with history, but they also test my reasoning.

I also enjoy adventurous spy stories because they are intriguing, although they are not as believable as classical literature. The situations in this type of novel are realistic enough and some could possibly happen, but when all of the situations revolve around one man, I know it's highly unlikely that it really could happen. This is the appeal these books hold for me, though. Because they depict reality carried to the extreme, they are exciting. Novels written by Robert Ludlum are excellent examples of spy novels. Most of his protagonists are antiheroes who have an almost superhuman will to live. Although stabbed, shot, blown up, and beaten up, his antiheroes always crawl to their victory over the villain. In addition, his plots always involve the salvation of the American government by eliminating the corrupt antagonists. Packed with action, Ludlum's exciting novels are easy to read and to escape into.

Classical literature and spy novels are two types of "escape" books I enjoy. A third type, the one I enjoy the most, is the horror/fantasy novel. Because most of the stories could not possibly happen, I find this type the most interesting. Novels written by Stephen King or Peter Straub are always exciting. Although their novels start out with normal characters and situations, the stories end up with weird creatures and circumstances involved. For instance, Stephen King's *Salem's Lot* opens with a middle-aged widower who returns to his hometown after his wife's tragic death. The town is eventually taken over by vampires. The bizarre elements are so carefully and subtly woven into the normal events, I can't determine exactly where the deviation between normal and weird begins. Plots that involve seemingly typical American small towns with creepy undercurrents, nightmare-like creatures with human traits, and bizarre events as well as the normal human anti-heroes make excellent "escape" reading. It's this type of novel that I find difficult to put down. My creative imagination is unleashed to fully appreciate the horror/fantasy novels. I feel relaxed when I let my mind flow with the unusual events as they happen.

Unlike television, reading novels is more satisfying because I have to use my imagination in order to visualize the story. Because of this, I become so involved in the story that I feel as if I'm one of the novel's characters. I enjoy this involvement; it can make me forget everyday conflicts that dampen my spirit. After escaping into my favorite fiction novels, such as classical literature, spy novels, and horror/fantasy novels, I feel refreshed and relaxed.

Microwave Ovens

by Debbie Stewart

Last Tuesday, I came home from school hot, tired, and starving. I had been through a grueling day, and all I wanted to do was eat. I opened the refrigerator door and searched for something edible. Luckily, I stumbled across a piece of left-over pizza from the night before. I slapped it onto a paper plate and popped it into my microwave oven. Presto! In less than two minutes, my pizza slice was ready for me to devour. This modern-day invention, the microwave oven, should be considered one of the "wonders of the world" because it is unbeatable as a food, money, and time saver.

As a food saver, a microwave oven is definitely hard to beat. Almost any kind of leftover can be reheated in this type of oven, and used properly there is no worry of the food drying out. For example, spaghetti is a mess to try to reheat on top of the stove. It dries out terribly and will stick to the bottom and sides of a saucepan. The spaghetti will also scorch easily if one is not careful. But with a microwave oven, this is a different story with a happier ending. The spaghetti will remain saucy, will not stick, and will not scorch. The Italian delicacy will be as good as it was the first time around.

Another "wonder" about the microwave oven is the money that it saves. Leftovers that would normally be thrown out can be saved and reheated. This saves food; thus, it saves money. Also, these ovens are faster, therefore, they save electricity. In these days that can be a blessing.

Best of all, however, is the time that a microwave oven can save. As a general rule, microwave cooking takes one-third the time that a conventional oven does. Imagine what a delight this would be after a tiring day at work, school, or, better yet, shopping! For instance, to bake a medium-sized potato takes only eight to ten minutes in a microwave oven. So in the time it would take to fry up a hamburger, one could have a piping-hot baked potato to go with it. In addition to speedy cooking, a microwave is wonderful for defrosting meat. On low power this oven can defrost any kind of meat in less than fifteen minutes. This is a real lifesaver when company drops in right at dinnertime.

Indeed, microwave ovens should be considered one of the modern wonders of the world. I know that it was a wonder for me last Tuesday. That slice of day-old pizza made me feel like a new woman!

Common Emotions during Pregnancy

by Christine Holt

Women who are normally calm and serene are sometimes surprised to find how excitable they become when they are pregnant. Women's emotions usually change during pregnancy. I've been pregnant twice, and both times I've felt like a different person. I felt as though I had lost control over my emotions. I became depressed, anxious, and extremely sensitive.

Depression during pregnancy is very common. The emotion is not constant, but even more distressing, it alternates back and forth with high spirits. Elation can quickly turn into despair. I can remember many times waking up in the morning feeling great and then suddenly feeling as if it were the end of the world. One minute I would be laughing and the next, crying. It all seems very funny to me now, but at the time I thought I was losing my mind!

Another common emotion during pregnancy is anxiety. I worried about everything. If my husband was five minutes late coming home, I was sure he had been in a car accident. I worried about the baby each time I saw the doctor. Most of all I was afraid that I wouldn't be ready for the baby when he came. I worried right down to the last little T-shirt and pair of booties.

There is another common emotion during pregnancy that was, for me, the hardest to deal with. I became quite sensitive—*over*sensitive. Everything that was not very carefully said to me hurt my feelings. On one of my visits to the doctor, I was feeling very pregnant, that is, very fat. Then, when the doctor told me that I had gained too much weight that month, I started to cry. I could not stop, and all my poor doctor could do was offer me tissues and console me that I'd lose the weight after the baby was born. I was so embarrassed that I didn't want to go back to the doctor for my next appointment. But I did. And we both had a good laugh about that one. By the way, I *did* lose the weight after my son was born.

I am glad that pregnancy lasts only nine months. I couldn't stand it for any longer than that. I went through a lot of changes, but the hardest to deal with were changing emotions.

Home-Style Entertainment

by Tom Eagle

In general, games played at home provide a wholesome activity for the entire family. Many people find that the time spent playing games at home contributes to feelings of closeness among family members, thus giving them time to relax together and promote familial ties. Three types of games played at home that have remained popular over the years are card games, board games, and outdoor or backyard games.

Card games have remained popular in many homes. Bridge, canasta, rummy, and whist are only a few of the hundreds of games that can be played with an ordinary deck of cards. The popular movie star Omar Sharif has given bridge popular advertisement in his latest book and nationally syndicated talk shows. This positive endorsement of the game has brought attention to the fever pitch. Canasta and rummy have always been considered staples of the card-playing crowd, particularly in the northern climates where people are indoors during the winter months. These card games provide a healthy way to spend leisure time together, and the popularity of these games has not diminished over the years.

Board games have also been very popular with the typical American family. Monopoly, Clue, Chinese checkers, checkers, chess, and newer games like Trivial Pursuit are but a few of the board games currently on the market. Clue has been so successful as a board game that it has been made into a video game. Monopoly is the true American standard board game. What family does not have one somewhere in a drawer or closet? Its premise lies at the heart of every American—to become successful and earn enough money to be happy. It is the ultimate success game. Trivial Pursuit, a newcomer to the board game market, has become very popular with the young urban professionals who play it at parties and weekend get-togethers. There have even been spin-offs of the trivia game like Bible Trivia. Movie Trivia, and the like. Yes, board games certainly have always been popular in America, and it appears that this style of home entertainment is still a family favorite.

Outdoor or backyard games round out the list of home games that have remained popular over the years. Touch football and baseball or softball are played in almost every vacant lot or large backyard in the country. Most homes inhabited by children have a basketball hoop somewhere on the premises. These games not only appeal to family togetherness, but also appeal to those who are concerned about physical well-being since these physical activities promote the concept of fitness.

These games promote healthy competition among friends and family members, provide a healthy release of frustrations, and aid in understanding sportsmanship. Many younger players learn to win—and lose—graciously while older players are reminded that how the game is played is the most important thing to consider. Home entertainment has remained popular for many years, and it appears that games that can be played at home will continue to remain popular for a long time to come.

Court Side Creatures

by Kolbi Rockhold

When it comes to sports, I find nothing more entertaining than watching the people who are watching the sports! The ten American universities with the best basketball teams, nicknamed the "Big Ten," lure interesting fans that I'd pay more money to see than for the game. I've decided that the three most amusing types of fans are the bored wives, the teenage girls, and the die-hard, beer-bellied men.

The bored wives are a riot to watch and easy to find; look for knitting. These devoted ladies are there to make sure that their husbands aren't drinking too much, swearing too much, or watching the cheerleaders with too much interest. If a drunk husband stands up and bellows at the court, you'll hear a bored wife scream, "HENRY! Watch your mouth, you old fool! Sit down! What do you think you're doing? HONESTLY, if you would just behave, I wouldn't have to come to these wretched things! You're worse than the children! I said, *SIT DOWN!*" Henry sits, and then she returns to her knitting. Bored wives also go to keep an eye on their teenage daughters.

Rosy, teenage girls have hopeful faces that are transparent, so everyone knows why they attend these college basketball games. They paint on their make-up and sit with the college crowd, hoping to meet handsome college men. Teenage girls want to find Prince Charmings who will treat them like Snow Whites and rescue them from boring hometown high schools. They wish they had relationships like their more fortunate peers.

Die-hard, beer-bellied men are the most colorful. These amazing specimens attend basketball games for two reasons: to yell without ceasing, and to guzzle rivers of beer. Die-hard beer-bellies who don't have bored wives with them are immensely popular. They are admired by their contemporaries because they can buy beer without being henpecked. When four or five die-hard beer-bellies congregate, between them they can down a keg of beer per game (unless their team is losing; then their intake doubles). The more beer they drink, the more belligerent they become. By the end of the night, these men are sloshed, but they still go out for "a few" after the game.

Whomever I choose to watch, "Big Ten" basketball games are exciting, not because of the players on the court, but because of the entertainment in the stands. From the saintly bored wives to the obnoxious die-hards, basketball will never lose its appeal as long as the fans keep showing up courtside to spice up the surroundings.

Betting at the Race Track

by Alison Erion

Not too many people know the different ways of betting on the horses. One of the most common types of bet placed is the Box Ticket.

The term *box* is used when you place a wager on two or more horses in one race and wish to cover their every possible winning order of finish. Betting the "Box" is no more than making multiple wagers on one ticket.

There are three basic types of Box Tickets:

- Exacta Box Tickets
- Trifecta Box Tickets
- Key Box Tickets

Let's describe these individually:

Exacta Box Tickets

Exacta means choosing in the exact order of finish. Let's bet the Exacta Box using three horses. Say you would like the number 4-5-8 horses and can't decide on only two to bet on. You would buy a three-horse box combination ticket costing $12.00, because you are covering six possible finish positions at $2.00 each. The combinations are 4-5, 5-4, 4-8, 8-4, 5-8, and 8-5. When making this bet you would say to the clerk, "$2.00 Exacta Box 4-5-8." You can buy $1.00, $2.00, or $3.00 Box tickets with as many as nine horses or seventy-two combinations.

Trifecta Box Tickets

Trifecta means choosing first, second, and third finish positions in exact order. Say you like four horses (2-3-6-8) in this race. This means there are twenty-four possible winning combinations. You can bet a $1.00 Box ($24.00), $2.00 Box ($48.00), or $3.00 Box ($72.00). You ask the clerk for "$2.00 Trifecta Box 2-3-6-8."

Key Trifecta Box Tickets

If you think you have picked the winner of the trifecta race and you wish to box the other horses for second and third, then you would use a "key entry." You would tell the clerk, "$1.00 key entry on number 1 with the 2, 3, 4." This means the number 1 horse has to come in first and the others can be in any order. This would cost you $6.00 and cover the combinations of: 1-2-3, 1-2-4, 1-3-2, 1-3-4, 1-4-2, and 1-4-3. Since three horses are boxed behind the "key entry" (number 1), the bet is a three-horse key entry.

These are the three basic types of Box Tickets used at any racetrack. It takes a while to understand what you are really betting and what you are supposed to tell the clerk, but "Box Tickets" are very helpful in winning some money.

Process

How to Lose Your Appetite

by Julia Waterbury

Fast-food restaurants advertise themselves as being quick and convenient. However, seldom does one live up to that image. Because of the slow service one encounters, the lousy food served, and the often incompetent help, eating fast food is a lesson in how to waste time and money, and how to lose your appetite.

First, decide that you do not have the time or the inclination to cook your own meal. Then remember or discover that there is a fast-food restaurant nearby. Proceed to the "convenient," quick-service drive-thru lane—and wait. Just the other day, I decided to grab a quick burger for lunch at the local fast-food burger place. Because I had only twenty minutes for lunch, I was immediately frustrated by the long line of cars ahead of me. After what seemed an interminable amount of time, I was able to inch my way up to the ordering telecom. When I finally made it to the pickup window, I was, to my disbelief, curtly told to "Please pull aside," as my order was not yet completed. By the time I got my food, my lunch break was over. Thus, I give you lesson number one on how to waste time: whenever you're in a hurry for fast food, use the quick drive-thru lane. It isn't.

Next, decide what taste-tempting delicacies you will eat at the fast-food restaurant. For most health-conscious people, "fresh" and "natural" are the catchwords to look for. Unfortunately, I have found fast-food places are notorious for their bad food. I have yet to eat a fresh hamburger bun from any of the fast-food giants. And though I've tried and tried, I still haven't figured out how "the hot" can stay "hot" and the "cold" stay "cold" when everything is under a heat lamp! Believe me, brown, wilted lettuce does very little for my palate. The food is consistently either too hot or too cold, too done or too raw. I'll never forget the day I almost chipped a tooth on a partially frozen chicken nugget. So lesson number two: leave all sense of culinary prowess at home when you eat at a fast-food restaurant. That way when you lose your appetite, you won't have lost much—except the money you wasted on food you couldn't eat.

Finally, when you go to a fast-food restaurant, be prepared to deal with people who probably had to fail a literacy test to be hired. It seems that none of the service help I run into can give change without the use of computerized registers. When I'm ordering food, I feel as if I'm playing the nursery school edition of Password. If I request a single with onions, tomatoes, and ketchup, more often than not, I'll end up with a single with mayo, lettuce (brown and wilted), and pickles. I hate pickles! Lesson number three: when you go to a fast-food joint be sure you can pay with exact change, bring flash cards to *show* what you want, and learn to eat pickles—just in case.

Without a doubt, fast-food restaurants, with their slow service, bad food. and incompetent help, are truly a waste of time and money. Perhaps fast-food restaurants are Nature's revenge on a society whose inhabitants have gotten too busy to cook for themselves!

Hawkeye

by Jim Meeks

For some time now television has been the primary source of entertainment for America's people. Probably a show that will remain deeply embedded within our memories is "M.A.S.H." The most distinct character of that series was Dr. Benjamin Franklin "Hawkeye" Pierce. Hawkeye was, and through reruns still is, a character who has tremendous appeal to his audience. The reason for that appeal was that his portrayal of life in war-torn Korea made us very capable of empathizing with his plight. He was able to bring about the audience reaction with his brutal honesty, his sometimes highly depressed state, and his ability to draw light to an issue through humor.

First, Hawkeye gave us a great capacity for empathy by his forthright honesty. Throughout the "M.A.S.H." series Hawkeye was known to be the devil's advocate, the character who could be counted on to get to the heart of the matter. He constantly exhibited enviable distaste for the unjust. Whether it was the injustice of war itself (which he daily confronted in surgery) or the plight of Korean orphans, he could always be counted on to stand for the right by speaking loudly, without the typical military bureaucratic sidestepping. He, in essence, was a civilian trapped in an army uniform.

Another characteristic that made Hawkeye quite real to us was his oft depressed state. Most certainly if we were to put ourselves in his place, seeing death and suffering on an epic scale, we, too, could easily see ourselves becoming manic.

Oftentimes Hawkeye would write letters home that would allow him, and us, to review the torture of his life at the time. As he moved from one event to the next, his mood would change from bleak to bleaker. "M.A.S.H." itself was one of the few shows that would often end leaving the conflict of the episode unresolved. Thus, as we left Hawkeye at times in his desperate state, we, too, could feel his desperation.

Last, we could relate to Hawkeye's thoroughly nonsensical methods of maintaining his sanity through humor. This, perhaps, was his salvation, and ours as well, because it allowed him a means by which to cope. He often used Frank Burns as the focus of his jokes and tricks. We had little to no trouble justifying his rationale, seeing as Burns was completely unlikeable and worthy of the treatment he received. The bizarre pranks Hawkeye played were the type we could only dream of. His creative humor, which by the way was usually a method of obtaining some type of justice, was indeed admirable.

Through Hawkeye Pierce's multiple personality of his honesty, his depression, and his humor, we see his character come alive. Through the creative use of these aspects we were able to be transported back to the time of the Korean conflict and were able to learn of the tragedy of war, killing, and hatred. Perhaps through Hawkeye we have gained new insights and an objectivity that can help us avoid the travesties he had to endure.

COMMENT

The essay you just read veers a bit from the traditional "description of a mechanism in operation" paper. However, it does describe the process Hawkeye uses to affect audience reaction.

The next essay also shows a creative approach to the process essay: it describes the process a president used to gain power.

Andrew Jackson: Increasing the Power of the Presidency

by Michele Harding

Today U.S. citizens are accustomed to the notion of a strong president; our news is full of commentary evaluating how well the president is doing—particularly whether his is a strong presidency. Such was not always the case. Before Andrew Jackson's presidency, the executive branch of the U.S. government was regarded as inferior to the legislative and judicial branches. Because the United States is a republic, the people thought Congress to be the most important branch of government. As for the judiciary, John Marshall had increased the power of the Supreme Court by establishing judicial review—the power to declare something unconstitutional. Throughout his presidency, Andrew Jackson succeeded in increasing the power of the executive branch so that it was equal to the other two branches. One of Jackson's chief means of increasing presidential power was his treatment of the issue of the Bank of the United States.

Jackson's first major step against the bank came near the end of his first term, in July 1832, when the charter of the Second Bank of the United States was to be renewed. Jackson had great personal as well as political dislike of the Bank of the United States. He saw it as corrupt and nonbeneficial to the common man. When he vetoed the recharter of the Second Bank of the United States, he also issued a stinging veto message. Jackson declared that the bank was not only anti-Western, but also anti-American and unconstitutional. By saying this, Jackson defied the earlier Supreme Court ruling in *McCulloch v. Maryland,* which stated that the bank was constitutional. Jackson also ignored the theory of judicial review. He believed that *his* interpretation of the Constitution was just as important as that of the Supreme Court, so he used his constitutionally granted veto power. Jackson not only took advantage of the seldom-used veto, but with his veto message increased the power of the presidency.

Jackson saw his reelection as public endorsement of his positions and justification for his attacks on the Bank of the United States. The bank was a major issue in the election of 1832. When Jackson won by a landslide, he chose to interpret his victory as a mandate from the voters not only to reform the bank, but to destroy it. Jackson was the first president to claim that he was the direct representative of the people. As their direct representative, Jackson felt it was his duty to follow their mandate to destroy the bank regardless of the positions of the other branches of government. Here again, Jackson was grabbing power for the presidency. He was claiming that the president was an equal of Congress in representing the people. His subsequent moves on the bank issue demonstrated this philosophy.

Once he had decided to kill the Bank of the United States by placing federal funds in private banks, Jackson found that he had to change some of his Cabinet members several times to get people who would do his bidding. According to tradition, the Senate had to approve both the appointment and removal of Cabinet members. Jackson had no qualms about replacing Cabinet members even though Congress was in recess. He appointed a new Secretary of Treasury, Roger B. Taney, during such a recess, and Taney immediately moved against the Bank of the United States.

Under Jackson's direction, Taney began to remove funds from the Bank of the United States without informing the recessed Congress. Because the Constitution gives Congress jurisdiction over federal funds, the Secretary of Treasury was expected to report to Congress when anything unusual happened with the money. Taney, the unofficial Secretary of Treasury, could not inform Congress of his proceedings until they were well under way. When the Senate returned, it refused to approve Taney as Secretary of Treasury. Moreover, in reaction to what Congress saw as Jackson's overstepping his presidential power, the Senate censured Jackson, the first such act against a U.S. president. In his protest, Jackson again claimed that, as the direct representative of the people, he was required to act in their best interests and according to their wishes. Jackson felt that the redirection of federal funds was simply a fulfillment of the people's mandate to destroy the Bank of the United States.

President Andrew Jackson used the bank issue to increase presidential power significantly. He established the president as a direct representative of the people and claimed powers that previously had belonged either to the Supreme Court or to Congress. What Jackson actually did was bring the inferior executive branch to a position of equality with the legislative and judicial branches. As John Marshall used *Marbury v. Madison* to establish judicial review and therefore increase Supreme Court power, so Andrew Jackson used destruction of the Bank of the United States to increase presidential power.

Selling Crabs

by Karen E. Yeatman

Rappahannock Oyster Company—ROC—is a seafood company that deals mainly in processing and distributing crab meat. I know this name is a bit deceiving considering what the company does, but the truth is that it used to be a company dealing mainly in oysters. Who is to change the name of a good upstanding company just because the product has changed over the years? It is on a small creek joining the Chesapeake Bay—about two and one-half hours south of Washington, DC, if driving—in a small town by the name of Kilmarnock, Virginia.

The crab business is actually a large and relatively interesting one—not to mention a good bit smelly! Three main parts make up the business: buying crabs, cooking and processing crabs, and distributing the meat.

Buying crabs

Rappahannock buys crabs from local watermen—crabbers—and from larger organizations that deal only with buying large amounts of live crabs and distributing them to companies like ROC. This sounds like an easy job, but it is quite time-consuming and difficult. The problems often come in when negotiating prices. This affects everything—the price of crab meat, crabbers' income, and profits.

Cooking and processing crabs

Cooking the crabs is next after purchasing, and ROC does this by steaming them under high pressure for twelve minutes. The cooling process is next—first by letting them cool down to room temperature and then in a large refrigerator. Finally, they are taken into the picking room where thirty to fifty women pick three types of meat out of the crabs:

- *jumbo lump*—the best and most select part of the crab
- *special*—the rest of the good meat—just not in lumps
- *claw*—just as it says, claw meat, with or without the hard claw itself

Of course these types of meat have respective prices: jumbo lump is the most expensive and claw the least. The pickers work from 3:00 A.M. to noon so that we can pack, seal, and send the meat out that day.

Distributing the meat

At this time, we ship the meat out by refrigerated truck or overnight air using special "cold packaging" to restaurants, grocery store chains, and other larger distributors in Williamsburg, Richmond, Washington, West Virginia, and even Arizona.

We also offer a retail store and cafe right in our plant—offering fresh crab meat and some extra seafood goodies like shrimp, fish, scallops, deviled crab, and crab cakes to the local people.

APPENDIX A
Theme Format

Incredible as it may seem, English instructors are just like you and us (well—maybe a little more like us). Like you, they're human and have their little eccentricities. For example, they think that if students have done a good job writing their themes, they'll also want to make them as neat as possible. Silly idea—or is it?

That idea also has its corollary: the student who writes a theme at the last minute probably doesn't take—doesn't even *have*—the time to make it neat.

The moral is clear: be neat so that your instructors think they're looking at an A paper before they've read even the first word. Here are some guidelines, although your instructors may wish to make some changes to suit individual preferences.

- *Handwriting or typing?* Look at the two sample papers that follow. Which one would you rather read? If you can type at all, then do so. The early papers are short enough that typing them shouldn't take very long. If you don't type, use either black or blue ink. Other colors are hard to read.

- *Typing or word processing?* Should you use a typewriter or a computer with a word processing program? The answer is easy: If you have a word processor, by all means use it. It has several overwhelming advantages over the typewriter:

  - You can make corrections easily. That means you're far more likely to engage seriously in the revising process.

  - With most programs, you can use a spell-checking tool. That means you'll not only correct words you've misspelled but correct typos, too. By helping with the technicalities, the word processor frees you to think about the larger, more important matters of writing. Be careful, though, because spell-checking tools don't catch all errors—especially when your typo results in a legitimate word.

- Most important from our point of view, the word processor helps you get words on paper easily in the first place—especially if you can compose at the keyboard. People who have become comfortable with this method know that it is one of the primary benefits of the word processor, and often they refuse to write any other way.

- *Proofreading*   Do it—*always,* but especially if you type, and even if you use spell-checking with a word processor. Otherwise, you might be surprised by what your magic fingers did the night before.

- *Paper*   If you type, use standard-sized ($8^1/_2$-by-11 inch) typing paper. For a standard typewriter, the erasable kind is especially good because you can make corrections easily. However, most instructors don't like to receive work on erasable paper because it's hard to write on. You can overcome this problem by typing on erasable paper and then making a photocopy to hand in (if your instructor will accept a photocopy). Do not use thin "onionskin" paper.

  For a word processor, erasing isn't required, so stick to a reasonably heavy bond paper (twenty-pound paper, a good weight, is readily available in separate sheets or, for tractor-feed printers, continuous form).

  If you don't type or use a word processor, find a standard-sized tablet or pad of high-quality, lined theme paper. Don't use ordinary notebook paper (or paper torn from a spiral notebook) unless your instructor approves.

- *Corrections*   On a short assignment (such as the one-paragraph essay), avoid handing in a paper with obvious corrections. If, however, you're torn between making a correction at the last minute or handing in a neat paper, of course make the correction. What good is a neat error?

- *Spacing*   If you're typing, double-space except where format requirements call for different spacing. If you're writing by hand, write on every other line.

- *Margins*   Allow an inch on the top, left, right, and bottom. On page one for a theme assignment, begin the identification block (see sample on page 487) one inch from the top of the page, quadruple-space (double-space twice) to find the line for the title, and then quadruple-space again to find where to begin the first line of your theme. (For research papers, you'll probably use a title page for identification information; see the sample research paper for the format for a title page and for the first page of the paper's body. Some of the comments on the pages facing the sample research paper discuss format requirements for students who need to follow MLA page layout guidance.)

- *Page numbers*   Don't number the first page, but do count it as page one. For other pages, use Arabic numerals (2, 3, 4, and so on) and put the number in the upper right-hand corner, half an inch from the top of the page and in line with the right margin. (Chapter 19 shows the MLA format, which uses a somewhat different pagination style for the research paper.)

- *Identification*   Put your name, your instructor's name, the course number, and the date in the upper left-hand corner of page one, one inch from the top of the page. Your instructor may direct you to put this information on a title page for your research paper, as the sample research paper demonstrates.

- *Fastening the paper*   Unless your instructor directs you to put your paper in a binder, use a stapler to fasten pages together. Paper clips are fine in theory, but in a stack of themes they tend to clip themselves onto other themes.

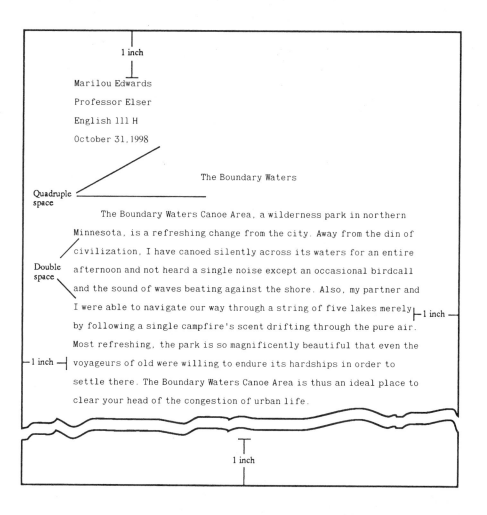

1 inch

Marilou Edwards

Professor Elser

English 111 H

October 31, 1998

The Boundary Waters

Quadruple space

      The Boundary Waters Canoe Area, a wilderness park in northern Minnesota, is a refreshing change from the city. Away from the din of civilization, I have canoed silently across its waters for an entire

Double space

afternoon and not heard a single noise except an occasional birdcall and the sound of waves beating against the shore. Also, my partner and I were able to navigate our way through a string of five lakes merely by following a single campfire's scent drifting through the pure air. Most refreshing, the park is so magnificently beautiful that even the voyageurs of old were willing to endure its hardships in order to settle there. The Boundary Waters Canoe Area is thus an ideal place to clear your head of the congestion of urban life.

1 inch

1 inch

1 inch

Marilou Edwards
English 111 H
Professor Elser
October 31, 1998

The Boundary Waters

The Boundary Waters Canoe Area, a wilderness park in northern Minnesota, is a refreshing change from the city. Away from the din of civilization, I have canoed silently across its waters for an entire afternoon and not heard a single noise except an occasional bird call and the sound of the waves beating against the shore. Also, my partner and I were able to navigate our way through a string of five lakes merely by following a single campfire's scent drifting through the pure air. Most refreshing, the park is so magnificently beautiful that even the voyageurs of old were willing to endure its hardships in order to settle there. The Boundary Waters Canoe Area is thus an ideal place to clear your head of the congestion of urban life.

APPENDIX B

Commonly Confused Words

These are some words college students sometimes have trouble with. The list isn't complete—we've kept it short purposely so you can read through it rather than just use it as a reference.

accept / except

Accept is a verb meaning to receive something or to be favorable toward something; *except* is a verb meaning to leave out, a preposition meaning excluding, or a conjunction meaning only: "I'd like to *accept* your invitation to dinner, *except* I can't go out tonight."

affect / effect

Affect is almost always a verb: "What you learn in college will *affect* your decision-making process for the rest of your life."

Effect is almost always a noun: "What you learn in college will have an *effect* on your decision-making process for the rest of your life."

a lot / alot

A lot is the correct spelling.

all ready / already

All ready means that everyone or everything is ready; *already* means previously: "I *already* told you that we are *all ready* to go."

all right / alright

All right is the correct spelling.

all together / altogether

All together means collectively; *altogether* means entirely or completely: "It is *altogether* possible that we will travel *all together.*"

among / between

Use *between* when you're dealing with two items; use *among* for three or more: "*Between* you and me, I don't think there's much honor *among* all those thieves."

amount / number

Use *amount* with things involving weight, bulk, or sums—things measured with a total; use *number* with things that must be counted individually: "The *amount* of water in the pot should be sufficient to cover the *number* of beans you intend to cook."

awhile / a while

Both imply for a short time, but *awhile* is an adverb, and *while* is a noun: "I may stay *awhile* or I may leave for *a while.*"

complement / compliment

Complement means to go along nicely with: "Her scarf *complemented* her blouse."

Compliment is a nice thing to say to someone else: "He *complimented* her on her scarf."

council / counsel

Council refers to an assembly of people; *counsel* refers to a discussion, advice, or a plan: "The employee *council* met yesterday and accepted the company lawyer's *counsel.*"

disinterested / uninterested

Disinterested means impartial; *uninterested* means bored: "Thank goodness the referee was *disinterested* because, believe me, the fans weren't *uninterested* in the outcome of the game."

farther / further

Farther refers to physical distance; *further* refers to figurative or notional distance (degree, time, quantity): "The evidence shows *further* that my client was *farther* from the door than the prosecution claims."

fewer / less

Use *fewer* to compare things you can count (teeth, cars, glasses); use *less* for things that are amounts (wheat, sugar, syrup): "*Fewer* people came to the fair, so we'll need *less* food to feed them."

imply / infer

You *imply* something to a listener when you don't quite say it explicitly; the listener *infers* what you as a speaker haven't quite said explicitly: "The teacher *implied* that the work needs to be handed in on time. I *inferred* that the teacher wants the work turned in on time."

irregardless / regardless

Regardless is standard. *Irregardless* is nonstandard.

it's / its' / its

It's is a contraction of "it is" or "it has"; *its'* is always incorrect; *its* shows possession (many pronouns show possession without an apostrophe: *his, hers, ours*): "*It's* a good time to put the desk back in *its* place."

lie / lay

Lie means to recline or to rest; *lay* means to place something, but *lay* also is the past tense of *lie*: "If I forget to *lay* my car keys on the dresser, I'll *lie* awake for hours, just as I *lay* awake most of last night."

principal / principle

Principal can be a noun (the person who ran your high school) or an adjective (meaning main); *principle* is a noun that means a basic truth, rule, or law: "The school's *principal* said that the *principal* reason for the snow holiday is that it violated her *principles* to have students traveling on dangerous roads."

sit / set

Sit means to rest or remain inactive or to be in an upright position; *set* means to place something: "After I *set* this bag of groceries on the table, I intend to *sit* in front of a fan for a while."

stationary / stationery

Stationary means still; *stationery* is paper that you write on: "Hold that *stationery stationary* or I'll never be able to write this letter!"

suppose / supposed

Suppose is the present tense form of a verb meaning to assume or believe, while *supposed* is the past tense form of the same verb and is used with a helping verb: "I *suppose* she was *supposed* to return yesterday."

than / then

Than is a conjunction used in comparisons or statements of preference; *then* is an adverb referring to time: "Sometimes I feel inadequate because he is more successful *than* I am; *then* I remember how unhappy he is."

their / they're / there

Their is the possessive of *they*; *they're* is a contraction of "they are"; *there* is an adverb meaning at or in that place: "After the banquet to honor my parents, I'll remain *there* until *they're* finished opening *their* gifts."

who's / whose

Who's is a contraction for "who is"; *whose* is the possessive of *who* or *which*: "*Who's* going to worry about *whose* turn is next?"

your / you're

Your is the possessive of *you*; *you're* is a contraction of "you are": "*You're* sure to want *your* sweater tonight."

Index